LATIN LYRIC AND
ELEGIAC POETRY

GARLAND REFERENCE LIBRARY
OF THE HUMANITIES
VOL. 1425

LATIN LYRIC AND ELEGIAC POETRY

An Anthology of
New Translations

edited by

Diane J. Rayor
William W. Batstone

with an introduction by

William S. Anderson

GARLAND PUBLISHING, Inc.
New York & London / 1995

Library of Congress Cataloging-in-Publication Data

Latin lyric and elegiac poetry : an anthology of new translations /
edited by Diane J. Rayor and William W. Batstone.
    p. cm. — (Garland reference library of the humanities ;
v. 1425)
    Includes bibliographical references.
    ISBN 0–8153–0087–5 (hardcover). — ISBN 0–8153–1540–6
(paperback)
    1. Latin poetry—Translations into English. 2. Elegiac poetry,
Latin—Translations into English. 3. Rome—Poetry.   I. Rayor,
Diane J. II. Batstone, William Wendell. III. Series: Garland
reference library of the humanities ; vol. 1425.
PA6164.L38 1995
871'. 0108—dc20   94–37902
                                             CIP

Paperback cover art: Flora. Fresco from Stabia. Museo Archeologico
Nazionale, Naples, Italy. By permission of Art Resource.

Paperback cover design by Patti Hefner.

Printed on acid-free, 250-year-life paper
Manufactured in the United States of America

Contents

Acknowledgments

I am indebted to Seth Schein for sending this project my way. I warmly thank Patricia Clark, William Levitan, and Connie Rayor for their suggestions on the Appendix epigrams, and Helen Deutsch and Stanley Lombardo for their help on the Note on Translation. Garland Publishing's general editor, Kennie Lyman, provided valuable assistance throughout. I am also grateful to Ron Dwelle and Nancy Brown in the English department at Grand Valley State University for technical support. My husband, David Hast, gave me the gifts of time and encouragement, which made completing this book possible.

DJR

The debts we acquire over even a few years in academics rapidly exceed our ability to enumerate or recall. Even if I could trace down and acknowledge every influence from every book or article I have read, I would still be left with an essentially unpayable debt to those teachers, friends, and colleagues whose conversations inside and outside of the academy have helped shape my sense of how to read and of what we are doing. I suppose that in the long run we repay this debt by being the best teachers, friends, and colleagues that we can be, trying to offer to others what was so generously given to us. However, at the inevitable certainty of leaving out several important influences, I would like here to acknowledge two classicists whose influence on my work might, but cannot, go without saying: The first is the author of our Introduction, William S. Anderson. As a scholar and teacher he has done more (whether he likes it or not) to shape my understanding of Latin literature than anyone else in the profession. Others certainly in individual cases have had greater influence over my understanding of a particular point, but as the teacher who raised me from a second-year Latin student to a Ph.D., his influence has been the most consistent, and now I discover that the standards he represents as a teacher and reader continue to appear stronger and better with time. The second, appropriately enough, is a student of William S. Anderson, W. Ralph Johnson, that inimitable poet/teacher/scholar who has been the inspiration for many of my generation. I would also like to thank my assistant Bart Brown for his particularly close attention to details of all kinds.

WWB

Introduction

The six poets whose works comprise the material of this volume represent the sudden flowering of lyric poetry in Rome at the end of the Republic and in the first decades of the Augustan principate. All six poets, though by birth separated by a generation or two, composed what we have in a period of approximately fifty years, from 60 to 10 B.C.E. All but Horace and Ovid were dead by 10 B.C.E., most of them prematurely. Horace died in 8 B.C.E., but Ovid, who turned away from these short poems before he was thirty, had a long productive career ahead of him in other forms (e.g., the tragedy *Medea*, *The Art of Love*, and the *Metamorphoses*), before his exile brought him back to an impressive series of personal meditations on his banishment.

It is tempting to speculate as to why lyric poetry appeared, almost like a meteor, in Roman literature, dazzling the talented writers and their cultivated audiences, then passing on into the darkness after Ovid. Was it some last assertion of personal freedom? Was it the result of the chaotic political times? Was it the beginning of personal freedom in a social class that heretofore had not been privileged to speak out? Was it one of the last creative surges of the Hellenistic culture? Or had there been a steady, perceptible growth of personal awareness in Rome that at last secured its moment to flower in the heady instability of the First Triumvirate and the half-century that followed? I leave such speculations to the reader. There are numerous other tempting possibilities and all sorts of combinations, I am sure.

Lyric poetry assumes the value and interest of personal experience and highly personal responses to situations. The characteristic voice of such poetry is the first person, I myself. Our earliest Greek poetry gives expression to an individual viewpoint and often allows it to express itself; but it conditions it against the views of the community or the family. Thus, in Homeric epic, we study the clash of the self-assertive hero Achilles with the purposes and needs of the Greek army to which he has responsibilities; and we watch the slow maturation of the self-serving Odysseus to the status of a husband, father, and householder who at last deserves home and family. In Greek tragedy and comedy, we watch the actions and listen to the self-centered words of heroes who challenge, sometimes magnificently but fatally or ridiculously, the public responsibilities that belong to them. But it was not until the dawn of lyric verse in the seventh century B.C.E. that the personal voice was allowed to express itself without the limitations of a defined community voice that qualified or negated it. Then, we encounter such strong personalities and personal viewpoints as those of Archilochus, Sappho, Alcaeus, Anacreon, Theognis, and others.

The Romans did not lack subjectivity or personal awareness, but they were far behind the Greeks in developing its literary expression. It was not until they came into contact with the Hellenistic world during the third century B.C.E. and observed and admired the achievements of Greek poets in the representation of personal feelings that Roman literature even came into existence. Before the first Latin writers began to borrow the forms and manner of Greek poets, there was no Roman poetry that we can discover. The principal media for self-expression and personal assertion set very definite constraints on what could be properly said. Public speeches, in the Roman Senate or before the voters or in court, inscriptions that commemorated the public achievements of military victors or benefactors, and the epitaphs that were carefully carved on funerary monuments to assess the life of the dead person—these were the conventional forms of personal presentation before Greek poetry liberated the fuller personality. During the late third and much of the second century, the early poets who now appeared in Italy and found patronage in Rome experimented with the major genres of epic and drama. In the late second century lived a unique man who developed the genre of satire, Gaius Lucilius. He made satire very much the medium of outspoken personal expression, and he certainly influenced the subsequent experiments of Catullus and his generation. But satire was not lyric poetry: it was a pronounced assertion of personal importance, not as an individual of rich and sensitive feeling, but as a moral judge of others. And so it was another fifty years before Catullus would claim pride of position in extant Roman lyric. (His contemporaries, many of whose names we know, survive today only as tantalizing words and broken lines.)

If we go back to the third century, when Roman poetry had its start adapting Greek techniques and genres, we realize that that poetry arose as part of a general public movement to celebrate the steady expansion of Roman power into the Greek world and to signal the appropriation of its art. Roman poets followed in the train of conquering commanders and wrote epic poems, in Greek hexameter, on their victories. Roman poets adapted Greek tragedies and comedies for the festivals in Rome that collected the Roman populace in the Roman Forum and later in stone theaters to enjoy Roman prosperity. No doubt there were some feelings of dissent at the militant policies of the Roman Senate, but the obvious profits which were accruing to Rome and Italy during the third and second centuries encouraged poets to share in the public celebration of Roman success. But that unanimity of patriotic optimism did not survive the second century. Factionalism developed at the political level, and the first omens of the civil war appeared when the Senate crushed and killed the Gracchi for daring to challenge traditional class advantages. Some historians, indeed, like to describe the next century, from the death of Tiberius Gracchus in 129 to the battle between Antony and Octavian at Actium in 31 B.C.E., as a period of intermittent civil war.

As political unity degenerated, other aspects of culture and individualism, both bad and good, came to the fore. The first century B.C.E. is the age of individualism in Roman history. We easily think of the great dynasts, Sulla and Marius, Caesar and Pompey, Antony and Octavian, who tore Rome apart for their own personal advantage and dubiously creative purposes. We think of an ambitious lawyer like Cicero whose oratorical skills allowed him to become a significant figure even though he did not come from a ruling family. Many men of the business (equestrian) class were able to make fortunes and to affect policy quietly with their riches for their private advantage. Some men from famous families even started to turn their backs on politics, once the only way to go, and instead adopted the foreign ways popularized by Epicurus of living in comfortable and pleasurable "obscurity." And the poets, too, found themselves alienated or liberated from ties to the senatorial self-interest, from politics, and from confidence in the rightness of Roman policies—so alienated that they began to explore Hellenistic poetry in a new way and discovered a new common ground with its themes and its writers. The large public genres and their grand schemes lost reality for the poets, who instead found the private experiences of themselves and their apolitical friends of primary significance. What was important to the poets of Alexandria two centuries earlier—art, love, poetic craftsmanship, and personal feeling—dominated in the considerably different environment of first century Rome, the attention of the poets of the 60's and 50's, who were called, perhaps derisively by the conservatives, neoterics (Greek and hence contemptuous for "new poets"). These, then, are the subjects of Catullus, the earliest of our six poets, who must represent for us the revolutionary developments of lyric poetry in Rome in the era of Julius Caesar, especially during the tensions of 60-50 before Caesar crossed the Rubicon and started the worst stage of the civil war.

Lyric poetry has its own personal subjects, which openly reject or quietly ignore traditional public themes. It also has its own style and form. The grandiose events of epic and drama required a large expanse and spacious meters; the events that affect the lyric poet are often ordinary and everyday and, even though viewed with much personal feeling, do not want the heavy hand of the epic writer but the light touch of the sophisticated poet. The principal critical values of the new poets put emphasis on lightness, delicacy, smallness, self-awareness that could even be self-ironic as well as self-admiring, and sheer delight in wit, in small crafted images, in suggestion rather than total description. Catullus and his fellow poets experimented with many new Greek meters and started the process of Romanizing them, a process which in the next generation Horace furthered.

The topic which later Roman and modern readers most closely associate with Catullus is that of love, and this selection properly emphasizes that aspect of his creativity. I shall, accordingly, give most of my attention to Catullan love lyric. However, this selection also duly recognizes that the personal range of Catullus was not limited to amatory situations and the pathos of largely unsuccessful, unrealistic passion. At least eight focus on the various interests of what we might call neoteric society, the seemingly idle but eagerly engaged activities of young men and women whose life was not political but interpersonal. (cf. poems 6, 9, 10, 13, 32, 50, 55, and 95.) Catullus likes to expose himself and his friends in "embarrassing situations," likes to play with the intricacies of friendship, is intent on showing how writing poetry and thinking of poetry form a necessary part of daily, normal activity. There are poems which are about poetry (cf. 50), about the self–conscious poet (cf. 49), or exhibit the experimentation of the neoteric interest (cf. 4, 34, 46). Other poems adopt a satiric vein, mocking men and women for trivial faults like halitosis or self-confidence, or even advertizing contempt for Caesar and his corrupt friends (cf. 29, 39, 41, 43, 57, 93). In other words, Catullus projects a personality that seems bright, friendly, irreverent, and anti-political. It is very easy to feel sympathetic to the neoterics and assimilate their modern interests to those of our day.

The trend of Catullus's successors will be to abandon most of these wider interests and subjects and to concentrate on the one topic of love, which Catullus had explored so impressively. (Horace alone is an exception: he will continue to write of broader social concerns, though deliberately changing the Catullan point of view.) What does Catullus contribute to love lyric that his successors were impelled to develop? Catullus situates himself (that is, his lyric speaker) in a love affair that has struck his audience as powerfully real and has evoked deep sympathy from generation after generation. He loves a beautiful and thoroughly entrancing woman whom he calls Lesbia. The name is Greek and invented, for the woman is Roman, almost surely an aristocrat, wealthy, educated, and talented, but very "modern" in her own way, much more interested in her own pleasure than in her responsibility to her class, her husband, or to her Catullan lover. She has usually been identified with a sensational beauty of the old family of Appius Claudius, who allowed her aristocratic name of Claudia to be given an everyday pronunciation of Clodia, whom Cicero attacks in one of his famous orations for her degenerate self-indulgences. It is, however, less important to identify Lesbia than to recognize the qualities which Catullus put into this woman in his poetry and how he made the two characters in the love relationship, the personal male "I" and the loved and hated female, interact. That was what preoccupied Tibullus, Propertius, and Ovid.

From the start (cf. 5 and 7), Catullus focuses on rendering his own feelings exclusively. How Lesbia feels, how much she really loves him, is not a subject for consideration. Catullus declares at the start of 5 that love should be the essence of living, that he and Lesbia should ignore everything else, calculating only the countless number of their kisses. Counting kisses also is the subject of 7, though now with a flourish in the direction of Alexandrian Callimachus (of Cyrene) and an open admission that the lover Catullus is "demented." The various flourishes in defiance of public opinion and practical numbers, even in the face of time, are bold and attractive, but they simultaneously invite our critical distance. Is the lover's dementia simply heroic, or is it dangerously unrealistic even about the beloved? Does she want to spend her life kissing this young man, talented and impetuous though he may be? (I suppose he was handsome, too, but that never comes up for discussion.) The very next poem, 8, reveals to us a lover who is totally disillusioned and trying to talk sense into himself, to escape from his dementia. He insists that he has been an extraordinarily devoted lover, yet she isn't interested any more. He is suffering intensely; she is apparently not at all, and so he turns from his self-pity and self-urging to address Lesbia, angrily, but also wistfully, as a "sorry bitch." It is not hard to read between the lines that, while Catullus fumes, his once-loved Lesbia is actively involved with new lovers.

Here then is the essential drama of this Catullan love affair, real or invented or at least touched up, that the poet so masterfully evokes in many variations in poem after poem: a love that is largely one-sided and fed by illusion and disillusion. The impetuosity of the male speaker/lover attributes to Lesbia the same passion that he feels, erroneously, and he never troubles to understand her—what she needs and demands. She could be passionate at times, and tell him things that he loves to hear at the time, but later holds against her (cf. 72, 92). But I think that she was the kind of woman that did not want to be tied down, especially to a poet of no social status, and I don't doubt that she told him so. However, everything we learn about Lesbia is focalized in the impetuous passion and disillusion of the poet, and so is flawed and emblematic of the lover's hopelessly unreal demands. Poem 85 in two perfect lines epitomizes that situation as excruciatingly painful hate and love over which the lover has no rational control, and we sympathize with that condition, but perceive it, too, as one for which the irrational lover is himself finally responsible. Poems 11 and 58 show that tormented love/hate far more dramatically.

I would like to emphasize Catullus less as a pathetic self-conscious lover than as a brilliant self-conscious artist who represented a disastrous love relationship in this utterly striking and convincing manner. Thus, although he wrote mostly brief lyrics, he also produced some haunting longer poems, and this collection includes two of them (cf. 63 and 68). In 68, Catullus is frankly subjective, and the speaker is the lyric lover, "I Catullus," once again engaged with passionate memories of mutual love with Lesbia in the past and with the desperate contrast now of her sovereign indifference to his love and anger. But now the poet introduces an added dimension, seeing the affair in the perspective of a famous Greek myth in which passionate Laodamia loses her beloved husband, the first Greek casualty in the landing at Homeric Troy. Because of the elaboration of the lover's disappointment through this mythical distancing (note the sexual inversion) scholars often describe Catullus 68 as the "first Roman love elegy." We will see why later in the works of his successors. I wish here to emphasize the distancing of subjectivity and the aesthetic control that is implicit in 68. In 63, that distancing is even greater. The poet narrates the experience of a young Greek he calls Attis, who sails across to the coast of Asia Minor, plunges enthusiastically into the rites of Cybele, and, at the height of dementia, castrates himself. Only at the very end does the poet enter personally and pray to Cybele that no such madness ever possess him. As we now realize, Catullus here is presenting his favorite topic objectively through the myth of Attis. Attis is an image of the irrational, self-destructive lover devoting himself to a woman of impossible confidence, who therefore dominates him and their relationship. It does not take much effort to interpret the symbolism of castration.

Catullus seems to have died before hostilities broke out in 49 B.C.E. between Caesar and Pompey. Horace, Tibullus, and Propertius were each, in different ways, involved in and affected by the troubled period of the civil wars, the five years that led up to Caesar's victories over his opponents and then to his assassination in March, 44; and the thirteen years of chaos which were finally resolved by the defeat of Antony and Cleopatra at Actium in 31 and the amazing sole rule of Caesar's great-nephew Octavian, who was awarded the honorary name of Augustus by vote of the Roman Senate in 27. Horace, born in 65, was just starting his university education in Athens when Caesar was murdered. A patriotic radical at that age, he joined the forces of Brutus and followed him to defeat at the battle of Philippi. From defeat and financial loss, he rose to be the special kind of Augustan poet we meet here. Tibullus, a decade younger, had active military service under one of Octavian's most trusted generals, Valerius Messalla, who then became his patron. Propertius was about the same age as Tibullus, born in northern Italy, probably at Assisi. His region favored the family of Antony against Octavian, and during the war around nearby Perugia, he lost a close relative. He never entirely forgot this trauma and never exhibited much warmth for Augustus and his political order.

Chronologically, then, Horace comes next, but thematically and generically the closest successors to Catullus are the other four, of whom Tibullus and Propertius, born in the mid 50's, will be my concern now. They are masters of what we call Roman love elegy. That means that, unlike the more versatile Catullus, they write exclusively in elegiac meter, a system of alternating couplets well exemplified in the present translations. (It has become conventional in English to use rhyming couplets, but the Romans did not rhyme, their couplets working quite satisfactorily for them without this additional element.) And they give up his broader canvas to concentrate solely on his wonderfully-developed topic of disillusioning love.

We saw how Catullus represented his disillusioned lover: he was an impressionable young man, of modest status but striking poetic ability, who falls in love with a somewhat older woman, of aristocratic status, lovely, independent, imperious, and selfish. He gives everything to the relationship, he claims; she gives while it diverts her—which, unfortunately for Catullus, is not very long. He expected too much without understanding her limited purposes and moral limitations. In the next generation appeared a poet named Cornelius Gallus, a friend of Vergil and of Octavian, who seems to have been the intermediary between Catullus and the love elegists. Gallus's work has been lost, but his reputation is assured both by Vergil and the canon of elegy that becomes recognized: he is the true founder of love elegy because he wrote in the meter and he modified the patterns of Catullus in a way that others follow. The principal modification came from the trans-formation of the beloved woman from an aristocrat, who was superior to the male lover by right of status, to a courtesan, who was by definition inferior to the lover. Whereas Catullus seems to portray an adulterous liaison, Gallus represented the kind of permissible, if not altogether approved, relation between a young man and a prostitute that had been dramatized for at least three centuries in New Comedy and had been known in actual Greco-Roman life.

The romance of two freeborn Italians could, of course, result in legitimate marriage, and so the Catullan lover had some reason to hope for happiness from Lesbia (if he had not so badly misjudged her intentions). But the romance between a freeborn Italian and a prostitute could not eventuate in marriage, only in concubinage (which meant a permanent taint on children). So the male poet/lover could not indulge in the romantic illusions of the Catullan lover. Loving his woman, whom he called Lycoris, Gallus projected himself not into the heady world of aristocratic self-indulgence, but into the environment of courtesans, who make their living from "love," if you want. But no lover like Gallus could impetuously say to his courtesan, as Catullus said to Lesbia, "Let's live and love, forgetting everything else." The male lover might indeed feel strong love for his girlfriend, for she might be as beautiful and talented as Lesbia was (the model for Lycoris was apparently a very famous actress of the time), but she needed money from him to live, usually more than he alone could afford, so she had to have multiple lovers, rivals of the poet. All of this introduces, then, obvious anti-romantic elements—commercialization and plural lovers—which make enduring love impossible. Although the poet/lover may then wax passionate and think himself profoundly in love, the audience of Roman love elegy stands at an ironic distance from this lover, his beloved, and his so-called love, knowing that this love cannot, and indeed should not, last. (Horace uses an ironic stance in some of his *Odes* to mock conventional elegiac love.)

Gallus moved into politics and won and lost favor with Octavian, dying in disgrace a suicide, having long given up poetry for troubled power. Tibullus and Propertius took up his kind of love situation and developed it in different directions shortly after Actium ended the civil war and Octavian (hailed as Augustus in 27 B.C.E.) gained sole power. Tibullus had a short decade of productivity: he has left us sixteen poems of modest size but considerable originality. In the mixture of fact and fiction which emerges from his poetry, almost our sole source of information about the poet, we learn that he was closely associated as a friend with his patron, Valerius Messalla. He accompanied Messalla on one campaign in Aquitania (France); and he may have started out on another trip with him to the East to help restore order after the defeat of Antony, but had fallen sick before getting too far from Italy. Tibullus mentions Messalla and includes him in the amatory settings of I 1 and I 10; he makes him central to I 7 and II 1. In spite of that, contemporary politics is of almost no interest to this poet: his lover is so utterly unrealistic that he cannot stay focused on the present time, whether of politics or of his love. He is a dreamer, fondly wishing for the impossible.

The dream of the Tibullan lover takes two main directions:

1. He loudly proclaims aversion to war and the acquisition of wealth by warfare, and so peace is his passionate ideal. That is not irrelevant in this age, for Augustan propaganda increasingly stressed the achievement of peace (i.e., the definitive end of civil war) after Actium, and the blessings of peace for the Italian peninsula were basic themes of coins, reliefs, and public worship, to say nothing of other poets. But the larger Roman world did require constant military intervention, so that total peace remained a dream; the Roman army became a magnificent permanent element of the empire that Augustus founded. Tibullus seems to use the anti-war theme to define his poetic distance not from Augustus, but from Messalla, to imply his personal nonpolitical status.

2. Much more pronounced is the Tibullan love of the Italian country, not of the bustling excitement of Augustan Rome. The very first elegy longs for the country and talks with considerable ardor of a small family farm that has seen better days. Poem I 10 seems planned as a reminder and corrector of that wishful dream, and II 1 places us in a rustic religious ceremony. The ideal of this lover is to be with his girlfriend Delia in a rural setting, snugly cradled in her arms while the wind howls and the rains beat down on their roof. I daresay that most of us can respond to that picture, but what we should be doing is smiling at its unreality. Delia is no country girl. As a courtesan, her talents are exclusively urban, and it doesn't take much effort to realize that her life-style, indeed her very existence, depends on a steady income from various affluent

lovers in Rome. The dreamy Tibullan lover is always in conflict
with reality, with the fact that Delia cannot, and does not want to,
leave Rome for the farm. You would never catch her, in her high
heels and tight skirts, stumbling through the straw and manure of
a barn or farmyard. Never. The art of Tibullus, then, invites us to
indulge ourselves briefly with his dream, then return, amused, to
our reality. None of the Tibullan dreams is ever realized in his
verse.

Propertius is of tougher, more exciting substance. Though he, too, by
definition is doomed to failure, and indeed repeatedly suffers disappointment, misery, and outrage, he faces his troubles squarely and struggles to
overcome them. Not by coming to his senses, of course, but by straining
every effort to combat difficulties or to find reason to boast of the troubles
that this love costs him. At least, he claims, this misery has more value than
the goals to which most young Romans commit themselves: he rejects the
political career pursued by Tullus in I 6, and he mocks the epic poetry that
Ponticus doggedly composes in I 7 and I 9. His Cynthia, whom he introduces
in her powerful mastery in his first poem, has totally inverted the everyday
relationship of superior Roman male and inferior courtesan: she has such
power over him by her multiple attractions and personality that he responds
to her (or feels he does) like a helpless slave to his owner. She is in Roman
terms his *domina*, his legal mistress (entirely different from our contemptuous word for the so-called "kept woman"). He cannot gain his freedom
from this amatory slavery. Aware of his public status, he resents his
humiliation and simultaneously exults in it. It is the only way to live, the
only "reality" worth experiencing. The excitement with which Propertius
explores the various possibilities of this variant on the amatory situation
devised by Gallus emerges in the seven poems from his first book of elegies
that he published about 28 B.C.E. Cynthia and her wildly passionate,
impetuously unrealistic lover are indeed a marvelous pair. The passionate
engagement with Cynthia, rivals, and friends engages Propertius's audience
more immediately than do Tibullus's dreams, and so our awareness of his
self-destructive contradictions also acts more strongly and humorously.

Later stylists valued Tibullus for his smoothness: that goes well with
his dreamy manner. Propertius, on the other hand, has a nervous, irregular
style that enhances his wild diversity of feeling. Propertius also uses
mythological allusion where Tibullus largely ignored the device. In the very
first poem, for instance, the eight lines of personal introduction are
immediately followed by a sudden eight-line narrative about Milanion and
Atalanta. Propertius tells the myth as a success story of lover's devotion:
Milanion finally won Atalanta. But then he bemoans the fact that in his own
case such devotion produces no results: he is worse off than Milanion, or, he
implies, his love is grander, more tragic than that of the myth. This is a
highly artful, self-conscious use of myth, along the neoteric and Alexandrian

lines. In I 3, the poem starts with a triple mythical allusion which we are invited to explore. Among other things, it implies the drunkenness of the lover as he arrives and his erotic interest in the sleeping Cynthia. But self-irony also has its expression, as in the subsequent comparison of the unsteady male to hundred-eyed Argus. In I 19, Propertius retells the story of Laodamia and Protesilaus that Catullus had used so skillfully in poem 68: now, the lover asserts, passionately but without proof, that love will impel him to come back even from the dead in his total loyalty to Cynthia. And I 20* displays Propertius's finesse as a modern poet by narrating the complicated story of Hylas and the lustful nymphs, who robbed unwary Hercules of his boyfriend.

The final poems of Book I are I 21 and I 22: I 22 gives an important self-presentation of Propertius, not as a lover, but as a man whose boyhood was scarred by the effects of civil war on his native region of Perugia in northern Italy. It is assumed that the poet in fact came from the nearby town of Assisium (a small hill town of little importance before the life of St. Francis), but the whole region suffered badly when it sided with the enemies of Octavian. One of Propertius's close relatives died at the time. (That is the subject of I 21, in which the dying soldier acts as speaker.) When asked about his origins, then, he does not boast or tell some fabulous story about the Muses' blessing of his birth; he ignores everything except the fact that Umbria was his homeland, Umbria the victim of war. It is more than fifteen years since those terrible times, but Propertius still cannot hail Octavian or celebrate his victory in the civil war (even though it provides favorable conditions for his poetry and his affair with Cynthia). At this point, he has no prominent patron.

Propertius never does become much of an Augustan. By the time he publishes his second book of elegies about three years later, he can address Augustus's closest advisor, Maecenas. But the relationship is not intimate, and Maecenas appears in none of the other thirty-three poems of the large book. The connection does not resemble that of Tibullus with Messalla or of Horace, as we shall see, with Maecenas. The poet essentially uses the great man as a foil, representing political issues and epic themes, to set off the elegist's choice of Cynthia, a subject worth many *Iliads*, and an Alexandrian manner modeled on Callimachus. Propertius now is more overtly a love poet than a poet/lover. He is writing Cynthia, artfully constructing scenes of love; and, as he admits in II 10, he can foresee the day when "his girl will have been written," and he then can begin on a more "noble" epic theme. Meanwhile, however, he mainly concentrates on various situations that allow him to dramatize his reactions to Cynthia the courtesan (cf. II 4 and II 5). He has one rare night of erotic happiness in II 14, but even that trails off with an imaginary picture of the excluded poet dying on Cynthia's doorstep.

In another three years, Propertius had produced a third collection of twenty-five poems; it appeared just after Horace published his magnificent three-book volume of *Odes*, and the elegist borrows some of Horace's proud claims in his opening elegies (cf. III 1 and III 2). It should be noted that the poet does not mention Cynthia by name in any of the four poems translated. He is more concerned to talk of himself as an Alexandrian poet or, as in III 4, to point up the clash between love and war, between himself and Augustus. Only in the last elegies does Cynthia appear, in contexts where, by calling a determined end to the relationship, Propertius is obviously concluding his preoccupation with love elegy of Gallus's kind. He has set the stage for the major transformation and masterful poetry of Book IV.

Five of the eleven poems from the new book are given here, good representatives of its achievement. We can see that the love theme has been changed, sometimes obliterated by pseudo-patriotism (cf. IV 6), refined by marriage (IV 11), or assigned to a myth about early Rome (IV 4). Even when in two poems (in fact, the only ones in the book) Cynthia does play a role, the situations do not parallel those of traditional love elegy. In IV 8 Cynthia has gone off with her latest lover to be an ironic spectator of a rite connected with virginal maidens, and Propertius tries to comfort himself with two local prostitutes—not very successfully. Even more ironically, imperious and self-righteous Cynthia storms in and utterly routs her rivals and cows Propertius. The ordering of that elegy makes an ironic comment on the previous one, where the poet imagines Cynthia coming back from the dead and accusing *him* of perfidy, then confidently describing her assignment in death to the Elysian Fields, where utterly faithful lovers have their final reward! The new art of Propertius has left the formulae of love elegy behind; no longer does the personal "I" who speaks have to be identified with the male poet, because he creates female speakers who become dominant. The feelings of IV 4, IV 7, IV 8, and IV 11 are all focalized in the different female characters. Although the narrator argues that Tarpeia in IV 4 is a sinner and traitor, she makes a powerful case for herself; and significantly, Propertius has attenuated her traditional guilt by making it spring from love, not simple greed. I encourage the reader to compare IV 7 and IV 11 and try to decide whether we are to favor the persuasive liar Cynthia or the piously arrogant matron Cornelia in their self-presentations after death. Keeping in mind Propertius's childhood experiences near Perugia, his continuous alienation from the Augustan program, and his earlier advocacy of dramatically passionate love, I hope you will choose Cynthia, as I do.

I move next to the six poems of Sulpicia and to the three that are listed under Tibullus as the "Garland of Sulpicia." Both groups of elegies come from the manuscripts of Tibullus, part of a third book, but are considered to have been the work of other writers in the circle of Messalla (Tibullus's noble patron). Sulpicia identifies herself as the speaker of her poems in III 16; and she connects herself with Messalla in III 14. One likely possibility is that she is Messalla's niece, daughter of his sister and Servius Sulpicius; and that after her father's death she has become Messalla's ward.

What is especially interesting about these six short poems, which come only to forty lines in all, is that they not only dramatize a woman's personality, but are presumably the authentic voice of a female lover, the first such Roman voice to survive. As an aristocratic woman, still unmarried, Sulpicia lacked the freedom of a pleasure-loving, irresponsible woman like Catullus's Lesbia, and she could not operate in public like the courtesans of Tibullus and Propertius. Yet the situation that is assumed in her poems is that she passionately loves a young man named Cerinthus and that she risks her good name to communicate with him by these elegies, as though by letter.

If we follow the order of the elegies as given in the manuscripts, the love affair goes downhill: in III 13 Sulpicia defiantly proclaims her sexual success, regardless of reputation. In III 14 and III 15, she encounters diffi-culties over where her birthday will be celebrated. Like Delia, she has no wish to go to the country, and she ends by staying in Rome, where Cerinthus is. In III 16, Cerinthus is proving disloyal, and Sulpicia proudly compares herself, an aristocratic catch, with the whore, her rival. In III 17, she wonders, when sick, whether health without Cerinthus is of any value. And in III 18, she lets us glimpse a scene in which she was burning with passion, in response to his, but she ran away (out of modesty or perversity?) and now she bitterly regrets it. We don't have to adopt the chronology suggested by the manuscript order, and older Victorian critics liked to place the first poem last, to make a happy ending. Nor do we have to assume that these poems offer a little chronicle. Readers today find most interesting the open passion of this woman, her defiance of the typical Roman constraints on free women, and the persistence with which she woos her silent Cerinthus. Now, it seems, the delusions of love are experienced by a young woman. The "Garland of Sulpicia" is a little group of six poems which may have been inspired by the Sulpicia collection, and so they deal with the same person on several of the same occasions. The speaker is a friendly third individual who favors both the girl and Cerinthus. We hear about the birthday in III 12, about the sickness in III 10; and III 8 admiringly describes Sulpicia on the occasion of March 1, when Roman women received special presents.

The last elegiac love poet of this fertile era was Ovid. He came to Rome as an adolescent from his home town of Sulmo just as Tibullus and Propertius published their first collections, and he quickly set out to apply himself to their fascinating genre. Immensely gifted and highly productive, Ovid had a large quantity of poems that he could publish when he was not much older than twenty. That would have been not long after 23–22 B.C.E., the years when Horace and Propertius appeared with new poems. A decade or so later, Ovid revised the collection, cutting it from five to the three books that we possess today. It is a fair guess that some of the present poems were added at the time and that the poet then worked out the arrangement for this edition. What we have now is the representation of a typical male Lothario who confidently launches himself into the "game of love" with some success at first—until the game starts to go against him. Then he flounders for a while and ends up, I think, discredited. If so, that should mean that Ovid has seen through (and makes us see through) the glib and witty facade of the male lover of elegy to suggest that what the men have been talking about, with the exception of Catullus, has been a pretty shoddy, self-serving kind of "love." The silence of the beloved amid these verbal effusions of the male poets has indeed been meaningful: the men want little but sexual pleasure, not the mutuality of friendship and real love. The very outrageousness and insouciance of the Ovidian lover, then, can earn smiling admiration for a while, but his shallow opportunism ultimately condemns him, as, I think, the perceptive Ovid planned.

To start his first book, the poet claims that he has been prevented from writing epic by the forcible intervention of Cupid, who laughed at his grand efforts, then stole a foot from his second hexameter. The result was that the second line turned into a pentameter and a standard elegiac couplet appeared. Trapped in a meter without the appropriate material, the poet complained and, lo and behold, Cupid struck him with an arrow and so subjected him to love (the conventional topic). Does that sound like the usual lover, impelled to write of his beloved by passion? Not at all, and so we encounter here a witty poet making a game of love. In I 4, the Ovidian lover tries to control the game in a triangular situation, where he is currently the loser. His girl is going with another man, and all three are to attend the same dinner party. He attempts to arrange ways of communicating during the party, ways of reducing the success of his rival, but he can't win despite his cleverness. In the end, he merely requests that the girl lie to him tomorrow about what she did when she went home with the rival. He prefers deception to the bitter truth. What emerges, then, is that this kind of love thrives and depends on dishonesty and deception—which everyone practices.

The long monologue of the Ovidian lover drowns out and ignores the words, feelings, and personality of the woman. In I 5, we get the narration of a rare moment of erotic bliss, told exclusively from the male viewpoint. The girl, named Corinna, arrives at his room during the noon siesta. He sees her only as a sex object (that is the implication of the allusions) and proceeds to rip off her clothes. He says that she put up faint resistance and really wanted to lose, but that is a self-serving excuse with which we are all too familiar today. Once he has her naked, he briefly admires her (and enjoys recollecting the scene now), then moves wordlessly, lovelessly to the sexual act. He assumes that he describes love; to many in this audience, it will sound like date-rape at best. Or consider the self-serving rhetoric of I 10 and II 13. Our "fond lover" smoothly protests that the girl expects a tangible fee for her favors. Why shouldn't she? Since the man doesn't really love at all, but simply wants sexual gratification, he has destroyed the romantic relationship and its codes of behavior and replaced it with the commercial code by which she accordingly operates. All his specious protests merely mean that he is trying to weasel out of the money he owes her, and to bad-mouth her into the bargain. Even worse in II 13, our "fond lover" is worried over Corinna, who has just had an abortion and is terribly sick. He has been very angry with her, he states, but yielded to concern. He admits, in fact, that he probably got her pregnant. Now he busies himself in bribing the gods to spare her life so that he can have her to "love" again. Only in the final couplet does he address Corinna herself, to reveal his total lack of comprehension of her situation, his obvious self-interest. She must never risk another abortion, he declares. Will he assume reponsibility for his bastard? Will he give her some long-range protection as his concubine? No way! His interest is in having her sexually available. Ovid paired II 14* with this scene to show the lover railing at Corinna over the abortion, a major display of male heartlessness.

This voluble Ovidian lover tries to manipulate the amatory situation by words in place of real feelings, by wit that fails to mask his selfishness. As I said earlier, the poems of Book III seem placed there to mark his failure. The most obvious failure appears in III 7: our "fond lover" suddenly finds himself, in spite of the availability of desirable sex, impotent. For all his words, addressed in a stream to us and to what he considers his offending member, nothing, of course, happens. It is symbolically appropriate. The elegy on the death of Tibullus, III 9, has its position, I think, because it too ignores the lover and focuses on the poet's death. (Of course, it is also a superb appreciation of a dead predecessor.) In III 12, the poet/lover moans over the fact that his poetry about Corinna has advertized her attractions and thus prostituted her! Witty, ironic, and apt: he treated her as a prostitute after all, not as a woman he really loved and would make sacrifices for. In III 13, for the only time in the collection, the speaker is not involved with elegiac courtesans, but has a wife whom he accompanies out of Rome, away from temptation, to a country religious festival. In III 14, the lover reveals how far he has sunk below the ethical level of the Catullan lover. He pleads with his girl, whom he frankly recognizes as a "harlot," to pretend virtue in his presence. He will be totally content if only she does not talk about her love affairs. He wants her to deceive him and will cooperate in the deception. What arouses the tides of love and hate in him (cf. Catullus 85) is her admission that there are others. That does not say much for this loser. The final poem, III 15, which bids farewell to love elegy and promises grander works, shows a confidence in birth and achievement that invites comparison with the unhappy self-presentation of Propertius in I 22. Ovid has exposed the inner workings of love elegy, its predominantly male orientation and its primary concern with sex, not love, through the witty rascal he has created to speak his poetry.

I have said that the first edition of Ovid's love poetry appeared not long after the *Odes* of Horace, so I have not violated chronology too seriously when I insisted on treating as a group the poets after Catullus who wrote in the genre of love elegy. But I have not intended to slight Horace, whom most Latinists regard as the greatest lyric poet of Rome. He produced some excellent love poems of a special kind, only a few of which appear in this selection. He was so versatile in his subject matter, so special in the manner that he adopted, that nobody could satisfy others when choosing only a quarter of his output, twenty-five out of slightly more than a hundred odes. Unlike the other poets in this volume, Horace did not begin as a love poet or composer of odes. Already a successful publisher of two collections of satires and one of epodes, between thirty and thirty-five years old, he embarked on these lyrics as a mature, practiced poet, close to the seat of power in Augustan Rome as the confidential friend of Maecenas and associate of many other successful politicians. That maturity gave him range and inspired him to modulate his personal expression so that many readers at first find his quiet moderation disappointing, especially in comparison with Catullus and the elegists. Let us see whether we can dispel such disappointment early.

Ode I 22 has won much fame in itself, and also because its first two stanzas became the lyrics of a popular school song of the nineteenth century still popular with modern glee clubs. Horace has gone back to Catullus and Sappho for his meter and clearly cited Catullus 51.5 in his penultimate line about his "sweetly smiling" girlfriend Lalage. Latinists can point out how carefully he has "tidied up" the permissive aspects of the Catullan meter: after Horace, this stanza had a definitive pattern. The sense of control that can be felt in the meter extends its range over the topic and its presentation, too. Note the clear articulation of units: two stanzas for a large generalization about how an upright person is utterly secure; two stanzas to provide a personal illustration of the statement, from an experience that seems somewhat inappropriately invoked; and a final two stanzas to reapply the generalization to the speaker, now not a vague man of moral probity but simply an ordinary devoted lover. The basic theme is a topos that both Tibullus in I 2 and Propertius in III 16 have incidentally exploited for different elegiac situations, both with some self-irony: for them the lover is sacrosanct, and he consoles himself amid the dangers of the night, in Rome or on the roads outside the city, that, though he shivers with fear, he really need not be afraid: Venus is with him. Horace makes the topos his central concern, building it up into a universal statement about morality, not merely love, and then wittily reducing it by applying it to his own speaker's somewhat slight experience of its "truth." How was his love-probity demonstrated? Why, there he was out in the Sabine hills singing about Lalage, and a monstrous wolf, incredibly big, he insists, which could have killed and eaten him up, weaponless as he was, just ran away from him. Does that prove that love has irresistible power to protect; or are we allowed to be irreverent and suspect that the sound of Horace's voice frightened the quite ordinary beast? The enthusiasm with which the speaker develops his conclusion, that he will march across Arctic snows and Saharan sands, goes far beyond reason, and we distance ourselves, amused, from his amatory confidence. Horace regularly injects a cautionary note of self-irony into his love lyrics that serves to amuse and distance us from the speaker. (cf. III 9, IV 1 and IV 10.)

Ode I 22 also exhibits self-irony about the lyric poet himself. In many other poems here translated we hear that note extended beyond love lyric to other genres. We have the first and last poems of Books I, II, III, and IV, all of them designed to be "programmatic" and present the poet's view of his material and task as he approaches and later completes them. Consider I 1 and I 38. In the first, the speaker affects to show that being a poet is superior to all other vocations in life. His organization, however, proves to be anticlimactic, descending from what everybody recognized as greatness— being an Olympic victor or consul at Rome or the richest man in Italy—to shivering in the forest, far from wife and warm home, while hunting a deer or dangerous boar. It is from that dubious forest scene that he makes his transition to the fauns and nymphs, mythical denizens of the same sylvan scenery, and his ideal dream of poetic inspiration. Though the poem, then, argues the superiority of being a poet, it constructs its argument so as to invite our ironic distance. And the final picture of the speaker, bumping his head against the stars, concludes that ironic development. Again, in I 38, Horace, who has just presented one of his most powerful representations of tragic greatness in Cleopatra's suicide, suddenly imposes a diminuendo on that strident lyric. His speaker's insistence on simple pleasures, drinking under the vine of his little farm, brings us sharply down to earth, far from Cleopatra and also far from the stars he was bumping his head against in I 1. We usually conclude from reading the *Odes* that Horace devoted himself utterly to his craft and vocation as poet, but was cautious about how he made claims for his achievement. That modest self-irony wins our hearts.

Another favorite mode of Horatian lyric is that of protreptic, giving advice on life. Here the speaker adopts a general Epicurean stance and urges his addressee to abandon the anxieties of conventional ways of "success" through politics and business, and instead to take advantage of the simple pleasures available to us all while we live our short span of life. By and large, this is advice for the middle-aged, not for young people (who, like Catullus and Propertius, defy the thought of death in the excitement of love), and so the addressees are important men of Rome: Dellius, consul of 23 B.C.E. in I 4; Plancus, well-known supporter of Augustus in I 7; Maecenas in III 29; and Torquatus in IV 7. They are invited to leave the concerns of the city and to enjoy the ready delights of the country in a setting that today we would associate with a grand picnic. Nature has many comforts to offer; it also has an important lesson: that everything changes and that our human existence does *not* match the regular return of the seasons. We live but once; there is no second chance for pleasure.

Not bad advice, as I said, for the middle-aged business person. It, too, has its ironic side, however. Maecenas would not be Maecenas if he were not characterized as a preoccupied politician. So his essential personality is oriented toward the valid responsibilities of political life; he can afford only temporary letdowns from his necessary activities. Few people can give themselves over to a permanent existence on a South Sea island. We are not to imagine the whole Roman political and business community suddenly flocking to the hills, woods, and beaches. That is but part of life, as other odes make clear. The other aspect of irony focuses on the adviser, the lyric speaker. He seems to hide behind a pose of Epicurean wisdom and rural comfort, but at other times he reveals that the country makes him anxious with its wolves (cf. I 22) or its falling trees (cf. II 13)—that he is drawn into the city and involves himself with the serious goals of Augustan politics as a concerned Roman, if not an elected official. The poems of advice in Book I proceed from I 4 and I 7, addressed to major leaders in their late forties, to young people in I 9 and I 11, whose ideal activity is not a picnic but loving. It is not sure about how objective the speaker in I 9 may be, but we can give him the benefit of the doubt. In I 11, there is not the slightest doubt that the speaker is advising the young Leuconoe to yield to love because *he*, not she, will be the beneficiary. The generally appealing Epicurean advice of the early poems has been ironically diminished to serve the interests of the adviser.

Horace's hesitation to commit himself unreservedly to any single goal or moral system, his insistence on minimizing his enthusiasms and claims of achievement, his note of self-irony and gentle laughter at others' ardors, those are his characteristic lyric qualities. That is why he comes across as a peculiarly *personal* poet. Today, many poets have adopted that same stance of cool irony that masks serious, hard-thought and hard-felt engagement with the problems of existence. By contrast with his Epicurean, nonpolitical stance, Horace often engages himself directly with the major issues of the Augustan era with an earnestness that reminds some of the committed Stoic. It is not shallow and thoughtless patriotism, though, as the ode on Cleopatra I 37 shows. Together with his Roman exultation in an enemy's total defeat, the speaker links growing admiration for the queen's heroic fortitude: her suicide, then, symbolizes both the Roman victory and her personal "triumph."

The major political poems in this selection, namely, III 1, III 3, and III 6, come from a cycle of six successive works which it is customary to label the "Roman Odes." Announcing in the first lines of III 1 that he speaks like a priest inspired to reach out to the young, Horace then proceeds to denounce the crass materialism of his day. Although many of the moral details fit the Epicurean as well as Stoic language, nevertheless, the priestly urgency is new. Yet in the final stanza the priest withdraws and turns into the poet on his Sabine farm: Horace never pretends to be an active politician, only a concerned Roman. In III 3, he executes a similar move to engage and then disengage his commitments. He begins by describing how the Stoic virtues of selfless involvement with government, regardless of mob demands, ultimately earn apotheosis for the hero. Then he makes a transition to the Roman myth of how Romulus (a model ruler) became the god Quirinus, escaping death and ascending to Olympus in spite of the instinctive opposition of Juno. Although this founder of Rome is a descendant, through his mother Ilia, of the hated Trojans of Ilium, Juno can accept Romulus, provided that his Romans establish an absolute barrier in their new land against the corruptions that have marked Troy for destruction. Horace, in this dichotomy between Troy and Rome, symbolically alludes to the same major theme that we find in Vergil's *Aeneid* (focused on Aeneas's spiritual journey from fallen Troy to a new home in Italy): the need of Augustan Rome to break the curse of civil war in its past century, to become a new nation. Horace puts most of the preaching into the mouth of his character Juno, who is certainly fiercer and more truculent than the usual lyric "I" of the *Odes*. And so it is no surprise when, in the final stanza, the Horatian speaker disengages himself from her tone and from a wayward Muse who, he claims, has defied his characteristic light congeniality.

Although III 6 never undercuts its bleak pessimism about the general impiety and decadence of Rome and seems to predict an unbroken decline to extinction, the next poem in Book III* abruptly abandons that grim patriotic fervor with a question to its amatory addressee that seems also to apply to Horace's speaker in III 6: "What in the world are you crying about?" With politics and patriotism, as with all his other themes, Horace keeps reminding us that there are larger issues, other attitudes, and that the world can be enriched by recognizing its polarities, preferably with a smile, a generous indulgence of others' inconsistencies, and a ruefully ironic admission of our own foibles. Thus, in the final poem here offered, which is the last ode of Book IV (published when the poet was now fifty), we encounter the poet balked when he starts to overreach himself and attempt epic poetry like the *Aeneid*. Retreating, then, from exaltation of wars and conquest, certainly one real aspect of the Augustan era, the poet settles for praising the more humane achievements of the emperor: peace, security, and economic stability for the Roman world. It is as though the poet, after repeated misses in earlier poems like the Roman *Odes*, has at last found the right note for his genial lyre.

We can, if we choose, discern a double influence radiating from the works of Catullus as lyric poet and represented here in the five poets that postdate him. On the one hand, we studied the Catullan lover and his total, sympathetic, but self-deceiving personal engagement with the woman Lesbia, whom he never could understand. As she did or did not respond to his desires, she was either a goddess or a slut. That version of love was a truly unique lyric creation in Catullus's time. The later love elegists proceeded to study and develop it, limiting it to the elegiac meter, changing the status of the aristocratic Lesbia to that of a talented courtesan, and then exploring the levels of infatuation and self-deception in the lover/poet. With Ovid, that exploration ends in a lover so selfish, so in love with his own words and the gamesmanship of sex, that love becomes bankrupt in this medium. The other strand of Catullus's new poetry was his ironic observation of himself and others in the larger Roman world, its politics and its social interests and its daily preoccupations, encapsulated in carefully wrought, newly crafted lyric meters. That strand of broader personal and public concern, with its self-irony and artistic commitment, connects Catullus with Horace. Rarely has a poet found such talented and diverse admiration as Catullus did in the half-century that links him with two such different personal voices as those of Ovid and Horace; Roman lyric poetry is one of the great literary creations of an era which revolutionized the ancient world.

William S. Anderson
Berkeley, California

* Not translated in this anthology

Note on Translation

Notions of translation change through time. New translations reflect both current language usage and current expectations of what translations are and are supposed to do. In translating a poem by Sappho (see Appendix) into Latin (Catullus 51), Catullus transforms the Greek into a poem of his own. The new poem reflects Roman sensibilities and Catullus's own concerns. While the beloved addressee in Sappho's poem is nameless, Catullus addresses his beloved "Lesbia" in the second stanza and himself in the last stanza. By inserting Lesbia and himself, Catullus literally inscribes his signature on the poem.

    Catullus also substitutes his own fourth stanza for Sappho's:

> Idle ways, Catullus—they cause you trouble.
> Idling turns you on—and you've grown addicted.
> Idle ways have left bygone kings and wealthy
>   nations in ruins.

> > *(Otium, Catulle, tibi molestum est:*
> > *Otio exsultas nimiumque gestis.*
> > *Otium et reges prius et beatas*
> >   *Perdidit urbes.)*

for:

> cold sweat rushes down me,
> trembling seizes me,
> I am greener than grass,
> to myself I seem
> needing but little to die.

> But all must be endured, since . . .

> († κὰδ δέ μ' ἴδρως ψῦχρος ἔχει,† τρόμος δὲ
> παῖσαν ἄγρει, χλωροτέρα δὲ ποίας
> ἔμμι, τεθνάκην δ' ὀλίγω 'πιδεύης
> φαίνομ' ἔμ' αὔτα.

> ἀλλὰ πὰν τόλματον, ἐπεὶ . . .)

This entirely different final stanza changes the meaning and direction of the whole poem. Catullus makes it obvious where he diverges from Sappho's poem; he was not trying to fool his readers.

Throughout the ages poets have used their literary ancestors to influence, oppose, and stimulate their own poetry. Catullus uses Sappho's poem as inspiration and matrix; his goal was not to provide an accurate representation of Sappho for his contemporaries. Valerius Aedituus's epigram (see Appendix) is a condensed version of the same Sappho poem that emphasizes the stuttering tongue attempting to communicate passion:

> Attempting to tell you the love, Pamphila, in my heart,
> what I ask of you, words fail my lips.
> Down my roused breast runs sudden sweat:
> silent, aroused, I am ashamed, I die.

The twentieth-century poet H.D. (American Hilda Dolittle, 1886–1961) embedded many of Sappho's extant fragments within her own longer poems. No one considers H.D.'s Sapphics or Valerius Aedituus's epigram "translations."

It is a poor translation that turns a good Latin poem into a bad English one, however literally the English words translate the Latin. The translators in this anthology follow Catullus's example of providing good, lively poetry for the contemporary reader, but they also try to represent the original poems as accurately as possible. To the editors, accuracy means that reading these translations comes as close as possible to the experience of reading the Latin poems. The translators provide a medium for readers to discover the original poems. Each Latin poem is filtered through the translator's individual insight, and its translation becomes the expression of whatever the translator perceives as most important in the original.

The translators in this volume have used various strategies to convey their perception of the essential poem. All chose to translate verse into verse. Virtually all the translations contain the same number of lines as the Latin. Most kept very closely to the sense and specific imagery of the originals, while some occasionally updated images for effect. Jane Joyce sought to trigger in the modern audience a response equivalent to that of Catullus's poetry on the Roman audience by using modern images, such as the "needle-jab in the vein" to represent excruciating pain and addiction (Catullus 85). Other translators, such as Helen Deutsch for Propertius, tended to hold to the Latin images precisely, letting modern readers compensate for the difference in time and culture.

Each poet and poem calls for an individualized strategy. Because the Latin poems are all in strict lyric or elegiac meters, each translator had to wrestle with the task of developing a meter that worked for the English poem. For her Ovid translations, Diane Arnson Svarlien alternated roughly six-beat lines (occasionally sprawling to seven) with fairly strict iambic pentameter lines: "With this loosening-and-tightening scheme I have tried to recapture some of the metrical flavor of the original elegiac couplets. I have slipped in rhymes in just a few places, reflecting (though not exactly, of course) Ovid's play of sounds." John Svarlien followed the same metrical scheme but allowed himself a bit more freedom: "The modern English reader has metrical expectations different from those shared by Ovid's contemporaries. Neither Ovid's meter nor his syntax, moreover, can be reproduced successfully in English. In my translations I have tried to convey some sense of the sound patterns in the Latin. Above all else, I have aimed at producing couplets capable of effectively expressing Ovid's poetic voice and tone in the *Amores*." Svarlien and Arnson Svarlien had the added challenge of composing one Ovidian voice out of their two. Although they worked independently, they read and critiqued each other's translations.[1]

Although Tibullus did not compose in rhyme, Rachel Hadas's heroic couplets best convey his metrical elegance: "When I attempt to render elegiac couplets directly into English verse, rhymed iambic pentameter is the stubborn result. Tibullus's verse is elegant, often ruefully witty; his thought process tends to straggle, but the meander of ideas is easy to trace with accuracy. Heroic couplets may give my Tibullus more finality or gusto than the dying fall of the long elegiac line, and yet the shorter concluding line of the elegiac couplet has, to my ear, rather the same brisk effect as the second, rhyming line, of the heroic couplet—something snaps into place."

Stanley Lombardo strove to reproduce the serious and playful language and tone of Horace's *Odes*: "You are constantly aware of technique—verbal mosaics and virtuoso metrics—most of which cannot be replicated in English. You do what you can: work with rhythms and line breaks to get some of the shape and movement, pay constant attention to tone and diction. Horace takes pride in his craftsmanship, but he also is often the poet at play, and I have tried to get across his sense of fun."

Joyce's translations seek to recreate Catullus's innovative and sophisticated linguistic play. To do that, she created "a stable, central vocabulary of slang terms that set up the constant cross-references in the translations which exist in the originals. I wanted this core of slang to be racy, breezy, but not too period-specific. I have also invented words to echo Catullus's neologisms, employed coarseness and archaisms where he does."

Mary Maxwell's challenge was to replicate Sulpicia's fresh, innocent tone (as if her poems were spontaneous letters) crafted in skillful elegiacs. For Maxwell, the essence of Sulpicia's poetry is her "rhetorical (and frankly social) strategy that manipulates in very clever ways audience expectations in a 'courtly' society. The trope of the private letter read aloud makes

---

[1] John Svarlien translated the selections from Book I and poems 6, 7, 8, 10, and 11 from Book II; Diane Arnson Svarlien translated the selections from Book III and poems 1, 4, 13, 14, 17, 18, and 19 from Book II.

possible public expressions of desire, for one thing; it also uses this public 'announcement' as something of a threat. Sulpicia suggests that she can put a 'spin' on reports of her lover's behavior in ways that will cause her lover social embarassment. She is conscious of the power of her class, and her social superiority to potential 'competitors.'"

Like Sulpicia, all the poets in this anthology read their work publicly. For Deutsch, "Propertius makes the inherited tradition of elegy come alive through the spoken quality of his poetry. Propertius is playful, deliberately obscure, ironic, and also sincerely passionate, all at once. He uses myth as a tool to contrast with the immediate passion in his love poems, and to make political statements that he could not make otherwise. His tone frequently surprises. He succeeds in presenting how it feels to be a woman when he gives the Roman matron Cornelia or his lover Cynthia voice. When Cornelia speaks in IV 11, Propertius's tone is unexpectedly and seriously moving, even though the Roman virtue she represents is antithetical to much of his other poetry. Reading Propertius, one hears each voice performing on the stage of elegy."

The translations in this anthology reflect the various choices the translators and editors made in order to put these Latin poems into English, these strange and wonderful old wines into new bottles.

DJR

POEMS

Catullus

We know little for certain about either the life of Catullus or the publication of his poetry. He was born in Verona, probably between 87 and 84 B.C.E., and probably died at about thirty during or shortly after 54 B.C.E. In his poetry, he refers exclusively to events between 56 and 54, which would suggest an extremely short creative life for the young poet, but he himself tells us that he took up both poetry and sex at about fifteen. We do not know when he came to Rome from Verona, but there he knew some of the most prominent men in politics and literature; some he befriended, others he hated and attacked in his poetry. We learn from his poetry that he went to Bithynia as a member of the staff of C. Memmius; this was probably from the spring of 57 to the spring of 56, and that some time before that his brother had died while away from home in the Troad.

As a poet he offers a remarkable combination of intensity and flippancy, of passion and obscenity. It has been estimated that of his shorter poems, one-third include explicitly sexual material. As a love poet, he precurses the elegists in that he writes a series of poems about a single woman. She is called Lesbia, a name chosen as the metrical equivalent of her real name, Clodia, but also as a reference to the Greek poet, Sappho of Lesbos. We do not know which of the three sisters named Clodia she was, but it is generally believed that she was Clodia Metelli, the wife of Q. Caecilius Metellus, cos. 60 B.C.E.

The poetry which has survived seems to divide into three parts: sixty short poems in lyric and iambic meters; some longer poems (variously grouped as 61–64 or as 61–68), and several poems in elegiac meter (either grouped by meter as 65–116 or by length as 69–116). Many believe today that at least the collection of short poems was arranged and published by the poet in his lifetime; some believe that all three collections reflect Catullus's intentional arrangement; and a few believe that all 116 poems were published together as a book. We must see Catullus's relationship to his poetic output as carefully self-conscious and professional, a new attitude in Rome.

Catullus and his generation of poets opened the door to a range of literary expression and culture that made possible the achievements of Vergil, Horace, and Ovid: to explore their own depths of feeling and their relationship to society, to reflect on the power and limits of poetry, and to adapt the learned and allusive poetry of Alexandria to Roman realities.

Catullus

1

My dedicatee for this snazzy Slim Volume?
(its edges new-slicked with assiduous pumice):
you, Cornelius! for you always did
reckon something would come of my scribbles,
even back then when you, alone of us all,   5
boldly unfolded THE HISTORY OF THE ITALIANS
(Complete! Unabridged! 3 Brief Scrolls!)—talk about
discernment! my God, what fine work!
So, here you go: one volume (slim),
such as it is and for what it's worth,   10
which I pray (O Miss Muse, preserve me!)
may last out—outlast!—one generation.

2

(Passer noster:
Our Sparrow, which art in Heaven . . .)

Sparrow! my little maid's fancy-tickler,
the one she teases, the one she tucks in her pocket,
the one she gives her fingertip to (how he
wants it!) and constantly rouses to peck her—hard—
any time my shining heart's desire feels   5
the need for some sweet amusement or other,
a smidgette of balm for her misery, which
(I believe) eases her grievous fever:
would I could tease you just the way she does,
relieving *my* mind of its rasping anguish.   10

* * *

I'm pleased as the little maid in the fable,
the sprinter who picked up the gilded pippin
that loosed her ceinture, so long tight-laced.

3

Weep, oh weep, ye Venuses and Cupidses
and every single Venus-elect!
Sparrow is No More, my little maid's

Sparrow, my little maid's fancy-tickler,
the one she loved beyond her own eyes.   5
For he was honey-dew, knew his own
mistress, much as a maid her mother;
never did he stir a step from her lap
but, hopping about now here, now there,
peep-peeped all ways for his lady alone.   10

Now he makes his darksome way
down there, whence they declare none return.
But you be damned, you damnable Dark
Destroyer, who all things lovely devour!
You've carried my lovely *Sparrow* away!   15
O damnable deed! O poor little *Sparrow*!

Now look! you've made my little maid's eyes
red and swollen—a little—with crying.

4

The cockleshell you see before you, visitors,
declares that once she was the speediest of boats,
that not one other spar afloat could pass her—not
when she went all out; and whether we're talking sail-
power or the quick swim-strokes of oars, it matters not.   5

The ship denies that the rough Adriatic coast
denies this boast—so, too, the Cycladic Isles, and
historic Rhodes, and the wild and woolly Thracian
Bosporus and the unkind Black Sea's remoteness

(where previously our latter-day cockleshell was   10
a leaf-haired grove—for on those slopes where boxwood grows,
her long, loquacious hair tossed off near-ceaseless sounds).

O Amastris on the Black Sea shore and Cytorus, thick
with box—to you these facts neither were nor are news,
declares our cockleshell: from earliest seedlinghood   15
she stood (she says) atop your topmost mountain peak;
her oars first took a dip in your calm salt-water.

And then, Master on board, she sallied forth, crossing
a thousand stormy seas, whether a breeze to port

or starboard called, or whether God smiled and issued   20
a fair wind to fill the sails in even measure.

And not a single plaque did this ship's crew vow
to the Coast Gods until she left her seventh sea
abaft and sailed upstream to this bright backwater.

Ah! those were the days! but now, well stricken with age,   25
bemused, becalmed, she dedicates herself to you,
Castor the Twin, and to you, the Twin of Castor!

5

Live, my Lesbia, and love—let's do it!
and austere old men's aspersions,
all of them, value at ten for a penny.
The sun, new each day, can sink and return,
but we—? once sunk, our brief light's   5
night, endless, one we're bound to sleep through.
Give me a thousand kisses. Then a hundred.
Then another thousand. Then a second hundred.
Then a further thousand. Then a hundred.
Then, when we've achieved untold thousands,   10
we'll jumble them all up, so *we won't know*—and
no one spiteful can evil-eye us, since he
won't know either!—the Grand Total of kisses.

6

Flavius! you should *want* to tell Catullus
about your fancy—mum should NOT be
the word! or perhaps she's unsnazzy? unstylish?
Hmmm. . . Are you hooked on some red-hot
hooker? You *are*! and ashamed to confess it!   5
Yet your all-too-telltale bed, reeking of
scented (!) wreaths and exotic massage oil, shrieks
of the non-celibate nights you're spending.
Ditto the pillow dented equally
left side and right, the shudders and thumps   10
your peripatetic mattress attests to.
Keep a one-night stand under wraps—no way!
You wouldn't be so fucked-out *languid*
were it just a bit of slap-and-tickle!

So whatever you're onto, good or bad,   15
tell me. I want to call you and your lady-love
up sky-high by way of my snazzy verses.

7

You inquire how many of your kissimizations
would, Lesbia, suffice and sate me.
A total to equal grains of Libyan sand
spread across aphrodisiacal Cyrene
between, say, the oracle of Jove Most Torrid   5
and aged Battus's sacred sepulcher;
or else, a sum to match the many stars
which, in hush of night, observe
humans and their stealthy passions:
that's how many kisses you'd kiss   10
to suffice demented Catullus and sate him—
enough to muddle the meddlers' accounts
and stop witches wagging their evil tongues.

8

Poor dear Catullus!—would you please stop this foolishness?
Get this and get it right:
if you see that a thing has died? it's dead. Gone. *LOST.*
The sun shone, once, radiant, all yours each day,
when you went wandering right where she led you,   5
the maid we loved as no other shall ever be loved.
Then, when first those many amusements saw the light,
the ones you so wanted and the maid did not *not* want,
the sun did shine (truly!) radiant, all yours each day . . .

Now she does not want: you too, weakling, stop wanting!   10
if she runs off, don't chase her, don't *be* 'poor dear,'
but, iron-willed, plan to get past it. Be firm.
Good-bye, little maid! Catullus has now become firm.
He won't plead or invite you out, Ms. Don't-think-I-will!
But you'll fret when you find yourself uninvited!   15
Sorry bitch! shove off! What kind of life awaits you?
Who now will go near you? who'll find you appealing?
what man will you love now? whose will they call you?
whom will you kiss? whose lips will you bite?
But *you*, Catullus! stick to your plan: BE FIRM.   20

9

Veranius! of all my friends the best,
one in a million, the way I see it!
Have you come back to your hearth and home,
your agreeable brothers and aged mother?
You *have* come! O happy news! Will I   5
see you? (you're well?) and hear your tales
of Spain—scenery, customs, natives
(I know you!)—and, hugging your neck,
will I buss your cheeks and sweet eyes?
Oh, of all happy humans on earth,   10
who more delighted or happy than I?

10

Varus (a pal) had steered me out
of the Forum to see his lady-love
(I had nothing better to do):
a tart—that was my first impression—
not entirely unsnazzy and not   5
a non-Venus-elect. So
we arrived and fell to chatting of this
and that—'What's it like in Bithynia
these days? how's it going out there?
How much grease did you get anyway?' So I   10
told them how it was—zip for the natives,
let alone for the Governor or his staff,
barely the price of a dab of pomade,
especially for guys with a suck-my-cock
Gov who cared not a straw for his staff.   15
'But still, *surely*,' (they said) 'you purchased
what the place is known for—a set
of sedan-chair toters?' 'Well,' (I said,
wanting to make his little maid think
I was One Lucky Guy) 'I didn't   20
let the fact that I was assigned
a rotten province stand in my path—
I got my set: eight males in great shape.'
(*Fact was, I didn't own a one,*
either here or there, who had the strength   25
to hoist the splintered foot of an old
army-cot as high as his collar-bone!)
Then she said (Just Like a Slut!), 'Oh,

please, Catullus, won't you lend 'em to me
just for a while? I want to be chauffeured   30
to Serapis's Shrine.' 'Hold it!' I told her,
'the, you know, what I said just now
was mine? I got mixed up—my *confrère*,
Cinna Gaius, uh, Gaius Cinna—
he bought them! But his or mine, who cares?   35
I use them just as if they were mine.
But you! what a bubblehead *you* are—
you don't cut a man much slack, do you?'

11

Furius and Aurelus, Catullus's comrades
whether he makes tracks for the wilds of India
where the sunrise surf, far resounding, gives the
                    shoreline a pounding,

or if he treks off to effete Arabia,   5
or to Parthian backcountry thick with bowmen,
or to seas stained black where the seven Nile-streams
                    empty their waters,

or if he sets out to traverse the high Alps,
touring Caesar's trophies, his trail of glory,   10
namely, Gaulish Rhine and the Britons (fierce, re-
                    motest of races)—

you two, though you're ready to face these hazards
with me, face "whatever is Heaven's pleasure,"
take my *Little Maiden* a message, short but   15
                    not sweetly-worded:

Live it up. Farewell. Hope you like your lovers,
hug and squeeze them tight—all three hundred jointly—
true to none but, matter-of-factly, help them
                    all get their rocks off.   20

Tell her *she can look someplace else for my love*
which she, by her crime, cut to pieces—like a
flower at meadow's edge that the plow, in passing,
                    brushed and left broken.

12

Marrucinus Asinius, the way you employ
your light-fingered left hand is most un-
lovely: in jest and your cups, you pinch
the dinner napkins of unwary fellows!
You think that's witty? Wrong, lamebrain!   5
It's just plain mean and *not* the deed
of a true Venus-elect! You don't
believe me? Believe your brother
Pollio, who'd shell out a million
to silk-purse your larceny—and him   10
a lad chock-full of snazz and high jinks!
So: either prepare for three hundred
pasquinades, or else RETURN MY NAPKIN,
an item which rouses my Warmest Regard
no matter what it cost. Then, too,   15
it's *un souvenir de mes confrères*:
the napery we're nattering about
hails from Spain—a keepsake Fabullus
and Veranius sent me for free—
wherefore I must, I can't help but   20
love it the way I do my friends
'Ranius the Runt and Little Fab.

13

You'll dine well, dear Fabullus, *chez moi*
all in good time (if God obliges you!),
if you bring with you a gourmet (jumbo size)
dinner! Also your radiant maiden,
wine, salty wit, and the latest guffaws.   5
If, as I say, you bring all this
with you, then you, our dear Venus-
elect, will Dine Well: for your friend
Catullus's wallet is full of cobwebs.
But! in return, you'll receive my 100-   10
proof undiluted Pure Love—or,
better yet, something sweet and stylish:
for I shall give you a whiff of the scent
granted my Maid by Venuses and Cupidses
and, when you smell it, Fabullus, you'll   15
implore God to make you All Nose!

29

Who can see this, who can stand it?
None but a rutting hog of a gambler!
Mamurra's grabbed the fat of two lands—
Long-haired Gaul and remotest Britain!
Will twinkletoed Romulus see and condone it?   5
And will that supercilious superspender
ramble round from bed to bed, all
Romeo-ish, like a white love-birdie?
Will twinkletoed Romulus see and condone this?
Yes! he's a rutting hog of a gambler!   10

Was it for *him*, my singular Leader,
you went to the West's remotest isle?
so your fucked-out dick-head buddy there
could gobble down two, three thousand thou?
What's that but open-handed gone wild?   15
Did he shell out too little? scarf up too little?
First, he ripped through his family fortune;
second, the Black Sea booty; then third,
Spanish gold from (where else?) the Tajo.
Now Gaul's panicked and Britain, too.   20
Why favor him, dammit? What can he do
but devour fat patrimonies?
Is it for *him*, O Holy Father-
and Son-in-law, you've ruined Rome?

32

Pleasepleaseplease*please*, DEAR little lady-oh,
my fancy-tickler, my clever-puss,
ask me to take my siesta at *your* house.
And, if you *do* ask me, it'd be
Highly Desirable for you to arrange   5
to have the side door left unlocked
and *not to go out yourself*: no,
you stay home and get ready for our
Nine Continuous Fornifuckations.
But seriously—if you've got plans,   10
ask me *NOW*: I've had my breakfast
(protein aplenty), and I'm just lying here
on my back, making the bedclothes bulge.

34

Diana's wards are we
innocent girls and boys:
Diana! innocent boys
and girls, we sing of Thee!

O Child of Leto! high-   5
born daughter of Jove Most High!
whose mother bore Thee beside
the Delian olive tree,

to be Mistress of Mountains
and of woodlands green,   10
of forest groves well-hidden
and the river's rushing stream!

You they call Juno Lucina,
women in throes of childbirth;
You they call Lady-of-Crossroads,   15
stealthily luminous Luna.

You, Goddess, in monthly course
measure the march of seasons,
filling the farmer's barn
with all good fruits of harvest.   20

Hallowed be all Thy names:
and, as was ever Thy way,
with Thy good help, keep Thou
the race of Romulus safe.

39

Just because his teeth are dazzling white, Egnatius
flashes his grin any- and everywhere: if he goes
to court, and Counsel for Defense is wringing their withers,
he flashes a grin; if he's a mourner at a good boy's wake,
bereaved mother lamenting the loss of her only son,   5
he flashes a grin. Whatever the case, wherever he goes,
no matter *what* he's doing—he flashes a grin.
He's got this Condition which, if I may be
the judge, is neither stylish nor urbane. So,
let me give you a piece of advice, good Egnatius: 10

were you an urbane Roman, even a hick from Italy's
outback—if you were Sabine, say, or Tiburtine,
raw-boned Umbrian, plump Etruscan, or swart and toothy
Alban hillsman; were you a Gentleman of Verona
(allow me to mention my own country cousins!)—take your   15
pick of the Men Who Do Rinse Their Teeth in Pure Springwater—
still I would not want you to flash that grin just any-
old-where. What's more out-of-place than an out-of-place smile?

Now, you're a Spaniard, right? and in Spain, we hear,
the water a native makes each morn serves as his   20
mouthwash (*"Swill it around! give those red gums a good rub!"*).
Therefore, the gleamier the gloss each tooth of yours displays,
the clearer the evidence, the bigger the swig of piss!

41

Ameana's a maid with her brains fucked out—
hit *me* up for ten thousand clams,
she did, that maid with the out-sized snout,
friend of the Bankrupt Playboy of Formiae!

You next-of-kin, who look out for this   5
maid, convene her friends and physicians!
She's Not Well, this little maid—she fails
to consult her brazen reflectiose mirror!

43

Greetings, little maid with nose not teeny,
foot not comely, eyes not inky,
fingers not slim, lips not slobberless,
and tongue distinctly short on taste!

Friend of the Bankrupt Playboy of Formiae,   5
does the province proclaim *you* lovely?
and is our Lesbia compared with *you*?
O times uncouth and unclever!

46

At last! spring thaws bring back balmy bloom-time!
At last! the blustering days of in-like-a-lion
skip off like lambs to Zephyr's pleasant airs.

Come, Catullus, let's leave the plains near Troy,
grainfields plump and hazy under Nicene heat: 5
to Asia's fabulous cities let us fly!

At last! my mind quivers, eager for elsewhere.
At last! my feet thrill, new-nimble with glee.

O sweet band of companions, fare ye well!
long since, we set out from home together: 10
high roads and low lead us back, no road the same.

49

Of all the great-grandsons of Romulus,
dead or living or as yet unborn,
you are the most eloquent, Marcus Tully.
To you profoundest thanks are due
from Catullus, Worst Poet of All—   5
the Worst Poet of All as *you*
are the Best Attorney of All!

50

Yesterday, Licinius, we put in a hard
day's work, fooling around with my notebook—
a game we'd agreed would amuse us:
we each wrote lines of verse in turn,
fooling with one meter after another,   5
passing everything back and forth—
wine punch flowed fast as the punch lines.

And I came away from there, Licinius,
so fired up by your wit and wisecracks
that (poor me!) dinner had lost its appeal   10
and night spread no sleep on my eyes
but, in unbridled frenzy, I bucked

and tossed, longing for dawn, when I
could talk to you and be with you.

Later, bone weary with stress and strain, 15
lying semi-expired on my pallet,
I made this poem for you, sweet friend,
by which you may gauge my anguish.

Careful now! don't be heartless! Careful,
bright-eyes, I beg you, don't curl your lip 20
at our pleas—or you'll get yours from
Nemesis. That's one implacable goddess—
don't upset *Her*, you hear? Take care!

51

He appears, to me, to be God's own equal,
he (may God forgive me!) surpasses all Gods,
he that sits so matter-of-factly near you,
        watching and hearing

your delicious laughter—a thing which (ah me!) 5
rips out all my senses for, when I see you,
Lesbia, I disintegrate, nothing's left of
        [me, I am speechless.]

Yes, my tongue goes numb, tender fire is
seeping down through bone marrow; ears re-echo, 10
belling their own notes; over both bright eyes, night
        knots double blindfolds.

(Idle ways, Catullus—they cause you trouble.
Idling turns you on—and you've grown addicted.
Idle ways have left bygone kings and wealthy 15
        nations in ruins.)

55

We implore you—if perchance it's no trouble—
to point out just where your Shady Nook is.
We've looked for you at the racetracks (both Bijou
and CircMax), checked out all the bookstores, even
cased the temple sacred to Jove Most High. 5

Likewise, my friend, I collared all the femettes
strolling in Pompey's Portico—but not
one of those innocents batted an eye.
"Give him back!" (that's how I accosted them)
"Give me Camerius, you *wicked* little maids!"   10
One of them, making a clean breast of it, said:
"C'm'ere yourself: he's hiding—between my pink tits!"

To put up with you now is Ye Labor of Hercules,
you keep your distance with such disdain, dear friend!
Tell us your schedule (when and *where*), broadcast it   15
boldly, **trust me**. Step into the Light of Day!
The Peaches 'n' Cream Girls are keeping you, right?
If you keep your tongue sealed up in your mouth,
you'll waste all the tasty fruits of love—
Venus Verbosa likes *lots* of gossip!   20
Or, if you want, you can keep your hatch latched,
so long as *I* get a load of your love(s)!

57

It all comes together for no-good butt-fucks,
for Mamurra and cock-sucking Caesar.
And no wonder: double trouble,
those two; Roman lesions I and II,
Formian rank and defilement; twin   5
zits—squeezed, they ooze indelible ink.
A loathsome twosome, little inseparables,
litteratini on one weeny couch,
eager other-fuckers, the pair of them,
rivals, allies—even of sub-debs.   10
It all comes together for no-good butt-fucks!

58

Caelius, our Lesbia—you know, *Lesbia*,
that Lesbia, the one woman Catullus
loved more than himself or his kinsmen—
now at crossroads and down back alleys,
she's jerking off Mighty Remus's grandsons.   5

63

Over the deep seas he sailed,
     Attis in his racing ship,
and when his eager, speeding feet
     reached the Phrygian grove,
stepping into the shadows,
     the Goddess's tree-ringed precinct,
goaded to raging frenzy,
     crazed with hallucinations,
he struck off the hanging weight from his groin
     with a sharp, flint knife,   5
and then, conscious his sex had been cut
     away from his body,
drops of bright blood still falling,
     splashing the soil of Earth,
in hands deft and snowy,
     she took up the light tambourine
(*Your tambourine, Cybele,*
     Your holy instrument, Mother!);
slender fingertips tapping
     the taut membrane of bull's hide,   10
she rose up to sing
     this quavering song to *her* companions:

"Up, Gallae, up!
     to the high groves of Cybele! Come with me,
come with me,
     dazed flock of the Lady of Dindymon!
Eager as refugees seeking asylum,
     you fell in behind me,
followed my footsteps,
     up the gangway, onto the cutter,   15
heedless of turbulent surf,
     the ocean's sullen rage, and
you unmanned your flesh
     in fanatic hatred of Venus: now,
with steps swift and far-ranging,
     fill our Mistress with ecstasy!
Slow hesitation must slip from your minds.
     Come with me, follow me,
on to Cybele's Phrygian abode,
     the Phrygian grove of the Goddess   20

where gongs give clamorous tongue,
    where tambourines rattle response,
where Phrygians coax low notes
    from their oboes' flaring bells,
where Maenads fling back manic heads,
    brows entwined with ivy,
where, with piercing shrieks,
    they shake the sacred insignia,
where the Goddess's wandering troupe
    delights to swoop—   25
there must we hasten,
    dancing our swift tarantellas!"

And when, to *her* companions,
    Attis the sham woman sang,
at once they raised a cry,
    ululating tongues aflutter,
tambourines bellowed in rapid response
    and hollow gongs clashed,
feet beat a quick riff as revelers
    tore up Ida's green slopes.   30
Delirious, panting, reeling, *she* went
    rushing at once through
shadowy groves, a tambourine in attendance;
    fighting for breath,
forcing *herself* to lengthen *her* loping stride,
    Attis surged ahead
like an untamed heifer
    shying away from the onerous yoke;
Gallae scrambled to
    follow *her* fleet-footed lead.   35
And so, when they, spent,
    reached the abode of Cybele
in utter exhaustion, they feasted on
    sleep, not on bread, while
stumbling Stupor, heavy-lidded,
    fumbled their eyes shut.
Soothed by repose,
    that frenzied rage of the mind seeped away.

* * *

But, when the Sun
    with his golden face and blazing eyes, swept   40

in solemn procession across
      crystal sky, massed lands, untrammeled sea,
and his steeds dashed away dark of night
      with fast-drumming hooves,
then Sleep, eager to flee,
      abandoned the now-wakeful Attis
and sought the arms
      his divine wife held out in tremulous welcome.
Then, deserted by soothing repose
      and by fast-paced frenzy,   45
Attis at once began
      to relive in *her* mind what *she*'d done,
seeing by reason's cold light
      where *she* was and without what.
Head spinning,
      she made *her* way back to the beach once more;
there, surveying the vast ocean,
      eyes streaming with tears,
she called out to *her* country—
      an anguished, abject cry: 50

"Dear land, source of my origin,
      dear land, site of my birth!
Poor fool that I was,
      I left you as runaway houseboys
flee their master,
      guided my steps up to Ida's groves,
bent on a life in the snow,
      in the freezing lairs of wild things,
wanting (demented!) to march
      right up to their shadowy dens—   •   55
where was I thinking to find you,
      where to locate you, my land?
The very pupil of my eye
      longs to light upon you,
while, for a brief time,
      my mind is clear of wild raging.
Shall I be borne to these groves,
      torn away from my home?
Shall I from my land, my goods,
      my friends, my parents be absent?   60
absent from plaza and track,
      from wrestling ring and gymnasium?
Wretched! ah, wretched mind,

again and again you must wail:
'What manner of form exists
    which I have not assumed?'
I am a woman,
    I who was once a man, a youth, a boy. . .
I was an athlete in full bloom,
    glistened supreme among wrestlers,   65
fans flocked to my door by day,
    warmed my doorstep nightly,
ringed my house 'round
    with their chaplets of fresh-cut flowers
each day I was due
    to make my way from my bedroom at dawn.
Shall I now be called
    the Deity's handmaid, Cybele's
slave-girl? Shall I be a Maenad,
    a part of myself, a eunuch?   70
Must I haunt the green slopes
    of chilly, snow-capped Mount Ida?
live out my life
    at the foot of Phrygia's lofty peaks
with doe and boar,
    with woods-haunter and grove-wanderer?
Now, *now* I regret my deed,
    now I rue it, now."

* * *

When those rapid words
    went forth from *her* rosy lips,   75
conveying unwelcome news
    to the twin ears of the Deity,
then Cybele
    loosed the linking yoke from Her lions and,
goading the carnivore on the left,
    She called to it:

"Come up!" She cried,
    "Up, my fierce one! Make madness attack
him, turn him back with the blow of madness,
    back to the groves!   80
this man who too freely
    desires to flee my commands!
Come, thrash your flanks with your tail,
    endure its lashing,

make all the region resound
>with your thunderous roar,
shake the tawny mane on your brawny neck,
>my fierce one!"

With this, dread Cybele
>undid the yoke with Her hand: 85
the beast worked itself up,
>rapidly rousing its bloodlust;
it prowled, it roared, it paced back and forth,
>trampling brambles underfoot,
and, when it approached
>the damp expanse of foam-flecked shore,
spying slender Attis
>beside the sparkling sea,
it sprang.
>Demented, *she* ran back into the wild groves,   90
there to remain for all *her* days,
>forever a slave-girl.

* * *

Goddess, great Goddess, Cybele,
>*Goddess, Mistress of Dindymon,*
far from my house
>*may You keep Your madness, my Lady:*
drive other men wild,
>*other men drive to this frenzy!*

68

Bowed down with bad luck and bitter misfortune, you send me
>this *petite lettre* scribbled with your tears:
Please lighten the load of a shipwrecked man the sea and foaming
>*waves have tossed ashore—save him from Death's threshold.*
No release through velvety sleep does holy Venus   5
>*allow him, abandoned in his lonely bed,*
nor do the Muses charm him with sweet-spelling writers
>*of old, when his anguished mind turns sleepless. . .*

Your appeal I find pleasing, for you say you hold me dear and
>ask to sample my Musings—also erotica.   10
But, should you not know my unhappiness, Mallius,
>or think I scorn a protégé's obligations,

consider what seas of bad luck I drown in myself—
    don't ask a poor wretch for trifles and trinkets!
Since first I put on young man's dress whites, when my youth   15
    bloomed in its heady green age, I had my fun
and then some: no stranger to me, the Goddess who cuts
    love's bittersweet draught with lacings of woe!
But all such concerns have been swept away in grief
    at my brother's death.
                           (Brother, taken from me—   20
poor wretch: dying, you—oh, you have shattered all my happiness,
    our whole household lies in the grave beside you,
all things perished the instant you did—each and every
    pleasure that, in life, your sweet love nourished.)

Because of his untimely death, I've emptied both   25
    mind and heart of all sweet frivolities.

So, Mallius, when you write, *'Tis a shame to stay in Verona,*
    Catullus, since here, anyone worthy of note is
thawing his frozen flesh in the bed you left abandoned—
    it's no shame: say rather, *'Tis a pity . . .*   30

And thus, you must forgive me if I do not oblige you
    with those gifts that grief has taken from me—
I can't help it: my stockpile of sample writings
    is low, for Rome's where I **live**. That's where I make
my home, that's where I've put down roots, there I'm most alive;   35
    here, I make do with but one box of books.
Such being the case, please don't imagine I'm acting this way
    with malice aforethought, intending to slight you:
my stock cannot supply you with either of your requirements;
    if I had them in stock, I'd gladly deliver.   40

                    * * *

I cannot keep quiet, Muses, in view of how
    and how often my *Allius* has come to my rescue,
lest, in eons of obliteration, fleeting Time should
    cover this kindness of his with sightless night.
No, I'll tell you the tale: do you, in years to come, tell   45
    thousands more, making this page speak in its old age.
[Muses, grant me words to bring my friend joy in his lifetime;]
    may he in death receive ever-increasing fame!
Let no spider, spinning her gossamer thread high up, work
    her web across *Allius's* neglected name.   50

For, what agony Cyprus's two-faced Goddess has given me,
      what means she's used to torment me, you know well,
since I burned with fires as hot as Sicilian Etna's,
      hot as the boiling springs near Thermopylae,
my unhappy eyes welling up with incessant tears,   55
      ever splashing my cheeks with their dismal rain
the way a stream, sparkling high on the peak of a wind-swept
      mountain, leaps down ledges bearded with moss:
plunging headlong, it rolls out onto a sloping valley,
      then veers across a highway thronged with people—   60
sweet relief for the traveler in his sweaty exhaustion
      when sweltering heat leaves the fields parched and cracked.
But, as to sailors caught in a black and turbulent gale
      there comes a kindly breeze with breath more gentle,
one they prayed for, imploring Pollux first, then Castor,   65
      so has *Allius* proved to be my ally!

For he opened wide the way into a narrow field
      (that is, he lent me and my mistress a house)
where we could exercise our mutual fascination.
      Here my radiant angel directed her tender   70
steps; the sole of her shining foot brushed the polished threshold;
      her sandal squeaked; she hesitated . . .
just as, long ago, Laodamia, blazing with love
      of her husband Protesilaus, approached his house,
a house unfinished—for no victim had yet bought   75
      the High Gods' blessing with its holy blood.

(Nemesis! may I never want something badly enough
      to go after it rashly, without Gods' good will!)

How much the starved altar craved sacrificial blood
      Laodamia learned when she lost her husband,   80
forced to unwind her arms from about her bridegroom's neck
      before one winter and then a second came
with the long nights that would see her greedy passion sated,
      giving her strength to endure the separation
that the Fates knew all too well was not far off if ever   85
      he went for a soldier against the walls of Troy;
for in those days, given the rape of Helen, Troy was
      finding the chief heroes of Greece lined up against her:
Troy (atrocity!), the mass grave of Asia and Europe,
      Troy, acrid ash of heroes and all heroism—   90

why, *why* has she also inflicted a wretched death on my
    brother?
                Ah, brother, taken from me (poor wretch!);
ah, light of joy taken from my brother (poor wretch!);
    our whole household lies in the grave beside you,
all things perished the instant you did—each and every   95
    pleasure that, in life, your sweet love nourished.
Now he is so far away—not among tombs well-known,
    not laid to rest near the ashes of kinsmen,
but buried at Troy, that bleak and baleful ghost town! buried
    deep in the distant clay of a strange land . . .   100

To Troy, then, they sped (so goes the tale)—the bravest
    and best in all Greece, leaving hearth and home,
lest Paris have time for the harlot he'd abducted,
    leisurely hours at peace and ease in her bed.
Misfortune for you, Laodamia, loveliest of women!   105
    that's when you lost your husband, sweeter than life
or breath: the hot tide of passion, a whirlpool drawing you
    down, had swept you into an underground cavern,
deep as the one near Cyllenian Pheneus which (claim the Greeks)
    drains the swamp and leaves the rich soil dry,   110
the one (we hear) which, long ago, pseudo-Amphitryo's
    son dug, hollowing out the mountain's core
in the days when, with his surefire shafts, he picked off monstrous,
    man-eating birds at his mere-mortal master's behest,
so that yet more Gods could polish Heaven's threshold   115
    and Hebe need not be a virgin long.

But your deep love, deeper than that underground cavern,
    taught you, untamed till then, to bear the yoke;
for Protesilaus was dear to you, wasn't he, lovely
    Laodamia?—dearer to you than his grandson's head   120
is to an old man, the baby so long awaited,
    nursing at the breast of his daughter, his only child:
the infant arrived only just in time to be named
    heir to the family fortune in the old man's will
(Cousin found he'd been cut off without a dime!),   125
    driving away the vulture circling the white-haired head.
No dove ever found her snow-white mate such a source
    of pleasure—and she, they say, will bill and coo,
forever nibbling kisses, more wanton than any
    woman, even a downright flighty one.   130

Laodamia alone has outdone the doves' fierce ardor
    from the day she wed her golden-haired husband.

No difference (or not much) that day the light of my life,
    nestling in my arms, gave herself to me—
Cupid, dazzling white in his robe of crocus-yellow,   135
    fluttered about her this side and that—more than once.
She—well, though she's not content with Catullus alone,
    we'll endure Milady's occasional indiscretions:
we would not want, in the fashion of fools, to make a fuss.
    Even Juno, Heaven's Queen, has often   140
choked down rage that blazed when Her spouse strayed—*She* knew of
    omnamorous Jove's numerous indiscretions!
Still, it's not fair that humans be compared with Gods.
    Thankless task, to play the querulous elder . . .
And it's not as if she'd walked down the aisle on her father's arm,   145
    come home with you to a rose-covered cottage,
no—that wondrous night, she gave you stolen goods, trifles
    taken from the very arms of her husband.
So this is enough—that she should keep her calendar clear,
    dazzling white, on days appointed for *us*.   150

This gift, *Allius*, such as it is, composed of a poem,
    I present to you for your many favors
that this day and the next and tomorrow and tomorrow
    should not touch your name with corrosive rust.
To this the Gods will add as many blessings as,   155
    in bygone days, Justice gave the upright.
May you prosper, you and the light of your life together,
    also the house where I and my mistress made sport,
[and the bed where, in the beginning, we two got no sleep,]
    and where, at first, all good things were begotten,   160
and she, who beyond all others is dearer to me than myself,
    my life who, living, makes life sweet for me.

70

My woman says there's no one she'd want to marry
    more than me—not if Jove Himself proposed.
Says she. But what a woman says to her urgent lover
    should be written on wind and white water.

72

You used to say, once, that you knew only Catullus,
    Lesbia, that you'd not take Jove before me.
I cherished you then, not the way men do their sweethearts,
    but as a father cherishes sons and sons-in-law.
Now *I* know *you*: so, though the burn's deeper and costs me more,   5
    still I find you cheaper and much more trifling.
How can that be, you ask? Simple. This kind of wrong
    makes a lover *love* more but *like* less.

73

Don't even *want* to expect anything from anyone
    or think someone can be made conscientious.
All deeds are thankless, no kindness shown ever wins
    a medal—no, it's just *tiresome*, it's *meddling*.
So say I, speaking as one hard-hit—and by whom?   5
    the man who claimed I was his one and only friend.

75

To this has my mind been reduced, Lesbia, by your crime,
    and by its own devotion so doomed itself,
that now it *can*not like you—though you change for the best,
    nor cease to love you—though you do your worst.

76

If a person feels any pleasure in recalling
    past kindnesses when he thinks, with clear conscience,
that he has shattered no hallowed faith nor broken
    any true allegiance to play someone false,
much is in store for you in the long years ahead, Catullus—   5
    joy on joy derived from this thankless love:
for whatever one person can in kindness say or
    do for another, that have you said and done.

Everything you entrusted to a thankless mind is lost—
    so why put yourself through further torment?   10
why not stiffen your will and pull back from where you are now
    and, as God is against it, don't *be* 'poor dear.'

No easy thing, to set old love aside of a sudden . . .
    No easy thing but, somehow, you've *got to do it*.
This is your one hope, this is a fight you must win,   15
    you've just **got** to, possible or not.

O God, if mercy is Thine, or if Thou hast ever
    succored mortals at the last—even in death—
look upon me (poor me!) and, if I have led a pure life,
    rip from my flesh this poisonous putrefaction   20
which, creeping like cancer into my deepest marrow,
    has squeezed all happiness out of my heart.

No more do I pray either that *she* should cherish *me*
    or—since it's not possible—want to be true:
I yearn to be well and to set this loathsome illness aside: 25
    God, grant me this, for I am a man of good conscience!

83

Lesbia gives me (husband right there!) a good tongue-lashing—
    an act which affords that fathead the rarest
felicity. Oxbrain! you don't get it. If she cold-
    shoulders us, she's cured; but, because she's
squawking a blue streak, (A) she remembers and (B) what's more
    to the point—she's enraged. Cold talk, hot pants.

85 Two Versions

        I loathe and I love. Why do it, perhaps you ask?
            I don't know—I just feel it happening,
                needle-jab in the vein.

                        *

        Hate/love, love\hate: cross-purposes.
            You want to know how come?
        Don't know. *Do* know I feel it come.
            Flesh, spike: I'm both, I'm torn.

86

To many, Quintia's a "10." To me, she's glossy, long-legged,
    clean-limbed—a number of fine points, I grant you.
But Total Perfection? I think not. There's no sparkle,
    not a pinch of wit in all that Great Bod.
Lesbia's perfection: utterly lovely, yes—and more!   5
    all other starlets dim beside this Venus!

92

Lesbia's always giving me a good tongue-lashing—
    I'm what she can't shut up about.
    GodDAMN if Lesbia doesn't love me!

What's my proof? the fact that, in every particular, I'm
    just like her: I slam her persistently
    but—GodDAMN if I don't love her!

93

Do you like me, Caesar, or not?
Do I care? does it makes much diff?
I can't be bothered to figure out if
you're six of one, or not.

95

Zmyrna! begun by my good friend Cinna nine long harvests,
    nine long winters ago—brought into this world at last!
(The Horror of Hatria has, in the meantime, whelped five hundred
    zillion lines of his mangy doggerel per day . . .)
Zmyrna! will reach the undercut banks of the river Satrachus;   5
    Zmyrna! will please readers from age to white-haired age.
(Scrolls of Volusius's *Annals* float by, belly-up in the Po—
    shoals of dust jackets, loose-fitting mackerel wrappers.)
So what if turgid Antimachus tops the list of bestsellers?
    Philetas's slim edition is dear to my heart!   10

101

Many the nations and many the oceans I have crossed
 to come here, brother, to this poor gravesite,
for I wanted to make you the mourner's parting gifts
 and speak these words (useless!) to your mute dust.
But, given that mischance has carried you off—*you*!—   5
 (ah, my poor brother, taken from me so young),
still, even so, accept these—prescribed by custom,
 age to age, the mournful gifts at graveside:
accept them, wet as they are with a brother's tears,
 and now and forever, brother, farewell.   10

109

Proposal, dear heart, or proposition? that this love
 we share shall be ours, ours alone, forever.
Ye mighty Gods, enable her to make a promise
 honestly, to speak sincerely and from the heart,
that we, for all our days, may jointly constitute   5
 one couple, under God, indivisible . . .

Tibullus

We know little about the life of Tibullus. We do not even know his *praenomen*, or "first name." It is thought that he came from Gabii, a town in Latium, but that depends on an unproven conjecture. Beyond his own statements in his poetry, we have two poems addressed to him by Horace, of which one describes the poet as a good critic who is at that time living in Latium, philosophical and depressed; Horace encourages him to enjoy his good looks, his wealth, his health, and his "art of enjoyment." In Rome, Tibullus was a close friend of Messalla and a member of Messalla's literary circle. He was probably younger than Propertius, and died before the age of forty shortly after Vergil died in 19 B.C.E. This will place his date of birth between 58 and 50 B.C.E. He spent his youth, then, in the last days of the Republic, just after J. Caesar, M. Crassus and Cn. Pompey had formed the First Trium virate. He lived to see the victory of Octavian over Antony in 31 B.C.E., the so-called "Restoration of the Republic." Given the political turmoil of the time, and given the fact that Messalla, who had been quick to shift his allegiance from Antony to Octavian, had played an important role in politics as augur, consul, and triumphant general, it is striking that Tibullus remains entirely silent about particular events and policies. He never mentions Augustus, Maecenas, or Actium. He is concerned with peace and the country side, but as general poetic and personal concerns, not as direct reflections of political realities or of a partisan ideology.

Following Catullus and Gallus (see the Introduction for the role of Gallus in elegy), Tibullus wrote of his love for a certain blond-haired and blue-eyed Delia. We are told that her real name was Plania, but some find it altogether too convenient that the pseudonym Delia which has clear associations with Delian Apollo, god of poets, and his sister Diana, goddess of the countryside, would be both the metrical equivalent of Plania and a direct translation of that name into Greek. We gather from the poems that she was a freedwoman, probably living in concubinage to another man. Historicity, however, is not so much to the point. She remains in Tibullus more the literary locus for contemplating the Tibullan dream of leisure, love, contentment, and the ancestral countryside, than a real flesh and blood person. In Book I, Tibullus also wrote of his love for a young man, Marathus, and, after the affair with Delia, Tibullus wrote in Book II of an affair with a girl named Nemesis.

Tibullus

I 1

Let someone else heap up a bulging pile
Of gold, and own vast acres of rich soil.
He toils away, forever on the watch
For enemies; sleep shuns his anxious couch.
Let peaceful poverty be my tranquil lot,   5
The home-fires always glowing in the grate.

When planting season rolls around, I'd graft
Young vines; tend apples too with rustic craft.
Bountiful Hope would yield a bumper crop,
Filling each bin and wine jar to the top.   10
For lonely stumps can be my prayers' abode,
Or flower-decked stones that mark a triple road.
Whatever first-fruits harvest season yields,
I offer to the patron god of fields.

Ceres, let a crown of homegrown wheat   15
Hang up to decorate your temple gate.
And in the garden let Priapus stand
To frighten birds, his sickle in his hand.
Poverty-stricken gods of property
Once prosperous, Lares, take your gift from me: 20
Countless heifers once upon a time,
But the small plot now yields one meager lamb.
To grace the feast at which the country boys
Pray for "Good crops! Good wine!" with joyful noise.

If only I could make my home right here   25
And not keep moving on forevermore,
I'd seek out shade, the Dog Star rising high,
Under a tree, some burbling brook nearby.
I wouldn't be too proud to wield a spade
Or urge on lazy oxen with a goad;   30
Any abandoned kid or little lamb
Left by its mother I would carry home.

Robbers and wolves, please spare my little flock;
Do your plundering from some richer stock.

Both flock and peaceful Pales are my care;   35
Offerings and milk I sprinkle every year.
Oh Gods, be present at my humble feast!
My simple pottery is clean, at least.
(A farmer first invented pottery,
Molding goblets out of the soft clay.)   40

My father's fortune, Grandfather's rich crop,
Carefully garnered—these I can give up;
A humble income is enough for me,
And my own bed to sleep in peacefully.
Delicious, hearing the wild wind's alarms   45
While cuddled up within my mistress's arms,
And when harsh gales drench all the world in mire,
To sit and snooze in safety by the fire!
I ask no more; all riches cheerfully
I give to those who weather storms at sea.   50

Let all gold rot, and every emerald too,
Rather than one girl weep to see me go!
Messalla, you through land and sea must roam
To show your captured booty off at home;
While to a woman's beauty captive here,   55
Janitor-like I guard her stubborn door.

What I want, Delia, isn't praise but you—
Let them call me sluggish, lazy too.
You I will gaze at in my dying hour,
You I will touch with my hand's failing power.   60
And when upon the funeral pyre I lie,
Your tears and kisses will gush forth for me.
Yours is no brazen heart, but flesh—and sore;
Your tender bosom hides no flinty core.
From my funeral no one will go home   65
Dry-eyed, neither maiden nor young man.
But violence, Delia, wounds my ghost; so please,
No hair-tearing, cheek-scratching—omit these.

All this will come. Turn now to love instead,
Before dark Death sneaks up with muffled head   70
And feeble Age limps forward. It's not right
To say sweet nothings when your hair is white.
Grab hold of Venus! Now's the time to break
Down doors, be riotous for love's sweet sake.

I am both general and private here.   75
Let greedy men be wounded—I don't care—
And wealthy too. My livelihood's secure;
I can look down on both the rich and poor.

12

Fill up my glass again! The anodyne
For this poor lover's pain is sleep—and wine.
And when I've swilled enough to sink a ship,
No busybody better wake me up.
A cruel door stands between my girl and me,   5
Double-locked with a determined key.

Damn you, door! May rainstorms mildew you,
Or well-aimed lightning rot you through and through.
Aren't you moved by all my misery?
Please, door, open just a crack for me,   10
But carefully—don't creak. If I just said
Harsh things, may curses light on my own head.
I hope you've not forgotten all my prayers,
And all the times I hung your knob with flowers.

You, Delia, must be bold and cunning too;   15
Venus helps those who help themselves, you know.
Whether a boy sneaks to a strange room or
Stealthily a girl unlocks the door,
Venus teaches sorties out of bed,
Teaches our footsteps soundlessly to pad,   20
Or lovers to communicate by sighs
Before the hoodwinked husband's very eyes.
But you must have initiative, and dare
To prowl around at midnight without fear.

Take me—I wander through the streets all night.   25
Plenty of thieves and muggers are in sight,
But Love protects me from the switchblade knife
Scenario ("Your money or your life!").
In holiness a lover's safety lies;
It's needless to envision plots and spies.   30
No frosty winter night can do me harm;
Rain falls in torrents, but I'm safe and warm.

True, now I'm suffering; that could turn around
If Delia beckoned me without a sound.

Whoever sees us, please pretend you didn't;   35
Venus prefers her lovers snugly hidden.
Don't make a racket, do not ask my name
Or blind me with an outthrust torch's flame.
If you were fool enough to see us, then
Pray to the gods that you'll forget again.   40
The tattletale must learn the parentage
(Tempest and blood) that fuels Venus's rage.

But even if some busybody tells
Your husband all about us, magic spells
Will seal his eyes. A witch has promised me.   45
I've seen her pull the stars down from the sky.
Her charms can change a running river's flow,
Split open graves and let dead spirits go.
From pyres still smouldering she can wheedle bones,
Commanding ghostly troops with weird groans;   50
Then, sprinkling milk, she orders them away.
Clouds she disperses from a sullen sky.
In midsummer she can make it snow;
She knows Medea's herbs and where they grow;
The hounds of Hecate she can tame at will.   55

To cheat him, she's concocted me a spell
To chant three times, and each time spit as well.
From that time on, no matter what he sees,
He'll be unable to believe his eyes.
But keep away from other men! He'll be   60
Suspicious of every man but me.
This sorceress claimed that she could cure me too;
Her charms and herbs could set me free—of you.
She purified me at the witching hour
By torchlight, and slew victims with her power.   65
But what I prayed for was a love to share;
Life without you would be bleak and bare.

Ironheaded fool, who had you in his bed
But chose a military life instead!
Let him parade his troops of prisoners forth   70
And pitch his tent on bloody captured earth.
His armor's silver worked with gold, of course,

So let him preen in it astride his horse.
For myself, let me yoke up my two
Oxen and plow, so long as I'm with you.   75
When we are intertwined in one embrace,
Sweet sleep on the bare ground is no disgrace.
Why toss on purple counterpanes, awake
And weeping all night for a lost love's sake?
Down comforters, rich bedspreads cannot bring   80
Sleep, nor can soft water murmuring.

Have I offended with my blasphemy,
Venus, and do I pay the penalty?
Can it be said that I've profaned the shrine,
Despoiled the altar of its boughs divine?   85
If this were true I'd go down on all fours
And plant a kiss upon the temple floor;
Kneeling in supplication on the ground,
Against the door my wretched head I'd pound.

Whoever finds this laughable—you'll see!   90
You too will suffer from Love's cruelty.
An oldster thinks a lovelorn youth's a joke,
But soon his wrinkled neck is in the yoke.
He whistles senile ditties to the air
And carefully arranges his white hair,   95
Loiters for hours at his beloved's gate
And buttonholes her servant in the street.
Children pursue him, a malicious flock
Who spit in their own bosoms for good luck.

Venus, I've always served you faithfully.   100
Don't burn your harvest in your rage at me!

I 5

I claimed in anger that our separation
Left me cold—ah, what a foolish notion!
For now I'm helpless, twirling like a top
Driven by clever boys—I cannot stop.
Bring irons, fire, all instruments whose pain   5
Will keep me from such silly boasts again.

Be good to me. I beg you by our bed,
By loving memories of my sleeping head
Near you, and by my kindness. When you lay
Fever-racked, who else snatched you away   10
From death? Who sprinkled sulfur here and there
While an old woman hummed a magic air?
Who else subdued the evil dreams of night,
Fed them with meal lest they should cause you fright?
Who else with loosened tunic bowed before   15
The nether powers at the witching hour?
But everything I've done has been in vain;
Another tastes the fruits of all my pain.

Happily ever after, so I thought
(Madman!), we'd live. The gods appended "not."   20

With Delia at my side, said I, I'll farm.
She'll oversee the threshing of the grain
In blazing noon, and watch the steady beat
As laborers tread the grapes with flashing feet.
She'll learn so much! to count the flocks; to play   25
Sweetly with the hired man's little boy;
And how to please the hungry gods as well,
Offering corn, grapes, or a brimming bowl.
She shall be mistress of the whole domain;
My great delight will be to stay at home   30
Doing nothing. Let Messalla come;
Delia can pick the ripest fruit for him
And wait on him with her white hands, to show
How deep the veneration that's his due.
Such were my dreams—mere figments, tempest-tossed   35
Now to remote Armenia—all lost.

I've often hoped that wine would drive my cares
Away—alas! pain turned the wine to tears.
To other women, true, I've turned as well,
But memories of you broke Venus's spell   40
Upon fulfillment's brink. Thus rumor ran
I was accursed, bewitched, a doomed, damned man.
No magic spells for this does Delia need—
Only that face, those arms, that golden head,
Fair as the sea-nymph Thetis when she rode   45
Upon a fish, Peleus's future bride.

I'm ruined. Watch some rich successor come!
Of course some clever bawd concocts my doom.
Oh, may her meals be soaked in blood, her vile
Lips drink from cups befouled with bitter gall!   50
Let snickering spirits flit and moan their fate
Around her head, while screech owls scream all night.
Let her haunt tombs in ravenous hunger, snatch
At graveside weeds or bones the wolves have touched,
And naked in the plaza wail aloud   55
While packs of dogs pursue her down the road.
Oh may this happen! Venus will allow it;
When lovers break their promises, gods know it.

Meanwhile, my Delia, break the witch's spell.
Remember love is always up for sale.   60
A poor man will be faithful, first and last,
Constantly cleaving to your tender breast;
On crowded city streets this lover true
Will make the shoving throng give way for you.
He'll lead you to the house of secret friends   65
And take your sandals off with his own hands.

What am I singing for? The door stays shut.
First grease whatever palm can open it!
So swiftly does the wheel of Fortune spin,
My rival now should fear a fate like mine.   70
This very moment, lurking somewhere near,
Some patient suitor glances here and there,
Pretends to leave, then ambles back once more
To meaningfully cough before the door!
Oh, what's love up to now? Best take your boat   75
And sail away while you are still afloat!

I 6

Cheerfully smiling, Love, at first you come
To draw me in; but once I'm caught you're glum,
Sullen, and savage. Is it worth your while
To have entrapped a mortal by your guile?

Spread out your snares, now Delia secretly   5
At blackest midnight kisses—well, not me.
A fig for all her fervid protestations

Of innocence!—familiar proclamations
To my ear, for it isn't long since she
Made them to her husband about me.   10
Yes, I was fool enough to teach her how
To play the tricks whose victim I am now,
Like cooking up a need for privacy
At bedtime, and then tiptoeing to me,
Or using herbal remedies to smooth   15
The telltale blemishes left by Love's tooth.

And you, dimwitted spouse of this deceiver,
Take it from me: you never should believe her.
A friendly gossip session may appear
Harmless, or a dress cut down to here—   20
Watch out! She'll dip her finger in a cup,
Trace assignations on the table top.
Or she'll develop endless rendezvous
At women's rites—men, these are not for you.
I'd follow, if you left it up to me,   25
Straight to the altar. Trust what you can see.

Pretending to admire her wedding band,
I often found a way to touch her hand;
I'd send you off to sleep with wine while I
Watered my own and drank adultery.   30
Pardon me, please; I never meant to harm you.
Love forced me to it, and such gods disarm you.
I am he—discretion, now take flight!—
The man your dog was barking at all night.
Why have her, when you treat her carelessly?   35
The door is shut, but you forgot the key.
In bed she's breathing hard—for other men;
Then suddenly that migraine's back again.
Leave her to me. I wouldn't mind the whip;
Cheerfully I'd let them chain me up.   40
Away, all you who preen for hours on end,
Languorous togas flowing to the ground.
Whoever sees us, keep your conscience free;
Cross the street or look the other way.

All this is by arrangement of a god,   45
Or so a priestess prophesied out loud,
Who when the war god whirls across her mind
Leaves fear of fire and torture far behind,

Cuts her own flesh, and doesn't hesitate
To raise an idol in the scarlet spate,   50
And having pierced herself right through the chest
Chants oracles, blood flowing from her breast:
"Since Love is this girl's guardian, treat her well;
Who touches her will suffer from my spell.
As blood from me, so shall his money flow   55
Away and vanish, dust to winds that blow."

Some punishment she also meted out,
Delia, to you. I pray that it be slight.
Not on your account, you understand;
Your good old mother stays my angry hand.   60
Trembling in darkness she leads you to me
And joins our hands in silence, secretly.
My footsteps sing an individual song
To her who's waited by the door so long.

Long life to you, old woman! And I'd give   65
You, if I could, some of my years to live.
Because of you I'll always love your daughter;
You know the saying about blood and water.
But though a matron's gown is out of place,
Do teach her to be faithful nonetheless.   70
I too will be all virtue. If I praise
Another girl, she may scratch out my eyes,
And if I cheat her, drag me by the hair
Upside down right through the public square.

Sooner than ever lift a hand to you,   75
I'd have it cut off—and the other too.
Let it be not fear but fidelity
That in my absence keeps you true to me.
The girl who's true to no one in old age
Turns to a crone who's weaving for a wage,   80
Guiding her wool through someone else's loom,
Working her shaky fingers to the bone.
The young men laugh at this pathetic sight
And all agree it serves the old bag right.
From high Olympus Venus too beholds her: 85
"See the rewards of sluttishness!" she scolds her.

Let whom the shoe fits wear it, Delia. We
Will be a model couple till we die.

I 7

This is the day the Fates sang, who arrange
Destinies not even gods can change,
The day the Aquitanians would take flight
And Adour tremble at our legions' might.
And so it happened; our whole generation   5
Sees captive chiefs on show from every nation,
While you, Messalla, steeds and chariot bear
Forward, victorious laurel in your hair.

This honor did not happen without me;
The Pyrenees bear witness, the North Sea,   10
And the great rivers Saone, Garonne, and Rhone,
And the blue Loire, the blond Carnutes' home.
Or shall I sing of Cydnus, peaceful tide
Whose azure waters in smooth silence glide?
Or icy Taurus whose great shaggy head   15
Touches the clouds and keeps Cilicia fed?
Why mention the white dove that, sacred, flies
Unharmed through bustling towns 'neath Syrian skies?
How Tyre, the school of seafaring, surveys
From her high towers the vast ocean's ways?   20
Or how in summer when the great Nile bursts,
Its flooding waters quench the dry fields' thirst?

Oh Father Nile, I know not for what cause
Nor in what region you hide your source.
Thanks to you, your land demands no rain,   25
No grass is woven to coax water down.
Your folk, who for the bull of Memphis weep,
Worship you in the god Osiris's shape.

Osiris, the inventor of the plow,
First tore the tender earth with iron claw.   30
In unaccustomed soil he planted seeds;
Apples he picked from unfamiliar trees.
He showed us how to tie the slender vine
And with a sickle slice its shoots of green.
Trodden at first by unaccustomed feet,   35
Grapes yielded up their flavors of delight.
That wine which first taught voices how to rise
In song, moved awkward limbs in rhythmic ways.
Bacchus eases with his joyful spell

The hearts of farmers grim with endless toil.   40
No matter if they're chained by miseries,
Bacchus gives unhappy mortals ease.
Troubles and woes do not belong to you,
Osiris. Dancing, singing, loving do;
Armloads of flowers; heads with ivy crowned;   45
And robes of saffron rippling to the ground;
Tyrian purple; fluted melodies;
The holy vessel for your mysteries.

Head drenched with wine, come celebrate with us
The games and dances of the Genius!   50
Let ointment from his gleaming locks run down,
And let his head be wreathed with a soft crown.
Come today, spirit! For your offering
Incense and rich Greek honeycakes I'll bring.

Messalla, may each increasing generation   55
To your old age display its veneration.
Pilgrims to Tusculum, to Alba and its god
Will all proclaim your monument—the road,
Its pavement laid by your munificence,
Great blocks of stone fitted at your expense.   60
Farmers returning from the City late
Will sing your praises for their unbruised feet.

Your birthday candle ever brighter burns.
Good years ahead! Many happy returns!

I 10

Whoever first invented swords was more
Than merely fierce, but feral to the core!
First battles and then warfare, genocide—
A whole new way to death he opened wide.

Poor devil, can we blame him in the least?   5
We make ill use of weapons meant for beasts.

I lay the blame at riches' gilded door.
People used beechen cups in times of yore.
Safely flocks wandered, and when day was done
Among his ewes the lordly ram lay down.   10

Had I lived then, I never would have known
Weapons, or shuddered hearing trumpets blown.
But now I'm dragged to war. Some enemy
Already wields the sword that will slay me.

Save me, you household gods! Remember, it   15
Is I, the child who frolicked at your feet.
Even a carved log can be put to use;
You're the ancestral guardians of our house.
Religion meant more when a humble shrine
Sheltered a god small, wooden, but divine,   20
Who favored any man who brought him fruit
Or bound his carven head with ears of wheat.
Prayers satisfied, whole families would bring
Wheatcakes and honey as an offering.
You Lares, ward off weapons from us; I   25
Promise you a hog fresh from the sty.
I'll follow, robed in white from head to toe,
My temples wreathed in myrtle as I go.
But let it be another man who (Mars
Aiding him) is triumphant in the wars   30
And tells me every last exploit again,
Sketching the troops' position out in wine.

Insanity, pursuing Death this way!
Soon enough she approaches stealthily
To take us to the land where nothing grows,   35
But Cerberus barks and horrid Charon rows
Across the Styx forever. Throngs of souls
Pallid and ashen-faced drift past dim pools.

Leave that. The patriarch whose family
Surrounds his ripe age—that's the man for me!   40
He is a shepherd, his son tends the lambs;
His wife heats water for their weary limbs.
May I thus, tranquil, hair as white as snow,
Tell stories of what I did long ago.

May radiant Peace, who first taught bulls to plow,   45
Cultivate our fruitful acres now.
Peace pressed the juices from the swollen vine
So sons inherit the paternal wine.
In peacetime hoe and plow gleam, free of rust,
While neglected weapons gather dust.   50

Homeward wends the farmer (he's none too
Sober) with his family in tow.
Then Venus's war heats up. The woman's hair
Is torn, cheeks scratched; he's beaten down the door.
She weeps; but he, victorious, weeps too   55
To think of all the damage he can do.
Love plants himself between the angry pair
And mischievously makes their quarrel flare.

A man who strikes his girl is iron, is stone;
He drags the gods down from their heavenly throne.   60
Sufficient if he peels her thin dress off her,
Sufficient if he musses up her coiffure
And makes her cry. What blessings that man bears
Who can move a tender girl to tears!
But nothing rough—or let him take his shield   65
And march himself right out of Venus's field.

Come, fostering Peace, the harvest fruits bestowing,
A cornucopia filled to overflowing.

II 1

Keep silence! As our ancestors have taught us,
Let's purify the crops our work has brought us.
Ripe grapes drooping down from either horn,
Come, Bacchus; Ceres, gird your brow with corn.
The heavy plowshare idle on the wall,   5
Both earth and plowman rest for festival.
Each to his stall let oxen now be led,
Yokes undone and garlands on each head.
All chores are for the god. No spinner may
Touch her allotted task of wool today.   10
And keep far from the altar, all of you
Whom Venus last night granted pleasures to.
Put on fresh clothes—gods love what's chaste and clean—
And with washed hands cup water from the stream.
See: toward the altar the doomed lamb is led.   15
White-robed crowds follow; olive wreathes each head.

Both farmers and their fields we purify;
Gods, drive out evil from each boundary.
Let no field run to seed at harvest time,

No swift wolf terrorize the slower lamb.   20
Then confidently the sleek farmer piles
Massive logs upon the glowing coals.
A healthy index of his good estate,
His servants' children frolic by the grate.

My prayers are answered! For this liver—see?   25
Shows that the gods are nodding graciously.

Now bring a smoked Falernian of prewar
Vintage, and uncork the Chian jar.
Wine makes the feast—go on and celebrate!
No need to blush if you can't stand up straight.   30
But "To Messalla!" each must drain his cup;
Messalla's name must sound on every lip,
Who, glorious for triumphs near and far,
Brings honor to each long-haired ancestor.
Hero, inspire me while my verses yield   35
Thanks to the patron gods of flock and field.

The country is my theme; those gods who showed
Men how to plant, not gather up their food;
They taught us how to bind together boughs
And with green branches roof a little house;   40
They taught us first to tame the mighty bull
And move a load with (one more gift) the wheel.
Wild food forgotten, orchards striped the hills,
And fertile gardens drank from gurgling rills.
Golden grapes pressed, juice came oozing down: 45
Men mingled sober water with strong wine.
At harvest time under a starry tide
Of heat, Earth lays her golden hair aside;
In springtime bustling bees transport each bloom
To pack their hives with honey to the brim.   50
A weary farmer was the first to sing
His rural ditties with a metric swing;
Tired of plowing, this first poet piped
Songs to honor gods whose forms he'd draped.
Another farmer was the first to lead   55
The Bacchic dance, his face besmeared with red,
And won a gift of memorable note
Added to his scanty stock: a goat.
A country boy first wove a crown of flowers
To celebrate the ancient Lares' powers;   60

And in the countryside snow-white sheep bear
Soft fleeces destined to be maidens' care.
Hence ever since—see how the distaff twirls—
Spinning is work for women and for girls:
They hum at work, and sing Minerva's tune   65
In rhythm with the clattering of the loom.

The god of love himself was country-born,
Right in among the horses, cattle, corn.
There clumsy Cupid practiced with his bow;
Alas! he's gotten better at it now.   70
No longer are dumb animals his game;
He pierces maidens, at grown men takes aim.
Thus a young man once wealthy he makes poor;
An old man curses at a vixen's door;
Cupid her escort, a sly girl steps out   75
To meet her lover. Guards sleep sprawled about;
She feels her way along with careful tread
Over rough places, groping on ahead.
Such are Love's poor victims in their blindness.
Fortunate he on whom Love breathes with kindness!   80

Come, holy one, and grace our festal day,
But leave your torch and arrows far away.
Celebrants, hymn the god aloud for your
Flocks; in silence for your heart's desire.
No, rather call upon the god out loud—   85
No one will hear you in the boisterous crowd.
Play now! Night yokes the horses for her car.
After its mother many a yellow star
Dances; then silently, wings furled and black,
Comes Sleep, with dark Dreams faltering at his back.   90

Propertius

Propertius was probably a slightly younger contemporary of Tibullus. He was born between 54 and 47 B.C.E., the son of local aristocracy at the town of Assisi in Umbria. His father died around 41–40 B.C.E., just after the Perusine War and at the time when Propertius's family suffered from land confiscations at the hands of Octavian. We do not know exactly when Propertius came to Rome. After the publication of his first book of poetry, called the *Monobiblos* (29–28 B.C.E.), when he was in his early twenties, he came to the attention of Maecenas and eventually joined Horace and Vergil as members of Maecenas's literary circle. He published four books of elegies (or perhaps five, if our Book II is, as some believe, really two books) whose dates are open to some dispute. Since a friend of Pliny, a writer of the first century C.E., is recorded as claiming descent from Propertius, we infer that he was married. We do not know when he died, but a reference to him by Ovid suggests that he was certainly dead by 2 B.C.E.

In publishing his *Monobiblos*, Propertius indicated his decision as a poet to remain with the personal, elegiac poetry of his immediate predecessors rather than move in the new directions that Vergil and Horace were taking. Throughout the next ten to fifteen years the publications of Propertius's and Tibullus's poetry alternate as their concerns complement each other. The dates are approximate, but can be roughed out as follows: Tibullus I, 26 B.C.E.; Propertius II, 25 B.C.E.; Propertius III, 22 B.C.E.; Tibullus II, 19 B.C.E.; and Propertius IV, 16 B.C.E.

Like Gallus and Catullus before him, Propertius writes of his love affair with a single woman. His mistress, Cynthia, is introduced in the first poem of the *Monobiblos* where she plays a most important role. She is addressed less and less frequently in Books II and III, and we are told in the last poems of Book III that the affair is at an end. She reappears, however, in two poems of Book IV. According to convention, her pseudonym, Cynthia, stands in place of her real name, which we are told was Hostia. While few doubt the existence of such a mistress as inspiration for his poems, the historical accuracy of Propertius's portrait is called into question by certain inconsistencies and ambiguities in Propertius's portrayal. It is not clear, for instance, whether we are to think of Cynthia as a prostitute, a courtesan of the highest standing, or a married woman; and in poem I 3 there is even a certain domesticity to Propertius's and Cynthia's circumstances. It is perhaps wisest to think of this mistress, when she is explicitly called Cynthia and even when one just assumes that the woman in a poem is Cynthia, as a generic locus or occasion for the exploration of questions and feelings about poetry, power, love, passion, individual identity, and empire. She can be read as an allegory for poetry, or for an individualistic, if not political, opposition to Augustan conformity.

By the end of Propertius's poetic career, the poet who began fiercely defending individual experience and passions had turned his attention to more public subjects. It is a major transformation, in its own way no less momentous than the *Monobiblos* must have been. What began as an exploration of the embattled individual, captive of love and struggling against the pressures of the world around him, ends by viewing Roman topics and concerns, for instance the myth of Heracles, the etiology of the Tarpeian rock, the history of the battle of Actium, and the ideology of Roman marriage, through the lens of elegy.

Propertius

I 1

Cynthia's eyes first captured poor me,
who before was immune to desire.
Then Love subdued my arrogant gaze,
his adamant feet bowed my head,
until he taught me to spurn chaste women   5
(perverse Love!) and to live foolishly.
A year now, and this madness won't leave me.
Despite myself I cross the gods.

Milanion, Tullus, by refusing no trial,
beat down harsh Atalanta's cruelty.   10
Crazed, he would wander Parthenian caves,
head-on face hairy beasts;
beaten, smitten by Hylaeus's club,
struck, he moaned on Arcadian cliffs.
Thus he conquered the swift-footed girl: 15
so prayers and feats prevail in love.

In me sluggish Love plots no schemes,
forgets even to plod down old paths.
But you, whose tricks tempt the moon from heaven,
on magic hearths performing sacred rites,   20
now come, change my mistress's mind:
make her face blanch paler than mine!
Then I will believe that you rule rivers
and move the stars with Colchian song.

Friends, you call me back too late—I've fallen: 25
seek help for an unsound heart.
Bravely I'll endure knife blade and flame,
so long as my anger can speak freely.
Carry me through exotic lands, over the sea,
wherever no woman can track me down.   30

To you the god lends an easy ear: may you stay,
always equal in a safe love.
Against me our Venus wields sleepless nights
and untiring Love never rests.

I warn you—shun this evil. Let each one's love   35
hold him. Don't change love's home.

But, oh, the one my warnings touch too late—
repeating my words will make him ache.

I 3

Picture Ariadne, lying limp on a barren beach,
Theseus's ship departing in the distance.
Picture Andromeda, fresh with first sleep,
freed now from the rough rocks.
Think of the Thracian women, weak from frenzied dancing,   5
collapsing on Apidian grass.

So she seemed to breathe in easy peace,
Cynthia, head resting on sprawling hands,
as I dragged in on wine-drunk feet
while the boys brandished the late-night torch.   10

Not fully senseless yet, softly pressing
against her bed, I approach her,
seized with double fervor, and though they urge me,
now Love, now Wine, each a hard master,
to slide my arm lightly beneath her lying there,   15
to attack, to begin battle with a kiss, the hint of a hand

(yet I didn't dare disturb my mistress's rest,
afraid to rouse war-tested rage),

still, I cling with pinioned eyes
like Argos to Io's horns, in awe,   20
now undoing the garlands from my brow,
I place them, Cynthia, on your temples,
now delighting to compose your undone curls, now bestowing
furtive fruit on your hollowed hands,
lavishing all those gifts on ungrateful sleep   25
as apples roll from your prone lap,

and each time you stirred with a sigh,
I stood paralyzed, struck by an empty sign—
what if unknown fears haunt you in dreams?
what if someone makes you, unwilling, his?   30

Meanwhile, the moon, hastening by the windows,
officious moon with lingering light,
opened your eyes with its flighty beams. Thus,
elbow propped on the soft bed, she spoke:

How did you offend her? she must have locked you out,   35
sending you home to our bed at last.
Where did you waste my endless night, alas,
you, so limp now as the stars fade?
If only, thoughtless one, you could suffer
such nights as you inflict on poor me,   40
who deceived sleep by weaving with purple thread,
and again, exhausted, by Orphean song,
while lightly lamenting with myself, all alone,
your endless absence in another love,
until weariness overwhelmed me, borne by sleep's sweet wings.   45
This was my final worry as I wept.

I 6

Fearless, I'd face the Adriatic with you,
Tullus, I'd set sail on the rough Aegean;
with you I'd scale Rhipean peaks,
penetrate furthest Ethiopia even,

but my mistress, clinging, crying, holds me back   5
with insistent prayers, and pallor's punctuation.
All night she raves that she's aflame for me;
should I leave her, she swears, there are no gods.
Already she refuses me, threatens, menaces,
she the spurned woman, I the hardened heart.   10

Not for one hour can I stand such complaints.
He who does love unmoved—let him die.

Can all of Athens's learning matter,
or the sight of Asia's ancient wealth,
if Cynthia weeps as my ship embarks,   15
with maddened hands marks my face
and credits my kisses to the adverse winds,
claiming nothing crueler than a faithless man?

Prepare to herald your uncle's prestige.
Restore forgotten allies' ancient rights.   20
Since your life never stayed for love,
your nation's arms your only care.
May that Boy never crush you with my pains,
with the hard-won wisdom of my tears.

Let me, whom the fates want to conquer,   25
utterly lose my soul to shame.
Many have freely died for lasting love—
buried in their number may the earth cover me.
I am not fit for glory, not born for war.
In this struggle the Fates demand I fall.   30

But you, whether where gentle Ionia tends,
or Paclotus's stream flows through Lydian farms,
whether to seize the earth by foot, the sea by oar,
you go, a partner in a popular rule,
if an hour should come to remind you of me,   35
rest assured: I stay beneath this tyrant star.

I 7

While you sing, Ponticus, of Cadmean Thebes
and the grim arms of brotherly battles,
and contend, so help me, with Homer himself
(may the Fates be tender to your verse),
as usual, I'm busy with my love,   5
trying anything to soften her hard heart.
Compelled, I give up wit to obey
pain, and to complain of daily trial.

Thus erodes my prime, such is my fame,
the only name my poetry pursues.   10

Praise me for this alone: I pleased a learned girl,
Ponticus, and often suffered her unjust threats.
May a spurned lover one day read me, desperate,
and find solace in my sorrows understood.

Should that Boy hit you too with ruthless bow   15
(I sadly pray our gods won't so decree):
useless your camps, useless the seven armies, lying

silent in perpetual neglect. You'll mourn them, miserable.
In vain you'll long to write love poems,
but a late love informs no verse.   20

How you'll marvel at me then—no humble poet—
preferring me to all the wits of Rome.
Young men will break the silence at my tomb:
"Great poet of our passion, here you lie."

Take care—don't let your pride condemn my poems—   25
Late love too often makes you pay too much.

I 9

I told you, scoffer, Love would come,
your words would not be free forever.
See—beggar, you lie flattened, coming when she calls,
now some bought girl rules you with her whims.

No one, in love matters, not even Chaonian doves,   5
could better tell how woman conquers men.
I earned my expertise with pain and tears—
how gladly I would stammer, free of love!

How does tumid epic help you now,
lamenting walls Amphion's lyre once raised?   10
Mimnermus, more than Homer, delights lovers:
smooth songs suit gentle love.
Go, I tell you, lose those tragic tomes.
Sing something more to woman's taste.
What if winning her was hard? Insane,   15
you crave water mid-torrent.
You're not even pale yet—you haven't touched true fire.

This is future evil's first spark.
Later, you'll take on Armenian tigers,
test the bonds of Ixion's hellish wheel: 20
easier than Love's shaft rankling in your marrow,
and no resistance to an angry girl.

Love never lifted anyone's wings
without his other hand weighing him down.
Don't be deceived if she seems well-won—   25

she'll undo you piercingly, Ponticus, if yours.
Love forbids wandering eyes to turn where
unpermitted, bans watches kept in any other name.

To him, yet unafflicted, until his hand grips your bones:
whoever you are, flee love's relentless charms.   30
Such suavity fells sharp stones, strong oaks—
how much further might you, frail spirit, fall?

If you have shame left, now, confess your faults.
It lightens love to speak of why you die.

I 16

I, once thrown open for mighty triumphs,
door renowned for Tarpeia's chastity,
my threshhold mobbed by gilded chariots,
damp with captives' suppliant tears;
now, nightly beaten by drunken brawlers,   5
still pounded by unworthy fists, complain.
To my ceaseless disgrace I'm festooned with garlands
and strewn torches, the shut-out's tokens.
I can't stop my mistress's notorious nights,
betrayed, infamous in dirty verse.   10
In sum: mindless to spare her reputation
she lives more grossly even than her shameless age.
Heavy with grief, I'm forced to mourn,
made doleful by this suitor's long watching.
He never allows my posts to rest,   15
reciting his verse with plangent charm:

"Door, crueler even than my mistress herself,
Why, so silent with stern gates, are you closed to me?
Why never, unbarred, do you admit my loves,
Don't you know how, moved, to send secret prayers?   20
Will no end be given to my pain?
Will I even sleep here—shameful!—on the warm threshhold?
Midnights, full stars, frigid breezes grieve
for me prostrate here with the morning star's frost.
You alone, pitiless to human pain   25
answer with silent hinges.
If only a twisted crack bearing my weak voice
would turn it toward my mistress's startled ears!

Then were she more unyielding than Sicilian rock,
were she harder than iron or steel,   30
still, she couldn't restrain her eyes,
and her breath would surge in reluctant tears.
Now she lies resting on another's happy arm,
while my words sink with the night's west wind.
But you are the only, the worst, cause of my woe,   35
door never swayed by my bribery.
You no petulance of my tongue ever hurt
(so used to telling all when angry),
that so long you should let me, hoarse with complaining,
pass sleepless nights on this crossroads in anxious waiting.   40
How often I spun songs for you with fresh verse,
and pressed fervent kisses to your worn steps.
How often, traitress, I prayed before your posts,
and bore the promised offerings in furtive hands."

With this, and whatever you miserable lovers invent,   45
he drowns out the morning birds.
Thus I, for my mistress's vices, and her lover's endless
mourning, am famous in eternal shame.

I 19

I don't fear now, Cynthia, sad shades,
or mind the fate I owe my pyre—
but a death bereft of your love,
this fear is crueler than funerals.
Cupid didn't cling to my eyes so lightly   5
that my dust could lie empty with love forgotten.

In that dark place, Protesilaus the hero
could not forget his delightful wife,
but longing to grasp joy with weightless hands,
returned to his old home, a ghost.   10

There, whatever I'll be, I'll always be called your shadow:
great love crosses death's shores.
There though the troop of beauties come,
Trojan spoil, the prize of Argive men,
not one shall please me more, Cynthia, than the sight   15
of you; and (may just Earth have it so),

however long the Fates may hold you in old age,
my tears will cherish you when you are bones.

May you, alive, feel this when I am ashes—
then my death, no matter where, will not be bitter.   20

How I fear, Cynthia, my tomb scorned,
a rival dragging you away, oh, from my dust,
forcing you, unwilling, to dry your falling tears.
Ceaseless threats sway even faithful girls.

And so, while we can, let's take our joy as lovers: 25
Love is not long enough for all time.

I 21

"You, soldier, rushing to escape our fate—
wounded beside beseiged Perusia's walls—
why, when I moan, do you turn shocked eyes?
I was your comrade in arms just now.
Save yourself so your parents may rejoice,   5
so your sister won't read my fate in your tears:
Gallus, snatched from Caesar's jaws,
could not fly death from unknown hands;
whatever scattered bones she'll find
on Etruscan hills, tell her these are mine."   10

I 22

Who and where I come from;
who are, Tullus, my household gods;
you ask, since we are friends forever.
If you know Perusia, our country's grave,
Italy's ruin in cruel times,   5
when Roman strife drove out its own—

my grief most of all, Etruscan dust:
on you my kinsman's limbs lie cast away, long-suffering,
you do not cover his poor bones—

Umbria, touching nearest the plain beneath,   10
bore me, rich with fertile earth.

II 1

You ask why I'm always writing of love, where
does she come from, my sweet book about the town?
Not Calliope, not Apollo, sings such things to me:
my girl alone creates my genius.
If I see her moving, alight in Coan silk,   5
all Coan cloth will be my book.
If her curls wander freely across her brow,
pleased, she'll walk proudly, her curls praised.
If her ivory fingers beat a song on the lyre,
I marvel—with what art she presses her nimble hands.   10
Should she close her eyes, seeking sleep,
I find a thousand new causes for poetry.
If she casts off her clothes and naked strives with me,
Then surely I compose long *Iliads*.
Whatever she does, whatever she says,   15
The greatest history is born of nothing.

Had the Fates granted me, Maecenas, the prowess
to lead heroic armies into war,
I would not sing of Titans, nor Ossa atop Olympus
transforming Pelion to heaven's path,   20
nor ancient Thebes, nor Troy—Homer's way to fame,
nor how Xerxes joined two seas by his command,
nor Remus's first reign, nor haughty Carthage's pride,
nor the Cimbrian threats and the feats of Marius:
Your Caesar's wars and deeds I would record, and you,   25
beneath great Caesar alone, would be my second care.

For I would sing of Mutina, or the Philippan
civil wars I'd sing, the Sicilian rout at sea,
the profaned hearths of the old Etruscan race,
the captured shores of Ptolomaean Pharos;   30
or I would sing of Egypt and Nile, how he went maimed,
drawn into the city, his seven tributaries captive,
or the necks of kings enclosed with chains of gold,
and Actium's beaked ships speeding down the Sacred Way.
Amidst these warlike scenes my Muse would imbricate you,   35
and your loyalty in peace won or lost.

Theseus in hell, Achilles in heaven,
bear witness for Pirithous, for Patroclus.

But to intone the titanic tumults of Jove and Enceladus
did not suit Callimachus's narrow chest.   40
Nor does my heart harmonize in rugged lines
to trace Caesar's name to a Trojan source.
The sailor tells of winds, the farmer of bulls,
the soldier recounts wounds, the shepherd sheep.
I wage wars on a narrow bed: 45
With whatever art he can, let each wear down the day.

It is glory to die in love, yet more glory if it is given
to enjoy one love alone. Oh to enjoy my love alone!
If I'm not mistaken, she always condemns loose girls,
and because of Helen deplores all the *Iliad*.   50
Whether I am destined to drink Phaedra's poison,
a draught not meant for Hippolytus's harm,
whether I am to die of Circe's herbs,
or Medea heats her kettle on Iolchus's hearth for me,
since one woman has preyed on my senses,   55
my funeral proceeds from her home.

Medicine cures all human ills.
Only love does not love the artist of disease.
Machaon cured Philoctetes's sluggish blood,
Philyridean Chiron the eyes of Phoenix,   60
the Epidaurian god restored dead Androgeos,
with Cretan herbs to his father's hearth,
and the Mysian youth wounded by Achilles' spear,
by that same spear he felt the cure.

He who takes this pain from me, he alone   65
will pull down apples to Tantalus's hand;
fill leaking casks with the virgins' urns,
unbend their necks from endless water's weight;
release Prometheus from Caucasian rock,
drive off the bird who devours his breast.   70

Thus when the Fates reclaim my life,
And leave me a brief name on a little marble,
Maecenas, envied hope of our youth,
proper glory of my life and death,
if perhaps your path should lead you near my tomb,   75
turn your British chariot with its wrought wheels,
and weeping toss these words to my mute dust:
A cruel girl was death for this poor wretch.

II 2

Free for good, I planned an empty bed,
but love, having made peace, deceived me.
How could this human face remain on earth?
Jupiter, I forgive your former lapses.
Tawny-gold her hair, her hands long, dazzling in all   5
her body, she walks as if Juno's equal,
or like Pallas striding to Ithaca's altars,
her breast blazoned with the Gorgon's snaky curls,
or Ischomache, Lapith's heroic daughter,
the besotted Centaur's drunken plunder,   10
or like chaste Brimo, who by Boebeis's waves,
united, they say, with Mercury.
Give up now, goddesses, whom Paris once judged,
tunicless on Ida's peak!
If only time declined to change this face,   15
though it grew old as the Cumaean Sibyl!

II 4

You'll complain, first, of her many wrongs,
you'll continually beg, she'll as often refuse,
you'll punish your innocent nails with your teeth;
impatient, tap the ground with peevish foot.

I wasted my time, with my perfumed hair,   5
my loitering walk with its measured tread.
Here herbs were worth nothing, no night-dark Medea,
no grasses boiled by Perimede's art:
we can't locate the causes, the blows hit us blind,
yet still they come down invisible paths.   10
This patient needs no doctors, no soft beds,
Immune to the weather, to the air,
he walks—shocked, his friends gape at his corpse!
Whatever love is, it is indefensible.
To what charlatan seer am I not a windfall?   15
What crone doesn't read my dreams ten times over?

If one will be my enemy, let him love girls.
Delight in a boy, if he will be my friend.
In a safe boat you descend down a calm stream—
how can such paltry waves harm you?   20

For one word he hands over his heart;
She will scarcely soften, though she takes your blood.

II 5

Is this true, Cynthia? All Rome talks of you,
your unsavory life no secret?
Did I deserve this? Betrayer, you'll pay the price,
the wind will blow me away somewhere,
and among you pack of she-liars I'll still find one   5
who longs for my poems to make her known.
Her cruelty won't touch me, but she'll tear you apart:
too bad, too late, my long-time love, you'll weep.

Leave now, while anger still smarts:
Once the pain goes, love always returns.   10
The Carpathian waves shimmering with the north winds,
the black clouds buffeted by the fickle south breeze,
don't change as fast as lovers with a word.
While you can, free your neck from the unfair yoke.
You won't grieve at all, except the first night;   15
All pain in love—be patient—is light.

But you, by Queen Juno's sweet rule,
stop hurting yourself, my life, with your pride.
Not only bulls with curved horns kill—
even wounded sheep retaliate.   20
I won't tear the clothes from your lying breast,
nor break down your closed doors, enraged;
I wouldn't dare rip your woven locks,
nor bruise you with unforgiving fists:
Let brutes seek out such painful fights   25
whose heads the ivy does not crown.
I will write, therefore, what your lifetime won't erase:
"Cynthia, masterful beauty: Cynthia, trivial words."

Trust me, though you dismiss rumor's whispers,
this verse, Cynthia, will make you pale.   30

II 7

You must have rejoiced, Cynthia, when the law was lifted,
that once laid down we both lamented

lest it divide us—still, not Jupiter himself
can separate unwilling lovers.

"But Caesar is great." Caesar is great in war: 5
conquered nations in love count for nothing.
More swiftly I'd suffer this head to leave my neck,
than waste torches at a bride's whim,
or parade past your closed door, a husband,
turning damp eyes back toward my betrayal.   10

Ah, my flute would sing such sleeps to you,
flute more morose than horn's funeral note!
Why should sons of mine feed my country's triumphs?
None of my blood will be a soldier.

But should I serve in my love's army,   15
Castor's horse could not be great enough.
Thus, truly, my glory has earned such a name,
glory widespread to the snowy wilderness.

You alone please me; let me please you, Cynthia, alone:
This will be more than my father's name: love.   20

II 10

Time to traverse Helicon with different notes,
time now to give way to the Thessalian horse.
I'm determined to tell now of troops brave in battle,
of the Roman camp of my leader.
Should my strength fail, surely my boldness   5
will merit praise: in great affairs, will suffices.
Let youth sing Loves, maturity uprisings:
wars I shall sing, since my girl has been written.
Now I want to march with brow gravely furrowed,
now my Muse shows me another strain.   10

Arise, soul, from lowliness; now songs, gather strength;
My work now will come, Muses, from mighty mouth.
Now Euphrates denies that Parthian riders can see
behind their backs, and regrets that he held the Crassi:
India even, Augustus, gives her neck to your triumph,   15
Arabia's realm, untouched, trembles before you;
even if some land recoils to the earth's farthest borders,

captive, she will soon feel your hands.
This camp I'll follow, I will be a great prophet
singing your camp: the Fates preserve that day for me!   20

As when great statues' heads evade our reach,
we place our garlands at their lowly feet,
so now, for praise's triumph-car too poor,
I burn cheap incense in a pauper's rite.
My songs fall short of the Ascraean fount;   25
Love washed them only in Permessus's stream.

II 13

More darts than Persian arrows arming Susa
Love buried in my chest.
He forbade me to scorn the delicate Muses
and directed me to Ascraea's grove.
Not to lead Pieria's oaks with my words,   5
nor to lure wild beasts from Ismaria's valley,
but to strike Cynthia dumb with my verse:
then I'll eclipse Inachian Linus in fame.

I don't love a beautiful body alone,
nor a woman's mention of famous forebears: 10
may I delight to have read in a learned girl's lap,
and to have tested my verses by her pure ears.
When I've attained this, farewell common clamor:
my mistress, my judge, will keep me safe.
If perhaps she'll lend a kind ear to peace,   15
then I could suffer Jupiter's enmity.

Then whenever death will close my eyes,
hear and observe my funeral rites:
No long procession of family portraits,
no trumpet's empty lament of my fate,   20
no bed laid for me with ivory headrest,
my corpse won't lie on a gold-draped couch.
No line of attendants with fragrant platters.
Instead: small funeral, modest ritual.
Lavish enough, if three books follow me,   25
I will bear them to Persephone, my greatest gifts.

Surely you'll follow, bare breast nail-torn,
nor will you weary of calling my name.
You will place the last kisses on my cold lips,
as the onyx jar pours forth Syrian oils. 30
When the pyre's flame has rendered me ash,
let a little earthen urn take my remains.
Plant laurel above my meager tomb,
whose shade shall cover my death's remnants.
Two verses: HE WHO NOW LIES GRAINY DUST 35
ONCE WAS THE SLAVE OF ONE LOVE ALONE.

Nor will my tomb achieve less fame
than did Achilles' bloody grave.
You too, when you come to death, remember:
white-haired, take my path to these watchful stones. 40
Meanwhile, beware, don't spurn me dead:
the conscious earth observes the truth.

If only some Sister of the Three had ordered
my life snuffed out in the cradle!
Why is my spirit saved for a doubtful hour? 45
Three generations until Nestor was ashes;
yet if some Greek soldier on Ilium's ramparts
had cut short the thread of his endless old age,
he wouldn't have seen Antilochus buried,
or have cried, "Oh Death, why come to me so late?" 50

Still, you doubtless will mourn your lost lover:
it's right always to love men who have died.
Witness the harsh boar who struck down
snow-white Adonis, hunting on Idalia's peak.
They say he lay, breathtaking, in those marshes 55
where you came, Venus, your hair streaming.
But in vain you'll call back, Cynthia, my silent corpse:
for how could my crumbled bones reply?

II 14

Not Atrides rejoicing at the Trojan triumph,
when Laomedon's great labor fell,
nor Ulysses, elated, his wandering over,
when he touched dear Dulichia's shore,
nor Electra, when she saw Orestes safe 5

(holding her brother's false bones, she'd wept);
not Minos's daughter beholding Theseus unharmed
when he mastered the Daedalian maze with her guiding thread,
gathered such joys as I from the past night.
I will be immortal if there be another.   10

As long as I begged with my neck bent,
she counted me cheaper than a dry well.
She won't oppose me now with unjust scorn,
nor sit indifferent as I lament—
if only I hadn't learned the rules too late.   15
Now the medicine goes to ashes.
The path was lit for me—a blind man.
No one can see in incurable love.

I learned what works: scorn her, lovers!
This way she'll come today, who spurned you yesterday.   20
While others were knocking in vain and calling her mistress,
unmoved she held me, and laid her head near mine.
More powerful to me than Parthia beaten, this victory,
my booty, my captive kings, my chariot this will be.
On your column, Cytherea, I will fix a great gift,   25
and this song will bear my name:

THESE SPOILS, GODDESS, I, PROPERTIUS, PLACE BEFORE YOUR SHRINE,
FOR ONE WHOLE NIGHT A LOVER BELOVED.

It rests with you, my light. Will my ship reach the shore
safe, or burdened in mid-shallows run aground?   30
For if somehow by my fault you should change toward me,
let me lie dead before your door!

II 26a

I saw you in a dream, my life, shipwrecked,
drawing your weary hands through Ionian foam,
and confessing all the things you had lied to me.
Your hair dragged you down, heavy with water,
just as Helle was tossed on purple waves,   5
borne on the golden sheep's soft back;
this I feared—lest the sea might bear your name,
and a sailor, gliding through your deeps, lament you!

What things I saved then, for Neptune, for Castor
and his brother, and for you, now a goddess, Leucothea! 10

While you, barely raising your palms above the flood,
about to die, would often call my name.
If Glaucus had beheld your eyes, you'd be
transformed to an Ionian sea nymph,
and the Nereids would upbraid you with envy, 15
radiant Nesaee, heavenly-blue Cymothoe.

But I saw then a dolphin speeding to your aid,
who once, I think, saved Arion's lyre.
And I was about to hurl myself from the highest peak,
when fear dashed my visions to pieces. 20

II 29a

Last night, my light, when I was drunkenly wandering,
no servant to guide me by the hand,
a band of who knows how many little Loves
blocked my way (fear stopped me from counting),
holding tiny torches, some brandishing arrows, 5
some even preparing chains for me.
But they were naked. One, bolder than the rest,
said, "Seize this man, you know him well!
That angry woman put out a contract on him."

He spoke: the noose was on my neck. 10
Just then another called to surround me, but
another, "Let him die, who denies our divinity!
She waits eternally for you, who don't deserve it;
while you search for anyone's door, fool.
When she undoes the nightly bonds 15
of her Sidonian turban and raises her heavy eyes,
scents will inspire you—not Arabian herbs,
but those which Love made with his own hands, himself.
Spare him now, brothers, now he pledges true love,
and now, behold, we come to the house commanded." 20

And thus, having thrown my cloak back on,
"Go now," they said, "and learn to spend your nights at home."

II 29b

It was dawn, and I wanted to see: was she sleeping alone?
but Cynthia was in bed alone.
I stood stupefied: never had she seemed more beautiful,
not even when, dressed in a purple tunic,
she went to tell her dreams to chaste Vesta,   5
afraid they might bode harm for her or me.
So she seemed to me, just released from sleep.
How her radiant beauty triumphed all alone!

"What," she cried, "you, a morning spy on your mistress?
Do you think I share your ways?   10
I'm not so easy: knowing one man will suffice for me,
whether you or someone capable of constancy.
No traces whatsoever on this pressed bed,
no signs of two lying rolling around.
Look: no breath rises from all my body,   15
a known sign when adultery's been done."

She spoke, her right hand pushing away a kiss,
and leapt up, feet bound in loose slippers.

Thus I, a jailor of such sacred love, was duped:
since then I've spent no happy night.   20

III 1

Shades of Callimachus, Coan mysteries of Philitas,
allow me, I pray, to enter your grove.
I, the first priest, proceeding from the pure well-spring,
to bear Italian emblems in Greek dances.
Tell me, in what cave did you refine your song?   5
With what step did you march? What water nourished you?
Away with him, who detains Phoebus in arms!
Verse should go polished by a fine pumice
for which lofty fame lifts me from earth; my daughter,
my Muse, triumphs on garlanded steeds;   10
and with me in our chariot ride little Loves,
a mob of writers dogging my wheels.
Why waste time competing, your reins let loose?
You can't run to the Muses on a wide road.
Many men, Rome, augment annals with your praise,   15
who sing Bactra the destined end of empire. But what you'll read

in peace, this work from the Muses' mountain,
my page has borne down an untraveled road.
Muses, give your poet soft garlands:
hard crowns will not suit my head.   20
All a jealous mob steals from me while I live,
Honor will redouble after death.
After death age betters all things:
funeral rites make a name grow greater.
Who would have known—the towers pummeled by a wooden horse,   25
that rivers fought hand to hand with Achilles,
Idaean Simois, Scamander the offspring of Jove,
that wheels befouled Hector three times through the fields?
Deiphobus, and Helenus and Polydamas, and whatever he was
in arms, Paris, hardly even his homeland would have known.   30
Ilion, you would be small talk now, and you
Troy, twice captured by Hercules' force.
Even Homer, that rememberer of your fall,
felt his work grow with posterity.
And me, in generations to come, Rome will praise;   35
I myself prophesy that day past my ashes.
A stone will mark my bones in a tomb unscorned:
Apollo saw to it, approving my vow.

III 2

Time to return to my song's usual round,
so that the girl might be glad, touched by accustomed notes.
Orpheus, they say, soothed beasts, stilled
rough rivers with his Thracian lyre.
Propelled to Thebes by art, the story goes, Cithaeron's rocks   5
willingly leapt together, parts of a wall.
Polyphemus, even Galatea beneath wild Etna
turned back her dripping horses toward your song.
Any wonder, with Bacchus and Apollo behind me,
that a mob of girls cherishes my words?   10
What if no Taenarian columns hold up my house,
nor ivory ceilings between gilded beams;
my orchards can't compare with Alcinous's groves,
no Marcian stream moistens my artful grot.
The Muses are my followers, and poems dear to the reader;   15
Calliope never wearies of my dances.

Fortunate girl, should my book celebrate you,
my poems will form your beauty's monument.
For neither the price of the pyramids, built to the stars,
nor Jove's temple at Elis, mimicking heaven,   20
nor the luxury of Mausolus's tomb,
are exempt from death's final contract.
Fire or water will steal their honor,
or by time's blow, crushed by their own weight, they'll fall.
But the name genius earns time will not   25
forget: glory by genius stands deathless.

III 4

Divine Caesar plots war against wealthy India,
his fleet splits the gem-rich sea.
Great reward, men! the farthest earth readies triumphs;
Tigris and Euphrates will flow at your command.
Belated, this province will fall to Ausonian rods;   5
Parthian trophies will come to know Latin Jove.
Go now: war-tested prows, set your sails!
Martial horses perform your service!
I sing good omens. Avenge the Crassi and the slaughter!
Go, and remember Rome's history!   10

Father Mars, fateful lamps of holy Vesta,
I pray that day will come before I die,
when I see Caesar's chariot, spoil-laden,
often halt the horses at the crowd's applause;
lying in my dear girl's arms I'll endeavor   15
to watch; I'll read the names of captured towns,
javelins seized from fleeing horses, bows of barbarian
soldiers, captured leaders posed beneath their arms!
Venus, preserve your child: may he live forever;
you see in him the Aenean line's survival.   20

Let the spoils be theirs, whose labors earned them;
for me, to applaud from the Sacred Way will suffice.

III 16

Midnight—a letter comes from my mistress.
She commands me: appear at Tibur immediately,
where gleaming roofs flaunt twin towers,

and Anio's nymph falls into the spreading lake.
What should I do? Commit myself to consuming darkness,   5
so I can fear being mauled by ruffians?
But if fear prompts me to put off her orders,
her tears will be fiercer to me than a night-thief.
I offended once and for a whole year she spurned me:
against me her hands are far from gentle.   10

All the same, there's no one who'd hurt holy lovers:
they can stride down the middle of Sciron's road.
Whoever will love, may walk on Scythia's shore
with none barbarous enough to do him harm.
The moon lights his way, stars reveal the rough spots,   15
Love himself shakes his lit torches ahead,
fierce mad dogs avert their gaping jaws—
to him the way is always safe.
For who, so heartless, could spatter his scanty blood?
Venus herself befriends the shut-out man.   20

But if certain death should come from my adventure,
I'd purchase that demise at such a price.
She will bring me ointments and adorn my tomb
with wreaths, and guard me, sitting at my grave.
Gods, don't let her place my bones in common earth   25
where the public way beats a constant path!
After death lovers' tombs are thus defamed.
May secluded earth cover me with leafy shade,
or bury me in a marked mound of foreign sand.
My name posted in the street disgusts me.   30

IV 4

Tarpeia's crime, Tarpeia's shameful grave
I'll tell, Jove's ancient temple taken.
A prosperous grove nestled in an ivy-draped hollow
where many trees conversed with local waters,
Silvanus's branching home. Here sweet flutes   5
summoned the sheep to come and drink.
Facing this place, Tatius surrounds his camp
with maple fence, circles it safe with piles of soil.
What was Rome then, when the Sabine trumpeter
shook Jove's nearby stones with lasting roar?   10
Where now commands resound to conquered lands,

where the Roman forum is, stood Sabine spears.
Rome's walls were mountains; our Curia, sheepfolds;
and from that spring war-horses drank.

Here, drawing water for the goddess, Tarpeia came   15
the clay urn pressing heavy on her head.
Would one death suffice for this evil girl
who longed, Vesta, to betray your flame?
She saw him, maneuvering on the sandy fields, Tatius,
raising his painted weapons over his horse's golden mane: 20
stunned at the king's beauty, his regal arms,
she dropped the urn from her forgetful hands.
Often she feigned omens from the innocent moon,
insisting her hair be washed in the spring.
She would bear silvery lilies to indulgent nymphs,   25
lest Romulus's spear wound Tatius's face.
Climbing the cloudy Capitol as the morning smoke rose,
heading home, arms cut by prickly brambles,
sitting on her own Tarpeian rock, she lamented
her insufferable wounds to neighboring Jove.   30

"The martial fire, the guards of Tatius's troop,
the Sabine weapons lovely to my eyes,
if only I, a captive to your Gods,
could gaze, a prisoner, on my Tatius's face!
Roman mountains, Rome who crowns their height,   35
and Vesta, shamed by my disgrace, farewell!
That horse bears home my love, Tatius
himself directs his mane toward his right hand.
What wonder Scylla raged against her father's locks,
her shining groin transformed to rabid hounds?   40
What wonder the brother monster's horns betrayed,
when the gathered thread opened the twisted way?
What a warning I'll be to Ausonian girls,
a wicked servant picked for the virgin hearth!
Should anyone marvel at Pallas's flame put out,   45
may she forgive: the altar is wet with my tears.
Tomorrow, rumor says, all Rome will be drunk.
You—seize the dewy backs of the thorny hills.
Slippery and treacherous all the road, hiding
silent waters on its deceiving path.   50
If only I knew the Magic Muse's charms!
This tongue too would embolden my fair one!
The purple toga will become you, not that bastard,

suckled by a monstrous wolf's hard breast.
And I'll be feared, a foreign queen on her native throne.   55
I bring you no humble dowry in Rome betrayed.
If not, at least avenge the Sabines' rape;
seize me, with your own law repay their crime.
As your wife, I'll sunder battles joined;
Make peace with my wedding's mediation.   60
Hymen, start your song: trumpeter, stop your fierce roars.
Believe me, my bridal bed will blunt your weapons.
And now the fourth horn sings the coming light,
the stars themselves, fallen, sink to the sea.
I shall try sleep, and seek my dreams of you: 65
come, sweet shade, before my eyes."
She spoke, surrendering to fitful sleep,
not knowing that new frenzy lay with her.
For Vesta, kind guardian of Trojan embers,
nurses her fault, buries torches in her bones.   70
She rages, like—near quick Thermodon—a Thracian
Amazon, breast bare, robe ripped apart.

In Rome a festival (*Parilia*, our fathers' name.
On the first such day our walls began).
Each year a shepherds' feast, games in the city,   75
when rural dishes flow soused with riches,
when over scattered heaps of burning hay
a drunken crowd leaps with blackened feet.
Romulus released his sentries into idleness,
interrupted the trumpets, commanded the camp be silent.   80
This was her time: Tarpeia calls the foe:
she binds her pact, a member of their party.
The hill was hard to climb, unguarded on the holiday.
No time wasted: his sword silences the noisy dogs.
The whole scene was asleep, but Jupiter alone   85
kept vigil for his vengeance.
The gate's honor, her prostrate country, she betrayed,
and asks him to name the wedding day.
But Tatius replied (not even a foe could honor her crime),
"Marry and ascend my royal bed!"   90
He spoke: they crushed her with their massive arms.
Fit dowry, virgin, for your service.

From this leader comes the name "Tarpeian Mount":
Reward, oh watcher, of an unjust fate.

IV 6

The priest begins the rite: keep holy silence,
let the victim collapse before my fires.
May the Roman garland vie with Philitan ivy
and Callimachus's urn pour forth water.
Give me soft spikenard, honors of smooth incense,   5
three times around the hearth turn the woolen orb.
Sprinkle me with water, sing a song to fresh altars,
let the ivory flute pour from Mygdonian vessels.
Away with lies, let evils find another landscape;
purifying laurel smooths the poet's new road.   10

Muse, I'll tell of the temple of Palatine Apollo:
a subject, Calliope, worthy your favor.
These songs are spun in Caesar's name: while I sing
Caesar, I pray, let Jupiter himself attend.
Where Phoebus's harbor flees toward Athamanian shores,   15
and stills the murmur of the Ionian Sea,
the Actian Sea makes a monument to Caesar's ship,
a friendly path for sailors' prayers.
Here the world's navies met: their pinewood walls
stood on the waves, but the bird sign favored one set of oars.   20
One fleet: condemned by Trojan Quirinus,
and shameful spears hurled by a woman's hand;
The other: Augustus's ship, sails swelled by Jupiter's favor,
and standards used to conquering for their country.
At last Nereus double-arcs the battle line   25
and the water trembles, dappled with armor's rays,
When Phoebus, leaving Delos firmly fixed in his protection
(a mobile island, swept before the south wind's wrath),
stood above Augustus's stern, and a strange flame
flashed, zig-zagging with oblique fire.   30
Not with hair falling loose on his neck,
nor the tortoise shell lyre's defenseless music,
but with the face that looked upon Agamemnon of Pelops,
discharged the Grecian camps to greedy death-pyres,
and flattened the Python through the coils of its orb,   35
the serpent feared by the peaceful Muses.
Soon he said: "Oh preserver of the world from Alba Longa,
Augustus, better known than your ancestor Hector,
conquer by sea. The land is yours; my bow enlists
in your service, and all my quiver favors you.   40
Free the country from fear. Trusting you as protector,

the people loaded your prow with prayers.
Unless you defend them, Romulus, prophet of the walls,
saw the Palatine birds pass to no avail.
Their oars dare too near: Latin waters are ashamed,   45
with you foremost, to suffer under a queen's sails.
Don't fear her fleet with its hundred oars:
she floats on a hostile sea;
and though Centaurs brandish rocks on her prows,
you'll find them hollow logs, mere painted frights.   50
It's the cause that makes or breaks a soldier;
unless it's just, shame dispels arms.
It is time. Summon your ships. I, maker of the moment,
with laurel-bearing hand shall lead the Julian fleet."

He spoke, and fed the bow his quiver's weight: 55
following the bow was Caesar's spear.
By Phoebus's pledge Rome conquers: the woman pays her price,
the broken scepter borne through the Ionian Sea.
And father Caesar marvels from his Venusian star:
"I am a god; this proves my paternity."   60
Triton takes up a song, all the sea nymphs
applaud, circling freedom's flags.
Vainly trusting to a fleeing skiff she seeks the Nile,
wanting only not to die on the day commanded.
God forbid! what a triumph one woman would make,   65
led through the same streets Jugurtha walked chained!
Thus Actian Phoebus won his monuments:
each arrow fired felled ten ships.

Enough of war: victorious Phoebus seeks the lyre,
puts off his arms for peaceful strains.   70
Now let white-robed guests enter a gentle grove;
let elegant roses adorn my neck,
let wine flow, crushed in Falernian presses,
let Cilician saffron drench my hair.
Let the muse provoke wit in reclining poets: 75
Bacchus, for Phoebus you always prove fertile.
One shall remember the slaves of the marshy Sycambri,
another sing Cephean Meroe and his swarthy empire,
another Parthia conceding to a late treaty.
"Let him return Remus's standards, soon he'll surrender his own: 80
or should Augustus spare something to the Eastern quivers,
he only leaves his sons future triumphs. Rejoice,
Crassus, if knowledge comes to you deep in the dark sand,

we can cross the Euphrates now to your tomb."
Thus with drink and with song shall I pass the night,   85
until the day casts its light on my wines.

IV 7

Shades do exist. Death does not end everything.
A haggard ghost escapes the abandoned pyre.
For she seemed to lean over my bed—Cynthia—
just buried at the rumbling of the roadside,
when sleep shunned my love's death rites   5
and I complained of my bed's cold dominion.

Her hair was arranged as at her burial,
the same eyes, her dress burnt into her side;
the flames had charred the familiar stone on her finger,
Lethe water had frayed her lips.   10
Breathing spirit, she uttered speech; but her reaching hands
reproached me as she snapped her brittle fingers.

"Traitor—though no girl could hope for better—
so soon sleep masters you?
So soon you've forgotten how we tricked the watchful Subura,   15
my windowsill worn by nightly deceit?
How many times I dangled down a rope to you,
hand over hand descending into your arms!
How often we made love at the crossroads, chest fused with chest,
while our cloaks made the street warm.   20
Pity our silent pact, those false words
the south winds tore apart and would not hear!

As my eyes faded, no one called me back.
Had you begged me to stay I might have gained one day.
No guard rattled behind me with cloven cane,   25
the broken tile bruised my resting head,
and last, who saw you bent with grief
or warming a black toga with your tears?

If going beyond Rome's gates displeased you, there at least
you might have asked that my bier had gone more slowly.   30
Why didn't you beg the winds, ingrate, for my pyre?
Why didn't you oil my flames with nard?

Was it too much even to scatter cheap hyacinths,
to honor my tomb with a broken wine jar?

Let Lygdamus burn—that slave of yours deserves white-hot metal—   35
I knew it, when I drank wine spiked with treason;
and though crafty Nomas hides her arcane potions,
a fiery brick will brand her guilty hands.
And she who once put herself on show, cheap nights for sale,
now sweeps the ground with her golden train   40
while a garrulous maid repays with labor
if she lets fall a word about my beauty.
Since old Petale remembered me with garlands,
now she's hobbled with a dirty block;
and Lalage bears blows, hung by her own hair's rope,   45
because she dared to plead in my name.
You let that woman melt my image's gold
and steal a dowry from my burning pyre.

Still, I don't blame you, though you deserve it, Propertius:
my reign in your books was long.   50
I swear by the Fates' thread, never to be unraveled,
and may Cerberus bark at me softly:
I was faithful. If I lie, may vipers
hiss on my tomb and coil over my bones.

Beyond the grim Styx, two seats are allotted,   55
and the river carries all on a twofold course.
One boat bears Clytemnestra's shame, and Pasiphaë's crime,
whose fraud devised the wooden cow's horror.

But behold the other group, wafted on a garlanded skiff,
where happy breezes soothe Elysian blooms,   60
where myriad lutes, Cybele's round brass,
and Lydian lyres sound with turbaned choirs.

Andromeda and Hypermestra, wives free from fraud,
recount the famous stories of their perils:
the first bemoans her arms bruised by maternal chains,   65
her hands ill-used by cold rock.
Hypermestra tells of the great deed her sisters dared,
though her soul lacked strength for the crime.
So in death we heal life's loves with tears.
I conceal your perfidies.   70

But now I command you, if perhaps you will be moved,
if Chloris's potions don't enslave you totally:
let my nurse Parthenie want for nothing in her tremulous age—
she could have been, but was not, greedy with you.
And forbid Servilla, my delight, whose name comes from her use,   75
to hold up the mirror to any new mistress.
And whatever verses you crafted in my name,
burn them for me—let go of my glory.

Lay ivy on my tomb, with full-clustered berries,
let it bind my brittle bones with twisted leaves.   80
Where fertile Anio caresses the gently-branching fields,
and ivory, by Hercules' power, never yellows,
here, on a column, write a song worthy of me,
but a short one, that a rider hastening from Rome might read:

HERE IN TIBER'S EARTH LIES GOLDEN CYNTHIA.   85
HER FAME, ANIO, ADDS LUSTER TO YOUR SHORE.

Don't ignore dreams that come from ivory gates:
when holy dreams come, they carry weight.
Wandering, night carries us out, night frees all captive shades,
even Cerberus roams when the door stands unbolted.   90
By law we return to stagnant Lethe with the light;
we are freight, the boatman checks his cargo.
Let others possess you now. Soon I alone will have you.
You will be with me: and I will grind your bones, fused with my bones."

Having convicted me with her bitter complaint,   95
the shade escaped my embrace.

IV 8

Hear and learn: the rainy Esquiline's fright last night,
when neighbors came running from the New Gardens,
when the old tavern roared with a drag-out brawl,
not with me, but with my name disgraced.

An ancient dragon guards old Lanuvium; here,   5
if anywhere, your inquisitive hour won't be wasted,
where a black abyss swallows the sacred way,
where the tribute (virgin, beware such a road entirely)
to the ravenous serpent enters, when he demands food,

hurling yearly hisses from beneath deep ground. 10
Sent down, girls pale at such sacred rites,
as they rashly trust their hands to the snake's mouth.
The virgin proffers, he seizes the offering;
the basket trembles in the maiden's grasp.
If chaste, they return to their parents' embrace, 15
and the farmers shout, "The year will bear fruit!"

Here came my Cynthia, clipped ponies carried her:
Juno was her reason; Venus the true cause.
Appia, tell me please, what a triumph you witnessed,
as she careened, wheels let loose over your stones! 20
She herself—a spectacle!—hung from the chariot's front,
daring to guide the reins over the rough spots.

As to that depilated scion's silk-hooded coach,
and his Molossan dogs with their ringed necks,
who'll sell his life for cheap gladiator's mash, 25
when a beard will make those smooth cheeks blush—I say nothing.
Since our bed suffered so much insult,
I wished to move camp to a new locale.
There's a certain Phyllis near Aventine Diana,
not much when she's sober; when drunk, all over charms. 30
Another, Teia, lives in the Tarpeian grove;
pretty, but soused and one man won't suffice.
I decided to call them and lighten the night,
and revive my affair with novelty Love.
One small bed for three in a secret court— 35
You ask our position? I lay between them.
Lygdamus manned the wine ladle, the table shone
with summer glass, the Greek flavor of Methymnaean wine.
Nile, yours was the flautist, Phyllis the castanet dancer,
and roses, artlessly elegant, ready for sprinkling, 40
and Magnus, concisely collapsed into himself,
waved stumps of arms to the hollow pipe.

But the filled lamps' flame did not stand firm;
the table collapsed at our feet.
And for me, shooting dice for luck in love, 45
always the damn dogs leapt up.
They sang to a deaf man, bore their breasts to a blind man:
I was alone, ah me, at the gates of Lanuvium.

When suddenly the raucous doors creaked on their hinges
and whispers issued from the front entrance.   50
Instantly Cynthia flung back the folding doors,
her hair in disarray, beautifully angry,
the cup dropped from my slackened fingers,
and my lips, wine-loosened, whitened.
Her eyes flashed lightning, her rage superlatively feminine,   55
no less a show than the taking of the city.

She hurled angry nails at Phyllis's face:
terrified Teia calls to the neighbors, "Fire!"
brandished torches wake up the district,
and the whole alley rings with the crazy night.   60
With their hair torn and tunics ripped,
they retreat to the first tavern in the dark road.

Cynthia rejoices in the spoils, runs back victorious,
wounds my face with a back-slashing hand,
brands my neck with a bite, and my eyes especially,   65
which deserved it, she strikes.
When finally her arms tired of hitting me,
she drags out Lygdamus, hiding at the bed's left end:
prostrate he beseeches my power.
Lygdamus, I was helpless, like you, a slave.   70
At last I begged peace with beseeching hands—
she barely held out her feet to be kissed,
and said, "If you want me to ignore your confessed crime,
you will live under the rule of my law.
You will not stroll, dolled-up, in Pompey's shade,   75
or on the Forum's lascivious sands.
Beware—don't crane your neck to the theater's top,
or dawdle before an open litter.
Lygdamus first, main cause of my complaint,
must be sold, feet bound with double chains."   80
She laid down the law. I replied, "I submit to your conditions."
She smiled, puffed up at the power I'd given.

Then wherever the alien girls had touched,
she fumigated, scoured the thresholds with pure water,
commanded all the lights to be changed,   85
three times touched my head with flame of sulfur,
and when each sheet on the bed was new,
I responded—over the whole bed we made peace.

IV 11

Paulus, don't oppress my tomb with tears;
no prayer opens death's dark gate.
Once a corpse comes under hell's jurisdiction
inexorable adamant blocks all exits.
Though the god may hear your plea in his dark hall,   5
the shores are surely deaf. They'll drink your tears.
Vows move the gods above: once the ferryman takes his pay;
the pale door shuts in the ruined pyre.
So the sad tubas sang when the cruel torch
beneath me burnt my life away.   10

Marriage to Paulus, my family chariot,
all those pledges of my fame, how have they helped?
Cornelia has found the fates just as harsh:
I am freight, now, for five fingers.
Doomed nights, sluggish waters, you marshes,   15
waves enfolding my feet,
untimely I came here, but not guilty:
may Pluto deal lightly with my shade.
Or if Aeacus sits, avenger, by his urn,
my lot drawn, let him judge my bones.   20
Let his brothers sit by, Minos's chair beside him,
the severe troop of Fates in the listening forum.

Sisyphus, rest from your weight; let Ixion's wheel fall silent;
Tantalus, seize the deceiving water;
Let rash Cerberus attack no shades today,   25
his loose chain dangle from the silent gate.
I will speak for myself: if I lie, like the sinful sisters,
may a doleful urn oppress my shoulders.

If word of ancestral trophies brought anyone honor,
Africa's realms speak of my Numantine fathers.   30
The other troop, maternal Libones, sets the balance:
each house stands firm on its titles.
The *praetexta* set aside for the marriage torches,
when a new headband held my braided hair,
I was bound, Paulus, to your bed, so to be divided.   35
Read this stone: I was bride to one man alone.

Ancestral ashes, and Rome who will keep them, I call to witness,
beneath whose legends, Africa, you lie beaten;

Perses, goading his heart with dreams of descent from Achilles,
who destroyed your homes, puffed up by his ancestor Achilles,   40
I never weakened the censor's law:
your hearths blushed at no spot of mine.
Cornelia was no loss to your spoils;
to your great house she adds an example.
My life never changed: the whole is free from crime,   45
From marriage to funeral I lived distinguished.
Nature endowed my blood with laws,
so no one could outshine me by mere fear of judgment.
Whatever harsh votes the urn may carry,
to sit beside me will be no woman's shame.   50
Not you, who towed slow Cybebe with a rope,
Claudia, uncommon servant of the tower-crowned goddess,
nor you to whom, when just Vesta called for her fire,
white linen revealed the living hearth.
Nor have I harmed you, mother Scribonia, sweet source: 55
what except death would you wish changed in me?
Maternal tears praise me, and a complaining city,
Caesar's lament defends my bones, he cries
that a sister worthy his own daughter has died,
and I saw tears escape the god.   60

Last, I earned finery's generous honors;
I was not seized from a sterile house.
You, Lepidus, you, Paulus, after death my comfort,
I left this life in your embrace.
Twice I watched my brother take a Senate chair,   65
celebrating his consulship, he lost his sister.
Daughter, sign of your father's censorial rule,
imitate me: cleave to one man.
By succession secure the line: the ship sets sail
for me, willing, so many of mine extending my life.   70
For a woman's triumph this is the highest reward:
if free-spoken fame praise her worthy pyre.

I commend to you the children, our shared pledges:
their care branded deep, still lives in my ashes.
Father, do a mother's work; carry all   75
that mob of mine, clinging to your neck.
To your kisses when they cry, add their mother's:
now all the house begins to be your burden.
If you must mourn, weep without their seeing!
Deceive their kisses with dry cheeks!   80

To long for me, Paulus, let the nights suffice,
and dreams you believe embody me.
When you speak to my picture in secret,
offer each word to one who will reply.
But should a new bed face our front door,   85
and a wary stepmother take my place,
your father's wife, boys, praise and bear:
won over, she'll surrender to your manners.
Don't over-praise your mother: careless speech
and past comparison will cause offense.   90
But if he, remembering, stays content with my shade,
and holds my ashes at so high a price,
learn now to watch for old age to come,
leave no road open for a widower's cares.
What I lost, to your years shall be added: 95
thanks to my children, old age shall make Paulus rejoice.
As it should be: I never mourned as a mother;
all my brood attended my last rites.
My case is closed. You witnesses who mourn me, rise,
while the grateful soil repays my life.   100
Even heaven has opened to virtue: may merit prove me worthy,
may my bones be borne across the honored waters.

Sulpicia

The third manuscript of Tibullus is a collection of elegies by various poets affiliated with Messalla. Five poems go by the name, "Garland of Sulpicia" (see below), and concern Sulpicia. The next group of poems, III 13-18, are by Sulpicia herself. She identifies herself as "Sulpicia, daughter of Servius" (III 16. 3-4), and was, by our best guesses, a niece of the literary patron, M. Valerius Messalla Corvinus (see III 14. 5–6), and daughter of Servius Sulpicius Rufus, cos. 51 B.C.E., a jurisconsult, friend of Caesar, and according to Cicero, a man of noble character. She tells us that her lover is Cerinthus, a name which by the standard convention of elegy is a Greek metrical equivalent for the beloved's real name. Some have suggested that the real lover is the Cornutus of Tibullus II 2, but there can be no certainty. The name Cerinthus, which means "bee-bread," may imply both the sweetness of honey, which was a common metaphor for poetical sweetness, and the activity of bees, in whose movement from flower to flower poets found an analogy for their own work.

Although the poems ascribed to Sulpicia are not in any detectable chronological sequence, they do seem to show some evidence of a purposeful order: Introduction to the affair and Sulpicia's intention to publicize it; her uncle plans a trip and Sulpicia wants to stay in Rome for her birthday (persuasion); happiness at the cancellation of the trip (joy); Cerinthus as an unfaithful lover (invective); Sulpicia's illness and Cerinthus's indifference (doubt); Sulpicia's regret for not fully expressing her love (apology).

Sulpicia

III 13

At last it's come, and to be said to hide this kind of love
    would shame me more than rumors that I'd laid it bare.
Won over by the pleading of my Muse, Cytherea
    delivered him to me. She placed him in my arms.
Venus has fulfilled what she promised: Let my joys be told   5
    by one who is said to have no joy of her own.
I would hate to keep what I've written under seal where none
    could read me sooner than my lover, for pleasure
Likes a little infamy; discretion is nothing but a tedious pose.
    Let it be known I have found a fitting partner.   10

III 14

The hated birthday approaches. A grim celebration
    in the backwaters, without Cerinthus, is planned.
What's sweeter than the city? Could a cottage satisfy a girl?
    Could farms along the freezing river of Arretium?
You're overanxious about me, Messalla, it's time you calmed down;   5
    for journeys, dear kin, are by no means always opportune.
Here soul and sense will remain though my self is abducted,
    as compulsion makes no note of my opinion.

III 15

Did you hear? Your girl has been relieved of her onerous trip,
    so now I'm allowed to stay in Rome for my birthday.
That day I was born will be celebrated by all of us,
    and by mere chance will be shared by once-skeptical you.

III 16

I'm grateful that, now you've so blithely left me behind,
    I am saved from taking a precipitous fall.
You prefer the simple toga and a basket-burdened
    whore to Sulpicia, daughter of Servius:
Others worry about me and the pain it would cause   5
    should I yield my high place to an inferior.

III 17

Are you, Cerinthus, still devoted to your girl
      now my feeble body's vexed with fever?
I would not pray to overcome this grim disease
      unless I could suppose you wished me well.
What use to me is conquered distress if your heart   5
      remains indifferent to my suffering?

III 18

No longer care for me, my light, with such fervor
      as you seem to have felt for the last few days,
if ever in my youth I'd done something so foolish,
      anything at all I could regret even more
than what I did last night when I left you alone,   5
      desiring as I did to hide my own fire.

"Garland of Sulpicia"

We do not know the identity of the author of this group of poems, who was clearly familiar with Sulpicia's poems (above). Scholars have suggested that he might be Tibullus, or the young Ovid, or an unknown contemporary of Tibullus. Some striking echoes between lines of the Garland and Ovid's *Metamorphoses*, make a strong case for a date of composition later than the publication of the *Metamorphoses* in 8 C.E.

"Garland of Sulpicia"

III 8

Descend from heaven, Mars, if you know the way,
To see Sulpicia decked out for your day!
Take care; you'd blush (though Venus well might smile)
If in your awe you let your weapons fall.
From her eyes, when he's in the mood to scorch   5
Immortals, Love lights up his double torch.
No matter where she goes, do what she will,
Some Grace discreetly makes it beautiful.
Her hair looks lovely when it's flowing free,
But a coiffure becomes her equally.   10
In Tyrian purple she sets hearts aflame,
In pure white the effect is just the same.
Thus does Vertumnus on Olympus wear
A thousand costumes, and each one is fair.
She is the only girl who ought to boast   15
Purple-dyed woolens—never mind the cost!
All that the rich Arabian from his field
Of fragrance reaps by rights should be her yield;
The Indian by the waters of the dawn
Who gathers gems should give her every one.   20
Sing of her, Muses, at this festival;
Apollo, pluck your glorious tortoise shell.
This ritual will be hers for years to come;
No girl is more deserving of your hymn.

III 10

Glorious Apollo with your hair unshorn,
Come cure a gentle girl of sickness—come!
Speed's of the essence! You will always be
Glad to have healed a beauty such as she.
Let not emaciation wreck her frame,   5
Nor any blemish mar a languid limb.
Whatever evil lurks there, let it be
Carried by rushing torrents out to sea.
Come, holy one, with all your remedies
And chants that bring a sickly body ease.   10
Pity the youth who, fearing she will die,

Sends prayers past counting up into the sky;
Now praying and now—if she should seem worse—
Hurling at heaven many a savage curse.
Fear not, Cerinthus; god's by love disarmed.   15
Love her forever and she'll stay unharmed.
Also, no tears; it's not appropriate
To weep until you two have had a fight.
But all yours now, she thinks of you alone;
A mob of others waits on her in vain.   20
Please, Phoebus! Praises will be heaped on you
For having saved not just one life but two!
What joy and fame for you when each one vies
To heap your altar with the debts s/he owes!
And every single god above will pray   25
For special skills like yours to come his way.

III 12

0 Birthday Juno, take your incense now;
A clever girl is offering it to you.
This morning she's adorned herself with care
So at your altar the whole world can stare.
All this primping she lays at your door,   5
But there's some mystery man she's dressing for.
Goddess, be gracious, let the lovers be;
But for the youth please forge chains equally
So they're well matched: no other girl is he
Fitter to love; no other young man she.   10
If any guardian catch them at their wooing,
Love, find a thousand means for his undoing.
Come hither in your shining purple gown,
Divine one; thrice they're offering cake and wine.
Though mothers tell their daughters how to pray,   15
Each maiden makes her wishes silently.
As rapid flames traverse the altar, she
Burns—with a flame that suits her perfectly.
Juno, be kind! When next year rolls around,
May this old love of theirs stay safe and sound.   20

Ovid

Ovid was born into a well-to-do equestrian family on March 20, 43 B.C.E. in Sulmo, a town in the Apennines, about eighty miles from Rome. This was the year after Julius Caesar was assassinated; almost a year before Cicero was murdered; and twelve years before the battle of Actium brought an end to the civil war between Antony and Octavian. At about the time of Actium, Ovid, like others from his class, was sent to Rome for an education in rhetoric and law. To a large degree, then, he missed the century of civil wars that played such an important role in the experience of our other poets, and he reached his maturity in the new, peaceful, and urbane Rome of Augustus. He continued his education in Athens, toured Asia Minor, spent a year in Sicily. Then at twenty-five he prepared to stand for the quaestorship. This public office was the first office in the *cursus honorum*, or "course of offices," leading ultimately to the consulship. It would have meant admission to the Senate and would have made Ovid the first senator from Sulmo. He decided, however, not to stand for the office, but rather to write poetry, "a useless task," his father called it. He became a member of Messalla's circle of poets.

Ovid had begun his public recitation of verse around 25 B.C.E. at about eighteen years of age. At that time, Vergil had completed his *Eclogues* and *Georgics* and was working on his *Aeneid*; Horace had completed his two books of *Satires* and his *Epodes* and was working on his *Odes*; Propertius had published the *Monobiblos* and perhaps a second book of elegies; and Tibullus had just published his first book of elegies. Rome was vibrant with literary activity; and Ovid said that he felt compelled to turn to poetry because whenever he attempted a speech, it came out in verse. He became in his own lifetime the most popular and widely read Roman poet and has been popular in all generations. He claims to have published a first edition of his love elegies in five books (between 19 and 8 B.C.E.), which were later reduced by the poet to the three books of *Amores* which we have. At the same time that he was producing his elegies he was breaking new ground with a series of poems called the *Heroides*, letters written by the women of myth to their husbands and lovers. Here he explored most explicitly his interest in female psychology and demonstrated his sympathy for what he took to be a woman's point of view. After the *Heroides* he wrote his only tragedy, the very popular *Medea*, which is lost to us. Then he returned to love poetry, this time to write a series of three books called *The Art of Love* (2 C.E.) in which he assumes the role of "Professor of Love" in order to instruct would-be lovers in passion manipulation. Immediately thereafter he wrote a sequel, *The*

Remedy for Love. He is best known for his great mythologic/historical epic, the *Metamorphoses*, which was completed by 8 C.E.

At that time, due to some "error" unknown to us, he was banished by the emperor Augustus to Tomis on the Black Sea. This was an old Greek colony, now inhabited mainly by barbarians, where no one spoke Latin and few spoke Greek. He left behind, unfinished, a series of etiological/astrological poems on the Roman calendar, and from Tomis composed his *Tristia*, or *Poems of Sadness*, and his *Letters from the Black Sea*. He was unable to win a reprieve, either from Augustus or the next emperor, Tiberius, and died in exile in 18 C.E. He had been married three times; two brief marriages which produced one daughter, and a third wife who remained with him during his exile.

His poetry is generally noted for its ease and wit; sometimes faulted for its rhetorical self-indulgence. He has less interest in politics per se than any other poet in this volume, which is not to say that his urban sophistication, irreverence, and even mockery of old-fashioned Roman values did not have political consequences. The elegies of the *Amores* are all the work of a young poet, but they already show his major strengths: an irreverence toward tradition and convention, be it the austere conventions of Roman morality or the recently developed conventions of his elegiac genre, and an interest in and subtle sense of human (here particularly male) psychology. As with his predecessors, he writes in the first person of his love for a woman, called Corinna, whose actual status as either a real person or as the consistent subject of the poems is problematic. In one poem Ovid wittily recounts that he knows a woman who boasts that she is Corinna. If his mistress is, as seems most likely, a literary topos, the persona which Ovid adopts for himself is similarly literary. He often seems to be a parody of the Propertian lover, a conscious attempt to undermine the typical lover's sincerity with comic posturing. Ovid says, "My love embraces all mythology" (*Amores* II 4. 44).

Ovid

I 1

Weapons and war were my theme. I was ready to roll forth battle lines
    in meter to match my subject matter.
Ranks of verse stood in strict formation—when Cupid laughed
    (it's said) and stole a foot of hexameter.
"Barbarous boy, who gave you leave to meddle in the art of poetry?   5
    It's the Pierides, not you, we bards flock to.
What if you caught Venus trying on the breastplate of blond Minerva,
    or blond Minerva fanning the flames of love?
Who would approve Ceres ruling over wooded mountains, or put
    bow-bearing Diana in charge of farm work?   10
Should long-haired Apollo march and drill with a battle spear,
    while Mars sits drumming an Aonian lyre?
Your empire, boy, is enormous and far too powerful as it is.
    Why grasp after more? Let ambition rest.
Or do you rule the whole world? Is Helicon now your private resort?   15
    Is Apollo in hock to you for his lyre?
I had just unfurled my opening line on the wide-open page,
    when in the second you slackened my sails.
Don't you see I haven't the themes light verse is made of: no boy
    or girl with her hair nicely done up."   20
So I complained. He just reached into his opened quiver
    and found the arrow meant for me.
He stoutly gripped his bow and bent it back against his knee:
    "Here's something," he said, "to make you sing."
O unhappy me! That boy really knew how to use a bow and arrow!   25
    I'm on fire—Love's taken charge of my heart.
Now let my verse swell with one line and fall back with the next.
    Farewell war and iron-shod hexameters!
Muse, now bind your fair forehead with myrtle from the shore,
    and prepare to dance to a different tune.   30

I 4

So it's true. He's coming with you to this dinner party.
    Dear gods, let it be his last meal on earth.
What am I supposed to do? Mingle? And when I see you,
    do nothing but look? Must I watch
another enjoying your touch, watch another throw his arms   5
    around your neck whenever he likes?

Now I understand how those well-wined centaurs went berserk
    just looking at the lovely girl of Atrax.
Granted, I don't live in the woods and I'm not half horse; still
    it's hard work to keep my hands off you.   10
But listen to what I want you to do; memorize every word:
    this is for your ears, not for Eurus.
First, find an excuse to come before him—I really don't know
    what good it will do—but do it anyway.
Look the part of dutiful wife when you follow him to the dining couch,   15
    but rub against my foot as you pass by.
Watch me. I'll communicate by nods, the look on my face:
    decode my winks and secretly reply.
Who needs speech? What can't I say with the arch of an eyebrow
    or trace with a finger in air or wine?   20
When you find yourself thinking of our last lovemaking,
    touch your flushed cheek with your thumb.
If you're brooding over some wrong you think I've done,
    let me know by pinching your earlobe.
But darling, if I say or do anything that gives you pleasure,   25
    encourage me by twiddling your ring.
When you're praying that he will suffer his just deserts, touch
    the table as a suppliant would an altar.
Be wise and make him swallow the drink he mixed for you; calmly ask
    the slave to bring whatever you want.   30
When you've taken a sip and put down your glass, I'll snatch it
    and press my lips to the wet rim.
If he thinks to pass you the hors d'oeuvres he's sampled,
    turn up your nose at what he tasted.
Push him away when he tries to embrace you; don't rest   35
    your head tenderly on that tough chest.
Keep his hands out of your dress; shield your inviting breasts;
    make it clear there will be no kissing.
Kiss him once and you can forget this masquerade; I'll shout
    "she's mine" and throw my arms around you.   40
This much I'll be able to see, but I'm worried sick at the possibilities
    the folds of dinner clothes hide.
Don't squeeze up close to him; don't rub your thigh against his;
    don't pet his rough foot with your polished toes.
If I'm a nervous wreck, it's because I've played these tricks myself   45
    and now torture myself by thinking
how many times in the same position I have performed miracles
    with one deft hand working undercover.
I'm sure you wouldn't follow my example, but to ease my suspicions,
    leave your evening wrap at the door.   50

Keep him drinking (you needn't coax him with kisses);
　　keep filling his glass when he's not looking.
If we're lucky he'll get soused and fall fast asleep on the couch;
　　opportunity will provide our course of action.
When you get up to go home and all the rest of us are departing,　　55
　　find a way to get into the thick of the crowd.
In the push and shove at the door one of us will find the other;
　　then touch whatever part of me you can.
Damn! will you listen to me desparately planning to snatch one hour
　　of happiness—the long night will divide us.　　60
At night he will lock you in. Weeping, I'll follow as far as I can—
　　all the way up to the heartless door.
It will be he who kisses you, and he will not stop at a kiss or two:
　　what you secretly give me, he'll take legally.
Do your level best to act unwilling; make him know he's forcing you;　　65
　　do whatever you have to do in grim silence.
If Venus hears my prayers, his desire will be a joyless exercise;
　　I can only hope that you won't enjoy it.
But whatever happens during the night, tell me the next day
　　that nothing happened, and make me believe it.　　70

I 5

It was hot—the day already more than half gone.
　　I lay where I'd dropped on the bed.
It happened a window was half open. Light filtered in
　　like light falling in a forest;
like the afterglow of twilight or when it's dawn　　5
　　but the night hasn't quite faded.
That's the kind of dim light shy girls like—it gives
　　their modesty some cover.
The door opens. In comes Corinna, her dress half buttoned,
　　her hair fixed to show off that lovely neck.　　10
She looked as lovely as Semiramis on her wedding night
　　or Lais in anyone's bed.
I tore off the dress. To make it more fun she fought
　　to keep the flimsy thing half on.
We struggled; I won! Her protests betrayed　　15
　　the truth: she had wanted to lose.
Clothes littered the room. There stood Corinna nude.
　　God, what a masterpiece she was!
Looking was not enough; I had to touch those shoulders, those arms;
　　mold my hands round each round breast.　　20

Her belly's subtle curves coaxed my fingers on. Soon I felt
    the supple swell of hips and thighs.
But why catalog the store of pleasure her body held?
    I held her naked in my arms.
You can fantasize the rest. We were exhausted and slept.   25
    May many afternoons be so well spent.

16

What a shame, doorman, that you're locked to that hard chain!
    But open up this obstinate door!
I'm begging you. It isn't much—just crack it wide enough
    for me to squeeze through sideways.
Long loving has pared me down to skin and bones and honed   5
    my limbs for jobs like this.
Love shows you how to sneak by the sleepless eyes of guards
    and steers your feet straight and sure.
I used to fear the dark. I quaked at every empty shadow. I marveled
    that anyone went out at night.   10
Then he laughed. I heard. It was Cupid with his gorgeous mother.
    "Even you," he said, "will be made brave."
Before I knew it I was in love and not afraid anymore of night's
    rushing shadows or the assassin's knife.
But you scare me. No one has ever seen me groveling like this.   15
    You wield the bolt of my doom.
Just look at my tears—open the damn door and look! The pitiless
    wood is soaked through and through.
Have you forgotten how it felt stripped and trembling before the whip?
    I begged your mistress to be lenient.   20
Doesn't one favor deserve another? It's a crime if the value of my
    good deed has so much depreciated.
Give me my due. Kindness pays off. You'll soon get what you want.
    Night is passing. Slide back the bolt.
Slide back the bolt. Listen to me and be free of those shackles. You needn't   25
    drink the water of slavery forever.
Am I entreating a cast-iron statue? Doorman, are you listening?
    The hard oak hasn't so much as budged.
You'd think this front door were the portal of a city under siege.
    Haven't you heard? We're at peace.   30
Pity the armed foe attacking this gate if you treat a lover so!
    Night is passing. Slide back the bolt.
I carry no weapons. I haven't come with storm troopers for company.
    I'm all alone except for savage Love.

I can't send *him* packing even if I wished—I might as well vivisect   35
    my soul from my own body!
It's just the two of us. Yes, my face is a bit wine-flushed (I only had a sip!)
    and my slick hair wears its wreath askew.
But who would fear such panoply? Who'd not face the likes of me?
    Night is passing. Slide back the bolt.   40
Are you thick as wood or asleep? Snoring be your death if your ears let
    the winds snatch away a lover's words.
I'll never forget how vigilant you used to be when I would try to give you
    the slip in the starlight of midnight.
But maybe even you have a lover cooing close to your side right now.   45
    Oh, how much kinder has luck treated you!
I'd gladly take your place. Quick, chain me to that predicament!
    Night is passing. Slide back the bolt.
Are my ears tricking me or did I hear the doorpost shudder and creak,
    did the hoarse hinge give me a sign?   50
I'm dreaming. Just a trick of the wind whispering against the door,
    blowing my hope down the street.
Boreas, remember now how you ravished Orithyia, and come to my aid—
    blow down this tone-deaf door.
There's not a sound in the city and the crystal dew is falling fast.   55
    Night is passing. Slide back the bolt.
I'm not kidding. I'll come back armed with iron and with my torch
    assail this pretentious house.
Night, Love and Wine have never advocated moderation. Night knows
    no shame; Love and Wine are fearless.   60
I've tried everything. You're impervious to prayers and threats.
    You're harder than the door itself.
It's all wrong to set you to guard the beauty of my dear love.
    You belong at a dungeon's sad gate.
As I speak Lucifer's whipping up his team—frost flies from the axles.   65
    The cock is calling drudges to their toil.
O wilted wreath, torn from my unhappy hair, I entreat you:
    lie the night on this hard doorjamb.
You shall be witness to my mistress when she wakes at dawn
    of the long, wretched hours I wasted here.   70
Hard as you are, doorman, farewell. I'm leaving. Listen at least
    to praise. You did your job. Good-bye.
And you also, cruel locks, bars and soulless wood, his fellow slaves,
    I say good-bye to one and all.

18

There's a certain madame—if your interests run in this direction,
    read on—I'll tell you about Dipsas,
an old bawd who lives up to her name—she's yet to be sober enough
    to see Memnon's mother and her rosy steeds.
But she does know her magic and all the secret spells of Circe;   5
    she can make strong rivers run backwards.
She's an expert when it comes to herbs and the tools of sorcery;
    she distills a rare poison from a mare in heat.
The very weather obeys her will; at her command the whole sky
    turns black as pitch or opens wide with light.   10
Believe it or not, I have seen the stars drip drops of blood,
    and once saw the moon a bloody ball.
I have long suspected that at night her wrinkled hide sprouts wings
    and she flies and flaps about in the dark.
I believe what I hear: twin pupils burn in her bloodshot eyes   15
    and flash hot sparks of lightning.
Corpses shudder awake at her cry and come walking from ancient tombs;
    her incantations break apart solid rock.
This hag had set her mind on violating love's chaste bonds;
    and she's eloquent when the cause is malign.   20
I happened to be on the other side of the double doors and overheard
    what she said. This was her advice:
"My pet, surely you noticed how you bewitched that rich young man
    yesterday. He couldn't take his eyes off you.
And I'm not surprised either. You're as beautiful as they come.   25
    It breaks my heart to see you cheaply dressed.
How I wish the gods had subsidized your curves with some hard cash;
    properly outfitted, you'd draw in a fortune.
It must have been the stars and Mars ascending that worked against you;
    but now Venus is rising in the zodiac,   30
and just look how your luck has turned: you've hooked your first lover
    with the means to keep you in style.
And he's not hard to look at; in fact, his face mirrors your loveliness;
    if he weren't a buyer, he'd be bought.
Does that make you blush? Hmm, a little color adds tone to your
complexion;   35
    but dab on some rouge; don't rely on nature.
Keep your eyes leveled on your lap; gear your fetching glances
    to the price a customer's gift will bring.
Maybe in Tatius's time the Sabine girls went unadorned and
    refused service to any but a husband.   40

Now Mars leads our boys around the world to test their courage;
    but Venus rules the city of her Aeneas.
The fun's nonstop for sexy girls; the chaste are those no one asks out.
    Only a hick wouldn't ask the man herself.
As for prim matrons, take another look—those venerable wrinkles hide   45
    tales of debauchery that would shock you.
Penelope knew how to try the strength of young men: she had them
    straining to arch the bow's bone.
Time slips by unnoticed—it goes spinning along out of control;
    a year has raced by before you know it.   50
Bronze is polished bright by use; a lovely dress is made to show off;
    if a house stands empty, it rots.
The same goes for beauty: you have to use it. You can't save it for rainy days.
    Don't think one lover makes a spring.
Diversify your amorous interests. You'll earn more and incur less envy.   55
    It's flocks of lambs that make wolves fat.
Now, what does that bard of yours give you besides his latest love lyrics?
    You call thousands of lines to read a gift?
The god of poets knows how to get your attention—he dresses in gold
    and plays a gold-plated lyre.   60
Wise up. A rich man has far more gifts than great Homer ever had.
    Believe me, generosity takes talent.
It doesn't matter if he's an ex-slave who climbed the social ladder;
    pretend not to see his chalk-marked heel.
Likewise, don't let the family busts in fancy homes take you in;   65
    If he hasn't cash, he can have his ancestors.
And I don't care how handsome he is. In this business there's no free lunch.
    Let him wheedle your price from his own lover.
At first, when you're baiting the trap, work for rates they can't refuse;
    once hooked, milk them for all they're worth.   70
There's nothing wrong with canned passion—purr sweet nothings in his ear,
    say "I adore you"—all the way to the bank.
At the same time, often stop the lovemaking short; complain of a headache,
    or say you have to rush to church to worship Isis.
But don't push the hard-to-get stuff too far or he might get used to it,   75
    and his fire, doused, completely sputter out.
Turn a deaf door to penniless pleading; open it wide to the generous giver;
    time it so one lover hears another leaving.
If he complains that you've hurt him, cry and scream that he hurt you first;
    upstage his charges with countercharges.   80
But take care never to let his anger simmer too long in its own juices.
    Anger often can age into bitter feelings.
Make the most of your eyes; learn how to turn the waterworks on and off;
    at the least trifle let your cheeks swim in tears.

If deception sometimes requires perjury, there's no need to worry: 85
    Venus can fix it so the gods won't hear.
Coach your hired help to play their supporting parts on cue;
    they can drop him a hint at what to buy you.
Let them work for tips on the side; loose change soon adds up;
    you build a big heap grain by grain.   90
Bring in your sister, mother, wet nurse—they'll help you fleece him;
    get as many hands in his pockets as you can.
When you've finally exhausted all the excuses for demanding gifts,
    bake a cake and tell him it's your birthday.
Never let him feel secure; do little things to make him fear a rival: 95
    complacency drains the sap out of passion.
See that he discovers the evidence of another's pleasure in your bed;
    let him count the bruises on your throat.
But above all else, show him the gifts other admirers have sent you.
    If you haven't any, go shopping on the *Via Sacra*.   100
After he's spent a fortune, make double-sure you get his last cent
    by asking a loan he'll never see again.
Coax and cozen him down the garden path. He won't guess what hit him
    if you honey-coat his bitter pill.
Well, there you have the legacy of my long professional experience.   105
    Don't waste it. If you take my advice
you'll often find reason to thank me while I live, often remember me
    fondly when I'm dead and gone."
She was still rambling on when my shadow slipped and betrayed me.
    I could hardly keep my shaking hands   110
from tearing apart her mangy white hair, her booze-shot eyes,
    her withered cheeks wrinkle by wrinkle.
If the gods hear my prayer, you'll drag out your old age homeless,
    racked by long winter, dying for a drink.

I 9

Soldiers—that's what lovers are. Cupid bivouacs in the field.
    Believe me, Atticus—love is war.
Venus and Mars recruit the same age group. It's shameful to see
    old men in arms, old men falling in love.
A general expects his fighting men to be strong and courageous;   5
    a beauty expects no less in a mate.
One stands vigil at his mistress's door, the other before his lord's tent.
    If they sleep, it's on the ground.
A soldier's job takes him far from home. A lover on active service
    will follow his girl around the world.   10

Mountains and rivers swollen double with rain won't stop him;
    he'll trudge through drifts of snow.
If he must scour the seas to find her, he'll not wait for favoring stars,
    nor find an excuse in rising easterlies.
Who but soldier or lover would put up with the night's cold   15
    and snow thick with sleet?
The soldier is sent to spy behind the lines of the dangerous foe;
    the lover's eye is peeled for his rival.
Laying siege to mighty cities or the threshold of a hard-hearted girl,
    one breaks down gates, one a front door.   20
Soldiers armed to the teeth often will fall upon the sleeping enemy
    and slaughter heaps of unarmed men.
So the fierce troops of Thracian Rhesus perished in their nightshirts,
    and you, captured steeds, abandoned your lord.
Naturally, lovers make the most of husbands snoring in their beds,   25
    and wield their arms as the foe slumbers.
You'll find soldiers and wretched lovers sneaking through sentry lines
    and mobs of guards—it's their job.
Mars is fickle, Venus mercurial. The fleeing host can turn and rally;
    those you thought invincible fall.   30
Recant, if you've ever called a lover shiftless and lazy.
    Love tests a man's mettle.
Great Achilles is all on fire for Briseis stolen from his bed.
    Quick, Trojans, break the Argive ranks!
Hector went to battle still warm from Andromache's arms;   35
    his wife put his helmet on.
The sight of Priam's daughter, her hair wild as a maenad's,
    struck dumb the mightiest of generals.
Mars himself felt the blacksmith's nets pin him to a bed—
    every god knows that story.   40
As for me, I was born lazy; relaxation was my element.
    Lounging in the shade had made me soft.
But the passion for a beautiful girl dragged me from leisure
    and bid me earn wages in love's camp.
So now you see me leaping into the fray on night's battlefields.   45
    If it's action you want, fall in love!

I 10

Think of Helen shipped far from the Eurotas under Phrygian sail,
    bound to bring war between two husbands;
think of Leda deceived by the false swan's snow-white wings
    a cunning adulterer masqueraded in;

think of Amymone wandering in the thirsty plain of Argos,   5
    a water jug crushing her lovely curls—
you once were a woman to rival these, and I feared eagle and bull
    and every form Love has made mighty Jove purloin.
Now all that fear is gone; I'm cured of my infatuation;
    my eyes are slaves no longer to that beauty of yours.   10
Why this metamorphosis, you ask. It's because you ask for gifts;
    this is the reason you fail to please me.
While you were ingenuous, I loved you, soul and body;
    now I see your figure's marred by a character flaw.
Love is a naked little boy whose unclothed, unspoiled youthfulness   15
    is proof enough of his innocence.
Why do all you women command Venus's child to sell himself?
    He hasn't even a pocket for his money.
Venus and her son are not suited to the savage tools of war;
    it's wrong to make peaceful gods mercenaries.   20
A prostitute hawks her wares at a fixed price to any passerby
    and makes her body earn its wretched toll.
But she curses the greedy pimp's power to force her to perform
    what you do of your own accord.
Look at the unreasoning beasts and learn from their example;   25
    it's shameful to be less kind than an animal.
You'll never see a mare solicit a stallion, nor a cow fleecing a bull;
    nor a ram promising his ewe a legacy.
Only a woman feels triumphant at despoiling a man of his money,
    only a woman sells her nights, only a woman   30
auctions herself and merchandises a mutual pleasure
    at a price her own enjoyment sets.
Venus is even-handed in giving her gift to men and women;
    why is it sold by one and bought by the other?
Why should enjoyment cost me, while it makes you money,   35
    when it takes two to create the pleasure?
There's something wrong when witnesses profit from perjury,
    when called jurors answer to bribes.
It's shameful that the eloquence of cash pleads the defendant's case,
    that money tips the scales of justice.   40
It's shameful that patrimonies swell with revenues from a bed,
    shameful to turn one's own beauty to coin.
Things without price richly deserve gratitude's full reward;
    thankless the bed where love is bought and sold.
The buyer's absolved of all obligations. Once his money's tendered   45
    he's met his debt for services rendered.
Refrain, O beauties, from putting a price tag on your nights;
    sordid income brings no good outcome.

Do you think the Vestal virgin got a bargain for those Sabine armlets
  when Sabine arms crushed her head?   50
Do you think one pretty necklace was worth having one's very son
  drive a sword into the womb that bore him?
Now, there's nothing wrong in asking gifts from a rich man;
  the wealthy can afford generosity.
Go on, pick and enjoy the grapes that weigh down the full vine;   55
  Alcinous's orchard has fruit to spare.
But let the poor man pay his bill with faithfulness, service and passion:
  a mistress can take all a man can give.
My gift is to celebrate girls in song, girls who have earned praise.
  I can make you a celebrity, if I choose.   60
Frippery will be torn; jewelery crafted from gold and gems will break;
  the fame my verses give will last forever.
I don't mind giving, but to be asked rouses my scorn and hate.
  Stop asking, and you'll have what I now deny.

I 13

She's coming. Even now frosty axles whir. Gold-haired Dawn is flying
  over ocean, speeding from her old husband.
What's your hurry, Aurora? Rest awhile and allow Memnon's shadow
  the honor his battling birds give but once a year.
Now it's pleasant just to lie here, my darling's soft arms   5
  around me, her body close against mine.
Now sleep feels slow and lazy and the chill air of early morning is alive
  with the liquid song of soft-throated birds.
What's your hurry? No lover or his girl welcomes your coming—
  grip the dew-drenched reins; pull back your rosy hand.   10
Before your arrival sailors can better read the shining map of the stars
  and do not wander blindly in mid ocean.
The moment you appear the road-weary traveler must stumble from bed,
  the soldier again lift sword in his savage hand.
You are the first to see the farmer in the fields doubled over his hoe,   15
  you drag the slow oxen under the curved yoke.
You cheat little boys of sleep and pack them off to schoolmasters
  who will take a cane to tender knuckles.
The young dandies you bring to court to bail out some friend
  will lose a fortune at the drop of a word.   20
How can the prosecutor or the learned defense welcome you
  when your coming means only more casework?

It's you, when women might enjoy some rest from daily chores,
    who summon them back to work their looms.
All this I could put up with, but only a man who hasn't a girl could   25
    brook the thought of sweethearts up at dawn.
How often I've prayed that night would refuse to yield the sky to you,
    that the stars would not flee before your face;
How often I've prayed the winds to smash your axle to bits
    or your horses to trip over a thick cloud!   30
What's your hurry? You're not wanted. Your heart's as black
    as that black son you bore and mothered.
I'd just love to hear Tithonus talk about you, if he could:
    no goddess in heaven would fall so low.
You're so eager to get away from the dotard that you hop from bed   35
    and race to mount the hated chariot.
You'd sing a different tune if you lay in the arms of Cephalus.
    Then you'd cry "run slowly, horses of night"
Must my love life suffer because old age has drained your husband's sap?
    Was it I who arranged your marriage?   40
I'll remind you that the Moon gave her lover the gift of long sleep;
    and the Moon is no less lovely than you.
Even the sire of the gods, when he tired of seeing you so often,
    ran two nights together for a tryst.
She was blushing when I stopped complaining, so she must have heard.   45
    Day, nevertheless, arrived right on time.

I 14

How many times did I tell you—"Stop dyeing your hair!"
    Now there's nothing left to color.
If only you'd left it alone. No one had hair like yours.
    It tumbled down full to your hips.
Your curls were so fine that you feared to dress them;   5
    fine as the silk the tan Chinese wear,
delicate as the thread a spider spins from her thin leg,
    weaving her gossamer from a lonely beam.
Your tresses were not sable, they were not golden;
    but in each hair both colors blended;   10
like the hue of a tall cedar's skin stripped of bark
    in the steep dewy vales of Ida.
Not to mention its manageability. Have you ever winced
    as you arranged it in a hundred styles?
Did hairpins or the teeth of your comb ever tear a single   15
    strand? Your hairdresser was safe.

I often watched her fixing your hair and not once saw you grab
    a brooch to stab her in the arm.
In the mornings you loved to lounge on your purple-spread bed,
    your hair down and still uncombed.   20
It was lovely loose and wild. You looked like a Thracian maenad
    sprawled exhausted on green grass.
Just think of the horrible tortures those poor down-soft curls
    had to suffer at your hands.
How patiently they endured the rack of hot curling irons   25
    as you twisted them into ringlets.
Again and again I cried—"It's a crime, a crime to singe them!
    Is your heart cast iron? Have mercy
on your own head. Don't force the beauty nature gave you.
    What a perm couldn't learn from your natural wave!"   30
Now you've destroyed all that gorgeous hair. Hair Apollo or Bacchus
    would have loved to call his own;
full and heavy as the hair I once saw nude Dione lift aside
    with dripping fingers in a painting.
What's the point of complaining now that those abused bangs are gone?   35
    Why cry, silly, and hide your mirror?
Are your eyes shocked by what they see? Better get used to it.
    Forget how you looked before.
A rival didn't do *that* to you with a pack of enchanted herbs;
    no hag rinsed your hair with Haemonian water.   40
It wasn't the work of a wasting illness—thank the gods—
    no envious tongue made your hair fall out.
You alone bear the blame for the loss you feel. Your own hand
    poured the poisonous lotion on your head.
Now the spoils of our triumphant armies will save you;   45
    you'll wear braids captured in Germany.
But you'll blush every time someone raves about your new look;
    "I'm upstaged by a wig!" you'll cry.
"It's some Sygambrian woman he's praising. I remember when
    those compliments were truly mine."   50
Oh dear—she can hardly keep back the tears. Her hands try
    to hide the flaming red her cheeks confess.
She just stares at the ruins of her hair lying in her lap;
    a sacrifice, alas, so misplaced.
Now, dry your eyes. Compose yourself. The loss can be repaired.   55
    You'll soon be showing off your own hair again.

I 15

Why, biting Envy, do you hound me, why keep harping on how
    I've wasted my years and gifts on poetry?
How long must I go on hearing the same old cant: get a real job, Ovid—
    join the army, Ovid—you won't be young forever—
do what your father did—be serious—go to law school—you've got   5
    to sell yourself to make it in the marketplace!
You're asking me to pawn my life for things that neither matter nor last.
    I'm after immortal fame—a name to fill the world.
Maeonides will live as long as there is a Tenedos or Mt. Ida,
    as long as Simois runs splashing to the sea.   10
The Ascraean poet will not perish while grapes still swell on the vine
    and Ceres' golden hair falls under the scythe.
Down the ages the son of Battus will be sung the world over:
    if shy of raw genius, he was consummate in art!
No harm will ever come to the high-laced buskin of Sophocles;   15
    while sun and moon shine, Aratus will reflect their light.
As long as servants lie, fathers chide their sons, call girls have a calling
    and pimps make the money—there will be Menander.
Rough-hewn Ennius and Accius whose mouth roared and stormed poetry—
    these are names time cannot tarnish or destroy.   20
Can you imagine an age ignorant of Varro and his epic tale of the Argonauts,
    a time when no one can name the Aesonian lord?
Only when a single day will bring destruction upon the whole world
    will the sublime song of Lucretius fall silent.
Vergil will sing in Arcadia, will celebrate harvests, will tell of Aeneas and
war   25
    for as long as Rome is capital of the world.
Until Cupid's bow is broken and his torches burn out, lovers will learn
    love's subtle undertones from you, Tibullus.
Gallus will be known in the East, Gallus's fame never wane in the West,
    and Lycoris be immortal because Gallus loved her.   30
The years wear down high cliffs, the iron plowshare rusts to dust;
    but time and decay cannot touch poetry.
Kings who parade in the purple trappings of power must learn to bow
    before poetry—it is more precious than gold.
Let the great herd of mankind gape at cheap display—I shall drink deep   35
    from Apollo's chalice at the Castalian spring.
Give me poesy's crown—wreathe my hair with leaves of winter-shy myrtle!
    Troubled lovers will love my books the world over.
Envy feeds on the living; it quickly loses all interest in the dead:
    fame defends each man as he deserves.   40

When the funeral flames have burned and consumed my mortal remains,
    I shall live, so much of me will survive the fire!

II 1

I composed this, too—I, Ovid, from stream-crossed Sulmo,
    the famous versifier of my own
fecklessness. This, too, was commissioned by Cupid: Begone
    judgmental souls, whose ears are unattuned
to tender songs. My readers should be warm, responsive   5
    brides, or boys in love for the first time;
and some young man, his wound of the same origin as mine,
    may recognize the symptoms of his state
and wonder, "who described these flames in such detail
    to that poet, who has written how I feel?"   10
At one time, I recall, I'd had the nerve to recount celestial battles
    and hundred-handed Gyas—I had the ability, too—
when Mother Earth exacted her harsh vengeance, and Olympus
    bore the sheer weight of Pelion and Ossa . . .
I held in my hands the storm clouds, Jove, and the thunderbolt he'd hurl   15
    expertly, to defend his place in heaven—
My woman shut me out. She closed her door! I dropped Jove
    thunderbolt and all, put him out of my mind.
Forgive me, Jove, but your bolts were useless to me, insignificant
    next to the thunderclap of her slammed door.   20
I went back to sweet elegy, picked up again my proper instrument:
    smooth words have often made hard doors give way.
Songs can pull down from the sky the horns of the blood-red moon,
    turn back the snow-white horses of the sun,
snap apart the jaws of poisonous snakes, make rivers run   25
    back to their sources, open entranceways
that once were closed up tight; songs can make the bolt slide back
    from the most intractable of doors.
Where's the profit in yet another epic on swift Achilles?
    What can the sons of Atreus do for me?   30
What use do I have for the Man of Too Many Wrong Turns,
    or Hector, Troy's great sorrow, dragged through the dust?
But praise the face of a beautiful woman—as often as not
    the poet's prize will be the girl herself.
That's my idea of compensation. Farewell, illustrious names   35
    of ancient heroes! I can live without
your gratitude. Lovely women of Rome, come hear me sing
    the words that I am taught by blushing Love.

II 4

You won't catch me making excuses for my vice-ridden life-style
    or using lies to fortify my faults.
If confessing one's sins is good for anything, then I confess—
    I scourge my failings like a man deranged!
I hate what I am, and want to change, but still I am what I hate;   5
    this oppresses me beyond belief.
You see, I lack the strength of will to control myself;
    I'm swept along, a helpless skiff at sea.
It's not that there's any one type of woman I can't resist—
    a hundred motives incite my perpetual lust.   10
If a girl casts her eyes shyly downward, her modesty
    inflames me: how I love a quiet girl!
But if she's forward, I find her sophistication quite compelling;
    the knowing depths of those soft bedroom eyes!
The austere Sabine type intrigues me; I suspect she wants it,   15
    but hides her feelings very skillfully.
And you, my lovely reader, your refinement and taste are rare indeed.
    But if you don't read . . . ah! you're so unspoiled!
One woman says that compared to me, Callimachus sounds rustic;
    what could be more provocative than praise?   20
Another finds fault with my verses, says I'm an awful poet—
    I'd like to get my hands around her thighs!
This girl walks softly—I'm captivated. That one seems harsh,
    but could be softened by a lover's touch.
Here's a girl who sings beautifully, flexing her supple voice;   25
    I'd like to steal kisses from that mouth.
And here's one who plucks the plaintive strings with practiced thumb:
    who could help but love such learned hands?
That dancer is fantastic: the rhythmic way she moves her arms, the way
    she twists, and undulates her silky sides . . .   30
Never mind my response (I'm easily moved)—one look at her
    would turn Hippolytus into Priapus.
You're wonderfully tall; your body is as long as a bed! Your stature
    is equal to the ancient heroines';
this girl is small and compact: I'm equally corrupted by you both.   35
    Both long and short conform to my desires.
She's not dressed up, but just think how good she'd look if she were!
    She's stylish—she knows how to show herself off!
I'm a pushover for fair-skinned women; I'm crazy for yellow hair;
    and dark girls can be really sexy, too.   40
Let's say a woman has coal-black hair around a snow-white neck:
    Leda was stunning with her raven hair.

Let's say she's a blonde: Aurora's saffron tresses were exquisite.
    My love embraces all mythology.
A young girl attracts my attention, an older woman moves me;   45
    the one has looks, the other savoir faire.
In short, any passable girl in Rome—all of the above!—
    is just the kind of girl I'd love to love.

II 6

The parrot, that winged mimic from orient India
    is dead. Come, ye birds! Crowd round her pyre.
Come, all pious fowl, and beat your breasts with your pinions,
    with sharp talons tear your tender cheeks.
In lieu of grief-torn hair, rend your disheveled plumage;   5
    in lieu of long trumpets, let your song resound.
Philomela, do you still moan over the crime of the Ismarian tyrant?
    That lament has filled its span of years.
Turn now to the sorrowful funeral of this singular bird:
    great the grief for Itys, but that was long ago.   10
Grieve, all who speed and pirouette through the liquid air, and you,
    turtle dove, most of all, who were his friend.
The two of you went through life together in perfect harmony
    and stood by one another to the very end.
Only the devotion Orestes found in his friend from Phocis   15
    approaches the turtle dove's devotion to you.
But what good is such loyalty, what good the rare beauty of your colors,
    what good your talent for mimicking voices,
what good that you were a gift that made my darling so happy—
    you're dead, unhappy paragon of birds.   20
Your feathers made delicate emerald seem lusterless and faded;
    your beak blazed with crimson and saffron.
In all the world there was no bird better at sounding human,
    so well you lisped counterfeit syllables.
Envy snatched you from the living—never a promoter of war's savagery,   25
    you chattered away and loved placid peace.
Just look how quail behave: their life's one internecine battle;
    perhaps that's why so many are old widows.
You were satisfied with so little: your passion for conversation
    left your bill short time for the table.   30
One nut made a meal; you took a few poppy seeds to help you sleep;
    a drop or two of plain water kept thirst at bay.
The ravenous vulture is alive; the kite still draws circles in the sky;
    the grackle survives to usher in rain.

The raven, despised by well-armed Minerva, lives until death finally   35
    catches up with him in the ninth generation.
But the parrot, that loquacious echo of the human voice, that gift
    sent from the end of the earth, has perished.
Almost always death's greedy hands snatch away the very best first;
    the worst are left to wear out their stay in life.   40
Thersites was there to see the sad funeral of the youth from Phylace;
    when Hector was ashes, his brothers still lived.
Why now recall my darling's fear, her vigil, her prayers for you—
    prayers swept to sea by blustering Notus.
When the seventh day dawned it was clear you would not see another: 45
    the Parcae stood by holding an empty spindle.
Still, weak as you were, you would not stop struggling to speak,
    and you died crying "Farewell, Corinna!"
There is a shady grove of dark ilex at the foot of a hill in Elysium
    and there the well-watered grass is evergreen.   50
If we can believe what is said about the unknown, that place is reserved
    for pious birds and barred to fallen fowl.
There far and wide the harmless swan thrives; there you will find
    the long-lived phoenix solitary in paradise.
In that grove Juno's bird opens and spreads her fan of feathers,   55
    and the coquettish dove kisses her amorous mate.
These will welcome the parrot into their sylvan haven, his last home,
    and all will flock round to hear him speak.
His bones lie buried in a tomb no larger than his mortal size,
    and these words crowd his modest headstone: 60
"This monument tells how well I pleased my mistress:
    Mine a learned tongue uncommon in a bird."

II 7

Am I always to stand trial on one new charge after another?
    I win, of course, but it's such a bother.
If we're at the theater and I glance back at the gallery,
    you pick out a rival to complain about.
If a beautiful woman happens just to look my way,   5
    you claim her looks send silent signals.
I praise a woman and your nails are out and at my hapless hair;
    I fault another and you think I'm hiding something.
If my color's good, you're sure my feelings for you have chilled;
    I'm pale—I must be dying for someone else.   10
How I wish I could think of some crime to be guilty of:
    those deserving punishment know how to take it.

As it is, you're wild with allegations and so given to suspicion
    that you make your anger inadmissable.
Look at the pitiable long-eared ass and learn a valuable lesson: 15
    the more you whip him, the slower he goes.
Now, here's a novel charge! I'm accused of defiling your bed
    with Cypassis, your beautician!
Dear gods, if I'm going to err on the side of pleasure, grant me
    something better than a sordid fling.   20
What free man willingly has sex with a slave, preferring
    to caress a lash-scarred back?
Not to mention how busy you keep her just fixing your hair
    and how pleased you are with her work.
Oh yes, I'm going to proposition one of your devoted servants!   25
    She'd slap my face and tell on me.
By Venus and the bow of her winged boy, I solemnly swear
    I'm not guilty of the charge you bring.

II 8

Cypassis, you're so accomplished in styling hair a thousand ways,
    your brush should touch only a goddess's curls.
And the Cypassis I've known in our stolen fun is no country girl:
    yes, you suit your mistress, but you suit me more.
So who could it have been who went and informed on our lovemaking?   5
    How did Corinna learn you were sharing your bed?
Was I the one who blushed? Did I stumble over a telling word?
    Did I do anything to give our secret away?
Okay, I did say that anyone who would mess around with a slave
    ought to have his head examined.   10
But Briseis was a slave and the Thessalian burned for her;
    the lord of Mycenae loved an enslaved priestess.
Am I a better man than Tantalus's son, am I greater than Achilles?
    Would I disdain what's good enough for kings?
But wasn't it when she turned her angry eyes in your direction   15
    that I saw you blush from ear to ear?
If you remember, I showed a bit more composure and swore
    by Venus's great godhead I'd been faithful.
(It's a little favor I ask, goddess: order tepid Notus to blow that piece
    of harmless perjury into the Carpathian ocean).   20
For that service, my dusky Cypassis, it's time to pay the fair price:
    let me sleep with you this afternoon.
Now don't be ungrateful. Stop shaking your head and acting afraid.
    It's quite enough to satisfy one of your masters.

If you don't stop this foolishness and say yes, I'll turn informer and tell   25
  everything. I'll betray myself, Cypassis,
and give your mistress an account of where we met, how many times,
  and how many different ways we did it!

II 10

It was you, Graecinus. No doubt about it. I remember you telling me
  no one can fall in love more than one girl at a time.
I believed you and it cost me. It's all your fault I was caught off guard.
  Look at me now—it's indecent—chasing two at once!
Each one is beautiful. Both unsparing in keeping up with high fashion;   5
  in accomplishments, it's hard to say who comes first.
One's the loveliest thing I've ever seen, the other is even lovelier;
  she pleases me most; no, the other pleases me more.
I'm at sea—like a skiff driven this way and that by warring winds—
  I adore one, I adore the other: I'm torn.   10
Erycina, why are you doubling the woes that plague me incessantly?
  Didn't one lover give me worry enough?
Why add more leaves to a tree, why put another star in the crowded sky,
  why pour pails of water into the deep sea?
Still, I have to agree, a surfeit of love is better than having none at all.   15
  Give the stern life of celibacy to my enemies!
To sleep like a log in the middle of an empty bed is something
  I'd wish only on someone I truly hate.
Stolid sleep is not for me. I want wild love to drive me mercilessly:
  never let me be caught alone in bed!   20
My darling can try her best to undo me—no one's going to stop her—
  if she can't keep up, I'll take two at a time.
I'm up to any challenge! I may be thin, but my limbs are wiry,
  and I make up for weight in sheer virility.
Pleasure's adrenaline will keep pumping energy into my thighs: 25
  no girl yet has gone away disappointed!
Many's the time I've spent the whole night in wild lovemaking
  and the next morning felt the fitter for it.
Blessed and happy the man who is a casualty in the lists of Venus.
  That, dear gods, is the way I want to go!   30
The soldier can have his battles, can take a chestful of enemy arrows,
  and pay out in blood the price of eternal fame.
The money-hungry merchant can wear out the sea lanes chasing wealth
  until his lying lips taste the brine of shipwreck.
For myself I ask only to fade slowly as I give my last performance in bed: 35
  I want to die mid-act in the play of love.

At my funeral let someone say as he wipes the tears away:
    "Your death was so well suited to your life!"

II 11

We did not know the sea's evils until a pine felled atop Pelion taught us.
    In sheer astonishment the waves watched
that first ship recklessly rush through the Clashing Rocks and onward
    to carry back a cargo of golden wool.
How much better had the Argo sunk and carried its secret to the bottom   5
    so no oar had ever again vexed wide ocean!
Now Corinna's determined to take a cruise on those treacherous waters
    and turns her back on her own bed and dear Penates.
I'm sick with fear just imagining what disasters Zephyrus or Eurus,
    icy Boreas or balmy Notus might bring you!   10
Mid ocean has nothing to offer the sightseer—no cities, no forests—
    only the vast sameness of endless blue water.
You'll be disappointed looking for shells and mottled pebbles out there.
    Stay at the shore and you'll find plenty.
Leave the prints of your marble-white feet along the sand. But stay on the
beach.   15
    It's blind folly, girls, to go any farther.
You can always hear others talk of hurricanes, of the waters Scylla
    terrorizes, of the whirlpool in Charybdis's maw.
Others can tell you how they saw the sea break against Ceraunian cliffs,
    or the bay where greater and lesser Syrtes lie hid.   20
Let others tell you all about such things, and believe what they say.
    You can't get hurt believing a storm report.
But it's too late once the cable's cast off, when you see the land receding
    as the curved keel speeds toward the open sea;
too late when the winds are howling and nervous sailors freeze with fear   25
    at the sight of death cresting the prow.
All the lovely color would drain from your face the moment you saw
    Triton striking the waves in a choppy sea.
Then you'd pray to Leda's two fine sons shining high in the heavens
    and sob, "Why did I ever leave dry land?"   30
It's much safer to stay at home: to curl up in bed with a good book
    or play your Thracian lyre whenever you wish.
But if you won't listen, and storm winds blow away my sound advice,
    I'll still ask Galatea to keep an eye on you.
If my darling should be lost at sea, the blame will be on your head,   35
    divine Nereids, and yours, father Nereus.

Go, Corinna, if you must; but remember me. I'll be here praying
  that a stronger wind will send you home.
When that time comes, mighty Nereus, tilt the sea toward our coast
  so her ship will fly downhill on the tide.   40
Then, Corinna, pray to Zephyrus to blow and fill the homebound sails,
  with your own hands trim the swelling sheets.
I'll be the first lookout on the shore to spy that ship I know so well,
  and shout: "She brings my gods back to me!"
I'll carry you off the ship on my shoulders; I'll cover you with kisses;   45
  the victim I vowed for you will fall at the altar.
We'll lie down together on a couch fashioned from piles of soft sand
  and a little dune will make do for a table.
There, when we've poured the wine, you'll tell me story after story—
  how your ship nearly sank in high seas,   50
how you fearlessly faced black night and the sudden squalls of Notus,
  as you rushed home to see me again.
I'll believe every tale you spin; I won't care if it's pure fiction.
  Why not enjoy believing what I want to hear?
Whip up your horses, brilliant Lucifer, fast as they can gallop   55
  across the sky, and bring that day to me!

II 13

For trying to unseat the burden crouched in her swelling womb,
  for her audacity, Corinna lies near death.
I should be furious: how could she take such a risk! And without telling me!
  But anger fails me—I'm so afraid.
You see, I'm the one who got her that way, or so I believe;   5
  I might as well be, since I could have been.
Isis! Great queen of Paraetonium, of Canopus's joyful plains,
  of Memphis, and of Pharos, rich in palm trees,
and of the broad delta where the swift Nile spreads, and pours
  his waters to the sea through seven mouths,   10
I pray, by your sacred rattles, by the venerated face of Anubis—
  may faithful Osiris always love your rites!
may the unhurried snake forever glide amid your offerings,
  and hornèd Apis travel at your side!—
come here, look kindly upon her, and save two lives in one: 15
  for you'll give life to her, and she to me.
She's been devout: performed every service on your festival days,
  observed the Gallic laurel ritual.
And you, who comfort laboring women in their time of distress, when
  the lurking burden strains their bodies hard,   20

come gently now, and smile upon my prayers, Ilithyia—
    she's worthy of your intervention—please!
I myself, in white robes, will bring incense to your smoking altar;
    I myself will offer votive gifts
and lay them at your feet with the inscription, "For Corinna's Life."   25
    Goddess, give occasion for those words!
Scarred and scared as we are from this battle, Corinna, I warn you:
    please don't ever go through this again!

II 14

What good does it do for girls to be exempt from combat, freed
    from all the dangers that our soldiers face,
if they will suffer self-inflicted wounds far from the front lines,
    and blindly brandish arms against their own
bodies? The woman who first took aim at her helpless fetus   5
    should have died by her own javelin.
Can it be possible that, simply to avoid a few stretch marks,
    you'd make your womb a bloody battleground?
What if our forebears had foreborne to bear? Without willing mothers
    the world would be unpopulated—again   10
someone would have to seed the empty earth with flung stones.
    Priam's palace wouldn't have been sacked
if sea-goddess Thetis had refused to shoulder (so to speak) her load;
    if Ilia, her belly swollen big,
had terminated her twins *in utero,* who would have founded   15
    the City that was bound to rule the world?
If Venus, in her audacity, had aborted fetal Aeneas
    the Caesars never would have graced our land.
Even you (though you were meant to be born a beauty) would have died
    if your mother had attempted what you've tried.   20
I myself (though personally I plan to die of love) would not
    have seen the light of day, had mother killed me.
Let the swelling grapes grow sweet and purple on the vine,
    leave the unripe apple on the tree.
All things will come to fruition in their season; let grow   25
    what has been planted; a life is worth the wait.
How can you pierce your own flesh with weapons, feed deadly toxins
    to babies still unborn? The world condemns
the woman of Colchis, spattered with the blood of her young sons,
    and mourns for Procne's victim, poor Itys.   30
Horrible mothers! But at least a kind of dreadful logic moved them
    to spill, from their sons' throats, their husbands' blood—

Tell me, in your case, where's the Tereus or Jason that could compel you
    to move your outraged hand against yourself?
The fierce Armenian tigress in her lair, the savage lioness   35
    show more consideration for their young.
What wild animals won't do, young ladies will—but often
    the girl who tries it kills herself as well.
She dies, and is carried out to the pyre, her hair all loose,
    and everyone who sees cries, "Serves her right!"   40
What am I saying? Let my words be carried off by the winds,
    let all ill omens vanish—let her live,
benevolent gods, let just this one sin go unpunished—but
    let her have it, if she tries again.

II 17

Anyone who considers servitude to a woman disgraceful
    would say that I'm the worst disgrace in town.
I don't care. I'll trade my reputation for the warmth
    of the flames fanned by Paphian Aphrodite
queen of wave-washed Cythera. I only wish my mistress,   5
    who is so beautiful, were also kind.
Beauty makes women stormy; Corinna's looks are gale-force
    and she knows it, much to my regret.
Her arrogance comes from looking in the mirror, which she never does
    before her hair and makeup are in place.   10
Corinna, your face (my downfall!) may justify your pride,
    your confidence of winning the upper hand,[1]
but please don't think that because of that you're too good for me—
    great and small can fit together well!
They say the nymph Calypso was smitten with a mere mortal   15
    and kept the man with her against his will.
A Nereid of the salt waves bedded down with Phthian Peleus;
    Egeria slept with Numa, the just king;
Venus belongs to Vulcan, in spite of his misshapen feet
    and clumsy limping as he leaves the forge.   20
Or look at the verse form I use: another unequal match!
    And yet the heroic unites with the lesser line.
And so should you, my love, take me, on whatever terms
    you like: you be the one to call the shots.[2]

---

[1] Reading *animum dat et omina regni*
[2] I prefer the reading *toro* (found in a few mss) to *foro*, but I've translated noncommittally.

I'll never make you ashamed of me; you won't be glad when I'm gone;   25
    we'll never have to pretend we never met.
I'm not rich, but (better yet) my verse is very successful;
    lots of women want to be in my poems.
There's even one who goes around telling people she is Corinna—
    what she wouldn't give to make it true!   30
But I would no more write about any other woman
    than Po would share its tree-lined riverbanks
with chilly Eurotas. My little books will always be about you;
    my inspiration comes from you alone.

II 18

While your magnum opus builds to the heights of wrathful Achilles
    and you fit the sworn confederates with arms,
you'll find me, Macer, cooling my heels in Venus's shadow
    with Cupid calmly squelching my pretensions
to grandiosity. I've tried telling Corinna to get lost;   5
    she comes right back and sits down in my lap.
I've told her, "I'm ashamed"; she bursts into tears, and moans,
    "are you ashamed of love? ashamed of me?"
Then she twines her arms around my neck and kisses me
    until it's hopeless: I lose all control,   10
I'm vanquished utterly; I no longer have the slightest concern
    for Arms and the Man; I want that woman's arms!
Not that I haven't tried other genres: my tragedy was a triumph;
    I seemed to have a certain knack for it.
Then Cupid laughed himself silly at the sight of me in boots, cloak,   15
    and scepter, which I'd picked up eagerly
but held improperly, against my nature. My almighty mistress
    and Cupid curbed me, triumphing as I
was led off in my buskins. Now I stick to my rightful sphere:
    I give instruction in the arts of Love   20
(which, I might add, frequently backfires on me), or I write
    the letter that Penelope wrote Ulysses;
the tearful words of Phyllis (you poor thing!); epistles sent
    to Paris, Macareus, and to Jason
(the ingrate!); to Hippolytus and his father; what Dido cried   25
    with sword in hand; and what Sappho sang.
With marvelous dispatch, my friend Sabinus returns from his travels
    bringing letters from around the world:
Here's one for fair Penelope, bearing the familiar seal of Ulysses;
    one from Hippolytus, for his stepmother;   30

pious Aeneas has finally answered poor Elissa's letter;
    here's one for Phyllis, if she's still alive;
Jason sends his regrets to Hypsipyle; the songstress of Lesbos
    can go ahead and dedicate that lyre
to Phoebus, her admirer. As for you, Macer, I've noticed that despite   35
    your military theme, you sing of Love
from time to time: the far-famed adultery of Paris and Helen;
    the faithfulness of Laodamia.
If I'm not mistaken, you even prefer the amorous parts—
    are you defecting from your camp to mine?   40

II 19

Where's your self-respect? If you won't keep an eye on your wife
    for your own sake, then do it for the sake
of increasing my passion. There's nothing more tiresome than fair game,
    or more exciting than the out-of-bounds.
The man who could love a licit woman has a heart made of iron.   5
    Hope thrives on fear, desire on repulse!
What's the point of happiness if it's stable? What's the point
    of love, without the risk of injury?
Corinna, in her wisdom, has seen this weakness in me, and understands
    how to keep me in captivity.   10
She's feigned a million headaches, and sent me dragging my heels home
    when she was feeling perfectly all right;
she's taken me to task a million times on trumped-up charges
    when we both knew that I was innocent.
Then, when she had thus aroused me, prodded my embers into flame,   15
    she once again submitted willingly.
What words of love she whispered! What sweet talk! And, great gods,
    what kisses! A profusion of delight!
And as for you, my dear, you who have caught my eye just recently:
    avoid entrapment; when you're asked, say "no";   20
make sure you lock me out and leave me shivering on your doorstep
    all night long, when there's a heavy frost.
That's the way to keep my love alive and kicking;
    that's the nourishment my spirit craves.
A cozy, plump, too-compliant love simply turns my stomach   25
    like too much cake; let love be lean and hungry!
If Danae had never been confined in a bronze tower, she never
    would have been impregnated by Jove.
And Io, transformed and horned, was all the more attractive to Jove
    when Juno kept her guarded day and night.   30

If a man desires what is his for the taking, let him pick leaves from the trees,
    gulp river water by the bucketful!
A woman who wants to stay in power must delude her lover...
    (wait! what am I saying? where does this leave me?)
I'll say it again, to hell with the consequences: submissiveness is boring;   35
    I flee when I'm pursued, pursue when fled.
But as for you, absentminded guardian of a gorgeous woman:
    take my advice, and lock her door at night.
Pay attention! Ask questions! What was that rustling sound at her window?
    What made the dogs begin to bark at midnight?   40
What are those letters her maid is always carrying back and forth?
    Why does she always ask to sleep alone?
If you took the time to think about it, you'd be sick with worry,
    and there would be some point to my deceit.
Stealing the wife of an imbecile like you is about as thrilling   45
    as stealing sand from a deserted beach.
I'm warning you now: if you don't start supervising your wife
    then I'll start losing interest very soon.
I've put up with so much for so long, persisting in the hope
    that you would open your eyes, so I could pull   50
the wool over them. But you're so docile, enduring the unendurable!
    Your apathy is killing my appetite.
Am I supposed to just walk right in, with no one blocking the way?
    Sleep all night, untroubled by the fear
of vengeance, never to wake in terror, gasping for breath?   55
    Why won't you make me wish that you were dead?
What good is a husband who's so easygoing he's practically her pimp?
    Our pleasure is ruined by this negligence.
Why don't you find yourself another rival, one who can tolerate tolerance;
    I won't stay unless I'm asked to leave.   60

III 1

In a stretch of ancient virgin forest—the kind of place
    where one can somehow sense a divine presence—
there stands a sacred fountain, and a cave overhung with rock;
    from every tree the birds sing, sweet and sad.
I was walking in this place, wrapped in the wood's shadows,   5
    wondering where my Muse would lead me next,
when Elegy appeared before me, her fragrant hair bound back,
    her right foot slightly longer than her left.
She was a beauty: her thin, translucent dress, her loving face,
    even her mismatched feet were ravishing.   10

Then Tragedy stormed in, ablaze with passion: hair hanging down
　　　across her savage brow, cloak on the ground.
In her left hand she brandished a royal scepter; on her foot
　　　the Lydian boot, in proper Tragic style.
She spoke first: "When wilt thou have done with this amatory foolishness,　15
　　　O poet most besotted by thy theme?
The tale of thy fecklessness is told over wine at every table
　　　and heard at every crossing of the ways.
Many an onlooker marks the passing poet, and says,
　　　'There walks a man whose heart is scorched by love.'　　　　　　20
All unawares, thou hast become the scandal of the town,
　　　the messenger of thy own shamelessness.
The solemn thyrsus's rhythm now befits thee more;
　　　'tis time now to commence a greater work.
Confine no more thy talent in small compass: sing heroic deeds.　　　25
　　　This new terrain shall well content thy heart.
Thy Muse but dabbles in delicate songs for the voices of girls;
　　　thy meter is the cadence of a child.
Roman Tragedy needs you now to make her great;
　　　Thy resonant breath shall stir my stately line."　　　　　　　30
She ended her speech; then, standing poised upon her ornate boots,
　　　shook back and forth her ponderous coiffure.
Elegy (as I recall) gave me a mischievous look, and smiled,
　　　in her right hand (I think) a myrtle branch.
"Spare me your weighty words, Tragedy," she said. "Do you always　35
　　　have to be so solemn, so intense,
and so depressing? Nevertheless, I see you've deigned
　　　to speak in elegiacs; you've challenged me
on my home turf! Not that I'd compare your verse to mine—
　　　a royal palace to a tiny shack.　　　　　　　　　　　　　40
I'm a lightweight, and so is my darling companion, Cupid;
　　　I'm no stronger than my theme, you see.
And yet Venus herself, without me, would be hopelessly provincial;
　　　I am her confidante and procuress.
Doors that you—with your high-toned high-laced boots—could never get
past　　　　　　　　　　　　　　　　　　　　　　　　　　　45
　　　will open up quite easily for me;
all it takes is a little smooth talk. You see, I've surpassed you
　　　by putting up with things *you* would consider
beneath your dignity. It was I, Elegy, who taught Corinna
　　　to give her guard the slip, to pick the lock,　　　　　　　50
to creep carefully out of bed, her robe untied around her,
　　　and tiptoe skillfully into the night.

I tell you, my lines have often been fastened[3] to an unresponsive door—
    I've hung out in the street for all to read!
And once I hid folded in a maid's brassiere, eluding watchful eyes,   55
    waiting to be delivered on the sly.
Or what about the time I was a birthday present, and that bitch
    tore me up and threw me in the sink?
I came first with you, Ovid. I planted the seeds in your mind.
    I gave you the gift that Tragedy wants to take!"   60
She had finished. I began: "Listen, I beg you, both of you, please—
    you've scared me half to death—now hear my words!
Thou, Tragedy, hast adorned me with scepter and lofty buskin—
    listen to me! I already sound like you!
Elegy, you give my love a name that will live forever. Very well: 65
    let the long and short lines alternate!
Tragedy, grant your poet a short reprieve. You want eternity;
    all she wants is a little of my time."
She was moved; she let me go. Now onward, gentle Amores!
    A greater work is pressing close behind.   70

III 2

"Horses, thoroughbred or otherwise, do not interest me in the least;
    but I do want your horse to win, of course.
I'm sitting here so I can sit by you, and talk with you,
    in case you haven't realized how much
you've made me love you. I've got an idea: you keep your eye   5
    on the track, and I'll keep mine on you. That way
we both can feast our eyes. You know, the driver you favor
    has all the luck—what I wouldn't give
to hold your attention like that! If you were watching me
    I'd fly with my steeds from the starting gate   10
like a man possessed, plying the reins, flailing with the whip,
    grazing the turning-post with my inside wheel—
I'd have to be careful not to look at you; if I did
    I'd slow down, drop the reins … at Pisa, once,
Pelops nearly took a spear in the back while gazing   15
    at Hippodameia's face. He won the race
because she favored him, needless to say. So may we all
    win our races, with our ladies' favors!
It's no use trying to scoot away; the seats are too close together.
    Why do you think I brought you here? Excuse me—   20

---

[3]reading *infixa* in line 53.

you on the right, quit pressing your side into her elbow.
    And you behind us—please! pull in your legs;
get your bony knee out of her back! Oh dear, your skirt
    must be too long; it's dragging on the ground.
That's right, raise it a little . . . here, allow me. Much better.   25
    O jealous dress! What a fine pair of legs
you hid! And the more you look at them . . . O jealous dress!
    Such were the shapely calves Milanion
was hot to get his hands around, swift Atalanta's legs;
    such are the thighs in paintings of Diana,   30
her skirt hitched up, pursuing mighty beasts, and she
    a mightier goddess herself. I was on fire
before I saw your legs; what now, with an eyeful of the real thing?
    You're adding flames to flames, streams to the sea.
To judge from those legs, I imagine the rest must be fantastic—   35
    the delights you're hiding under your flimsy dress.
Listen, I think I ought to stir up a little breeze here;
    shall I fan you, darling, with my racing form?
Are you hot, or is it just me? Maybe it's not the weather,
    but just my captive heart, sweltering with love.   40
Oh look, while I was talking, some dust blew on your nice white outfit;
    here, let me get that—off with you, filthy speck!
Stay off her snow-white body! Ah, here comes the procession.
    Now is the time for silence—everyone, hush!
And now is the time for applause; the golden procession arrives.   45
    Victory leads the way, her wings outspread.
Goddess, approach, and grant that my love may win first place.
    Now here comes Neptune; you who trust in the sea,
foolhardy, reckless sailors, clap your hands! As for me,
    you won't catch me in a ship. I'll stick to land.   50
Soldiers, applaud for Mars, your god. I hate war, personally;
    give me peace, for peace engenders love.
Phoebus, smile on the augurs, and Phoebe on the hunters;
    receive the craftsmen's outstretched hands, Minerva.
Country people, rise to your feet for Ceres and youthful Bacchus;   55
    let the boxer turn to Pollux, the knight to Castor.
I've saved my applause for you, kindly Venus, and your Cupids;
    dear goddess, give me a sign—nod your head
and grant that my new mistress will allow herself to be loved.
    She nodded! She gave a sign! Now all I need,   60
sweetheart, is for you to promise too. No offense to Venus,
    but you're the one that I will worship more.
I swear to you—as this whole parade of gods is my witness!—
    you'll always be the mistress of my heart.

Oh dear, your legs are dangling. See if this will help—   65
    rest your toes up on this railing here.
They've cleared the track for the big race. The praetor gives a sign,
    the four-horse chariots hurtle through the gates!
Look, there's your guy. Whoever you back is an easy bet to win;
    the horses themselves can read your mind, it seems.   70
Oh no, he took the turn too wide. What are you doing?
    You let the guy behind you get the edge!
What are you doing, idiot? You're making a fool of my girl—
    listen to me! Pull hard on your left rein!
We've backed a loser. Romans, we must demand they start again.   75
    Everyone, wave your togas—give the sign!
Yes, they're calling them back! But all this toga-waving
    could ruin your hairdo—take shelter under my cloak.
The gates are up again, the teams are off: a flying blur
    of hooves and racing colors. Listen, you,   80
this time, try to win! The field is open—surge ahead!
    Answer my lady's prayers, and my prayers too.
Ah, he won. He has his prize. That makes one down
    and one to go, for I must still seek mine."
She laughed, and a promise seemed to flash in her glancing eyes.   85
    That's enough for here; the rest comes later.

III 4

You're strict, but your severity is pointless—a woman must be watched
    by her own conscience, or else not at all.
To test her fidelity, call off your guards; chastity under compulsion
    might as well be called adultery.
You can keep her body under surveillance, but what about her mind?   5
    no woman can be true against her will.
For that matter, even her body's beyond the reach of your vigilance:
    lock every door; you've locked an adulterer in.
The seeds of transgression grow poorly in the barren soil of liberty;
    a woman who's free to sin will seldom bother.   10
Believe me, your prohibitions are only making things worse;
    the only way to win is to give in.
I saw a horse the other day raging against the bridle and bit,
    storming and frenzied, running away, until
he realized the reins had been dropped, and were lying slack   15
    across the tangled mane along his neck.
We always strive for the forbidden, long for the out-of-bounds
    like sick men, yearning to disobey just once

our doctor's orders. Argus the watcher had two hundred eyes
    but he was tricked by Love, time and again;   20
Danae was shut in a prison of stone and iron, yet she
    went in a virgin and came out a mother;
Penelope, with no one to protect her from the suitors, remained
    inviolate, surrounded by young men.
Whatever is guarded is desirable; surveillance courts invasion;   25
    few men can love what they're allowed to take.
Your wife is irresistible, not for her looks, but because you love her:
    she must use good bait, if she caught you.
Security measures just make a woman seem all the more valuable—
    the sense of danger is really the whole point.   30
Get as mad as you want: the truth is, there's no woman so exciting
    as one who whispers, "what if we get caught?"
Besides, your wife is a freeborn woman; you can't just lock her up
    as if she were some slave or foreigner.
And what's the big deal, if she stays chaste under lock and key?   35
    All that means is you hired a competent guard.
Here in Rome, getting upset at your wife's infidelity is considered
    provincial, unsophisticated, quaint.
After all, our founding fathers were begotten by Mars out of wedlock:
    Ilia's son Remus, and Romulus, Ilia's son.   40
Why did you choose a beautiful wife, if you wanted a faithful one?
    You'll never find a woman who is both.
If you have any sense, you'll take advantage of this situation:
    don't be such a stickler—loosen up!
Give your wife some latitude, and watch your house fill up   45
    with interesting young men (no need to take
the trouble of making friends yourself!) and expensive gifts
    for which you didn't have to pay a cent.

III 5

"It was night, and my weary eyes were steeped in slumber;
    a vision came which terrified my mind.
Beneath a sunny hill was a dense stand of oak trees;
    the branches sheltered scores of silent birds.
Further below, a grassy meadow, brilliant green,   5
    watered in drops by inching rivulets.
I was there. Under a tree I tried to escape the heat—
    still it was hot, under a leafy tree.
Seeking meadow grass amid the mosaic of flowers
    a pure white cow appeared before my eyes.   10

Whiter than snow new-fallen, before time has turned
      the drifting powder to a running stream;
whiter than ewe's milk in the milking-pail, so fresh
      you still can see the foam, and hear the splash.
With this cow was a bull, her contented mate. The pair   15
      rested their bodies on the springy ground.
And as this bull lay on the grass, so calmly and quietly
      chewing his regurgitated cud,
sleep seemed to steal away his strength; his neck relaxed,
      his massive head sank down into a drowse.   20
A crow appeared, angling down through the breezes on light wings
      to settle, chattering, on the grassy ground.
Three times the crow thrust its rough beak in the cow's white breast
      and pulled from it a tuft of snowy hair.
She who had stayed so long left the place and her mate,   25
      a dark blood-bruise disfiguring her breast.
And when she saw, far off, bulls grazing the greensward
      (bulls were grazing on tasty grass, far off)
she went towards them, to join them and mingle with their herd;
      she sought out a more fertile pasturage.   30
Interpreter of night-imaginings, whoever you are, tell me:
      is there truth or meaning in this dream?"
These were my words and my question. The dream interpreter
      weighed each point within his mind, and spoke:
"The heat which you sought to escape beneath the tree's shifting leaves   35
      but could not truly escape, that was the heat
of love. The cow is your girl—the color is right for her.
      You were the bull, companion to the cow.
The crow which pecked at her breast with its pointed beak was a bawd:
      an aged hag will sway your lady's mind.   40
Since the cow, who had stayed so long, abandoned the bull in the end,
      you will be left alone, cold in an empty bed.
The bruise on the front of the cow's breast, the blood-dark smirch
      is the stain, in your girl's heart, of adultery."
The interpreter had spoken. The blood drained from my face, my skin   45
      went cold, and deepest darkness filled my eyes.

III 7

What's the matter? Isn't she beautiful? Isn't she, in fact,
      the elegant object of my every prayer?
And yet when I held her I was limp as yesterday's lettuce,
      a useless burden on an idle bed.

Although I wanted to do it, and she was more than willing,   5
    I couldn't get my pleasure-part to work.
She tried everything and then some. She twined her ivory arms
    (whiter than Thracian snows) around my neck;
she wiggled her eager tongue between my lips, and slipped
    her stimulating thigh beneath my thigh;   10
she whispered pretty words, called me her "sweet daddy,"
    and murmured all the usual naughty things.
It was as if my body had been stung numb by hemlock
    and would no longer carry out my plans.
A sorry sight! I lay there like a rotten log, a dead weight—   15
    I even thought that I might be a ghost.
What will my old age be like (if I live that long)
    if this is how my so-called youth turns out?
I'm a disgrace to my generation. What's the point of being a young man?
    As far as she knew, I was neither young   20
nor a man. She left me, pure as any Vestal virgin,
    polite as any sister to her brother.
(But not long ago, with blonde Chlide, I did it twice—
    three times with fair-skinned Pitho, three with Libas—
and I recall Corinna asked, and I performed   25
    nine times—yes, nine!—within a single night.)
Has my poor shrivelled prick fallen victim to Thessalian poison,
    incantations, herbs? Or has some witch
inscribed my name in a red wax tablet, driven a pin
    into the liver of an Ovid doll?   30
Magic spells can blast the crops, turning grain to dust;
    spells can dry up rivers at the source;
Spells cause the acorns to fall from oaks, grapes from the vine;
    apples drop from trees on windless days.
I wouldn't be at all surprised to learn that witchcraft lay behind   35
    my present torpor—yes, that must be it.
That, and shame, of course. The shame really made it worse.
    Shame was the secondary influence.
God, what a girl I saw, and touched—I wrapped myself
    skin-tight around her body, smooth as silk.   40
One touch of her, and old Nestor would feel like a teenager;
    the years would melt away from Tithonus.
Yes, I had her, but she couldn't have me; I was no man.
    Why should I ever bother to pray again?
No doubt the mighty gods regret their generosity to me,   45
    seeing how I've squandered all their gifts.
I prayed to be received: she let me in. I wanted
    kisses: granted. Caresses: there she was.

What good did my fortune do me? What use is a kingdom in exile?
    I was like a miser hoarding gold   50
or like indiscreet Tantalus, who now thirsts in midstream,
    reaching for the fruit he'll never touch.
What kind of man can leave a lovely girl in the morning
    and still be fit to approach the holy gods?
Well, you may say, maybe she wasn't so great. Maybe   55
    she wasn't the best kisser in the world,
or didn't try very hard. Didn't try! She could have moved
    solid oak, hard adamant, dull stone
with those kisses. Any man alive would have responded,
    but I was neither living nor a man.   60
Why should Phemius bother to sing to deaf ears?
    What good is a painted picture to Thamyras?
And yet, what joys had I not planned in the silence of my mind—
    each move premeditated, every pleasure
in its place, and a place for every pleasure! But I was dead: 65
    wilted, windblown as a faded rose.
Look at me now: I'm stiff and swelling. What wonderful timing!
    Now he's ready for action, ready to fight.
Down, boy! Have some shame. You're the worst part of my body.
    I've seen how you fulfill your promises.   70
You betray your master—there I was, all because of you,
    impotent, humiliated, shamed.
Even so, my girl was not too proud to take it
    softly in her conscientious hand;
but when it refused to rise, when she saw it just lie there   75
    oblivious of her and all she did,
"Is this some kind of joke?" she said; "are you crazy? who asked you
    to come into my bed against your will?
Either some potion-packing Circe has you under a spell,
    or you're worn out from loving someone else."   80
Without a pause she jumped up, her robe untied around her
    (she looked so perfect there, in her bare feet);
to hide the disgrace, and save face with her maids, she took some water,
    and made a little wet spot on the bed.

III 9

If majestic Dawn wept for Memnon, if Thetis grieved Achilles' death,
    if ever goddess mourned her mortal son,
now, Elegy, wet your face with tears, and loose your guiltless braids;
    now will you live up to your sad name.

Your greatest pride, your poet and protégé, Tibullus—his life   5
  extinguished—is now burning on the pyre.
Venus's boy approaches, his quiver slung at half-mast, his bow
  snapped in two, his torch unlit and cold . . .
Just look at him! His wings droop forlorn at his sides, his frenzied hand
  batters his delicate, uncovered chest.   10
His tears stream down into his straggling strands of hair;
  he shakes with sobs, reverberates with wails.
They say he was just like this at his brother Aeneas's funeral,
  emerging, lovely Iulus, from your halls.
Venus dissolves in tears at Tibullus's death, no less than when   15
  the wild boar incised Adonis's thigh.
Poets, you see, are sacred, and dear to the gods; and there are those
  who think that we may even be divine.
And yet impatient Death stains every sacred thing;
  her hands like shadows slide around each throat.   20
Thracian Orpheus wasn't saved by his parents, nor by his gift
  for mesmerizing wild beasts with song;
Linus, another of Apollo's sons, is mourned in the deep woods—
  his father sings out *"aelinon"* and strums
his reluctant lyre. Even Homer, everlasting source   25
  at which all poets wet their thirsty lips,
was in the end immersed in the black water of Avernus.
  Only song escapes the hungry pyre.
The poet's work endures: the fame of the Trojan enterprise;
  the promised shroud, unraveled late at night;   30
the name of Nemesis shall long be known, and that of Delia,
  the one his last, the other his first love.
My dears, what good were your devoted rites? What was the use
  of your seclusion, your Egyptian rattles?
When malignant death overtakes a good man, I am tempted   35
  (forgive me!) to believe there are no gods.
Live a pious life and you will be a pious corpse.
  Go to temple every day: you'll be there
on time for your funeral. Put your faith in poetry, and one day
  you too can be just like Tibullus here,   40
an urnful of ashes. Divine poet! Did the pyre's flames
  not hesitate to feed upon your heart?
Those flames could burn the golden temples of the sacred gods
  if they were capable of such an outrage.
Venus of Eryx turned her face away; and there are some   45
  who say that she could not hold back her tears.
Still, it's better this way than if you had died in Corfu,
  a stranger buried in dirt, anonymous.

Here, at least, your mother could close your damp, dying eyes
     and give your ashes all the proper rites.   50
Here, your sister came to share your poor mother's grief,
     tearing out handfuls of her uncombed hair.
And with your loved ones came Nemesis and her predecessor
     to offer final kisses, final words.
Delia cried, as she parted, "you were happier, Tibullus, with me;   55
     at least when you were mine you didn't die."
Nemesis shot back, "who are you, to lay a claim to my grief?
     I was the one his dying arms embraced."
If any part of us survives, beyond our name and our shade,
     Tibullus's home will be Elysium.   60
And you will go to meet him, ivy crowning your unwrinkled brow,
     learned Catullus, hand in hand with Calvus;
and you (if those charges against you are false), Gallus, who spent
     your life and blood too open-handedly.
In such company, refined Tibullus—if the body has a shade—   65
     your shade augments the number of the blessed.
May your bones rest contented, I pray, in their sheltering urn,
     and may the earth lie easy on your ashes.

III 12

When exactly did you pestilential ink-black birds
     chant your curse on me, perpetually
in love as I am? Or should I blame some unlucky star
     or open warfare from some hostile god?
The girl whom I called my own, and mine alone, is now   5
     mine, and everybody else's, too.
And my own books are to blame, if I'm not mistaken. My genius
     has made a prostitute of my true love.
I deserve it; I ballyhooed her charms like a sideshow barker.
     If she's on sale, I'm the retailer.   10
I'm the pimp who leads the customer in to her,
     smiling and bowing while I hold the door.
What good is poetry? There's no question of the harm it does;
     it interferes with everything I want.
Just think: I could have written on Troy, Thebes, the glory of Caesar . . .   15
     only Corinna stirred my creative urge.
If only the Muses had refused to cooperate with my earliest efforts,
     if only Phoebus had turned his face away!
And it's not as if people ever have faith in what poets tell them—
     why was *I* the one to be believed?   20

The stories we poets unleash! Scylla's furtive barbering—
    and lovely loins encircled with snapping hounds!
We're the ones who attached wings to heels, snakes to women's hair;
    we mounted Perseus on Pegasus.
We did the stretching job on enormous Tityus, and gave   25
    the snaky hound of hell his triple heads.
We made Enceladus, hurling the spear with a thousand arms,
    and men destroyed by the treacherous maiden's voice.
We confined the great East Wind in the Ithacan's sack of skins,
    and traitor Tantalus thirsting in midstream.   30
We turned Niobe to stone, and poor Callisto into a bear;
    the nightingale sings for Thracian Itys;
Jupiter transforms himself into a bird, or a shower of gold,
    or swimming bull, crossing the Aegean
with a girl on his back! Not to mention Proteus, or the dragon's teeth   35
    sown in Thebes, or fire-breathing bulls,
sisters who weep tears of amber, ocean-going ships transformed
    into goddesses who swim the waves;
the sun recoiling from Atreus's bloodstained table; the lyre
    whose plucked notes charmed the stones of Thebes.   40
The poet's vast and teeming imagination brings forth
    line after line, with no regard for truth.
My praise of Corinna should have gone with a grain of salt;
    now I'm destroyed by your credulity.

III 13

Since my wife happens to be from apple-growing Falerii, we went
    to see the town that once Camillus took.
The priestesses made ready Juno's festival: the ceremony,
    the popular games, the sacrificial cow.
It's certainly worth the effort to go and see these rites,   5
    although the road is difficult and steep.
You'll find an ancient grove, tangled branches casting a deep shade.
    Look around: you'll sense a divine presence.
An altar receives the prayers and votive incense of the pious—
    an old-style altar, plain and unadorned.   10
To this place the solemn flute-song leads the annual procession,
    traveling along decorated paths.
As the crowd cheers, snow-white heifers are led out
    (fattened on good Falerian pasturage),
and calves, butting the air with their not-yet-sprouted horns,   15
    pigs (the less exalted offering),

and the bellwether, horns curving around his hard head.
       The she-goat is anathema to Juno:
they say she revealed the goddess's hiding place in the woods
       where she had run, and foiled her planned escape.   20
Now the blabbing goat is harried by boys with javelins;
       first one to hit her takes her as a prize.
Young men and shy young women lead the way for the goddess;
       their heavy trailing robes smooth down the paths.
Each maiden's hair is piled with heavy gold and gemstones;   25
       rich mantles touch their gold-embellished feet.
Wrapped in white robes, in the manner of their Greek ancestors,
       they bear the sacred objects on their heads.
The goddess herself comes near! The crowd falls silent, watching
       as she is led on by her priestesses.   30
This golden procession is Argive in form; Agamemnon's murder
       drove Halaesus out from his rich homeland
to wander in exile over land and sea, until he came
       to found this place with providential hand.
He taught the rites of Juno to his people here in Falerii—   35
       for all time may these rites avail us!

III 14

You're gorgeous; I wouldn't dream of expecting you to be faithful,
       but when you're not, do you have to let me know?
I'm no censor: do the full, unexpurgated version!
       But please, dear, *try* to exercise some deceit.
It's only crime confessed that makes a harlot a harlot;   5
       a woman who can say she hasn't sinned
hasn't! What madness, to uncover what lies hidden in the night,
       and drag it into daylight for all to see.
A whore, before she couples with your average anonymous Roman,
       always remembers to close and bolt the door.   10
You're the star of your own gossip, a lurid full-color spread
       posed shamelessly in your own scandal sheet.
If you can't manage a change of heart, at least pretend
       you're virtuous, and I'll be taken in.
Do what you do, but do deny you did it. Don't   15
       be ashamed to appear respectable in public.
Let's say you've found a perfect spot for today's debauch;
       let the games begin! Let modesty
take the day off. But when you're finished, let your lechery
       dissolve into the air, and leave your sins   20

behind you on the bed. Don't hesitate to strip
        while you're there; snuggle thigh-to-thigh
while you're there, and let him slide his tongue between
        your painted lips; let every form of lust
while you're there, be acted out in every variation;   25
        let your words of love be whispered low,
let the bed shake wildly from your wanton flailing—but
        when you get dressed, put on, along with your clothes,
a look of pure innocence, quick to blush. Your modesty
        must make your actions seem impossible.   30
Fool everyone! Fool me! Let me be wrong about you, ignorant
        and happy. Let me enjoy my gullibility.
Why do I have to witness the daily flurry of love letters
        sent and received? Why is your bed indented
not just here, but there? Your hair didn't get that way   35
        from sleeping on it wrong. And who's been chewing
there, on your neck? At least you don't do it right in front of my eyes—
        not yet, that is. If you don't care at all
about sparing your reputation, at least spare me. I go insane,
        I feel like I'm dying every time   40
you spill out another True Confession; my knees turn to ice water.
        At times like that I love and hate in vain:
I hate to have to love you. I wish I were in my grave,
        but with you beside me, of course.
Listen: I'll never ask a single question, never pry;   45
        I'll play my part and duly be deceived.
Even if I can see for myself that you're a slut,
        even if I catch you in the act,
just deny to my face that I saw what I saw face to face:
        I'll believe your words more than my eyes.   50
Nothing could be easier than to beat a man
        who wants to lose; the key to victory
is four little words: "I didn't do it." Remember them! You'll find
        you'll always win your case; your judge is blind.

III 15

Mother of gentle *Amores*, find yourself another poet:
        my elegies have run their final race.
And I, the man who composed these (not unsuccessful) delights—
        from the country, yes, but hardly rustic—
claim descent (if you care about such things) from an ancient line: 5
        my status antedates these troubled times.

Vergil is Mantua's glory, Verona boasts of Catullus, and I
    shall be the pride of the Paelignians,
a race who took up honorable arms in the name of freedom
    when Italy beleaguered anxious Rome.   10
One day a traveler, looking at the fields and city walls
    of tiny, stream-crossed Sulmo, will exclaim,
"You who could produce a poet of such surpassing excellence,
    however small you are, I call you great."
Elegant Cupid, and Cyprian mother of elegant Cupid, please,   15
    remove your golden pennants from my field!
Horned Dionysus moves me now with his solemn thyrsus;
    my horses' hooves must strike on new terrain.
Farewell, tender elegies, and you, my joyous Muse—my work
    and fame will long outlast my little life.   20

Horace

Most of what we know about Horace comes from his poetry, and he tells us more than any other ancient poet. Horace was born in Venusia, a town in Apulia, on December 8, 65 B.C.E., a little more than a year before Cicero's famous consulship. He was five years younger than Vergil and two years older than Augustus. His father was a freedman who saved enough money to take his son to Rome for school where he would get the best possible education, the kind "any knight or senator would have his children given" (as Horace describes it). He completed his education in Athens where Brutus, the assassin of Caesar, came to talk of liberty and persuade young men like Horace to join his fight. Horace became a military tribune in Brutus's army and fought at the battle of Philippi (42 B.C.E.), from which he escaped and returned to Rome. In Rome he found that his father's property had been confiscated. He was apparently pardoned for his participation in the civil war and purchased a position as the keeper of the *quaestor's* records.

Soon his early poetry attracted the attention of the poet Vergil, who was a member of Maecenas's literary group. Horace was introduced to Maecenas, and he describes the scene in a satire addressed to his patron: "When I came before you, I spoke haltingly a few words, for a childlike modesty kept me from saying more; I did not say I was born of a famous father, nor that I was carried around my farm on a Saturian horse, but I told you what I was. You responded, as is your custom, a few words. I departed, and you called me back after nine months and bade me join the number of your friends." From this time until his death a few weeks after the death of Maecenas the two were close friends. He was given employment and his Sabine farm by his patron. Through Maecenas, Horace came to know Augustus, with whom he appears to have had a friendly relationship, and was eventually asked by the emperor to be his personal secretary. Horace refused. Later he agreed to write, as a kind of poet laureate, a hymn for Augustus's renewal of the Secular Games in 17 B.C.E. He died on November 27, 8 B.C.E.

Horace lived through momentous events in the political life of Rome. From Cicero's consulship, when he was one year old, to Caesar's crossing of the Rubicon when he was sixteen years old, the late Republic was an unstable entity, governed by violence, the threat of violence, and secret alliances between powerful men. After 49 B.C.E. things got worse. Horace was twenty-one when Caesar was murdered, twenty-three when he joined

Brutus's army, and about twenty-five when he retired to Rome to work in the *quaestor's* office and begin his poetic career. Thereafter he saw the alliance of Octavian and Antony fall apart; he watched as Octavian waged his war of words and armies against Antony and Cleopatra. His patron became the second most powerful man in Rome, entrusted with managing the city when Octavian was away. Octavian became Augustus and twice restored the Republic; but in the end Rome had a principate and a hereditary monarchy. Maecenas, some believe, fell from grace, or became less useful to Augustus. Horace retired more and more frequently to his Sabine farm, his books, and his friends.

Horace is perhaps the most difficult of the Roman poets to describe. His poetic output was diverse and impressive. By the time he was thirty, he had written a collection of poems mainly in the tradition of Greek invective, the *Epodes*, and his first book of *Satires*. By the time he was thirty-five he completed his second book of *Satires*, and moved on to the *Odes*, an extraordinary effort to recreate the power and presence of archaic Greek lyric traditions in a modern and troubled Rome. These poems were published together as three books in 23 B.C.E. For the next seven years, he returned to those questions of philosophy and friendship which had occupied him in the *Satires*, but he gave them a more intimate and reflective voice in his first book of verse *Epistles*. His second book of *Epistles* was written between 19 and 15 B.C.E., a period which also saw the publication and production of his *Secular Hymn*, and the beginning of work on his last book of *Odes*, Book IV, which was published in 13 B.C.E.

Horace

I 1

Maecenas, descendant of ancestral kings,
my patron and the glory of my life:

There are those who delight in collecting
Olympic dust on the course: their burning wheels
just graze the posts, and the noble palm branch   5
lifts them up, lords of the earth, to the gods.

One man is pleased if the milling Roman crowds
elevate him to the three high magistracies;
another, if he can store in his granaries
everything swept from Libyan threshing floors.   10

Never will you persuade the man whose joy
is to cleave the ground with a hoe—no,
not with Attalus's riches—to cut the sea
as a frightened sailor with a Cyprian beam.

Winds wrestling with the Icarian waves   15
the merchant fears; he will praise a while
the local countryside, but soon repairs
his battered hulls, incapable of poverty.

There's him to whom a cup of Massic wine
or noonday nap is no disgrace: 20
limbs stretched now beneath a wild arbute,
now near the head of some quiet spring.

Entrenched arms thrill some, the clarion's blast
mixed with the horn's, and war despised
by mothers. A hunter stays beneath   25
the freezing sky, tender wife forgotten,

whether it's a deer in the hound's eye
or a Marsian boar has ripped the nets.
The ivies though, grace of a poet's brow,
mix me with the gods, and the cool grove,   30

the light chorus of the fauns and nymphs
unmill me from the masses—if Euterpe
does not stop her flutes, if Polyhymnia
will not refuse to tune her Lesboan lyre.

But if you rank me among the lyric bards,   35
I will strike the stars with my exalted head.

I 3

    May the powerful Goddess of Cyprus
guide you, may the starlit brothers of Helen
    and the lord of the winds lead you,
and may only the breeze from Apulia blow you

    over the water with Vergil aboard,   5
and bear him back safely—this is my prayer to you,
    O ship entrusted with half my soul:
render intact your debt to Attica's shores.

    Solid oak triply rimmed with bronze
was the heart of the first man ever to commit   10
    a fragile boat to the open sea,
ignoring the gales that swoop up from Africa

    and squall with Northers, braving
the gloomy Hyades and the rabid Southwester
    that controls the Adriatic   15
like no other wind, leaving it whitecapped or calm.

    Can Death's footfall terrify the man
able to look dry-eyed on monsters from the deep,
    on the swollen sea heaving,
and on Acroceraunia's notorious crags?   20

    God's work was wasted when He
prudently divided earth's lands from each other
    with sundering Ocean
if impious boats dash across forbidden seas.

    Daring everything, the human race   25
crashes to ruin by violating taboos.

Daring treason, Prometheus
smuggled fire down to the races on earth.

After fire was suborned from heaven,
starvation and cadres of feverish diseases   30
        settled on earth, and Death,
formerly a remote and slow necessity,

        now picked up his pace. Daedalus
explored the vacant atmosphere on wings
        not meant for humans, and Hercules   35
in his labors shattered Acheron's boundary.

        Nothing's too steep for mortals.
In our folly we reach for heaven itself, and
        our own sin prevents Jupiter
from putting aside his wrathful thunderbolts.   40

I 4

Winter's icy grip relaxes: spring returns with mild west winds,
        and winches haul the dry keels down to shore.
Cattle chafe in their stables now, and plowmen by their fire,
        and the meadows glisten no more with frost.

Venus leads the dances now beneath the pendant moon,   5
        and Nymphs in step with lovely Graces beat
their rhythms on the earth, while smoldering Vulcan
        fires up his massive Cyclopean forge.

Your elegant brow should now be bound with myrtle's green
        or with a flower that stems from loosened earth.   10
Now is the time, in a shadowy grove, to offer Faunus
        the lamb he wants, or sacrificial kid.

Pallid Death with foot impartial beats at paupers' hovels
        and towers of kings. My heaven-blest Sestius,
life's brief sum denies us any long-reaching hopes.   15
        Night shall soon oppress you, the storied shades,

and Pluto's stifling realm. Once there, you will no longer
        roll dice at drinking bouts, nor look with wonder

at tender Lycidas, for whom the young men now
    are all on fire, and soon the girls will glow.   20

I 5

What slender boy has you bedded on roses
and, oiled and scented, urges you on
    in some pleasant cave, Pyrrha?
        For whom do you tie back your blonde hair,

voguishly simple? Oh, how many times will he   5
weep over 'fidelity' and 'fickle gods' and gape
    in innocence at seas suddenly
        rough with black winds.

Now he takes pleasure in your fool's gold, thinking
you will be always available, always lovable,   10
    and has no idea how the gales
        shift around. The poor wrecks

for whom you shine untried! As for me, a votive
plaque on the temple wall shows I have hung up
    my dripping wet clothes   15
        to the powerful god of the sea.

I 7

Some people praise Rhodes, Mytilene or Ephesus,
    or Corinth, with bi-coastal beaches,
or Thebes, famous for Bacchus, or Delphi,
    for Apollo, or the Valley of Tempe.

Whole careers have been devoted to epics on Athens   5
    with its virginal goddess and olive wreaths,
on horse-rich Argos in Juno's honor, or golden Mycenae.
    I am personally not so impressed with hardy Sparta

or the plains of fertile Larissa as I am with
    certain locales in the country near Rome.   10
I mean the orchards in the river country of Anio,
    and the Italian goddess at Tivoli, where

the woods cascade down the hills. Rain much of the year,
    but the south wind blows the sky clear at times
and the clouds are washed down the cataracts, a gentle reminder   15
    speaking to you, Plancus: times of distress

may be softened with wine, whether in your Tivoli's dense
    and lovely shade or with the silver Eagles
in the camps of the world.
                The hero Teucer, beaten
    from Troy to Salamis, from Salamis   20

to Cyprus, burdened with the cares of exile
    and a father's curse, unwound before sailing,
wine and poplar leaves weaving their spell,
    and spoke to his downcast companions:

"My friends, we are going to a land where Fate   25
    will be kinder than my father was.
Never lose hope while Teucer still leads you.
    Remember, Apollo promised us

a second Salamis in a strange new land. You are brave,
    and you are men. You have suffered worse than this   30
before with me. Drink now and forget your troubles.
    Tomorrow we cross another boundless sea."

I 9

See how the snow drifts deep and white
on Soracte's slopes, and its weight
    strains the woods, and glacial
        streams snap in the cold.

Thaw winter out, piling logs high   5
on the fire, and spirit up from the cellar
    a magnum, Thaliarchus,
        of Sabine beaujolais,

and leave the rest to the gods. When they
lay brawling winds to rest on the water,   10
    cypresses shudder no more,
        nor ancient ash trees.

Forget about tomorrow, count as profit
however many days Fortune alots,
    never scorn sweet loves and dances   15
        while you're still a boy

blooming green, before grey hair
shadows your life. On the parade grounds
    couples meet in the evening now,
        whisper in the plazas,   20

a girl's welcome laughter betrays her
hiding in a corner, a bracelet snatched
    from an arm, or a ring
        from a poorly resisting finger.

I 11

You shouldn't try to find out—it's wrong to know—what end the gods
have in store for me or for you, Leuconoë, and you shouldn't tinker
with Babylonian astrology. Better just to bear what will be,
whether Jupiter has assigned us many more winters or this is the last
that wears out the Tyrrhenian Sea on the eroding cliffs.   5
Wise up, strain the wine, and since life is short, cut back
on long hopes. While we are speaking, envious Time slips
away. Seize the day, with minimum trust in tomorrow.

I 22

The life unblemished and pure of sin
needs no Mauritanian javelins
nor quiver full of poison arrows,
Fuscus, my friend,

not even if a man's bound for the Syrtes'   5
steaming shoals, or through the inhospitable
Caucasus range, or the lands licked by
the fabulous Jelum:

I was wandering off my property
in the Sabine woods, not a care in the world,   10
singing about my Lalage, when a wolf
fled from unarmed me,

such a monster as the wide thornbrakes
in martial Apulia never bred,
or the Land of Juba, that dry nurse of lions,   15
ever engendered.

Oh put me down in the Arctic tundra, where
never a tree is freshened by summer's breeze,
in the zone where mists hang low beneath
a dismal sky,   20

Oh put me down where the sun's chariot
swings too low for human habitation—
still I'll love my sweetly smiling Lalage,
love her sweet chatter.

I 24

For such grief, what moderation? What limit
to mourning so dear a life? Begin, Melpómene,
the funeral dirge: your father gave you
        a liquid voice to go with your lyre.

So Quinctilius lies now in perpetual sleep.   5
When will Modesty, and Justice's sister,
Good Faith uncorrupted, and naked Honesty,
        ever hereafter find his equal?

He dies lamented by many good men,
by no one, Vergil, more than by you.   10
In vain you devoutly call back Quinctilius,
        not so entrusted to the gods' care.

Could you modulate better than Orpheus
a lyre so sweet even the trees would listen,
blood would not return to his empty shade   15
        once Mercury has folded it

into the dark with his shuddering wand,
no god to beseech to unlock death's door.
It is hard. But endurance makes more bearable
        what it is unnatural to change.   20

I 37

Now for some drinking, now for the earth
to shake under our dancing, high time now
   to deck the the gods' couches
     with priestly banquets, friends.

Unthinkable before this to break out Caecuban   5
vintage from cellars, while the insane queen
   plotted ruin for the Capitoline,
     doom for the empire

with her hordes of hideous, diseased
soldiers, mad enough to hope for anything   10
   and drunk with sweet fortune.
     She soon sobered up,

scarcely one ship saved from the fire;
and, her mind swimming in Mareotic wine,
   she learned the meaning of real fear   15
     from Caesar, who chased her

away from Italy in oared pursuit—a hawk
after soft doves, or a swift hunter
   after a hare in the fields
     of snowy Thrace—intending to chain   20

the deadly monster. And yet, anxious to die
a nobler death, she did not with womanly fear
   quail at the sword, did not make for
     hidden shores with her fleet.

She had the courage to cast a calm eye on her   25
crumbling realm, the resolve to pick up
   scaly snakes and absorb
     their black poison into her body,

steelier when she had resolved on death,
too much a woman to allow her enemies   30
   to parade her, a queen no longer,
     in an insulting triumph.

I 38

Persian finery, I hate it, my boy,
can't stand wreaths made of lime tree bark.
Stop looking around for hidden places
where the roses linger.

Plain old myrtle is all I want,   5
pure and simple. Myrtle's no disgrace
for you when you pour, or me when I drink,
under the trellised vine.

II 1

The civil war from Metellus's consulship,
it's causes, atrocities, and vicissitudes,
        the play of Fortune, the dire
            alliance of leaders, and arms

smeared with still unexpiated blood: 5
this is a hazardous and perilous theme
        you're taking up, walking on hot lava
            layered over with treacherous ash.

Give your tragic Muse a short leave of absence
from the theater, put these public events   10
        in order, and you can soon resume
            the grand style of Attic drama,

Pollio, premier counsel for the defense,
and pillar of the Senate in debate,
        decorated in your Illyrian Triumph   15
            with the laurel of everlasting fame.

Already now the low-pitched menace of horns
grates on my ears, the trumpets are blaring,
        the gleam of weapons frightens horses
            and flashes fear on their riders' faces.   20

My mind imagines voices of great leaders,
their bodies grimed with not inglorious dust,
        and everything on earth subdued
            except the iron will of Cato.

Juno and the other gods who loved Carthage   25
but had to leave it unavenged return now
    to sacrifice the conquerors' grandsons
        at the tomb of Jugurtha.

What field is not richer for Latin blood, or
does not testify with tombstones to unholy   30
    battles and the downfall of the West
        loud enough to be heard by the Medes?

What lake or river has not experienced
our lamentable war, what sea has not been
    stained with Apulian blood,   35
        what coastline is free from our gore?

But don't lose your playfulness, impertinent Muse,
and lapse into a Simonidean dirge.
    In some cave sacred to Venus
        we can try measures with a lighter touch.   40

II 13

Whoever planted you did it on a black day,
and tended you with a sacrilegious hand
    to be the death of his descendants,
        O tree, and the village's disgrace—

I could credit him with having broken   5
his father's neck, and having spattered his hearth
    with a guest's blood at night;
        he's trafficked in Colchian poisons

and whatever other abomination has
ever been conceived—the man who placed you   10
    in my field to fall, dismal timber,
        on the head of your innocent lord.

You can never be too cautious about what
to avoid. The Phoenician sailor shudders
    at the Bosporus but doesn't fear   15
        that Fate will blindside him elsewhere.

The soldier fears the arrows and quick escape
of the Parthian, the Parthian fears
   the Roman dungeon, but Death
      strikes unforeseen the world over.   20

How narrowly I missed seeing the realms
of dark Proserpina, Aeacus passing judgement,
   the precincts of the loyal and true,
      and, playing on her Aeolic lyre,

Sappho lamenting her island's girls,   25
and you, Alcaeus, your golden plectrum
   sounding more fully the rigors
      of sailing and exile, the rigors of war.

The shades give both the hushed, sacral wonder
their songs deserve, but shoulder to shoulder   30
   they throng to lap up battles
      and tyrants toppled from their thrones.

No wonder if the monster with a hundred heads
is dazed by those songs and droops his black ears,
   and the snakes entwining the hair   35
      of the Furies feel young again.

No wonder if Prometheus and Tantalus
are spelled of their torture by that sweet sound,
   and Orion loses his interest
      in chasing lion and shy lynx.   40

II 14

The years are slipping by, Postumus,
my friend, nor can virtue retard
   the onset of wrinkles and old age,
      or of Death who never loses—

not even if you offer three hundred bulls   5
each day to implacable Pluto, who restrains
   triply gigantic Geryon
      and Tityos behind the gloomy

water which—you can count on it—all of us
who feed on earth's bounty must sail across,   10
    whether we die rich men
        or destitute peasants.

Useless to have avoided Mars's bloodbath
and the Adriatic's roaring breakers;
    useless to have feared each autumn   15
        the malignant Sirocco:

You'll still have to visit the sluggish
black Cocytos, view the Danaids'
    infamy and Sisyphus
        sentenced to long labor;   20

still have to leave land, home, and pleasing wife—
and of these trees you cherish, only the cursed
    cypresses shall follow
        their temporary master.

A worthier heir will consume the Caecuban   25
you locked in the cellar, staining the mosaic
    floor with wine more pedigreed
        than at a high priest's banquet.

II 15

Too far gone: palatial heaps encroach
on plowland, fishponds stagnate
    on farm plots, extensive eyesore,
        and the sterile planetree

chokes the vineyard elm; violets   5
to sniff and myrtle for savor drown
    the smell of fertile olive,
        a former owner's stand,

and even sunbeat cannot pierce
the thick of shade laurel. Romulus   10
    and our unshorn
        ancestors had other norms:

Theirs was a commonwealth, no private land
for porticoes that stretch the north wind
    through forests of columns   15
        and artificial shade.

Their laws plowed such spare turf. Towns
were built at public expense, and lean
    new marble graced only
the temples of the immortal gods.   20

II 20

No ordinary or tenuous wing will bear me,
a bard with double shape, through the air,
    nor will I remain earthbound
        any longer: transcending envy

I will leave cities behind. Nor will I, blood   5
of poor parents, I, whose name you call,
    dear Maecenas, die or be
        confined by the waters of Styx.

The transformation begins: rough skin forms
on my legs, and I am turning into a white bird   10
    above, smooth feathers growing
        through my arms and fingertips.

More famous than Icarus, Daedalus's son,
I will tour the shores of moaning Bosporus
    as a swan, see the Gaetulean   15
        shoals, the Hyperborean steppes.

Colchians, Dacians who conceal their fear
of our Marsian cohorts, and outlying Geloni
    will know me, Spaniards and Rhone-
        drinkers become experts in my poetry.   20

Ban lamentation from my empty funeral,
no repulsive grief or ritual complaints.
    Suppress the clamor and omit any
        vacuous honors at my tomb.

III 1

I spurn the masses and shun the uninitiate.
Observe a reverent silence. Songs never before
   heard, I, a priest of the Muses,
      sing to virginal girls and boys.

A king's dreaded dominion is over his subjects;   5
kings themselves are the dominion of Jove,
   glorious in his Gigantic triumph,
      moving the world with a lift of his brow.

One man's vineyard stretches on in rows
longer than his rival's; another comes down   10
   to the Field as a candidate
      with more largesse, campaigns with superior

morals or fame; another has a greater
mob of clients. But impartial Necessity
   sorts out distinguished and low.   15
      The great urn shuffles every single name.

Sicilian feasts lose their elaborate savor
for the banqueter with a sword suspended
   above his disrespectful head;
      neither bird song nor lyre music   20

will restore his sleep. But sleep comes gently
to the lowly cottages of country folk,
   does not disdain a shady bank or
      Tempe rustling in the western breeze.

Whoever desires only what is enough   25
is not disturbed by the tumultuous sea
   or the fierce onset of Arcturus
      setting or the Goat Stars rising,

or by vineyards pummeled with hailstones
or a fallacious farm where the trees blame   30
   first the watershed, then the stars
      that parch fields, then unjust winters.

Fish feel their seas contracting as huge fills
are dumped into the deep where the contractor
    with his gang of workers lowers   35
        rubble and the owner stands

disdainful of the earth. But Fear and Menace
clamber up to where the owner stands.
    And on the bronze trireme, and behind
        the horseman, black Anxiety rides.   40

And if a man's grief cannot be eased
by Phrygian marble, by the use of purples
    more lustrous than stars, by Falernian
        wine or Achaemenian perfume,

why should I pile up an invidious   45
mansion, columns soaring in the latest style?
    Or exchange my Sabine valley
        for the greater burden of wealth?

III 3

The man who is just and steadfast of purpose
cannot be shaken from his rock-like resolve,
    not by angry lynch mobs, the threatening
        stare of a dictator, storm winds

that rule the troubled Adriatic Sea,   5
or the mighty hand of lightening Jove.
    If the sky should crack and cave in,
        the pieces would strike him unperturbed.

This is how Pollux and wandering Hercules
strove for and reached the fires of heaven,   10
    reclining among whom Augustus
        will stain his mouth drinking nectar;

how you, Bacchus, won the honor of having
your chariot drawn by tigers with necks
    unused to a yoke; how Quirinus   15
        fled Acheron on a chariot of Mars

after Juno had spoken her welcome
to the gods in council: "Ilion, Ilion,
      a doomed and adulterous judge
            and a foreign woman have turned you   20

into dust, a city condemned from the time
when Laomedon cheated gods of their pay,
      cursed by me and by chaste Minerva
            with its people and fraudulent lord.

The infamous guest no longer shines   25
for his Spartan mistress, nor does Priam's
      perjured house drive back the fighting
            Achaeans thanks to Hector's prowess,

and the war prolonged by our divine intrigues
has gone to rest. I will now renounce   30
      my wrath, and my grandson, born
            of a Trojan priestess and loathed by me,

I will restore to Mars, and allow him
to enter the halls of light, to drink nectar
      sweet, and to be inscribed among   35
            the quiet ranks of the gods.

As long as a sea seethes between Ilion
and Rome, let the exiles rule and prosper
      in whatever region they please.
            As long as the tombs of Priam and Paris   40

are trampled by cattle and wild wolves hide
their cubs there unharmed, let the Capitol
      stand gleaming, let Rome in her power
            dictate laws to the conquered Medes.

And let her extend her name, feared far and wide,   45
to the outermost shores of the sea that divides
      Europe from Africa, to the fields
            irrigated by the swollen Nile,

a nation stronger in that it spurns
gold hidden in earth, and better left so,   50
      rather than plundering everything sacred
            and forcing it into human use.

Whatever boundary is set to the world
let Rome touch it with her arms, eager to see
    where the heat plays itself out, and   55
        where the mists condense into rain.

But I foretell fate to the bellicose Romans
on this condition: that they not in an excess
    of devotion or confidence
        rebuild the roofs of ancestral Troy.   60

If Troy is reborn it will be under
evil auspices, its calamity repeated,
    I myself, the wife and sister of Jove,
        leading the conquering hordes.

If the bronze wall built by Apollo   65
rises a third time, it will be demolished
    a third time by my Greeks, a third time
        will captive wife lament husband and sons."

This is not the tune for your playful lyre.
Where are you headed, Muse? Don't keep   70
    repeating speeches of the gods and
        trivializing the great in minor modes.

III 6

You shall atone, though innocent, for the crimes
of your ancestors, Roman, until you repair
    the gods' temples, their moldering shrines,
        their statues blackened with grimy smoke.

You rule because you bow your heads to the gods.   5
It all begins here, look here for the end.
    Neglected, the gods have given
        multitudinous woes to Italy.

Twice already Monaeses and Pacorus
have crushed our inauspicious offensives,   10
    and their soldiers gleam with added
        Roman spoils on their necklaces' strings.

The City, beset by revolution,
was nearly destroyed by Dacia and Egypt,
    one formidible for its fleet,   15
        the other more for arrows in flight.

A generation fertile in sin has befouled
marriage first, and then, family and home:
    from this source the calamitous tide
        has overwhelmed our nation's people.   20

The grown girl loves to learn Greek dances
and to be schooled in other similar skills,
    already obsessed with illicit affairs
        down to her delicate fingernails.

She is soon seeking out young adulterers   25
at her husband's parties, and is not choosy
    about whom she hastily grants
        forbidden joys when the lights are low,

but rises openly and with her husband's
compliance, whether she is called by some   30
    salesman or Spanish ship captain
        who pays good money for shameful acts.

The youth who dyed the sea with Punic blood
were not born from parents like these, the youth
    who cut down Pyrrhus, the great   35
        Antiochus, and grim Hannibal:

they were rugged farmer soldiers, trained
to break up the earth with Sabine hoes,
    and at a word from their strict
        mothers, to cut and carry bundles   40

of firewood, when the sun elongates
the shadows and takes the yoke off weary
    oxen, leading in the pleasant
        evening hours with his fading chariot.

Ruinous Time, what does it not diminish?   45
Our parents' age, worse than our grandfathers',
    produced us, still worse, yet soon to beget
        a progeny even more degenerate.

III 9

When I was still dear to you
    and you preferred no one else to put his arms
around your glistening neck,
    my life was happier than a Persian king's.

When you burned for no one more than   5
    for me, and Lydia was not second to Chloë,
my fame as Lydia
    shone more brightly than Roman Ilia's.

Thracian Chloë rules me now,
    a skillful lyrist who knows all the sweet modes   10
and for whom I would not fear to die
    if the powers would spare my beloved's life.

For me, Thurian Calaïs,
    Ornytus's son, lights the fire that burns us both.
I would face death twice for him,   15
    if the powers would spare my darling's life.

What if Venus returned as before
    and reunited her strays with a brazen yoke?
If blond Chloë were ushered out,
    and the door held open for rejected Lydia?   20

Although he is lovelier
    than starlight, and you more unstable than a cork
bobbing on the angry Adriatic,
    with you I would love to live, with you gladly die.

III 13

Bandusia's spring, outshining crystal,
worthy of sweet wine and flowers,
    tomorrow you will be given a kid
        whose forehead swollen with the tips

of horns marks him off for love and battles.   5
In vain: the lascivious herd's offspring
    will stain your chill currents
        crimson with his blood.

You cannot be touched by the flaming Dog Star
in summer's heat. You offer your lovely   10
   coolness to oxen weary
      with plowing, and to wandering cattle.

You too will be one of the famous springs,
when I tell of the scarlet oak growing above
   the fluted rocks where your   15
      speaking waters come leaping down.

III 22

Protector of woods and mountains, Lady
called three times by young wives in labor,
   you hearken and deliver them from death,
      goddess with three shapes:

May the pine nodding over my farmhouse be yours,   5
so at year's end in joy I might sacrifice there
   a young boar practicing its sidelong thrust
      and give blood to the wood.

III 26

I have lived my life, kept in shape for the girls,
and as a soldier of Love had my share of glory.
   It's over now: my weapons will hang
      on this wall; my lyre is discharged

on the left flank of the temple of Venus,   5
Goddess of Sea. Put the torches up here, men,
   and the crowbars and crossbows we used
      to such effect on the opposition's doors.

And you blessed Goddess, with headquarters
in Cyprus and Memphis, far from Thracian snows,   10
   flick your lash just once, my queen,
      on the back of arrogant Chloë.

III 29

Scion of Tyrrhenian kings, for you
a cask of mellow wine not yet tipped,
    along with blooming roses
        and balsam pressed for your hair,

has long been at my house. Tear yourself away;   5
do more than simply *gaze* at Tibur's springs,
    the sloping field of Aefula, and
        Telegonus the parricide's ridge.

Leave your cloying riches and that pile
of a house that slants up to the clouds.   10
    Cease to marvel at the smoke, the wealth,
        the noise of blessed Rome.

A change is often welcome to the rich,
and a simple meal under a poor man's roof
    without tapestries or purple   15
        has often smoothed a furrowed brow.

Cepheus is rising in the evening now,
bright on the horizon; Procyon rages,
    and the stars of violent Leo,
        as the sun brings back days hot and dry   20

and the shepherd with his listless flock searches
wearily for shade, a streambed, a thicket
    of rough Sylvanus, and the river bank
        is steeped in windless silence.

Your concern is for the state of the nation;   25
apprehensive for the City, you fear
    Chinese machinations, Bactria
        ruled by Cyrus, and discord on the Don.

Provident when he shrouded time future
in mists of night, the Deity smiles   30
    whenever mortals take fright
        more than is justified. Remember

to deal calmly with the present. The rest
is borne along as on a river, at times
    flowing peacefully down   35
        to the Etruscan Sea, at times rolling

worn rocks, uprooted trees, cattle and houses
along in its flood as the mountains and woods
    roar all around and the wild
        deluge troubles its normally   40

quiet streams. Master of himself and happy
in his time is the man who can say each day
    "I have lived." Tomorrow let
        the Father fill the sky with black clouds

or pure sunlight; he cannot, however,   45
undo what is past, cannot reshape or render
    null and void anything once Time
        in its running has brought it our way.

Fortune exults in her cruel business
and loves to play her malicious game   50
    shuffling around uncertain honors,
        kind now to me, now to another.

I praise her while she stays. If she starts to beat
her wings fast, I write off what she has given,
    wrap myself in my virtue and court   55
        honest Poverty, who has no dowry.

It is not my way, when the mast creaks
in an African hurricane, to resort
    to panicky prayers and vows lest
        my Cyprian and Tyrian wares   60

add their value to the avaricious sea.
In the protection of my two-oared skiff
    the breeze and Pollux will bear me
        safely through Aegean storms.

III 30

Done. A monument more lasting than bronze,
towering over pharaonic pyramids,
impervious to corrosive rain, powerless winds
and dilapidation over countless aeons

of serial time. I will not wholly die.   5
A large part of me will elude Libitina,
and I will grow green with praise, as long
as a Roman priest ascends the Capitoline

with a silent virgin. And this will be told:
How from the land where the Aufidus roars,   10
where Daunus with little water once ruled
a rustic people, from humble origins I rose

to power, the first to have spun Aeolic song
into Italian verse. Take this just pride
as your honor, Melpómene, and wreathe   15
my hair with laurel, a Delphic crown.

IV 1

We've had a long truce, Venus,
    and now you're mobilizing again. Take it easy, please.
I'm not the man I used to be
    when Cinara was my queen. Don't be cruel

to a man pushing fifty,   5
    soft to your stiff injunctions, you mythological
mother of golden Cupidons.
    Get to where the action is, fly your purple swans

to the house of Paulus Maximus,
    commission yourself to tickle the glands   10
of young people, who beg for it.
    It's really more appropriate. Take Paulus:

handsome, aristocratic,
    a fine defense lawyer, a boy who knows
all the tricks. He will promote   15
    your cause everywhere, fly your flag in the face

of his defeated rival,
    and at the victory party frame you
in marble in a cedar shrine
    at his lodge on Lake Alban.   20

Incense, zithers,
    Phrygian flutes and reed panspipes
music you will inhale,
    while sexy girls dance barefoot with boys

morning and night   25
    beating out on the ground like orgiastic
Salian priests
    a triple-time rhythm to honor your godhead.

But no more girls or boys for me,
    or naive hopes of finding a responsive soul.   30
It's no fun any more
    drinking at parties, wearing flowers in my hair.

And yet, why is it, Ligurinus,
    I still find tears wetting my cheeks?
Why do I lapse into   35
    awkward silences, with nothing to say?

At night, in my dreams,
    I seem to hold you, follow you forever
over the fields of Mars,
    the grass, the waters, hard in their flow.   40

IV 3

      One glance from you, Melpómene,
on the growing boy, one immortally calm look,
    and it is not the Isthmian Games
will bring him fame as a boxer, no fleet stallion

      will pull him on to victory   5
in a Greek chariot, no wartime laurels
    decorate him as a general—
because he crushed the threats of some swollen tyrant—

in his Capitoline parade.
No, it is the waters that flow past fertile Tibur   10
  and the dense foliage of its woods
will shape his renown for Aeolic poems.

  Let the rising generation
of Rome, prince of cities, deign to place me among
  its cherished band of poets,   15
and envy's tooth will begin to lose its bite.

  The golden lyre's tumultuous sound
you modulate to sweet music, Pierian,
  and you could, if you chose, bestow
a swan's voice even upon the mute fish;   20

  and it is by your grace alone
that I am pointed out by passersby
  as the master of the Roman lyre.
The breath I take, such pleasure as I give, are yours.

IV 7

The snows have melted; grass returns to the meadows
  and leaves to the trees.
Earth goes through her changes, and the rivers withdraw
  to flow level with their banks.

The Grace with her sisters and the nymphs now dare   5
  to lead the circle dance nude.
"Don't hope for immortality," warn the circling seasons
  that whirl the warm daylight away.

Winter softens in the westerlies, summer tramples spring,
  itself doomed to perish   10
when appled autumn arrives and pours out its harvest, and soon
  the lifeless groundfrost returns.

Though moon after moon may recoup its celestial losses,
  we, when we make our descent
where father Aeneas lies, and rich Tullus and Ancus,   15
  are shadows, darkness, and dust.

Who knows if the gods to the sum of todays will add
        tomorrow's quota of time?
Your heir, though, will not lay his greedy hands on whatever
        you spend on your own dear self.   20

Once you are gone beneath the earth and Minos has delivered
        his dazzling judgement on you,
not eloquence, Torquatus, nor religion nor family
        will ever again bring you back.

For Diana cannot free from the darkness below   25
        her chaste Hippolytus;
nor can all Theseus's strength break the Lethaean chain
        from his beloved Pirithous.

IV 10

You stuck up little pretty boy, you've had it all your way
but now you're afraid of the shadow of that pubic hair creeping down
and all that fine stuff down to your shoulders has to get cut,
those used-to-be pink-as-a-rose cheeks are fuzzing up your face
a rank mutation, right Ligurinus? and you're going to say   5
when you see your new self in the mirror, oh god, you're going to say,
if only I knew when I was a boy what I know today
or if only my cheeks could get smooth again when I feel this way.

IV 15

Apollo sounded a warning on his lyre
when I wanted to tell of conquest and war,
        lest I spread my little sails on a
                Tyrrhenian Sea. Your epoch, Caesar,

has brought fertility back to our fields,   5
has restored to Capitoline Jupiter
        insignia ripped from insolent
                Parthian doorposts, has closed

the empty, war-free temple of Janus,
curbed unbridled licentiousness,   10
        expiated guilt, canceled blame,
                and recalled the ancestral ways

by which the Latin name and Italian strength
increased, and our empire's fame and dignity
    was extended to the sun's 15
        rising from his Hesperian rest.

With Caesar guarding our state, the madness
of civil war will not expatriate peace,
    nor the anger flare that forges swords
        and alienates anguished cities. 20

Drinkers of the deep Danube will not break
the Julian decrees, nor the Gaets, the Silks,
    the faithless Persians, nor
        the natives by the river Don.

And we, on workdays as on festal days, 25
in celebration of merry Bacchus
    with our children and wives,
        having duly beseeched the gods,

will sing of brave heroes as our fathers did,
verses with interludes of Lydian flutes, 30
    sing of Troy, Anchises, and all
        the progeny of kindly Venus.

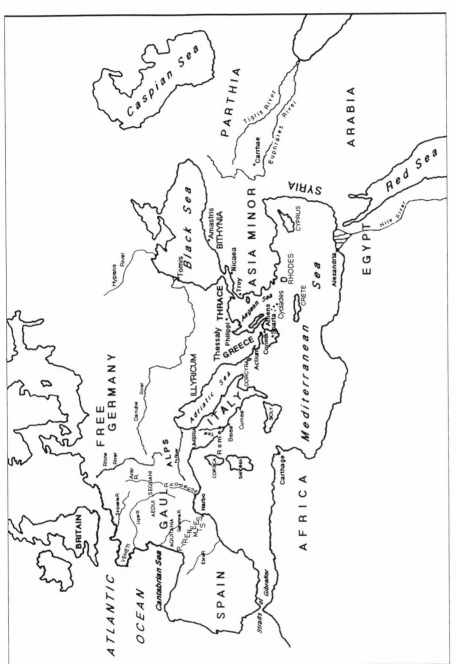

I. Roman World

II. Italy

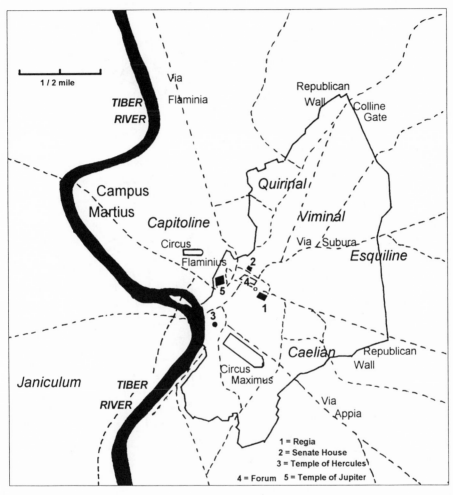

III. Rome

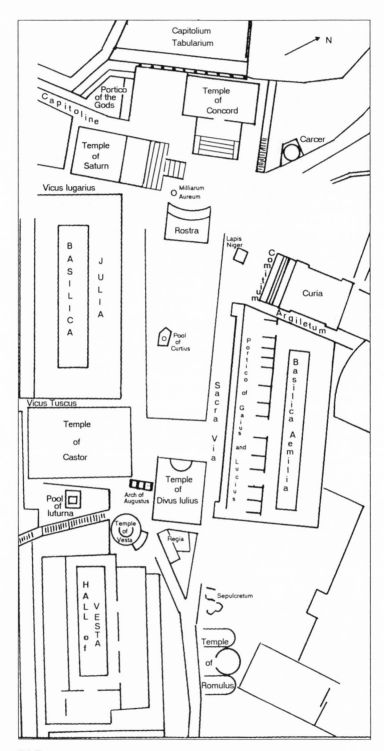

IV. Forum

NOTES AND COMMENTS

These notes are primarily for two audiences: undergraduates in courses on Roman literature and civilization who will read and discuss these poems with the aid of an instructor; and that diverse collection of general readers who with various levels of skill and knowledge will read alone for curiosity and other reasons. These audiences, I believe, have different needs. The undergraduates will generally need basic information about details, but will be able to rely on their instructors for guidance in the interpretation of the poems, while the more general readers may already be familiar with many details of the ancient world, but may appreciate some guidance in coming to understand and interpret for themselves these essentially foreign poems.

In my effort to satisfy both readers, I have tried to supply for undergraduates the kind of basic information that makes the poems readable. I have also tried on most occasions to supply more information than might be considered the bare minimum, or even the adequate facts—this is because allusion in Latin literature is a complex and often rich means of adding levels of implication and association. Each reader and teacher will have to decide for him or herself how far to take the implications of any allusion. I have thought it sensible to keep in mind the fact that one never knows what another will discover in an oblique or explicit allusion to a classical myth or a historical event.

The matter of interpretation is more difficult. As post-romantics, many of us still have a tendency to believe that good poetry should be immediately accessible to sensitive readers. Roman poets, however, were highly conventional and worked in a medium characterized by the learned manipulation of traditional features of form and content. Their poetry is as foreign to us as that of other distant cultures. Consequently, I have tried to offer information on details of form and content while suggesting something of the range of scholarly interpretation. I have not, however, tried to exhaust comment on every poem, but rather to offer, when it seemed possible and useful, perspectives and considerations that will give readers a way of beginning to understand some of the things these poets were doing. I have tried to make this commentary suggestive and useful, but neither a forum for my ideas nor an up-to-date variorum of scholarly interpretations.

I have appended to the notes for each poet a short and selected bibliography of books in English, and I have appended to this introductory note a short list of general works on Latin lyric and elegy. I hope that curious readers will be able to use these references as the first step in seeking further information, including further bibliography. I have not, however, tried to be comprehensive, nor have I cited articles (except in the case of Sulpicia, because there is no book in English about her). I make few explicit references to literary debates, but in general allow suggestions to speak for themselves. Experts in the field will readily identify my debts and contributions. I hope to be forgiven for not crediting the valuable work of others who have helped make these poems accessible to us all.

Poems marked with an asterisk in the Introduction and Notes and Comments are not translated in this anthology.

SOME GENERAL BOOKS ABOUT LATIN LYRIC AND ELEGY

Kennedy, Duncan F. *The Arts of Love: Five Studies in the Discourse of Roman Love Elegy* (New York: Cambridge University Press, 1993).

Luck, Georg. *The Latin Love Elegy* (London: Methuen, 1969).

Lyne, R.O.A.M. *The Latin Love Poets from Catullus to Horace* (New York: Oxford, 1980).

Catullus

BIBLIOGRAPHY

There are many books and articles on Catullus. Those most useful for the nonspecialist include the following:

Martin, Charles. *Catullus* (New Haven: Yale University Press, 1992).

Quinn, Kenneth. *The Catullan Revolution* (Cambridge: Heffer, 1969).

Wiseman, T. P. *Catullus and His World: A Reappraisal* (New York: Cambridge University Press, 1985).

1

Catullus's first poem, like the first poem of most Roman books of poetry, is programmatic. He begins with an echo of the Greek epigrammatist, Meleager, and continues with a description of the outside of his book's papyrus roll which suggests the stylistic and aesthetic qualities embodied in his verse. Similarly, his dedication to Cornelius Nepos provides an opportunity to praise qualities (learning, labor, brevity) which he, too, aspires to. Not only is Catullus's poetry and his urbane persona sometimes difficult to pin down, but it is possible that the ambiguous but appreciative relationship between this young, sophisticated poet and an older writer of prose history is for Catullus exactly what makes him exceptional and so ensures his poetic success.

1–2. snazzy, slim, new-slicked, assiduous: The Latin terms corresponding to or occasioning these terms all carry stylistic connotations associated with the learned, allusive, refined poetic style of Callimachus. See further the programmatic statement of poem 95.

3. Cornelius: Cornelius Nepos was a Roman historian who came from the same territory as Catullus. He was a friend of Cicero and Atticus, and wrote at least sixteen books on famous men, a lost history of Italy, lives of Cato and Cicero, and at least five books of anecdotes. The general opinion of his work, however, is that it was carelessly and hastily composed, plainly and indifferently written, and of slight value. Such an opinion seems to reflect values which are for the most part the exact opposite of the values Catullus exemplified. In his "Life of Atticus," written some time after Catullus's death, Nepos calls Catullus and Lucretius the most elegant poets of their age.

4. scribbles: "Scribbles" translates the Latin term, *nugae*, which means "trash, what is thrown away," and summarizes the attitude of men like Cicero to the poetry of poets like Catullus. Cicero had said, for instance, that, even if he had two lives to live, he would still never find time for lyric poetry.

6. THE HISTORY OF THE ITALIANS: The three-volume history of Italy by Nepos.

8. discernment, fine work: The Latin is tantalizingly ambiguous: "learned, by Jupiter, and laborious." The reference to learning and to labor is clearly a reference to Callimachean values; however, the reference to Jupiter and the use of the Latin term *laboriosus* undercuts Callimachean values with a suggestion of pretension.

2

The second poem of Catullus's book is a poem about a sparrow (Latin, *passer*), a pet sparrow, written in parody of hymnic style. Linguistic evidence points to the slang use of *passer* for the genitals, either male or female, which yields to both this poem and the next an erotic subtext.

1. Sparrow: Sparrows were common as pets in Italy; the name "sparrow" was used as a term of endearment, like "chick," as well as a slang term equivalent to "cock" and "beaver." Aphrodite's carriage was sometimes pictured as drawn by sparrows. And finally, as the first word of the poem, it would become the designation for Catullus's book of poetry, Catullus's *Sparrow*. Parodic hymns to animals are found in the Hellenistic literature on which Catullus so heavily relied, most notably in the poetry of Meleager.

6–10. amusement, balm, fever, tease, anguish: All terms which in other places, for instance in poem 50, recall poetry, the making of poetry, and the effects of poetry.

11–13. There is some dispute as to whether these three lines belong to poem 2 or to another poem. Even if they belong to poem 2, one must assume that something has been lost from the text.

11. the little maid: An allusion to the story of Atalanta, a virgin huntress who made her suitors race her: if the suitor won, he would marry her, but he was killed if he lost. One suitor tricked her by dropping golden apples in her path as he ran ahead. She stopped to pick them up, lost the race, and he married her. Catullus's version suggests she was pleased to be defeated. See Ovid *Amores* III 2. 28–29.

3

This poem takes form as a parody of a dirge or funeral lament whose traditional features would include: 1) address to the mourners, 2) praise and lament for the deceased, 3) the consolatory topics including the reception of the deceased in the underworld and clichés like "but all must be endured," and 4) a description of the funeral and memorial. Catullus breaks off in the middle of the fourth topic, just before the endurance theme comes up. Compare Horace *Odes* I 24, Ovid *Amores* III 9.

1. Cupidses: Catullus uses the plural of Cupid for the first time in attested Latin literature.

2. Venus-elect: The Latin term equates the charm of Venus, goddess of love, with the charm of a fashionable young gentleman.

9. now here, now there: As in poem 2, so here the language recalls other Catullan descriptions of poetry itself; poem 50 line 5 repeats this description exactly but applies it to the way Catullus and Licinius wrote "one meter after another."

13–14. Dark Destroyer: The Latin term, *Orcus*, is an archaic and epic term for the ruler of the Underworld.

4

The narrator relates the story of a ship's travels from its home on the Black Sea through the Adriatic and Aegean to its current place of retirement on a clear lake. As the narrative of an object dedicated to a god, in this case the Dioscuri, who are the gods of sailors, the poem's narrative recalls many Hellenistic dedicatory epigrams. The narrative moves back in time from the present to the ship's origins (1–15) and then forward again toward the present (15–27). The traditional view is that the journey recounted is the tale of Catullus's journey home from Bithynia. See poems 10 and 31 for other aspects of that journey.

1. cockleshell: The Latin for a light sea-going yacht is *phasellus,* or "bean-pod."

6. Adriatic coast: The Adriatic Sea lies between Italy and Greece; it was particularly unpredictable due to sudden winds.

7. Cycladic Isles: Islands in the Aegean off the coast of southern Greece; we are moving south and east from Italy toward Asia Minor.

8. Rhodes: An island off the coast of Asia Minor, slightly south and east of the Cycladic Isles. It had important historical and cultural associations.

8–9. Thracian Bosporus: Traveling from Rhodes north up the coast of Asia Minor one comes to Bosporus, the straits that lead east to the Black Sea.

9. unkind Black Sea's remoteness: The Black Sea was separated from the Aegean by the Bosporus; it was traditionally unkind to sailors.

11–12. leaf-haired grove, loquacious hair: The Latin word for "hair" is also used for the foliage of trees.

13. Amastris, Cytorus: Amastris was the capital of Paphlagonia, a port on the Black Sea; Cytorus was also a port, near Amastris, whose hills were famous for their boxwood.

20. God smiled: The god referred to here is Jove, or Jupiter. As god of the sky he was also a weather god.

22. plaque: Sailors who escaped from particularly dangerous voyages would hang a votive plaque to the gods of the sea or the gods of the shore to whom they had prayed in gratitude for their rescue. See Horace *Odes* I 5.

27. Castor: Castor and Pollux were twins, sons of Leda, who upon their death became the Dioscuri, the protectors of seafarers.

5

One of Catullus's most famous poems, imitated and translated many times. Lesbia, his girlfriend, who was presumably the girl of poems 2 and 3, is named for the first time here. We are told by Apuleius that "Lesbia" stands for "Clodia," one of three sisters whose youngest brother was the notorius Clodius, Cicero's enemy. Catullus finds in the prying eyes and envious leer of others an excuse for even more kisses by claiming that a sufficiently excessive number will confound the censors. Accounting imagery is curiously prominent in Catullus's poetry.

6

A remarkable exercise in poetic power and male bonding. Flavius, of whom we know nothing, has a girl and won't tell. By the time he makes his final request ("tell me"), his poem has already accomplished what it promises: to raise Flavius and his love to the stars.

    3. <u>unsnazzy</u>: "Snaz," as Joyce puts it, was one of the most important virtues of Catullus's circle; it combined sophistication, charm, and pleasure. By the time we get to the end of the poem, Catullus has left us with the impression that perhaps this girl is too snazzy, too stylish, and Flavius wants to keep her to himself.

7

This poem is a companion to poem 5, which when taken together with poems 2 and 3, seems to suggest an amatory narrative moving toward greater intimacy, but not without suggestions of danger and excess. The manner remains allusive and playful, and depends on a contrast between the learned style of Callimachus (2–6) and the common clichés of popular comedy (7–9).

    1. <u>kissimizations</u>: Catullus introduced into the literary language the common term for kisses which one still finds in the romance languages, *basia*. Here he has turned the colloquial term into a learned sounding polysyllabic abstract noun, *basiationes*.

    3. <u>Libyan sand</u>: One finds in the desert sands of Libya, in the province of Cyrene, whose chief town is Cyrene, the oracle of Jupiter Ammon and the tomb of Battus, founder and first king of Cyrene.

    4. <u>aphrodisiacal Cyrene</u>: The Latin refers to Cyrene's major export, asafoetida, a medicinal plant that grew wild in Cyrene and was used for a variety of purposes. John M. Riddle proposes that it was used as a contraceptive in antiquity (in *Contraception and Abortion*. Cambridge, MA: Harvard University Press, 1992). Today it is used in eastern cooking to ease the digestion.

    5. <u>oracle of Jove Most Torrid</u>: The temple of Jupiter Ammon in the Libyan desert was the seat of one of the most famous oracles of the ancient world. Such an allusion has complex associations, including the uncertainty of the future and Zeus's notoriously torrid sexual appetite.

    6. <u>Battus</u>: The legendary founder of Cyrene, but also the name of the father of Callimachus.

8

This is apparently the first Greek or Latin lyric poem in which a poet addresses himself. Some critics follow a dark underlying narrative account of the course of Catullus's affair, while others have noted the comic traditions out of which the poem grows. For a more compellingly serious exploration of the same situation, compare Catullus 76.

    1. <u>Poor dear Catullus!</u>: The term in Latin for "poor dear," *miser*, will become in all the elegists the specific designation of the lover.

9

Catullus welcomes his friend Veranius home from Spain. Veranius is mentioned in three other poems: 12, 28, and 47. Veranius and Fabullus were on the staff of L. Piso Caesoninus in Macedonia while Catullus was on the staff of C. Memmius in Bithynia. The poem organizes the traditional topics of a welcome poem (arrival, family, safe journey, places visited, tales to tell, and greeting) into a seemingly spontaneous and unmannered expression of delight.

10

Written after Catullus's return to Rome from Bithynia (perhaps the spring of 56) this lightly satiric poem is one that has divided critics into fairly exclusive camps. Some read the account of Catullus's encounter with Varus and his girlfriend as a condemnation of a girl who lacks the savoir faire to know how to act in the company of smart young men. Others have followed my suggestion that it is really the girl who has the upper hand and who, together with Varus, unmasks the pretense of this smart young man who wants to appear a little more favored than he is. This view allows both a serious political interpretation in which the poet undermines the aspirations of power and wealth inherent in the Roman imperial system, and a more comic perspective in which the poet celebrates the game of one-up(wo)manship, a game in which our masks of social pretense are manipulated by others, and in which the poet really does become one of the "favored few" by telling the story of his own discomfiture.

1. <u>Varus</u>: We do not know for certain who this Varus was. Quintilius Varus, a native of Cremona, was a friend of Horace and Vergil whose death Horace mourns in *Odes* I 24.

2. <u>Forum</u>: The chief public square in Rome, the center of civic life, the perfect place for an irresponsible young Roman with nothing to do to hang around.

4. <u>tart</u>: The Latin uses the dimunitive of the slang for a prostitute; a kind of "whore-let."

8. <u>Bithynia</u>: Catullus was in Bithynia, a territory in northwest Asia Minor near ancient Troy and the Black Sea, on the staff of the governor, C. Memmius, probably from the spring of 57 B.C.E. to the spring of 56 B.C.E. It was typical of a young Roman to begin his public career in such a position and it was generally expected that both the governor and the staff would make what profit they could from the provincials.

18. <u>sedan-chair toters</u>: The Romans themselves were on occasion uneasy about litters, associating them with images of luxury and arrogance.

28. <u>slut</u>: The Latin is impossible to translate. Catullus calls her by a name which elsewhere always refers to the passive male in a homosexual affair.

31. <u>Serapis's shrine</u>: The cult of Serapis had come to Italy from Egypt at the end of the previous century. Associated with the goddess Isis, Serapis was a god of healing particularly popular with the lower classes.

34. <u>Cinna Gaius</u>: In his embarassment the speaker mixes up the proper order of the Roman nomen and cognomen. C. Helvius Cinna was another countryman of Catullus, a neoteric poet whose learned verses required a learned commentary; his verses may even be echoed in

Catullus's dedicatory poem. On the basis of the fragments that have survived, it seems that he was in Bithynia with Catullus. See poem 95 for Catullus's praise of his epyllion on Smyrna.

37. bubblehead: In the Latin, the words the speaker uses make explicit the charge that the girl has no sense of wit and that she is a troublemaker.

11

The opening "cycle" of poems, 2–11, seems to recount the history of Catullus and Lesbia from initial attraction to this repudiation of love. Here the purpose is a stock *renuntio amoris* like that of poem 8, but varied in that the speaker does not directly address Lesbia. Instead he speaks to two comrades, Furius and Aurelius. The poem is in Sapphic stanzas, a verse form associated with Sappho of Lesbos, the Greek lyricist of bittersweet eros, who is no doubt recalled in Catullus's name for his beloved, Lesbia. Some believe that another poem in Sapphic stanzas, poem 51, which is a partial translation of a Sappho poem, was the first poem Catullus wrote to Lesbia. The implications of Catullus's "Lesbian" love for a woman who deflowers him, who cuts him down like a flower, continue to be the subject of critical fascination.

2. the wilds of India: For the Romans, India was the furthest eastern land. The geographical catalog, written in high epic style, celebrates the monumental extent of empire in heroic fashion.

5. effete Arabia: The Arabians in the Middle East were traditionally considered effeminate in Latin poetry, presumably because of their luxurious exports.

6. Parthian backcountry: The Parthians, a warlike people, had at this time extended their empire in the East from the Euphrates River to the Indus River. They were noted for a particular style of fighting on horseback whereby, as they seemed to retreat, they shot over their backs at the pursuing enemy.

7. seven Nile-streams: The Nile River stands for Egypt at the southern edge of the Roman world. Where the Nile flows into the Mediterranean it has seven mouths and discolors the sea.

9. the high Alps: The poet's catalog now moves to the north and the Alps that separate Italy from Germany and Britain.

10. Caesar's trophies: The connection of this catalog with Rome's imperial successes becomes explicit in this reference to Julius Caesar, who had campaigned in Germany during the summer of 55 B.C.E. and crossed the English Channel to Britain in 55 and 54.

15. short but: The expansive and epic range of the opening geographical survey is contrasted and compared with the private and intimate message of a few words which Catullus wants to send to Lesbia.

17. Live it up. Farewell: In the Latin Catullus uses an apparently conventional formula of separation, one used both to close letters and for the contemptuous dismissal of another.

18. all three hundred: While the intimate world of erotic feeling is explicitly contrasted to the public world of empire and monuments, it turns out that Lesbia's own achievements have an epic quality to them.

23. flower: Flowers are traditionally images of the female, and the cut flower, as in English, an image of deflowering.

12

The napkin thief, Marrucinus Asinius (or, in the proper order of names, Asinius Marrucinus), was, we believe, the brother of C. Asinius Pollio, an orator, historian, and friend of Horace and Vergil; see Horace *Odes* II 1. Born in 76–75, Pollio would be about seventeen when this poem was written (assuming that Catullus had not yet been to Bithynia), and, although the poem is not formally addressed to Pollio, it does offer him an oblique compliment. The poem belongs to the type known as a *flagitatio*, or "demand for restitution," in which Catullus asks for the return of a dinner napkin which has been boorishly taken by Asinius Marrucinus. This "demand for restitution" is neatly turned into an act of gratitude for Veranius and Fabullus, who had originally sent the napkin to Catullus, and a compliment to C. Asinius Pollio. One may see the poem itself as a form of "keepsake" or remembrance for the friendship of Veranius and Fabullus.

4. dinner napkins: The Romans ate with their fingers and used linen handkerchiefs at meals for wiping their hands and at other times to wipe their faces. The dinner guest who never brings a napkin to a dinner party but always takes one away was also attacked by the poet Martial.

18. from Spain: Spanish linen was reputed to be the best available at this time.

22. 'Ranius the Runt and Little Fab: Catullus uses an "affectionate diminutive" of the name of Veranius, "Veraniolus"; the name Fabullus already sounds like a diminutive.

13

This is an example of what is known as the Latin invitation poem—a genre in which someone is invited to dinner, given the time and place, and promised specific entertainment. The poem relies on reversals of expectation and tantalizing innuendo: you come to dinner, but bring the meal; my purse is full—of cobwebs; I'll give you something in return—undiluted love; you'll only think about your olfactory organ.

1. Fabullus: The friend of Veranius and Catullus, also addressed in poem 12. The poem begins and ends with Fabullus while Catullus is in the center.

29

Catullus's interest in politics, while always aloof from politicial agendas and factions, was nevertheless intense and personal. The great Julius Caesar had been a family friend and stayed with Catullus's father in Verona. This did not, however, protect him from Catullus's contemptuous indifference (see poem 93), or from his libelous and obscene invective (as in this poem and in poem 57). Suetonius, the Roman biographer of the emperors, tells us that Caesar took offense at some verses and that, after Catullus made amends, he continued his friendship with Catullus's family. We meet here for the first time Mamurra, a Roman of the equestrian class from Formiae, who had served under Pompey against King Mithridates and under Caesar in Spain. Mamurra was, apparently, from the same social class as Catullus: a well-to-do young eques without senatorial responsibilities. Unlike Catullus and his colleagues, Mamurra had done very well in his military service (compare poem 10) and become wealthy enough to attract Cicero's contempt. Catullus in this poem, most likely written in 55 B.C.E., blames both Caesar and Pompey for supporting the sexual and financial profligacy of their protégé, Mamurra. Although the addressee(s) of the poem is disputed, we will assume that Pompey the Great is addressed and ridiculed in the first ten lines for his association with Mamurra; then Catullus turns the same attack on Caesar for ten lines. The last four lines summarize.

2.   a rutting hog of a gambler: The line describes Mamurra himself. Catullus says that only someone like Mamurra could stand to see Mamurra.

4.   Gaul, Britain: Caesar's campaigns in Gaul lasted from 58 to 55 when he made his first expedition to Britain. Mamurra apparently returned to Rome after this expedition. Caesar's second expedition took place in the summer of 54 B.C.E.

5.   twinkletoed Romulus: Romulus was the founder of Rome and his name became synonymous with statesmanship and leadership. The compliment of addressing Pompey in this way is turned into an insult when he is designated as a passive homosexual (which is the precise meaning of the Latin). Insults like this were, however, part of the invective that soldiers might lavish on their generals during a triumph.

11.   my singular Leader: While there is some dispute about who is addressed in this poem and at what point, it seems to make best sense to take these lines as turning from Pompey, who would still be consul at this time and in Rome where Mamurra is, to Caesar, still on campaign.

12.   the West's remotest isle: Britain. The Romans had expected to find gold and other minerals there, but were disappointed.

15.   open-handed: Caesar had a reputation for liberality and generosity, which his enemies could make to seem like the vice of influence buying rather than a virtue.

18.   Black Sea booty: A reference to the wealth Mamurra would have brought back from his campaigns with Pompey against King Mithridates in 63 B.C.E.

19.   Spanish gold: In 61 B.C.E. Caesar led a successful campaign in Spain.

19.   Tajo: A great river in Spain and so associated with Spanish gold.

23.   O Holy Father: Caesar, although younger than Pompey, had given Pompey his daughter Julia in marriage. It was part of an effort to keep these powerful men allied. Caesar was also *Pontifex Maximus*, or head of the college of priests, an organization responsible for advising the state on religious matters.

24.   and Son-in-law: It apparently became traditional to refer to Caesar and Pompey as "father-in-law and son-in-law."

32

Another variation on an invitation poem—this time the poet has already eaten and is asking for an invitation to the home of Ipsitilla. The woman is unidentified, although some have seen in her name a reference to Orestilla, the wife of Catiline, of whom the historian Sallust remarks, "A good man never praised anything except her looks" and who may be the Orestilla of poem 64. 402.

9. <u>Fornifuckations</u>: Similarly, the Latin uses a "learned polysyllable"; compare the "kissimizations" of poem 7.

34

This poem adapts the formal style of Greek hymns to the celebration of Diana, an Italian goddess of the wild who had been assimilated to the Greek goddess Artemis in her three functions as Ilithyia, goddess of childbirth, as Hecate, goddess of the crossroads and the underworld, and as Selene, the moon goddess. The formal hymnic style entails a prooemium or introductory passage, an invocation of the goddess (including her ancestery), a catalog of the goddess's diffuse spheres of influence, and a petition based upon the goddess's powers. The poem should be compared with Horace *Odes* I 21.

2. <u>girls and boys</u>: In the innocent beginning lies the hope and future of the race.

5. <u>Child of Leto</u>: This was a common designation for Diana among the poets. She was the daughter of Leto and Jove (or Jupiter, or in Greek, Zeus) whom, according to some legends, Leto bore on the island of Delos assisted by an olive tree. Her twin brother was Apollo.

13. <u>Juno Lucina</u>: In her first aspect, Diana is invoked as goddess of childbirth; this aspect was identified with Juno.

15. <u>Lady-of-Crossroads</u>: In her second aspect, Diana is invoked as Hecate, goddess of the crossroads, with whom she was regularly identified.

16. <u>luminous Luna</u>: Either this is a third aspect or an extension of Diana Trivia. Formally, the repetition of "you" attaches this aspect of Diana to "Lady-of-Crossroads"; traditionally, however, this is another aspect of the goddess.

17. <u>You, Goddess</u>: The last aspect in which Diana is invoked, that of agricultural influence, an extension of her influence as moon goddess.

24. <u>the race of Romulus</u>: Romulus was the legendary founder of the city of Rome.

39

In poem 37*, we discovered Egnatius hanging out in a drinking house where Lesbia's lovers compared their lecherous achievements. Here we discover that he has other unpleasant characteristics: he has no taste, he smiles all the time, he brushes his teeth with piss. The poem has the underlying form of a joke with an ethnic punchline: Why shouldn't a Spaniard laugh in court?

11. <u>an urban Roman, even a hick</u>: The contrast is between the only recognized urban center of the Roman world, Rome, and anyplace else.

12–15. <u>Sabine, Tiburtine, Umbrian, Etruscan, Alban, Gentleman of Verona</u>: Territories of Italy outside of Rome, each cited with appropriately prejudicial ethnic epithets. When Catullus gets to his hometown, Verona, the designation becomes complimentary.

19. <u>and in Spain</u>: The ancient evidence of both Diodorus and Strabo agree with Catullus about this custom.

41

Invective and obscenity in public literary forms are foreign to the modern world and are still poorly accounted for in the scholarly literature on Latin lyric. Not so long ago, moral compunctions led to the censorship of such poems. This poem takes as its butt a certain Ameana (otherwise unknown), the girlfriend of some bankrupt playboy of Formiae. If we take this man to be the infamous Mamurra of Formiae, a friend of Caesar who is viciously attacked elsewhere (29, 94, 105, 114, 115), then the poem may be as much an attack on this man as on Ameana. What begins as an invective on Ameana becomes by implication an invective on Mamurra, who is bankrupt and whose ugly girlfriend is out trying to make ends meet.

1–4: The first four charges against Ameana are 1) she has no restraint in her sexual appetite, 2) she is asking for a couple of thousand, 3) she has a big nose, and 4) she's the girlfriend of Mamurra.

5–8. The last four lines respond to the situation as described. At first Catullus appears to offer advice or commiseration; but the final line shows that all this solicitude for the girl is really but foil for another attack: she does not know how ugly she is.

8. brazen: Mirrors were made of bronze.

43

This poem, complementary to poem 41, is separated, as are other poems in Catullus, from 41 by a related poem on another subject; compare poems 5 and 7. If poem 41 turned an attack on Ameana into an attack on Mamurra, poem 43 turns another attack on Ameana into a compliment to Lesbia. In poem 41, Ameana's looks and her request for money became a reflection of Mamurra's standards and masculinity; here the response to Ameana's looks becomes a reflection of a general degradation of taste and, perhaps by implication, of Mamurra's degraded politics. It is easy to infer that Lesbia possessed the qualities which are the opposite of those described here.

5. Bankrupt Playboy of Formiae: As in poem 41, probably a reference to Mamurra.

46

A lovely poem on the coming of spring which emphasizes change as opportunity— for travel, for stories, and for anticipating the return home. This poem should be compared with Horace's odes on spring: *Odes* I 4 and IV 7. It was apparently written in the spring of 56 B.C.E. when Catullus was preparing to return home from Bithynia.

3. Zephyr: The west wind whose gentle arrival meant the coming of spring.

4. plains near Troy: Bithynia was in Asia Minor near enough to Troy to justify such a reference.

5. Nicene heat: Nicaea was one of the two chief cities of the province of Bithynia.

6. Asia's fabulous cities: The language suggests a tour of the famous places of the east; such a tour was common for young Roman men.

49

This occasional poem has spawned diametrically opposed interpretations: 1) Catullus is flattering Cicero and thanking him for some real (but to us unknown) favor, and 2) Catullus is mocking Cicero for his pretentious rhetoric. There are irrefutable arguments for both sides: 1) Catullus recalls Cicero's real and substantial achievements: he was one of the greatest men of the period, a newcomer to Roman politics who attained the highest post in the Republic. Catullus even echoes the formal and ceremonial address of the senate in "Marcus Tullius," and 2) there is indubitable irony in Catullus's portrayal of himself as "the worst of all poets" and its rigorous and quantitative parallelism with "best of all patrons" cannot avoid the suggestion of a parallel irony. It may be more profitable to read the poem as a verbal image of the riddling relationship between Catullus, who can parade himself as the "worst of all poets" because that is what the serious voice of the Forum thinks of him, and Cicero, whose substantial and indelible achievements are important precisely because of their contrast with Catullan flippancy but who can nevertheless be treated with irony by the voice of this "worst of all poets."

1.   the great-grandsons of Romulus: Romulus was the founder of Rome; the expression is a quasi-heroic expression for all Romans. Cicero was not really a Roman, but, like Catullus himself, a man from the provinces.

1–3.   Rhetorically the shape of the Latin sentence is called a "tri-colon crescendo," which means that it is composed of three phrases of increasing length. Such a figure of speech was a mark of the high style and a particularly familiar feature of Cicero's rhetoric.

3.   Marcus Tully: The formal style of address to a member of the Senate; it was quite an achievement for a man from the provinces to come to Rome and succeed in Roman politics. One who did was called a "New Man."

7.   Attorney of All: One of Cicero's clients actually used the same phrase in a flattering address to Cicero.

50

A verse letter to Catullus's friend, orator and poet C. Licinius Calvus (also addressed in poems 14, 53 and 96). The poem provides a window on the values and pleasures of Catullus's circle of friends. It seems that he and Calvus spent yesterday exchanging verses in a kind of informal competition, and getting drunk. Last night Catullus found himself unable to sleep, aroused with an arguably erotic passion. The language is filled with double entendre and Catullus ends by threatening the vengeance of the goddess Nemesis if Calvus does not respond.

1.   Licinius: C. Licinius Calvus Macer was a close friend of Catullus who is described for us by Seneca as a small excitable man; he was slightly younger than Catullus and was frequently paired with Catullus by later poets. As an orator, he was known for his Attic, or dry and severe, style and was praised by Cicero. As a poet, he wrote satire and elegy, a mythological narrative poem, and marriage poems—much the same range as Catullus's. In poem 14 he was portrayed as having sent Catullus an anthology of terrible poetry and again Catullus imagined vengeance: he would send back an anthology of even worse poetry. In poem 96 Catullus offers consolation to Calvus on the death of his wife Quintilia.

2. fooling around: the first of several phrases which in the Latin may have sexual overtones as well as refer in general to the life-style of Catullus and his friends.

22. Nemesis: The goddess of retribution who brings about a change of circumstances for the proud and arrogant.

51

Many believe that this is the first poem Catullus wrote to Lesbia. It is, except for the final stanza, a fairly close translation of a Sappho poem which may be found in the Appendix to this volume. In that poem, Sappho observes while one of her young women sits and talks with a man. The translation of Sappho's poem, a poem in which the poet complains that she has lost her voice, is an elegant compliment to the continuing power of the voice that passion almost silenced.

2. may God forgive me!: A particularly Roman touch, added by Catullus, is this concern with religious propriety which is expressed in a very old religious formula.

2. surpasses all Gods: This hyperbole is another change Catullus made in Sappho's original.

4. watching: Lesbia is frequently the object of the gaze of Catullus and others, or so Catullus portrays her; to adhere to such a motif in this poem he must modify the Sapphic original.

5. (ah me!): This reappearance of the Latin word, *miser*, that tag for the unhappy elegiac lover, is another Catullan addition.

13–16. Idle ways: This stanza has been added by Catullus to Sappho's original which at this point seems to have put on a brave front: "but all must be endured" or "but all must be dared." The significance and value of Catullus's addition is the subject of continuing debate among scholars.

55

This poem had to be written after Pompey's portico was opened in 55 B.C.E. Catullus portrays himself on a sometimes frantic search for his friend Camerius in the portico, which after its opening had rapidly become a good place for a young man like Camerius to meet women. We do not know with certainty who Camerius was, but the name indicates that he was a young aristocrat. Catullus's final request, to be a participant in Camerius's love, is like the request that ends poem 6. It does not need any future action by Camerius because the poem has already become the "lots of gossip" that Venus loves and, since Camerius is also invited to be silent about their affair, the poem is all we are invited to know of how Catullus gets "a load of" Camerius's love.

1. We implore you: The first person plural may be mock-solemn or a reflection of Catullus's divided self, or both. He addresses Camerius.

3–4. racetracks, CircMax: The *Circus Maximus* was an oval where games, including horse races, were held in the hollow between two hills of Rome, the Palatine and the Aventine. It had been built by the first Tarquin and could contain more than 100,000 spectators. When the horses were not running, one could find in the *Circus Maximus* astronomers, soothsayers, jugglers, actors, and prostitutes.

3. Bijou: Catullus refers to the "Lesser Campus," a much disputed reference, possibly to be identified as an open area on the Caelian hill. We know that Mamurra, Caesar's henchman who is pilloried by Catullus in poems 29 and 57, lived on the Caelian and had spent much of his profits from Gaul on marble columns and inlaid walls. Apparently this was a preferred location for gentlemen of Catullus's social class.

4. bookstores: The meaning is uncertain. There were bookstores in Rome, but such a meaning for the Latin requires a reference to Greek usage. Another likely sense of the Latin would be "placards" or "public notices," but that makes an awkward parallel with the *Circus Maximus*, the *Circus Minor*, and the temple to Jupiter. In either case, we should imagine Catullus still looking in the crowded forum.

5. temple: The temple to Jupiter Optimus Maximus had been restored on the Capitoline hill in 69 B.C.E. and was, at least for the next generation and probably for Catullus, a place where a varied crowd of people assembled, including mimes, men down on their luck who prayed to Jupiter, women pretending to dress the hair of Juno, and, of course, prostitutes.

7. Pompey's Portico: An open rectangular court surrounded by trees and hung with tapestries which was part of Pompey's theater and was recommended later by Ovid as a place to find female company.

12–13. C'm'ere . . . Ye Labor of Hercules: The Latin is uncertain; it has been suggested that Catullus is playing with a pun on a supposed Greek word, camerion, meaning brassiere. If so, Catullus asks for "Camerium" and the prostitutes show him that they do not wear a brassiere. This interpretation seems to be confirmed by Catullus's complaint that it is a "Labor of Hercules" to put up with Camerius: one of Hercules' labors was to steal the girdle of an Amazon, Hippolyte.

57

This poem is the most virulent of Catullus's attacks on Caesar and so is generally thought to be the poem responsible for Caesar's statement that Catullus had placed an everlasting stigma on him. See the notes to poem 29 for the story of their reconciliation. Although the charges of literary pretension, of sodomy and promiscuity, were typical enough in the political invective of the time, the degree of Catullus's contempt and the appearance of this poem in a book which Catullus hoped would win him literary fame make his abuse particularly stinging. If the general background of the poem is Rome, then it was probably written before 58 B.C.E. when Caesar left Rome for Gaul.

1–2. butt-fucks, cock-sucking Caesar: Although homosexuality between freeborn males had been banned in Rome by the *lex Scantinia* (ca. 50 B.C.E.), homosexuality itself was more widely tolerated than it is in modern America. Homosexuality, especially in Roman political invective, was not so much itself the object of scorn as was being the passive partner in the act: the threat of being penetrated was a fundamental threat to male virility and power, the act of being the penetrator was a display of authority and manliness. This rhetoric is, of course, not unfamiliar to modern analysis of rape or to Americans who have listened to the humor of comics like Richard Pryor over the years (" . . . next thing I know I have my pants down around my knees an' I'm saying, 'Jus don't stick it in too far, yo' Honor!'"). One may also reasonably argue that "sexuality" in American prisons is a rhetoric which reflects political dominance and passivity much as it does in Catullus.

5. <u>Formian rank</u>: Mamurra hailed from Formiae, an ancient city of Latium; compare poems 41. 4 and 43. 5.

6. <u>ooze</u>: The political and ethical decline felt by many during the late Republic was often described as a disease.

6. <u>indelible ink</u>: Despite Catullus's differences with the particulars of a severe conservative Roman moral outlook, he often suggests that art and ethics are intertwined. Here the sexual perversity of Caesar and Mamurra is described as if it were writing. Both were poets.

8. <u>litteratini</u>: The charge of literary pretentiousness, like the charge of being uneducated and not knowing it, was common. In Catullus, however, literary failure often was expressed in vigorously sexual language (e.g., poem 16*), just as literary success had its sexual overtones (see poem 50).

10. <u>rivals, allies</u>: According to Suetonius, Caesar's soldiers often sang a short jingle about their general which went: "Gentlemen, watch your wives: We're leading in a bald adulterer. In Spain you fucked away your gold; here you took out a loan." It is also recorded that Caesar was called "a man for every woman and a woman for every man."

58

This poem is addressed to a Caelius whom scholars have been hesitant to identify with M. Caelius Rufus, friend of Cicero and the lover of Clodia after Catullus. The reason for the hesitation seems to be that Catullus addresses Caelius as a sympathetic friend when Caelius should be a rival for Lesbia's love.

3. <u>loved more than himself or his kinsmen</u>: An echo of poem 8. 6 above. The reference to "kinsmen" places Catullus's adulterous love for an older married woman in the context of Roman concerns with family and the connections within the political and social body that kinship provides. There is a tension in Catullus's poetry between the stock Roman values of piety, faithfulness, and integrity, and the nature of his love affair, which was a betrayal of those very values. If Lesbia betrayed his emotional commitment to her, he had himself already betrayed the only ethical and moral grounds on which he could claim to have been wronged.

5. <u>jerking off</u>: The exact meaning of the Latin term, no doubt a vulgar obscenty, is unknown to us. It is a metaphor from a word which elsewhere means "to strip the bark off of a tree." Speculation about the exact meaning of the obscenity includes masturbation, fellation, and vigorous intercourse. However this applies to Lesbia's actions, one senses that the image for a Roman would have been vivid, particular, and pornographic.

5. <u>Remus's grandsons</u>: In his poem to Cicero, poem 49, Catullus had similarly referred to the "great-grandsons of Romulus." The two, Romulus and Remus, were the twins who founded Rome. They fell into a dispute about the name of the new city and Romulus killed Remus. For later Romans the story became emblematic of the years of civil war in which Romans killed other Romans. Most scholars here refer only to the greatness of Rome's past and ignore the possible reference to Rome's foundation in a fundamental act of betrayal, the murder of one brother by another. It is at least arguable that, if Catullus felt his love for Lesbia rivaled the love of a man for the male continuers of his family, then her betrayal of that love could be imagined as a kind of fratricide. See also poem 68. 119–126.

63

This is one of the several great and powerful poems in Catullus's corpus. It is loosely based on the myth of Attis, a Phrygian god who, like Adonis, is a vegetative deity and whose death and resurrection symbolize the cycle of nature. In this poem, however, Catullus tells the story of a young Greek boy, Attis, who in fanatic devotion to the Great Mother Goddess Cybele (also known as Cybebe), castrates himself and then awakens from his trance to discover and regret what he has done. He is driven into the service of Cybele as one of her Galli, the eunich priests whose ritual castration was meant to re-enact the madness and self-mutilation of Attis, the god.

At this time in Rome, the cult of Cybele was celebrated under strict supervision annually at the Megalesia, a festival held on April 4. Roman citizens were not allowed to participate.

The poem is written in a strange and frenetic rhythm called the "galliambic meter." It may be read as an allegory on the vulnerability of male sexuality, as a lament for the political self-mutilation of the Roman aristocracy in the past and current years of civil war, as an evocation and deprecation of that mysterious implosion of divinity into our lives which may make us turn ourselves into something almost unrecognizable, as an awesome tribute to the ineluctable presence of the barbaric in the woods, in ourselves, in the march of priests, and in the goddess. The poem operates across the boundaries of male and female, civilized and barbaric, secular and divine, sane and possessed, and Greek and Roman. The critical challenge is to account for all of the poem's references; there are many fine accounts which privilege one or the other of these polarities.

The poem as a whole may be more easily grasped if it is outlined:

1–5	Narrative introduction	
6–34	Frenzy	
	6–11	Frenzy of Attis
		12–26 Attis's ecstatic song
	27–34	Frenzy of the Gallae
35–38	Sleep	
39–73	Repentance	
	39–47	Return to the shore
		48–73 Attis's speech of despair
	74–77	Escape
78–90	Return to Cybele	
	78–83	Speech of Cybele
		84–90 Recapture
91–93	Prayer to Goddess	

1. <u>in his racing ship</u>: Attis is not an oriental worshipper of the Great Mother Goddess, but a Greek who has been possessed to travel to Asia Minor to worship a foreign deity.

2. <u>Phrygian grove</u>: Line 30, ". . . up Ida's green slopes," indicates that the reference here is to the forests on Mt. Ida in the Troad near Troy, in the northwest corner of Asia Minor. Troy was important personally to Catullus as the place where his brother died; see poem 101.

3. <u>the Goddess's tree-ringed precinct</u>: This would be a grove consecrated to the goddess.

9. your tambourine, Cybele: The tympanum, a hoop stretched with oxhide, was especially associated with the worship of Cybele.

12. Gallae: The worshippers of Cybele were generally called the Galli (a masculine noun); the feminine, Gallae, is unusual.

13. Lady of Dindymon: Mt. Dindymon lay in eastern Phrygia.

17. Venus: Venus is the goddess of sexual, often procreative, love.

22. oboes' flaring bells: An Asiatic reed instrument with a curving horn-shaped bell.

23. Maenads: Properly, Maenads were worshippers of Dionysus; however, the ecstatic cults of Cybele and Dionysus had been conflated by other writers before Catullus. The Maenads traditionally held a thyrsus, a staff wreathed with ivy.

26. tarantellas: The Latin refers to the wild but ritual dances of the very Roman Arval brothers and the *Salii*, or "leaping priests." The effect of likening the ritual dances of the priests of Mars to the ecstatic worship of the Great Mother is strange. The *Salii* celebrated their festival in March and danced around the city carrying sacred shields (compare the tambourines above) and chanting ancient prayers that were probably not fully understood by the priests or their audience.

34. an untamed heifer: Heifers were sacrificed to the Mother Goddess.

44. his divine wife: This is a learned allusion to Pasithea, one of the Graces, whom Hera promises to Sleep during the Trojan War if he would put Zeus to sleep so that she can aid the Greeks.

61. plaza, track, wrestling ring, gymnasium: These are the places where a Greek young man would go to exercise and to be seen, often by an older male lover.

66. warmed my doorstep nightly: A popular young man would have a following of admirers, some of whom would serenade him in the evening after a dinner party; the speaker alludes here and with the flowers of the next line to a type of song that became a standard genre of love elegy, the *paraclausithyron*, or "song before the closed door."

77. Her lions: Cybele is typically represented in both literature and art as riding in a chariot drawn by lions.

80, 81. him, him, this man: It is striking that for Attis and for the narrator she is a woman, but for the goddess he is still a man. One may speculate that Attis's incipient noncompliance is a kind of "masculine" self-assertion in the eyes of Cybele.

81. too freely: Freedom of action and freedom of speech were becoming in the final years of the Republic important issues for the aristocracy which found these freedoms so often denied to them by their own fears or by the presence of naked power.

86. worked itself up: Just as Attis had done.

92–94. The concluding prayer is often noted as a closural technique of Alexandrian art. If the content of the narrative did not threaten to spill out of the poem into the lives of the poet and his listeners, there would be no need to pray.

68

This poem presents one of the most intractable problems in Catullan scholarship: was it originally one poem or two? The first forty lines are written as a verse letter to a man whose name remains disputed: Manius, Manlius, or Mallius. Then lines 41–162 address the Muses and concern a favor done to Catullus by Allius. Since the end of the poem returns to the language and concerns of the beginning in such a way that it seems to respond to the request of Mallius, some have accepted an emendation that gives the addressee of the letter the name Allius. These critics argue that it is difficult to believe that Catullus addressed lines so similiar now to Mallius, now to Allius. For others, however, that lines 20–24 are recalled almost identically in lines 92–96 suggests that we do have two poems here. Their argument includes the claim that in lines 19–26 Catullus has abandoned love and so these lines are incompatible with lines 133–162, in which his girl is "my life, who, living, makes life sweet to me." All in all, I am inclined to believe without strong conviction that we have two separate poems: one an apology to his friend in a poetic letter for not being able to write a poem; the other a Hellenistic poem, intricate in organization, experimental in its combination of mythology and personal experience, and a precursor of Roman elegiac poetry.

1–40: 68a

Catullus is at home in Verona shortly after the death of his brother in Asia Minor. He has received a letter from a friend, whose unhappy love life has moved him to ask from Catullus a gift of Venus and the Muses. Catullus complains that because of his situation he has neither the desire nor the resources to respond to Mallius's request.

3. shipwrecked man: Unhappy lovers were regularly cast in the figure of shipwrecked sailors, appropriate in part because Venus, the goddess of love, was also a goddess of the sea. See, for instance, Horace *Odes* I 5.

5, 7. Venus, Muses: The two essential ingredients of Catullus's life and that of his friends; not only were they necessary but they were inextricably joined: a poet's girlfriend must be herself poetic, a veritable Sappho, a Lesbia. Compare poem 50 where the writing of poetry is itself referred to in sexual terms.

11. Mallius: Otherwise unknown. See further below on line 42.

12. a protégé's obligations: Presumably, Mallius aided Catullus when he first came to Rome and so Catullus feels "a protégé's obligation" to the man. Others, convinced that this poem is a single work, believe that the *hospitis officium*, which could also be translated as "my obligation to my host" looks forward for clarification to line 68, "lent me and my mistress a house."

13. seas of bad luck: Catullus takes the traditional figure of unhappy love already employed by Mallius and turns it into a general image of unhappiness caused by both Venus and the death of his brother.

15. dress whites: The Roman boy would normally begin to dress in a plain white toga, a symbol of manhood, at about the age of fifteen or sixteen.

17. the Goddess: Venus herself, of course.

20. Brother taken from me: In the course of Catullus's book as we have it, the reader would already know from poem 65 that the poet's brother died near Troy. There he had said, "Will I never see you again, my brother, dearer than life? But I will certainly love you; the songs I sing will always be sad because of your death," 65. 10–12. The address to the brother, which here interrupts the letter to Mallius, recalls the expression of grief which is a traditional part of a ritual lament. The purpose of a lament is to express and then to set aside one's grief. Here the lament is not over, the grief is not set aside.

22. <u>our whole household</u>: This typically Roman concern for family is prominent throughout Catullus's poetry, most strikingly, perhaps, as the metaphor by which he imagines and measures his love for Lesbia; see esp. poem 72.

27. <u>Verona</u>: Catullus's home in northern Italy.

30. In other words, it is not something for which Catullus should feel shame, but rather something that increases his misery and for which others should feel pity.

33. <u>my stockpile</u>: A fairly clear allusion to the compositional needs of a Roman Alexandrian poet. He needed an extensive library, for he was expected to use the poetry of Greece, and especially Alexandria, for translations, models, and allusions.

41–162: 68b

At this point, Catullus's letter either ends and a new poem begins, or his letter, already a poem, becomes the poetic response to Allius's request for some poetry. The great Catullus scholar, Wheeler, compared the intricate organization of lines 41–162 to nested Chinese boxes. An outline of the structure will make apparent what he had in mind:

> 41–50: Allius, *actio gratiarum* ("expression of gratitude")
> > 51–72: Lesbia
> > > 73–86: Laodamia
> > > > 87–90: Troy
> > > > > 91–100: Catullus's brother
> > > > 101–104: Troy
> > > 105–132: Laodamia
> > 133–150: Lesbia
> 151–162: Allius, *actio gratiarum*

Critics have found the construction heavy and awkward, the composition garrish and overdone, the elements poorly fused. They have also, however, recognized the power of this poem, whether they preferred to speak of intense personal feeling, of guilt and psychological displacements, or of the familiar analytic pattern by which Catullus identifies with the feminine (here Laodamia) in his models.

41. <u>Muses</u>: Catullus reverses the typical pattern in which the Muses, daughters of Memory, convey a story to the poet who tells it to his audience. In the typical pattern, the poet inherits a public record and a public tradition which it is his duty to keep alive; in the Catullan version the poet gives life and significance to a personal experience which he relates to the Muses ("No, I'll tell you the tale," 45); the Muses thereafter preserve that experience.

42. <u>Allius</u>: We do not know who this Allius was.

47. [<u>Muses</u>]: A line is missing from our manuscripts; this addition maintains the meter and the flow of the poem.

49–50. The image seems to be that of a grave monument which has been abandoned and is covered with spider webs. The spider web is a common symbol of neglect going back to Homer, Od. 16. 34–35, where Odysseus's bed is said to lie empty of sleepers with webs upon it.

51. <u>Cyprus's two-faced Goddess</u>: Venus, goddess of love, who had several old and famous sites of worship in Cyprus.

53. <u>Sicilian Etna's</u>: Mt. Etna, the famous volcano in Sicily, was supposed to cover the workshop of Vulcan where he forged the thunderbolts of Jupiter.

54. <u>Thermopylae</u>: The pass of Thermopylae connected northern Greece to central Greece; the hot springs there gave the pass its name: *Thermopylae* means "hot gates" in Greek.

57–60. The comparison here has a Homeric heritage: tears with a stream recalls *Iliad* 9. 14f and 16. 3f, both instances of heroes weeping in despair of what to do. The image of a clear mountain stream recalls the Callimachean image of finely wrought poetry in the Alexandrian mode.

65. <u>Pollux, Castor</u>: Pollux and Castor were the twin brothers of Helen and were known as the Dioscuri. According to the *Iliad*, they died while Helen was at Troy. On their death they were made into gods, the protectors of sailors, and are identified with the constellation Gemini.

68. <u>mistress</u>: All commentators assume that this is Lesbia, and it is hard to imagine that she is someone else. If so, she is a married woman.

72. <u>her sandal squeaked; she hesitated</u>: Generally taken as bad omens; any hesitation by a bride at the threshhold was especially to be avoided.

73. <u>Laodamia</u>: In Alexandrian style, Catullus alludes to the myth of Laodamia and Protesilaus. Protesilaus had married Laodamia but had only one day of married life with her before leaving as commander of the Greek forces from Phylace to fight at Troy for the return of Helen. Protesilaus was doomed, however, to be the first Greek killed at Troy. Thus he left behind, according to Homer, a grieving widow and a half-built house. Latin authors elaborated the tale in various ways. See, for instance, Propertius I 19. 7–10. Catullus moves away from any heroic interest in Protesilaus to an elegiac interest in Laodamia. She is used to connect the theme of Catullus's love in Italy with death near Troy; she symbolizes the beauty and passion of Lesbia; and, then, she becomes a paradigm for the house unfinished and the grief that Catullus himself feels in regard to both Lesbia and his brother. She is thus both Lesbia and Catullus. In this regard, the common use of her by Latin poets as an image of fidelity to Protesilaus stands in contrast to the actions of Lesbia (especially above at lines 27–30), although she may adorn Catullus's own image of his fidelity.

74. <u>approached his house</u>: This important moment in the marriage ritual recalls line 68, in which Catullus is grateful to Mallius because he "lent me and my mistress a house," and in doing so measures the moral distance between Catullus's love for a married woman and the love of Laodamia for her husband on her wedding day. Note how the poem ends: "it's not as if she'd walked down the aisle on her father's arm, | come home...," 145–146.

75. <u>for no victim</u>: The notion that Protesilaus or Laodamia had neglected the appropriate sacrifice is either a Catullan invention or a Hellenistic allusion to an obscure version of the story. The idea that the "Gods' blessing" must be won, that a contract is established through sacrifice between gods and men, is a distinctly Roman notion.

77. <u>Nemesis</u>: Mentioned playfully at the end of Catullus's poem to Licinius, poem 50, Nemesis is the god of retribution, or of changed circumstance for the proud, the presumptuous, and the arrogant.

85. <u>the Fates knew</u>: A reference to an oracle that declared that the first Greek to set foot on Trojan soil would lose his life. There are two versions of the story: one, that only the Fates knew that Protesilaus would be first to set foot on Trojan soil; the other that Protesilaus, hearing the oracle, sacrificed his own life for his men.

87. <u>the rape of Helen</u>: Paris, the young and beautiful son of Priam, abducted Helen, the wife of Menelaus, from her home in Sparta and took her to his home in Troy. This was the cause of the Trojan War.

103.   the harlot: Helen is called a "harlot" because she is often represented as having gone with Paris willingly. This does not contradict the notion that she was "raped," for in the ancient world "rape" is literally the seizure of a man's property; it is something one man does to another, not primarily something done to a woman.

104.   leisurely hours: The Latin word here translated "leisurely hours" is the same word that is translated as "idle ways" at the end of poem 51.

109.   Cyllenian Pheneus: A characteristically Alexandrian allusion. Beside Mt. Cyllene, near the town of Pheneus in Arcadia, there was said to be an underground channel which had been dug out by Hercules. Hercules is called the son of pseudo-Amphitryo (line 111) because he was really the son of Zeus who, disguised as Amphitryo, slept with Amphitryo's wife, Hercules' mother. Hercules was compelled to endure twelve labors, the fifth of which was to kill the man-eating birds of Lake Stymphalus (see line 114). His "mere-mortal master" is Eurystheus, to whom he was at that time a slave. On his death he was rewarded by apotheosis (being made a god) (see line 115) and marriage to a goddess, Hebe (see line 116).

119–126.   The comparison of Laodamia's love to that of a grandfather for his only grandchild is a strikingly Roman image which puts the emotional emphasis on affection and family security rather than passion and desire. The reference in line 125–126 to legacy hunters, those who attempted to wheedle their way into the wills of old men without heirs, is a reference to a common Roman practice, one which like gold diggers today was probably more of a rhetorical topos than a real societal ill. "Vulture" seems to have been a common term for such legacy hunters.

127–132.   The second comparison of Laodamia to a dove takes a common image of marital fidelity and, by emphasizing the "nibbling kisses, more wanton than any woman," predicates that fidelity on erotic desire. Pliny, in his *Natural History,* says of the doves, "they do not violate their marriage trust and they preserve their common home; they do not abandon their nest, unless unmarried or widowed."

135.   Cupid: Cupid traditionally attended happy lovers, although he was usually naked. Here he appears as an attendant to a bride or to a goddess. The crocus-yellow of his dress suggests a marriage ceremony.

137.   Catullus: It is characteristic of Catullus to address himself in the third person.

140.   Juno: The wife of Jupiter, who had to endure his many erotic liaisons with others, both divine and mortal. Again Catullus chooses to compare himself to a female. Clodia Metelli, the woman most think was the real Lesbia, was given by Cicero the stock epic epithet for Juno; he called her "cow-eyed Clodia."

143–144.   There are apparently some lines missing in the manuscripts between line 143 and line 144.

147.   she gave you stolen goods: She was, then, more like Helen, the cause of the Trojan War, the reason that Troy is the "mass grave of Asia and Europe," than she was like Laodamia.

150.   dazzling white: Particularly lucky days were distinguished on calendars by a white mark.

151, 154.   The words, "this gift, . . . such as it is, composed of a poem," are often taken as reference to the request of Mallius in lines 9–10. The mention of "corrosive rust" seems rather clearly to be a reference to lines 43 and 49–50.

156.   Justice: A reference to the golden age when the goddess Justice walked among men and gave them just rewards.

70

In form and subject, this epigram recalls epigram 25 of Callimachus: "Kallignotos swore to Ionis never to hold another man or woman dearer than her. He swore; but they speak truly that lovers' oaths do not enter the ears of immortals. Now he warms with fire for a man, and of the poor girl, as of Megarians, there is no reckoning or account."

72

Poem 72 is paired across an intervening epigram with poem 70, as is often the case in Catullus's collection; see, for example, 5 and 7, and 41 and 43. Here the poet uncovers his response to what in poem 70 was portrayed as the facts of the case.

1. knew only Catullus: This may be a reference to the conservative ideal for a Roman woman, that is, to know only one man in her entire life, to be *univira*. It was an ideal more honored in the breach than practice. Compare Propertius IV 11.

2. you'd not take Jove before me: There may be here a reference to Cicero's nickname for Clodia Metelli, "cow-eyed," recalling the Homeric epithet for Jupiter's nagging wife, "cow-eyed Hera [=Juno]."

4. sons-in-law: While this emphasis may seem strange now, fathers would make sons-in-law the emblem of love and concern—this only reflects the traditional role of women as those who bring together the males of two different families in order to produce new males; it is a patriarchal concern. Catullus chooses such a conventional image from the conservative mechanisms of Roman family life to express his feelings of affection, fidelity, and self-interest in an essentially adulterous relationship. In poem 76 he will similarly characterize his part of this affair in terms of piety and contractual fidelity.

5. costs me more: Catullus typically uses the language of counting and accounting to express emotions.

7–8. A form of expression that makes a whole epigram by itself in poem 85.

73

A poem on the ingratitude of a friend, the language of which resembles the poems of Lesbia's infidelity, 72 and 76. The sense of trust and fidelity that Catullus appeals to in his relationship with Lesbia is one that was entirely borrowed from the language and concerns of male friendships, of *amicitia*, or the bonds of political and familial self-interest.

2. conscientious: The Latin term *pius* has, in addition to "conscientious," the ethical and religous connotations of "pious": all of one's obligations to the gods and to oaths, to family and friends, and to the state.

75

This epigram analyzes and develops the situation of poem 70 and the feelings of poem 72. If Catullus arranged these epigrams in the order in which we have them, the effect is striking: each effort to give epigrammatic closure to Lesbia's betrayal is inadequate and is followed by a new effort. First, Catullus encapsulates the betrayal; then, he summarizes his own emotional conflict about the event; now, he recognizes that for him there is no way out of emotional conflict whether Lesbia becomes faithful or not.

1. <u>crime</u>: The Latin term, *culpa*, may apply to infidelity and furtive affairs, but it also applies to legal negligence or liability.

2. <u>devotion</u>: The Latin term, *officium*, may also refer to the official and public duties of a statesman and citizen, or the mutual responsibilities of client and patron.

3. <u>like you</u>: The same expression ends poem 72 and refers to the good will that allows men to act together in good faith.

76

This is the longest of Catullus's epigrams (poems 69–116) and together with poem 68 is taken by many critics to mark the beginning of serious Roman love elegy. Its concern with self-expression and self-analysis and its mood of victimization all look in that direction. The poem recalls several other poems, but most especially poem 8. The crucial question in the interpretation of the poem is the relationship between Catullus's concern at the beginning with a clear conscience and Lesbia's infidelity and betrayal of an illicit affair.

2. <u>past kindnesses . . . with clear conscience</u>: Most of the terms of the opening are the same as those discussed above in the poems that lead up to this poem. "Past kindnesses," however, is a further escalation of the failed "good will" Catullus refers to when he says that his mind cannot like Lesbia. "Kindnesses" refer to the material actions which demonstrate his prior "good will" or "like" of Lesbia.

5. <u>Catullus</u>: Apparently Catullus was the first poet in the western tradition to speak to and about himself in the third person (compare 68. 137). The device had its origins in drama.

12. <u>'poor dear'</u>: Most likely a reference to poem 8, which began "Poor dear Catullus!"

20. <u>poisonous putrefaction</u>: The moral language of austere old men and the moral language of Catullus the lampoonist both saw the ills of the late Republic in terms of a disease infecting the body politic. Now, the same image is turned on Catullus himself, both in pity and in condemnation.

21. <u>into my deepest marrow</u>: Compare what is often thought of as the first poem to Lesbia, poem 51, especially line 10.

25. <u>set this loathsome illness aside</u>: Compare this with line 13: "to set old love aside of a sudden." The Latin further emphasizes the identity of Catullus's love (*amorem*) and Catullus's sickness (*morbum*) by two phrases that sound almost identical: "to set aside this love" = *deponere amorem*; "to set aside this illness" = *deponere morbum*.

83

An epigram from the happier days when love was a game, a light-hearted drama, where only fools did not understand their role. Compare this epigram with poem 92.

1. husband: If Lesbia was Clodia Metelli, then her husband was Q. Metellus Celer, who died in 59 B.C.E. This might help us date this epigram, but it remains speculative.

85

Perhaps the most famous of Catullus's epigrams. In a form that may recall the formal questions and answers of school recitations Catullus reveals his own inability to understand or to come to grips with his feelings. Joyce has offered two translations, which together help encompass the possible readings of the original.

86

An epigrammatic version of poem 43 in that it celebrates Lesbia and the totality of what makes her attractive. Here it is especially that elusive quality of "sparkle" and the inner quality of "wit."

1. Quintia: Unidentified.

6. this Venus: A veritable goddess, to be sure, but, since Venus is the goddess of sex, we may paraphrase this quality as "sex appeal"—which for Catullus means wit, sparkle, a pretty face, and a great body.

92

In the context of the other Lesbia poems, particularly 72 and 75, it is not easy to read epigram 92 at face value, as if all Catullus were saying was that Lesbia's anger reveals her love. If Catullus arranged the poems in this section of the manuscript, he has asked his readers to read against the grain of his own poem: perhaps Lesbia really is angry and this is the beginning of the end; perhaps Catullus just never heard her real anger, or did hear it and deluded himself; perhaps he didn't really come to grips with his own anger and covered it with a cliché about lovers' quarrels. Catullus has compelled his readers to not quite believe his own words in a poem which is about how we often do not say what we mean.

93

We are told that Catullus's family in Verona was friendly with Caesar. After Catullus wrote some contemptuous verses against Caesar, like those of poems 29 and 57, he made up to Caesar. Here Catullus is flippant, not contemptuous.

95

A programmatic epigram celebrating the *Zmyrna* of Catullus's friend and fellow poet, C. Helvius Cinna, and contrasting that poem and its Alexandrian poetics with the *Annales* of Volusius. The manuscript is in poor shape here and editors have supplied a line for the missing fourth to fill out the sense. The poem is carefully constructed: two lines on the *Zmyrna*; two lines on Volusius; two lines on the *Zmyrna* again, and two more lines on Volusius.

1. Zmyrna: Catullus uses the Greek spelling for Cinna's narrative poem on the incestuous passion of Smyrna for her father. The poem was an epyllion, or little epic, written in a learned and allusive style with elaborate mythological detail. We know that it needed a commentary shortly after it was published.

1–2. nine long harvests | nine long winters: The Alexandrian school of new poetry followed Callimachus in favoring short but carefully worked and refined poetry.

3. The Horror of Hatria: The line as translated relies on an editorial emendation which gives us an adjective meaning "of Hatria," a variant spelling for "of the Adriatic." This makes Catullus refer to a man from near the Adriatic, the region of the Po River, and this will be a geographical reference to the home of Volusius. The manuscripts, however, give the name Hortensius which is taken to be Quintus Hortensius Hortalus, Cicero's rival in oratory and a writer of light occasional verse. He was about thirty years older than Catullus, but from what we know, he seems to have been sympathetic to Catullus's verse. We do not know of any long poem that he wrote, and so editors and commentators guess that he must have attempted a longer poem, something in the more conservative tradition of poets who prided themselves on the quantity and speed of their often extemporaneous compositions, that is, something like what Volusius wrote. The real problem with accepting the manuscript reading is that with it the poem is unbalanced: why compare Cinna with Hortensius and then with Volusius?

5. the river Satrachus: A river in Cyprus connected with the legend of Adonis, Smyrna's son. The oblique and learned compliment, then, is that the fame of Cinna's poem on Smyrna has reached and so pleased the very river it celebrates.

7. Po: Volusius's poetry will not get any further than his home in Padua where it will be used to wrap fish. If in the reference to the river Satrachus above there is a reference to a rite for Adonis in which an image of the god is washed and ceremonially dressed; here Catullus provides a witty mock-ceremony appropriate for Volusius's poetry.

9. turgid Antimachus: Antimachus of Colophon was a contemporary of Callimachus who was ridiculed for his "fat writing." Some editors want to read lines 9–10 as a separate epigram; however, if we take lines 9–10 as part of the preceding, Catullus generalizes his own particular poetic disputes by reference to the polemics of his literary ancestors.

10. Philetas: A contemporary of Callimachus whose poetry exemplified the refined and learned style of the Alexandrians. Catullus's friend, Cinna, a poet of the Alexandrian school, is implicitly compared with one of his renowned Greek models. See Propertius III 1. 1.

101

In the imagined occasion of this poem, the poet stands before the tomb of his dead brother in the Troad, presumably sometime during or after his sojourn in Bithynia in 57 B.C.E. Such an occasion is the one assumed by most sepulchral epigrams, a traditional genre in which the dead halt and speak to passersby from their monuments.

Catullus has, typically, modified the conceit; he has chosen to stop and to speak to the mute tomb of his brother. The sad story is the tale of the living as well as the mischance of the dead. The simple change effects enormous pathos and allows a fairly limited form to gather to itself much more far-reaching effects.

   1.   Many the nations and many the oceans: As Catullus stands before his brother's tomb near Troy, he echoes the opening words of Homer's *Odyssey*. Homer's poem had told of the trials suffered by Odysseus as he returned home from the destruction of Troy to his wife and son in Ithaca. Catullus's journey is in many respects the inverse of Odysseus's journey, a point which seems even more apparent if we remember Catullus's words on his brother's death in poem 68: "our whole household lies in the grave beside you."

   3.   mourner's parting gifts: Offerings of wine, milk, honey, and flowers were generally made at gravesites to the spirits of the dead.

   4.   (useless!): The only vestige of the curse (e.g., "What good does it do? The gods are cruel!") typical of a formal lament. In the formal lament, such a complaint becomes in itself the ground for beginning consolation: since it does no good, we must endure; time makes it easier. Compare, for instance, Horace *Odes* I 24. Here Catullus does not construct such a forward movement; by line 6 we have returned in the lament proper to a point which usually precedes the curse.

   6.   This line is an echo of poem 68. 20 and 92.

109

This poem recalls Catullus's earlier struggles with the ultimate meaning of Lesbia's words.

   5–6.   Catullus casts his love affair in the terms of the severe traditional and conservative language of state, ethics, and politics in Rome.

Tibullus

BIBLIOGRAPHY

Ball, Robert J. "Tibullus the Elegist," *Hypomnemata* 77 (Göttingen: Vandenhoeck and Ruprecht, 1983).

Bright, David F. *Haec Mihi Fingebam: Tibullus in his World* (Leiden: Brill, 1978).

Cairns, Francis. *Tibullus: A Hellenistic Poet at Rome* (New York: Cambridge University Press, 1979).

Book I

Tibullus published his first collection of elegies between 27 and 25 B.C.E., at a time when Ovid was about fifteen and just after Propertius had produced his *Monobiblos*. It is a book of ten elegies, recalling in length and structure both Vergil's *Eclogues*, published in 37 B.C.E., and Horace's *Sermones*, published in 35 B.C.E. In this context, it seems clear that Tibullus intends his collection of elegies to be compared with his contemporaries' collections of hexameter verse. His poems are more intimate and withdrawn. In their length, in particular, being longer than the standard love elegy, they recall on the one hand the precedent set by Catullus 68 and on the other the general length of Vergil's *Eclogues*. Tibullus used "subjective love elegy" to examine and offer his own view of the major issues Vergil had addressed in the *Eclogues*: power, poetry and creativity, love, fantasy and withdrawal, war and peace. All these were subjects congenial to the melancholy and overly philosophical friend Horace has described. While the poems often indulge an escapist fantasy of love and a kind of soft country piety mingled with religious ritualism, the harder world of empire and war, especially as represented by the figure of Messalla, is never far away. It is against this world that Tibullus defines himself.

Tibullus rejects both the learned mythology and etiology of his Hellenistic predecessors and the Gallan emphasis in life and poetry on the world of military glory. Gallus had been the warrior poet, inventor of love elegy and friend of Augustus, ally in the campaign against Cleopatra, prefect of Egypt. However, by 26 B.C.E., he had offended Augustus and was forced to commit suicide. It is not likely to be accidental that Tibullus defined his elegiac vision as one dependent upon freedom from the public demands of military ambition.

I offer an outline of the entire contents of Book I so that the reader may have some sense of the book's structure and of what has been selected from what.

1: Introductory philosophy of life
    2 and 3: Delia
                2. separation by guard and husband
                3. separation by war and illness
            4: Priapus: a lecture on being a successful homosexual lover
    5 and 6: Delia
                5. take me back, Delia
                6. Delia is with another lover
            7: Messalla
    8 and 9: Marathus
                8. Marathus is in love: Phloe, be kind
                9. Marathus has had an affair with an older, rich man
10: Concluding philosophy of life

I. 1

As the first poem in a book of Augustan poetry is programmatic, so this poem can be and has been read as introducing the poetic biases and allegiances that will inform Tibullus's work. Two things, however, are striking about this poem: 1) it avoids the characteristically explicit rejection of the public and grandiose genres; 2) it indicates or exemplifies the characteristic features and concerns of Tibullan elegy but does not label them as such. Given the polemics of literary reference in the Augustan writers, this is, in itself, a striking posture.

The poem may also be read as a kind of introductory philosophy of life. Here we may emphasize Tibullus's Epicurean concerns with retirement and content-ment, his rejection of wealth and the ceaselessly acquisitive energies of war represent-ed by his patron Messalla, the generally conservative value he places on the farm and the gods of the household hearth, and his elegiac pre-nostalgia (following Propertius I 17) for the moment of perfect closure when Delia weeps for him as he breathes his last. The elegant, smooth, and sometimes dreamy surface of this poem belies and disguises its several tensions: the poet rejects wealth and glory, but expects all the young to weep at his funeral, and he finds Messalla's action fitting and proper; he wants the small poor farm he says he has but remembers his lost family wealth in the language of Vergil's complaint about the land confiscations; he expects Delia to be at his side as he dies but does not think love is appropriate for the old. As the poem and poet drift along, it is as if Tibullus's dream cannot find a point at which to rest: as soon as the pious countryside and poverty console and comfort him, Messalla appears with wealth and power and Delia and lethargy and dreams of death.

1–6: The opening lines are a version of a *priamel*, that is, a rhetorical form by which the choices and preferences of others are set in contrast to the personal choice of the poet. In the Roman tradition, the *priamel* is associated with the rejection of the common, the public, and the ambitious; see Horace *Odes* I 1. Here as elsewhere in this poem, one can read the philosophical preference as an allegory of the poetic preference: not the large and loud epic, but the slender, private elegy.

1–4:   Tibullus begins his elegiac career with reference to a significant feature of the career of his predecessor, Gallus. Military service was a traditional means of acquiring wealth in Rome. When Tibullus declares that his elegiac posture depends on an opposition to military ambition, he recalls a posture adopted by Catullus; but he also creates a contrast between his life as a poet with that of his patron Messalla. This contrast and its thematic implications will continue to concern Tibullus throughout his poetry.

7.   When planting season: Just as the rejection of military glory is a non-Roman posture, so this praise of the country and the farmer's piety is a distinctly Roman attitude. Tibullus has, in effect, split the old republican ideal, represented in the figure of Cincinnatus, and expressed by the elder Cato: "From farmers are born the most brave men and the most vigorous soldiers; pious and stable wealth follows. . . ."

9.   Hope: Arguably one of the most characteristically Tibullan responses to the world, and perhaps a reference to the goddess Hope who had several temples in Rome. Tibullus returns to eulogize Hope in the last poem of his second book: "By now I would have ended my ills in death, but Hope trustingly nourishes life and always says that tomorrow will be better."

11–12.   lonely stumps: Apparently a typical ancient superstition required one to pour libations or place flowers on stumps or stones at crossroads and to make prayers there. There may be a reference here to one or more of the following: Terminus, one of the gods of bound-aries; Hecate, whose worship typically took place at crossroads; and the *Lares Compitales,* or the guardian deities of lands that border on the crossroads.

14.   patron god of fields: The expression seems to be purposefully vague. In addition to the deities mentioned above, one may add Silvanus, god of fields and flocks; Mars, god of boundaries; and others. Vergil at the beginning of his *Georgics* was able to list twelve gods of agriculture while only repeating a few of the twelve that Varro had similarly listed at the beginning of his prose work on agriculture.

15.   Ceres: The Greek goddess of the grain and so of agriculture.

17.   Priapus: A god of fertility frequently found in gardens with an erect red phallus and a sickle.

20.   Once prosperous, Lares: The *Lares Compitales* mentioned above in the note to lines 11–12. Tibullus seems to allude to the recent history of land confiscations and the general disruption of agriculture caused locally by civil wars. There are several echoes in the Latin of Vergil's first *Eclogue*, in which one shepherd who is being forced from his lands meets another who has won his freedom and been allowed to stay.

20.   take your gift: Probably a reference to the Ambarvalia, an annual festival for the ritual purification of the fields by the farmers and of the state by the Arval priests. It is the occasion of poem II 1.

27.   Dog Star: The "dog days" of summer, so named because they set in after the rising of the constellation, *Canis Major,* or "the great dog," of which Sirius is the brightest star. They were proverbially days of unbearable heat, and it was a literary commonplace to associate the retreat to cool enclosures during the heat of these days with the poet's search for contentment, restraint, and protection. Such a cool, protected enclosure is also one of the major symbols for pastoral and by which pastoral is made to symbolize the poetic or academic life.

31.   abandoned kid: Another echo of Vergil's first *Eclogue*, in which a kid is abandoned by its mother and the shepherd does not retrieve it.

33.   please spare: The small and poor farm may have its attractions, but it, like Tibullus himself, is also vulnerable without the protections of size and wealth.

35. Pales: An ancient pastoral god whose festival, the Palilia, was also the birthday of Rome. She is offered milk and oil, as they were considered the earliest libations.

38. simple pottery is clean: Simplicity and cleanliness were ritual requirements for proper religious practice.

39. A farmer first: Tibullus represents the values of his way of life as a reflection of traditional rustic values. The Latin is filled with etymological wordplay, making this appreciation of rustic religious observance a kind of minietiology. Philosophically, this makes the farm the origin of piety; poetically, this places Tibullus in the tradition of Callimachus.

41. My father's fortune: We know that Tibullus was from an equestrian family; here we may surmise that his family had been fairly wealthy but had lost some land in land confiscation.

46. within my mistress's arms: Tibullus delays any mention of his mistress until he is considerably more than halfway through his introductory elegy, and when she does appear she is another version of protected withdrawal. The scene that follows here has several program-matic implications, none of which are explicit. First, since the pleasure felt by one secure from storms and war is typically the pleasure of Epicurean wisdom, Tibullus locates his philosophical bearing in that direction. Second, as he projects the values of his life in direct contrast with the life of action, he echoes the typical opposition between the Alexandrian interest in the small and discontinuous genres and the traditional poet's concern with war, the subject matter of epic.

53. Messalla: The first mention of the poet's patron is also postponed, although his military activities have been clearly suggested from the beginning.

55. captive: Unlike the conquering hero Messalla, Tibullus finds security in being a captive, even a slave, to his mistress.

56. Janitor-like: Tibullus recalls the setting for a *paraclausithyron*, a standard poem or song found in both comedy and love elegy which a lover sings while he imagines himself standing guard at his post outside the closed door of his mistress. Tibullus calls himself here a "Janitor" and, in so doing, both imagines himself as his mistress' slave, which may be true to his emotional state, and imagines himself as the one who controls the locked door, which converts the lover, typically locked out, into the guardian. In this and other ways, the poet attempts to convert his inert servitude into something desirable and responsible.

57. Delia: The name joins Tibullus's interest in poetry and his interest in the country in that it recalls both Apollo, the god of poets, and Diana, the virgin goddess of the hunt and of the countryside.

61. funeral pyre: Tibullus begins his collection with a reference to his final success; this is itself a confident and clever inversion of the typical procedure in which the poet is persuaded by Apollo (Delius) to write in the Callimachean fashion in the opening poem and lays claim to success and eternal fame (often in the context of his death) in the closing poem of the collection.

65. From my funeral: Here, for the elegiac poet, death becomes the fulfillment of love and elegiac nostalgia takes the place of the eternal fame sought alike by the epic hero and public man and granted by epic poetry.

66. neither maiden nor young man: By oblique reference Tibullus defines his audience; they are those who appreciate his poetry, those to whom his subjects are congenial, and those who represent the future of Rome.

68. No hair-tearing: These are the traditional signs of grief at a Roman funeral and are ordinarily thought to please the ghost of the departed. Delia is asked to spare her beauty because the Tibullan dream aspires to be a vision of perfection: the poet's corpse, the weeping cortege of youths, a few tears and tender kisses from the beautiful mistress.

69. <u>Turn now to love</u>: The topos is the amatory commonplace to "seize the day."

70. <u>Death</u>: The commentaries tell us that this is an unparalleled description of death: it is the sight of Delia that death takes away. The image is striking, both in its lack of conventionality, and because it contrasts starkly with the idealized funeral Tibullus has just imagined.

71. <u>feeble Age</u>: In the Latin the language is identical to that used in the phrase, "Let them call me sluggish, lazy too": here *iners aetas*; there (line 58) *iners vocer*.

75. <u>both general and private</u>: The metaphor of the lover as a soldier is a polemical inversion of the serious Roman distinction between what a more traditional Roman morality saw as the brave and meaningful life of manly military action and the luxurious and profligate life of the voluptary. This metaphorical equation, while found in the Roman comic writers, appears here for the first time in lyric or elegy. See Ovid *Amores* I 9 for an extended development of the metaphor.

76. <u>Let greedy men be wounded</u>: Tibullus returns to the ethical concerns of the opening. His rejection of military glory, necessary to secure his life of pleasure, has become simultaneously a rejection of an unethical life and the means to a pleasurable life.

I 2

This poem is usually thought to be a variation on the *paraclausithyron*, a genre referred to above in I 1. 56. Despite the claims of poem I 1, we are, therefore, in the city where such events apparently really took place. In the stock scene from comedy the lover, often drunk from a night of partying, stands outside his mistress's locked door and sings a song which may be part serenade and part complaint. The traditional elements of the genre as it was inherited by Roman poets include: a drunken lover with garlands and torches, a late night vigil at the door, complaints about the weather, attempts to persuade the door with violence and kisses (or the doorkeeper with bribes), and fears of the beloved's unfaithfulness. In Latin elegy, the addressee is usually the door itself, often treated as a divinity, which, because it never answers, is considered obstinate and insensitive, like the lover's mistress. Given the triangular nature of these elegiac affairs, some prominence is usually given to the girl's husband. When the lover's pleas to the door are, inevitably, ineffective, he may either depart leaving behind on the steps a token of his affection (a wreath or some verses) or simply fall asleep. (See also Propertius I 16 and Ovid *Amores* I 6.)

Having laid out and justified his vision of elegiac contentment in the first poem, he immediately discovers that the major obstacle to realizing this vision is Delia herself. Literarily, as the Tibullan lover struggles with his emotions, the *paraclausithyron* includes, adapts, and links several typical elegiac postures. There are echoes of the *praeceptor amoris* (see, for instance, Ovid *Amores* I 6), the sacred and protected lover (compare Propertius III 16, Ovid *Amores* I 6, and Horace *Odes* I 22), the lover's standard appeal to magic and witches (first appearing in love elegy in Propertius I 1), the contrast between the wealthy warrior and the simple life of the Epicurean lover (compare Horace *Odes* I 31), the lover's prophecy that others too will suffer the pangs of love (see Propertius I 7 or 9), and the lover's prayer of desperation. The *paraclausithyron* itself begins only at line 7, and critics have wondered why the scene is set in the opening verses as it is. Perhaps we really have here a drunken reverie in which the clichés of the love poet and the lover's dream of a satisfying, secure passion fail before the hard reality of Delia's closed door, symbol of her otherness. In any event, as Tibullus undercuts melancholy with self-mockery and restrains humor with gloom, his *paraclausithyron* is distinguished by its emotional and generic range and by its melancholic reflectiveness.

7.   <u>Damn you, door</u>: One may take these lines as the technical beginning of the *paraclausithyron*: the curse against the closed door, which is quickly regretted, and is followed by a curse upon the lover himself. Ovid's lover similarly changes his tone but the sequence of change is in the opposite direction: from pleading to threatening and insulting; the same is true of Horace in *Odes* III 10. Elegy I 1 had ended with the claim that "Now is the time to break | Down doors."

7.   <u>May rainstorms mildew you</u>: It was a distinctly Roman feature of the *paraclausithyron* to address the door as if it were a deity. Here the typical prayer to the door is inverted by the lover into a prayerful curse upon the door. The door is addressed in its more usual aspect in lines 13–14: "I hope you've not forgotten all my prayers . . . ."

15.   <u>You, Delia</u>: It is almost unparalleled for the lover to address the beloved in a *paraclausithyron*; our only example comes from Horace *Odes* III 7*.

22.   This scene is developed at length in Ovid *Amores* I 4. We discover here what we could not have known from elegy I 1—that Delia is married (or in concubinage) and guarded.

25.   <u>I wander through the streets</u>: Rome was a big city and streets were dangerous at night. From a later century, the Roman satirist Juvenal catalogs the dangers of the city streets at night: broken pottery flies from the windows, dirty water is poured on your head, drunks pick a fight, and robbers carry knives (*Satire* III 268–314). Tibullus here develops an erotic commonplace, that the lover has special protection from the gods. Compare Propertius I 17. 25–28; II 26. 45–46; II 33. 1–20; Ovid *Amores* III 6; and Horace *Odes* I 22.

31.   <u>No frosty winter night</u>: Finally the poet returns to the themes common in a *paraclausithyron*.

36.   The notion that Venus prefers furtive love is common; compare Catullus 7.

41–42.   An unobtrusive reference to the myth that Venus was born from the blood of Uranus when he was emasculated by his son, Saturn. The blood fell into the sea from which Venus arose. The sea was itself a common image of violent and unpredictable danger. Tibullus uses mythological reference less than any other elegist.

44.   <u>your husband</u>: The women of elegy are generally represented as freedwomen, sometimes as *meretrices*, or prostitutes. On occasion, as here, they are represented as married women; see Propertius II 23. 19–20, IV 7. 13ff and Ovid I 4. In general, there is no agreement among scholars as to their legal status.

45–55.   <u>A witch</u>: The catalog of magic powers is traditional and, like other passages in this poem, reads like a set piece.

51.   <u>sprinkling milk</u>: In primitive rituals, milk, not wine, was offered to the ghosts to appease them.

54.   <u>Medea</u>: The paradigmatic witch. With her powers she helped Jason retrieve the Golden Fleece and then escape from Colchis, first to Iolchus where Pelias has usurped the throne that belonged to Jason, and then to Corinth where Jason married the daughter of Creon. Among the various stories told of her use of magic herbs, she is said to have boiled Jason's father and renewed his youth, under the false pretext of renewing Pelias's youth to have simply boiled him, and to have given Jason's Corinthian wife a cloak that burst into flames when she wore it.

55. Hecate: One of the forms of the tri-formed goddess: Luna in the heavens, Hecate in the Underworld, and Diana on land. As Hecate, she was a goddess of boundaries and was worshipped at crossroads, particularly by witches.

62–67. A typical elegiac contradiction: when the lover sees that the precepts and powers that serve him may also serve others, he needs to claim a special dispensation or immunity. In this case, Tibullus offers the humorous proof of his immunity to the witch's power: the witch had promised to cure him of his love for Delia and she failed. Suddenly, the implied narrative background for the elegy must include desperation and an abandoned effort to leave Delia.

66. a love to share: At the moment when Tibullus cannot free himself from his love for Delia, he reverses the desperate prayer made by Catullus in poem 76: he wants the mutual love that Catullus had claimed to want no longer.

68–73. Ironheaded fool: The picture here of the wealthy soldier should be compared with the picture of Messalla in elegy I 1. 51–54, or of Tatius in Propertius IV 4.

72. silver worked with gold: An exaggerated (and perhaps bitter) allusion to the wealth that a military life could bring.

74. let me yoke: The Tibullan love of the countryside appears suddenly in this urban poem as a vision, not as a reality.

80. Down comforters: A Tibullan reworking of a popular Epicurean and Lucretian topic. Lucretius in his philosophical poem, *On the Nature of Things*, had written that the body needs little to remove distress and provide pleasure (II 20–33).

82–89. Have I offended: An extreme fantasy in which the poet imagines that he is charged with having plundered a temple of Venus, presumably in order to bring branches to his mistress's door. The supplication he imagines is equally extreme.

92. An oldster: The older lover is a common butt of jokes in comedy, satire, and elegy.

101. Don't burn your harvest: Both the dream of a secure love and the dream of a peaceful life in the country here go up in smoke.

I 5

In elegy I 3 the poet had been separated from Delia by war and the soldier's wandering life. Now, Delia has turned to someone else and much that Tibullus feared then seems to have come true. Lines 1–8 introduce the situation, especially through the emotional contradiction between "Bring irons, fire, all instruments of pain" which ends the introduction and "Be good to me" which begins the address to Delia. The poet's address to Delia occupies lines 7–68 and may be divided as follows: Delia's illness and Tibullus's past services (9–18); a fantasy of life in the country with Delia (19–36); the poet's sufferings and their past separation (37–46); curses on Delia's procuress (47–58); the future benefits of a poor lover (59–66). The range of situations is typical of Tibullus and here may serve both as an analog to the extent of his love or the range of his emotion and as a series of contexts in which to measure that love. The elegy concludes with an address to the poet's rival, a disquisition on chance and fortune, and the hesitant figure of a future lover on Delia's doorstep (67–76). Thematically, the poem may be described in terms of a general concern with madness and slavery which is developed in the contrast between Tibullus's dangerous dream of a do-nothing stability and the equally threatening motions of Messalla, passion and fate. The poem ultimately discloses the poet's failure to impose a secure and satisfying order on the elements of his world: his prayers may aid in Delia's recovery but Delia will not be the faithful farm wife; the poverty on which the security of his dream depends is the cause of his distress ("Watch some rich successor come!").

2. Left me cold: The situation here is a stock one, frequently played out in comedy; see Catullus 8 for another version of the jilted lover's prideful self-confidence.

3. twirling like a top: This image of love as a frenzy which drives the lover out of control was used also by Vergil in the *Aeneid*, and may have originated with Callimachus.

5. Bring irons: The instruments of torture referred to here would be used on a runaway slave. The lover conceives of his boast that he could endure separation from Delia as equivalent to a slave running away from his master; consequently, his request for the appropriate punishment is an effort to set things right so that he will not have to endure what now seems to be the consequence of his boast: a real separation from Delia.

6. silly boasts: The "claim" in line 1.

10. Fever-racked: Illness in elegy always provided the lover with an opportunity to display to his mistress his superior devotion. See also [Tibullus] III 17 [= IV 11]. The image of slavery and punishment has here shifted to a different but related concern with suffering and relief: I was the cause of your relief when you were sick, so you be the cause of mine. The implication is that the lover feels his love as a disease.

11ff: sulfur, magic, meal, loosened tunic: Ancient medicine seems to have been based in part on the notion that sickness was a demon that needed to be exorcised. Hence the combination of purifying agents, magic charms, and prayers.

12. a magic air: Similarly, this song is a magic charm to induce Delia's return to the poet; see especially the imprecation against the procuress in lines 49–58.

16. at the witching hour: The moon was thought to have a specific influence on disease and so the moon goddess, Hecate or Trivia, was often called upon to influence the course of an illness.

20. Madman!: Irrationality appears in variations throughout the poem: in the poet's "silly boasts" (6), in Delia's "evil dreams" (13), in the fantasy of country living ("such were my dreams," 35), in Tibullus's attempted escape to another girl ("bewitched," 42), and in Delia's enslavement to "the witch's spell" (59). One may say that the conflict between an imagined world and the real world is fundamental to Tibullan elegy and its use of prayer, wish, fantasy, and blurred vision.

21–34. With Delia at my side: The characteristically Tibullan fantasy of a happy life in the country; compare Tibullus I 1. 1–48. Here the poet brings together the peace, stability and fertility of the countryside, his beloved Delia, and his admired Messalla. One may see here all the essential elements of Tibullus's world; however, one may also note that, in an eerie literalization of line 18, Messalla now enjoys the fruits of Tibullus's domain and that Delia is in the precarious (for Tibullus) position of administering to Messalla's needs.

21. said I: The dream here narrated is described as a dream in the past. Tibullus's tactic above was, "See how I prayed for you." Now it becomes, "See what wonderful dreams I had." Tibullus will conclude this section with a pathetic appeal, "all lost," line 36.

31. Doing nothing: Peace and security in this fantasy is risky business. Here the Latin is even more explicit about the dangers, saying literally, "But it will be pleasant for me to be nothing anywhere in the house." Such absence-despite-presence brings Messalla immediately to the front: "Let Messalla come."

34. <u>veneration</u>: Delia will venerate, care for, obey, and serve Messalla. In this context, such devotion to Messalla's near divinity is not without its dangers. One may look forward to the picture of Messalla in Tibullus I 7 as a fertilizing river, as Bacchus himself, and we should recall that in poem I 2. 4 Tibullus complains of his unsuccessful and particularly fruitless love of Delia.

36: <u>Now to remote Armenia</u>: In accordance with a common proverb, the winds were said to carry off the fruitless words of empty oaths and unheard prayers. Armenia is probably chosen as a generally exotic and faraway place, not for any specific associations.

37–70: This section has been considered by some critics to constitute a separate elegy.

39. <u>To other women</u>: Not a typical recourse for the unrequited lover of elegy, but a common cure for passion prescribed in the philosophical literature.

45. <u>sea-nymph Thetis</u>: Tibullus does not generally use mythological exempla. The reference here is to the story of the mortal Peleus and the sea-goddess Thetis. Since Jupiter had heard that Thetis would bear a child more powerful than its father, he arranged for Thetis and Peleus to be married. Their son was Achilles, the greatest Greek warrior of the Trojan War.

47. <u>I'm ruined</u>: Thus Tibullus ends this section of his elegy, one in which the complaint, "See what you've done to me," reveals another variation on the Tibullan wish for inertia: impotence.

47–48: Here Tibullus finds the means to exonerate Delia's unfaithfulness by blaming "some clever bawd." This has the added advantage for the poet of allowing him to construct Delia's unfaithfulness as a function of her enslavement to this procuress; see line 59, "Meanwhile, my Delia, break the witch's spell." Earlier the poet's independent boast was likened to the unfaithfulness of a runaway slave; here Delia's unfaithfulness is imagined as a form of enslavement to this "clever bawd."

47. <u>some rich successor</u>: The rival in both elegy and comedy is typically rich; the poet complains that his devotion and poetic skill may not, although it should, successfully compete with this lover's gifts.

49–56. The formal curse against the procuress is a standard feature of both comedy and elegy; compare Ovid *Amores* I 8.

49–50. <u>blood, gall</u>: It was believed that drinking these substances would drive one mad; here it is an appropriate punishment for the old bawd who, from Tibullus's point of view, has driven Delia mad.

51. <u>spirits</u>: Presumably the unhappy souls of other lovers whose happiness has been destroyed by the bawd's mercenary persuasion.

52. <u>screech owls</u>: In popular superstition, witches were said to be able to turn into screech owls in which form they engaged in vampirism.

54. <u>At graveside weeds</u>: These plants were especially dangerous to eat because they were believed to be able to seek vengeance.

54. <u>or bones</u>: It was an ancient belief that anyone who ate food touched by wolves would eventually become a werewolf.

61–66: Tibullus mixes the language of lovers and the language of slaves. "His poverty makes him a slave, and his slavery makes him an ideal lover. The acts of servitude become more distinctly erotic until the two roles are completely combined." (Bright) All true, but when this lover/slave takes Delia to "secret friends" and unlaces her sandals, he begins to play the role of procurer. In this way his dream of impoverished devotion seems to make him vulnerable to the wealthy and powerful Messalla.

65. house of secret friends: These are private dinner parties to which "party girls" are invited. Secrecy is necessary for both to escape the notice of others, especially of Delia's guardians.

67–68: door stays shut: On the basis of these lines, some have thought that we suddenly realize that the poem has been a *paraclausithyron* all along. This is difficult to reconcile with all the details that precede and especially with the implied vantage point of line 71.

69. wheel of Fortune: Chance is a version of the familiar figure of Nemesis (see, for instance, Catullus 50) and often the locus of the unsatisfactory consolation that others will suffer as has the poet. Here, as the wheel of Fortune becomes the small consolation that Tibullus can hold onto, it also recalls the spinning top of Tibullus's passion in line 3.

72. Some patient suitor: This is the third lover, the future rival of Tibullus's rival. With these lines Tibullus composes a recrimination against Delia's established pattern, pity for his present competitor, and a nostalgic glance back at his own past.

75. your boat: The poet addresses his rival. Love is often represented as an ocean or sea where the sailing is not always smooth and whose presiding deity is the sea-born goddess, Venus.

I 6

The fifth elegy told of a quarrel caused by Delia's interest in a rich lover and ends with a vignette suggesting yet another lover is waiting at her door. The sixth elegy is the last to address Delia. Here the poet seeks to remedy his situation. First he describes his predicament by lamenting love's reversals (1–10); this leads to a rehearsal of all his successful tricks against the "dimwitted spouse" that now have turned against him (17–40); here his own cleverness encourages him to an extra-ordinary fantasy of wish fulfillment in which the husband entrusts the wife to the poet and he fends off other lovers (41–56); from this imagined position of strength, the poet now turns to Delia: first in order to pretend that it is really Delia's mother to whom he is beholding (60), so he can imagine Delia learning fidelity (57–74); then to protest to Delia that he'd never "lift a hand to you" (75), while picturing the threatening and sorry plight of unfaithful old crones: "See the rewards of sluttish-ness!" (86; 75–86). The final two lines are a brief prayer to Delia for faithfulness. All in all, it has turned out to be a desperate and not a very pretty affair, as one finds the Tibullan dream of mutual love and stability reliant upon both poverty and slavery while dependent upon treachery, infidelity, and violence. Pathos, however, is relieved by irony and by the poem's tendency to allow its characters and postures to recall the characters of the comic stage and their self-contradictions. In its topics and treatment, this elegy seems often to be a precursor of Ovid.

1. Love: Tibullus first addresses the god Amor, or "Love." The god's characteristics are arguably Hellenistic in origin: scheming, unpredictable, treacherous. Compare the picture of Cupid in Propertius II 12 and II 29 and Ovid *Amores* I 1.

4. your guile: Love's treachery has a long history, in Latin going back to Ennius; this complaint seems to be echoed by Vergil in his *Aeneid* (IV 93–95).

8. familiar proclamations: Ovid, in particular, will exploit the way in which a lover's own past experience comes back to haunt him; Catullus had already toyed with the topic in poem 8.

11. to teach her: The poet's erotic art, based as it is on duplicity, has turned against him. Compare Tibullus's earlier lines at I 2. 17–20.

17. dimwitted spouse: The cuckolded husband is always an object of ridicule; see, for instance, Catullus 17 and 83. In Tibullus's situation, however, it is difficult to keep the ridicule from rebounding on him.

24. women's rites: The rites of the Bona Dea, a Latin fertility goddess, were celebrated annually in the home of a high ranking Roman official by that official's wife and the Vestal Virgins. Men were religiously excluded, and so a husband normally would have no reason to follow a wife who said she was going to celebrate those rites. Blindness was the traditional punishment for sacrilege in these rites, especially the sacrilege of seeing what one is not supposed to see.

27. Pretending: As Tibullus attacks the husband for his stupidity, he also creates a record of his own success, a kind of victory catalog, as well as a warning for the future.

35. Why have her: A common topic in erotic poetry; for a witty variation, see Ovid *Amores* III 4.

39. the whip: Another echo of Tibullus's extreme literalization of the common figure of speech by which the lover was a slave to the beloved; compare, for instance, elegy I 5. 5.

46. priestess prophesied: This is the only mention of priestesses who served Bellona, a part Roman, part Cappadocian goddess of war who had her temple not far from the *Circus Maximus* in Rome. Her worship was ecstatic and had much in common with the worship of Isis and of the *Magna Mater*: priests would slash their arms, drink each other's blood, and prophesy.

47. war god whirls: The image, although typical, recalls the image of Tibullus at the beginning of elegy I 5. Here and in the next line, "leaves fear of fire and torture," Tibullus reconfigures his own experience as a kind of divine possession.

69. matron's gown: The stola was a long gown worn only by freeborn Roman matrons; on the basis of this passage, it would seem that Delia was a freedwoman, not a properly married Roman native. Because freedwomen could not improve their position by marriage or fidelity, they were characterized as especially promiscuous.

80. crone who's weaving: The aged prostitute is another typical object of ridicule; see Horace *Odes* I 25 and IV 13. Here Delia's task is appropriately the same activity that characterized the ancient world's model of fidelity, Penelope.

I 7

Usually referred to as Messalla's birthday poem, this poem celebrates both Messalla's birthday and his triumph in Aquitania, as well as his repair of the *Via Latina* and his mission to the East. Consequently, this elegy, in addition to being a birthday poem (a *genethliakon*), is also an heroic triumph ode, and, when one notes further that Tibullus has included a hymn (specifically a *kletic*, or invocatory hymn) to Osiris (who is taken to represent the great river of Egypt, the Nile, and Bacchus, the mystery god of fertility and wine), one is struck by the extraordinarily Callimachean mixture of genres and themes. Furthermore, the poem may be read as our first example of a private occasional poem in elegiacs, or as a public epideictic poem on an occasion of state. For many readers of the poem the feature most requiring explanation is the hymn to Osiris: Why does this Egyptian god of fertility, wine, and flowing rivers appear in the midst of Messalla's birthday poem? It is clear that Osiris is in some sense equated with Messalla; but on the one hand, Osiris is a vegetative god of rebirth, and on the other, as representative of Egypt he is what Messalla and Augustus have conquered and controlled.

1. the day the Fates sang: The day is Messalla's birthday and the reference to the Fates would recall for a Roman reader a poem not included in this anthology, Catullus 64. At the conclusion of that poem on the marriage of Peleus and Thetis, the Fates sing of the future birth of the great Greek warrior Achilles. A similar, though less assertively ambiguous song, is the Fates' prediction of a child who will occasion a new golden age in Vergil's *Eclogue* IV. The song of the Fates is appropriate to a birthday poem because they were said to spin at the hour of a man's birth the thread that measured the course of his life, the thread of his destiny. We do not know the exact day of Messalla's birth; it may have been the day on which he celebrated his triumph.

3. the Aquitanians: Aquitania is in the southwest of what is today France. Messalla had been sent there after the battle of Actium in 31 B.C.E. to put down an uprising. It is thought that Tibullus may have accompanied Messalla on this expedition.

4. And Adour tremble: The Adour is a river in southwest Aquitania. Roman poets were fond of referring to countries and territories in terms of striking or learned geographical features, especially rivers. Here one may see in the personification of the river Adour a displacement of the emotions of the Aquitanians. In this poem, rivers and fluids will play a very important role; the Latin for "would take flight" above is a word meaning "to make to pour out." Like Osiris, the god of the Nile which pours out and floods the delta yearly and keeps the land fertile, so Messalla's power to control and create is linked here to natural forces, specifically to fluids.

5. whole generation: Public and state events frequently made explicit their importance in terms of the youth, the next generation.

6–8. captive chiefs on show. . . : We know that Messalla's triumph took place on September 25, 27 B.C.E. A military triumph was a religious ceremony in which the triumphant general fulfilled the vows he had made to Capitoline Jupiter upon undertaking his military expedition as Jupiter's representative. This was as close as a mortal could come to divinity. To qualify for a triumph, a general had to have been responsible for the death of at least 5,000 of the enemy and had to bring the victorious army back to Rome to demonstrate that the war had been successfully completed. The procession moved from the *Campus Martius* through the *Porta Triumphalis* along the *Via Sacra* to the temple of Jupiter on the Capitoline, and included state officials and senators, musicians, captives, the spoils of war and sacrificial animals, soldiers who sang ribald songs about the general's sexual prowess or proclivities, and finally the general himself in a gold and ivory chariot drawn by four white horses. He carried an ivory scepter, wore a toga of purple and gold, and had his face painted red. Upon reaching the temple, he would walk or crawl up the steps to dedicate to Jupiter his laurel crown and the insignia of his rank. Afterward there was a banquet for the general attended by senators and other state officials.

9. This honor did not happen without me: This claim is suspect and some editors believe that the true reading would produce the meaning, "This honor did not happen without Mars (i.e., real fighting)."

10. Pyrenees, the North Sea: The Pyrenees are on the south of the territory of Aquitania; the North Sea borders Aquitania on the west.

11–12. Saone, Garonne, Rhone, Loire: From the North Sea on the west, Tibullus moves east to the Saone and then south to the Rhone; further south and to the west we find the Garonne (for the sake of euphony the order has been slightly changed in the English); and then to the north again we come on the Loire, where the Carnutes lived, near modern Chartres. In addition to cataloging the major rivers that bound and flow through the region, we seem to be moving through the territory in a circle or spiral.

13–16. Cydnus, Taurus, Cilicia: We now move to the east. Presumably we are following the eastern campaign on which Messalla was sent after the battle of Actium. The Cydnus is the major river of Cilicia, which is just north of Cyprus in Asia Minor; Taurus is the name of the mountain range which borders Cilicia to the north.

17–20. Syrian skies, Tyre: Syria is to the south and east of Cilicia, on the far eastern coast of the Mediterranean. Tyre was a Phoenecian island on the same coast, small but important. In addition to mentioning what were probably noteworthy stops on Messalla's campaign, Tibullus characterizes these places in such a way that he alludes to water (Cydnus), land (Taurus), and air (Syrian skies). When made explicit, this device is called a "universalizing triplet." Furthermore, the characterizations of these places from Cydnus to the Nile is in terms of peace, sustenance, piety, learning, and fertility.

17. white dove: The dove was sacred to the goddess Astarte, the Syrian/Phoenician counterpart to the Greek Aphrodite and the Roman Venus.

19. school of seafaring: The Phoenicians were sometimes considered the inventors of seafaring.

21. great Nile: The great river of Egypt comes as the "cap" to this catalog of places that bear witness to the presence and power of Messalla. The Nile's annual flood beginning in June and ending in October is responsible for keeping Egypt from being an uninhabitable desert. Just as the Nile was the great river of the ancient world, so too, especially at its flood, it was the quintessentially muddy river, a symbol for Callimachean poets of all that should be avoided by those who aspired to the pure fountain of the Muses. On the other hand, the poem is filled with allusions to Callimachus (in lines 22, 24, 28) which, if taken at face value, seem to equate Messalla's victories with the athletic victories celebrated by Callimachus.

24. nor in what region: Tibullus is being witty; the origin of the Nile was not known until the nineteenth century.

27–28. bull of Memphis, Osiris: The Nile River god Osiris was worshipped in the form of a bull, called "Apis," his reincarnation and living emblem, located in a magnificent temple in Memphis. When Apis died he became "Sarapis" and was mourned by priests in an extended ceremony at the end of which a new Apis was installed in the temple. According to the Osiris myth, the god was the brother and husband of Isis. He fought with Set, the god of darkness and evil, and was defeated, cut into pieces, and thrown into the water where he was brought back to life by Isis. He was the founder of civilization and agriculture, the inventor of the plow, and father of wheat, fruit, and wine. The Greeks readily identified him with Dionysus. He is easily construed as a god of fertility and civilization, of violence and vulnerability, of mutability and immortality.

30. the tender earth: This apt description of the irrigated alluvial land carries with it a suggestion of the ancient feeling that plowing was a form of violence done to Mother Earth.

38. song, rhythmic ways: Osiris teaches men to teach (or train) the vines and viticulture itself becomes the origin of other forms of culture.

39. Bacchus: The Roman god of wine, and so readily identified with Osiris. It is also recorded that Messalla was particularly fond of wine. The power of wine to relieve troubled minds has a long history; compare Horace *Odes* I 7 and the symposiastic themes in Horace's *Odes* generally.

45. ivy-crowned: Ivy was sacred to Bacchus and he was frequently portrayed wearing an ivy crown.

46. robes of saffron: Yellow, often associated with Bacchus, was also the color of the bride's veil and the eunuch's robe; it was thought to be a festal and an effeminate color.

47. Tyrian purple: Together with the saffron above, we have the purple and gold which characterized the triumphant general's toga.

49–54. come celebrate: A man's genius was the spirit born to him at his birth and accompanying him throughout his life. Consequently, one's birthday was the feast day for one's genius, a day on which the genius received offerings of incense and honeycakes. In this picture, the images of Messalla the birthday boy, Messalla the general, Messalla's genius, and even Osiris flow together. The image of ointment running down the hair might describe the genius or Messalla; similarly, the crown may also recall the crown Messalla wore at his triumph. Reference to the genius, as a reference to a kind of intractable nature, recalls the song of the Fates at the beginning of the poem.

57. Tusculum, Alba: Among Augustus's first projects was the repair of roads; he assigned Messalla that part of the *Via Latina* which runs southeast from Rome over the Alban hills and between Tusculum and Alba Longa until it meets the *Via Appia*.

62. Will sing your praises: Messalla is to the farmer, like the god Osiris, a bringer of blessings. After all its movement, the poem comes to a rest with a solid roadbed and a monument to Messalla, which, of course, the poem is also.

I 10

The last poem of Tibullus's first book can be seen as a return to the themes and general concerns of his first poem. Tibullus praises the peace, the religious traditions, and the simplicity of his elegiac countryside as he asks his household gods, the Lares, to rescue him from being dragged off to war. He employs many features of a solemn hymnic style to heighten his effects: repetitions of words (see notes on 41f, on 45ff, and 61f); contrasts of then and now, him and me; and direct appeals to the gods. The poet sets his standard peace/war antithesis, common to the elegiac poets, in a typically Tibullan context of praise for the religious piety of country life, and then develops the implications of this Tibullan peace through an equally common lover-as-soldier topos. In the end, the poem provides a witty (if typically male chauvinist) view of love. It has often been noted, however, that here Tibullus has in mind not the typical elegiac scene of lover and mistress, but an adaptation of elegiac love with its harmless quarrels to a conservative picture of married love. Marriage and married love play a role in all of the elegists.

1. Whoever first: The motif of the "first inventor" is a common topos, especially when a poet wishes to imagine eradicating a perceived evil at its very root.

2. fierce, feral: The Latin, too, contains a pun on the word for "iron" (*ferreus* = here, "fierce") and the word for "wild" (*ferus* = here, "feral").

6. ill use: This poem may be seen as attempting throughout to imagine the appropriate place for and the appropriate degree of violence in the world.

7. riches' gilded door: Wealth is commonly blamed for moral turpitude by most conventional moralists.

8. beechen cups: Wooden cups are traditionally associated with the simple rustic life. Rusticity itself, however, is not a conventional value of the elegiac poets.

9. flocks: Pastoral scenes are frequently used for symbols of golden age ease and golden age morality. This is in part, no doubt, because agriculture requires the property boundaries typically associated with the end of the golden age. Tibullus in this poem carefully weaves together the values of Vergil's *Georgics*, a poem on agriculture, and the values of Vergil's *Eclogues*, his pastoral poems.

15. you household gods: The Lares (see line 25) were originally the ghosts of the dead and farm land deities who were at this time worshiped at the hearth and who protected the home. Their function was, as here, apotropaic. They were originally made of wood, like the beechen cups above, or of terra cotta. See also poem I 1. 19ff. Sacrifices to them could include incense, wreaths, grapes, wine and other products of the farm according to the yield.

24. Wheatcakes and honey: See I 7. 54; these, together with grapes and wine, were common traditional offerings to the genius of a family. We actually have an ancient recipe for the honeycakes (Cato *de Agri Cultura* 75).

26. a hog: It seems that the pig was a favorite sacrificial animal among the Romans.

27. robed in white: White, symbolizing purity, was necessary for the proper performance of a sacrifice.

28. wreathed in myrtle: Myrtle was sacred to Venus but was used on many different festal and religious occasions. As in Horace *Odes* I 38, so here the myrtle seems chosen for its plainness.

32. the troops' position out in wine: For Tibullus, this is the right degree of interest in the military. Compare Propertius, who similarly enjoys Augustus's triumph with a girl and some wine; elegy III 4*.

35. where nothing grows: An appropriate image for the land of the dead in a poem that celebrates the values of the agricultural world.

36–37. Cerberus, Charon, Styx: Hades, the home of the dead, is pictured in ancient literature as a land inhabited by bloodless shadows. One arrives there by crossing the river Styx on the boat of Charon. The actual entrance to Hades was said to be guarded by a monstrous dog, sometimes portrayed with three heads, named Cerberus.

39. The patriarch: In many ways a surprising image of the ideal for an elegiac or lyric poet. Compare Catullus's attitude toward the severe old men of Rome with his image of his love for Lesbia as a patriarchal love for the family line; compare Ovid's attitude toward Augustus's marriage laws and moral legislation.

41. his son: And so everything is in its appropriate place—the father with the sheep, the son with the lambs.

45–50. An eulogy of peace, marked by repetition of "Peace . . . Peace . . . In peacetime . . . ." The virtues and effects of peace, including shiny plows and fruitful vineyards, are traditional.

51. Homeward: He is returning from some sacred grove and so some rural celebration in honor of a god.

55. he, victorious, weeps too: This ameliorative and self-justifying portrait of male violence is as traditional as it is today objectionable; it is as if Tibullus has replaced the need for violence to effect certain goals he finds desirable (and celebrates in I 7) with a soft-core violence that accomplishes nothing except an image of male domination. Tibullus here imagines a version of the lover as soldier; compare Horace *Odes* III 26, Propertius I 6, and Ovid *Amores* I 9.

59. is iron: A return to the topos of the opening, but here the poet measures degrees of violence within his elegiac world.

67. Come, fostering Peace: By the end of the poem the image and associations of peace have been assimilated to the proper functions of Demeter or Ceres, the most important agricultural goddess.

Book II

Tibullus's second book of elegies was published just before or just after his death, about 18 B.C.E. and about eight years after his first book. The affair with Delia is over; poems 8 and 9 of his first book had already been about a new love interest, the young man Marathus. Book II contains six elegies totaling only 428 lines and is thought by many to be incomplete.

II 1

Most scholars identify the rustic ritual represented here as the *Ambarvalia*, or the "purification of the field," which was celebrated annually in May. This was the time of year when the winter wheat began to ripen and so was susceptible to various diseases. The ritual itself was characterized primarily by a ritual walk three times around the circumference of the field with the sacrificial victims which were then killed on an altar. At the same time that this festival was celebrated by private individuals on their farms a similar festival was celebrated at Rome to provide for the ritual purification of the city. The poem's themes pick up many of the major interests of his first book, in particular the god-like power of Messalla and Tibullus's generally conservative aspirations. As the officiating priest of the festival, the poet is most likely imagining himself again in the role of *pater familias*, or "head of the household." The poem may be seen as a ritual symbol of the interrelation of the rustic values (peace, love, fertility, and piety) which the poet holds dear, but which always need the beneficent protection of Messalla. That the ritual is not exactly and undisputedly identified is perhaps a reflection of Tibullus's desire rather to generalize the spirit of rustic religion than to offer a strictly and merely historical narrative. The poem nevertheless follows the course of the ritual and so has more dramatic structure than most of Tibullus's soliloquies. Critics disagree about how to divide the poem; I have tried only to outline the poem's basic narrative movement.

1–14. Preparations for the ceremony. The priest or the *pater familias* summons to the ritual those who should properly attend and bids the profane to stay their distance. It is striking that the profane explicitly includes those who have enjoyed the pleasures of Venus on the previous night.

1. Keep silence: A ritual call for silence from the celebrants at a religious ritual; compare the beginning of Horace *Odes* III 1 and Propertius IV 6.

3. either horn: Bacchus, god of wine and the grape, did not always have horns; they seem to be an invention of the Hellenistic age. In any event, they were common on river gods and are

thought to symbolize fertility and strength. Here and below the god is adorned with and offered in sacrifice that which the worshippers themselves want.

4. <u>Ceres, corn</u>: The Italian goddess of agriculture and of grain; according to the Roman natural historian Pliny, the garland made of grain was the earliest garland used by the Italians.

5. <u>idle on the wall</u>: All work was to stop on festival days. As might be expected there was extensive theological discussion of exactly what was and what was not allowed.

12. <u>Whom Venus</u>: Perhaps this may seem to be an unusual prohibition for an elegiac poet; however, ritual purity was always important on festival days (see above on I 10. 27). Furthermore, the festival was apotropaic, and it is reasonable to expect that farmers would not want the various blights that threaten the crop to proliferate at this time. Venus has already done her job; the seeds have grown and the wheat ripens.

15–16. <u>The ritual begins</u>: Tibullus omits the triple circumambulation of the field and other details.

16. <u>olive wreaths</u>: The production of olive oil was particularly important to a farm.

17–24. <u>Prayer</u>: The gods here are not named, but include Bacchus, Ceres, the Lares, and the various gods of the countryside.

25–26. <u>Transition</u>: The poet transits to the examination of the entrails of the sacrificial animals; this was a task performed by special priests, the haruspices, in order to determine the will of the gods. If the entrails, particularly the liver, were normal, it was declared that the sacrifice had been acceptable to the gods.

27–36. An exhortation to celebration, including a toast and eulogy to Messalla.

27. <u>smoked Falernian</u>: Falernian, an Italian wine from Campania, was said to be a strong fruity wine which reached maturity at about fifteen years. In order for it to age properly it was kept warm above the hearth where it would become smoky in appearance and taste.

28. <u>the Chian jar</u>: Chian was a Greek wine, smoother and sweeter than Falernian, which was often mixed with Falernian.

31. <u>"To Messalla!"</u>: It was common to toast an absent friend. One critic has found Messalla's absence significant in that, if Tibullus celebrates the *Ambarvalia*, Messalla would at that time of year be in Rome celebrating the *Amburbium*, or the parallel ritual of purification for the city. If true, the toast unites country and city as it does patron and poet.

33. <u>glorious for triumphs</u>: See poem I 7, a poem celebrating both Messalla's birthday and his triumph over the Aquitanians. The plural here is a rhetorical amplification.

34. <u>long-haired ancestor</u>: Apparently barbers came to Rome about 300 B.C.E.; the older generations of Romans were frequently characterized as long-haired.

35. <u>Hero, inspire me</u>: Messalla is invoked both as a heroic divinity and as an inspiring muse.

37–80. <u>Praise of the countryside and its gods</u>: The transition effected in these lines, from "To Messalla!," a natural toast under the circumstances, to "inspire me," an invocation of the patron as muse, to "The country is my theme," a formal poetic announcement initiating a poem within the poem, is universally admired for its artful subtlety and apparent simplicity. Once again the values which Tibullus celebrates depend upon and are protected by the heroism and triumphs which also threaten his world. Compare elegy I 10. The lines that follow celebrate rural life in three movements as outlined below.

37–50. <u>A catalog of divine benefactions which forms a brief history of civilization</u>: The gods taught man to plant, to build houses, to plow, to use the wheel, to irrigate, to make wine, and to harvest honey. These are the traditional accomplishments of civilization and Messalla's connection to them as inspiring muse should be compared with the picture of him as a civilizing force in poem I 7.

42.   the wheel: The invention of the wheel is not common in the traditional catalogs of civilizational progress.

45.   Golden grapes: Golden because we are in an imagined golden age, not because the Romans had grapes of this color.

46.   water with strong wine: The ancient Greeks and Romans both drank wine mixed with water. It was considered excessive to drink unmixed wine.

48.   Earth lays her golden hair aside: Tibullus is the first to refer to the harvesting of wheat with this image.

49–50.   bees: Although Aristotle thought that bees built their combs out of flowers and that honey dropped from the sky, Tibullus is using "each bloom" as a metonymy for "honey"—note, "to pack their hives with honey."

51–66.   A catalog of rural inventions extends the history of civilization: Poetic song and dance are part of cultural development; the weaving of garlands is portrayed as a religious celebration; and the spinning of wool is characterized in terms of household care and honor to the goddess Minerva. All are described in their celebratory functions, and so they extend the poem's eulogistic mode. Compare the blessings of Osiris in poem I 7. 29–48.

54.   forms he'd draped: Images of the gods were dressed up on feast day.

56.   Bacchic dance: Tibullus begins with an enthusiastic element of a rustic celebration. To this he assimilates either a theory about the origins of comedy and satire, in which the face may have been painted red as a kind of primitive mask, or a theory about the origins of tragedy from singing competitions.

58.   a goat: The reference to goats here seems to suggest that Tibullus also has in mind another theory of the development of tragedy, so-called because a goat (Greek, *tragos*) was given as a prize to the victorious poet.

59.   a country boy: Of the various household gods (including Vesta and the Penates), only the *Lar Familiaris* looked over the whole household, including the slaves (here alluded to in the term "boy"). On the appropriate day for crowning the Lar and praying for his protection, it was the duty of a slave boy to offer a garland of flowers. The chief festival for the Lares, between December 17 and January 5, is probably not meant here. Again Tibullus seeks a general effect.

63.   the distaff twirls: The wool was held on the distaff in the left hand while the spindle was held in the right. The fingers of the right hand pulled the wool from the distaff while the thumb twirled the spindle and the spinning motion formed the thread.

65.   sing Minerva's tune: Minerva was the patron goddess of crafts, especially of spinning. The image of women singing at their work may be both true and sentimentally used.

67–80.   A description of Cupid as a country god: This final position is climactic. For Tibullus, as civilization progresses toward home, hearth, family, and spinning, the place of pride is reserved for elegiac love. Given the usual themes of love elegy, gold diggers and prostitutes, furtive affairs, drunken debauches, and urbane irreverence, this climax is more than a little extraordinary.

67.   country-born: The fertility of the world, the effect of Venus, and therefore of her son, Cupid, in the fields and among the animals in springtime made the power of love in the country a stock theme among poets and philosophers; compare Hamlet's "country matters." Most recently, Vergil in his *Georgics* had drawn a powerful picture of the effect of passion on bulls and stallions.

70. <u>Alas</u>: One of several "tags" which mark a speaker's recognition that he has fallen under the power of love.

73–76. <u>young man . . .</u>: These are the stock features of both elegiac love and of love as it was presented on the comic stage. In consequence of this, we are no longer imagining country scenes, but rather city scenes.

81. <u>Come, holy one</u>: Formally, an invocation of Cupid which returns to the ritual mode of the opening and recalls the invocation to Messalla in verse 35.

82. <u>leave your torch</u>: Cupid's bow and arrows and his torch were often considered instruments of torture. One must ask, however, exactly what the presence of Cupid would mean without his characteristic effects.

83–84. <u>aloud, in silence</u>: Prayers had to be made aloud in order for them to reach the ears of the gods. Consequently, by "in silence" the poet means "secretly, unheard by those around."

87. <u>Play now</u>: As in Catullus, the word "play" may refer to games, theater, or the writing of poetry. The latter is particularly appropriate to the first poem in a collection of poems. In this regard there is at least a hint of an ominous allegory in the poet's concern with "night" and "dark dreams." Compare Catullus 5.

87–90. The idea that Night had a chariot is very old, going back at least to the Greek tragedian Aeschylus. Stars were considered the children of Night as far back as Euripides. Sleep was also considered the child of Night by Hesiod. The picture of Sleep with wings seems to be a Hellenistic invention. But Dreams as the children of Night have a long history going back to Hesiod again. Thus all the elements of this elegant picture are traditional. The exact combination of elements, however, especially the image of Sleep and Dreams following the chariot of Night, is apparently a Tibullan invention.

Propertius

BIBLIOGRAPHY

Commager, Steele. *A Prolegomenon to Propertius, Lectures in Memory of L. Taft Semple,* University of Cincinnati (Norman, Oklahoma: University of Oklahoma Press, 1974).

Hubbard, Margaret. *Propertius* (New York: Scribner, 1974).

Stahl, Hans-Peter. *Propertius: "Love" and "War"* (Berkeley: University of California Press, 1985).

Sullivan, J. P. *Propertius: A Critical Introduction* (Cambridge [England]; New York: Cambridge University Press, 1976).

Warden, J. *Fallax Opus: Poet and Reader in the Elegies of Properius* (Phoenix Suppl. 14, Toronto; Buffalo: University of Toronto Press, 1980).

Book I: CYNTHIA MONOBIBLOS

Propertius begins his poetic career by explicitly introducing Cynthia, the first word of the first elegy, and by implicitly defining his poetic choices in terms of his predecessors in elegy and amatory poetry.

I 1

This poem is an extraordinary *tour de force,* simultaneously introducing us to the peculiar interests and dynamics of Propertian elegy and to Propertius's view of his place in contemporary poetic developments. Propertius's ability to address personal feeling and traditional form was facilitated by the ease with which the poet's mistress in Latin could stand for the poet's passion and for his verse. To talk about "Cynthia" was to talk both about the person Cynthia and about the poet's feelings; but in the Latin idiom, it was also to talk about the poet's "Cynthia": his book called *Cynthia.* (Similarly, Ovid's book of elegies is called *A Love Affair.*) For most Romans the kind of passionate emotion that Propertius speaks of was neither desirable nor even a sign of health. It was a disease, a form of helplessness, something to be cured. This allows the poet, then, to configure both his passion and his poetry as a form of compulsion, something beyond his control. Consequently, the poet's claim that magical charms cannot cure him of his passion can be developed both as an expression of how far beyond traditional remedies his passion is and as a rejection of the kind of (tradition-al) poetry he will not or cannot attempt to write because it does not address his feelings.

1. Cynthia: The first word or words of an ancient poetry book often became the title by which the book was cited by others. The name itself, however, recalls "Cynthius," another name for Apollo, the Callimachean god of poetry, and thereby (as the feminine of that title) also recalls Apollo's sister Diana, the chaste virgin goddess of the hunt and cold goddess of the moon. Propertius's choice of pseudonym carries associations and connotations that reverberate throughout his poetry.

2. was immune: Propertius tells us in elegy III 15 that he had had an earlier love affair with one Lycinna. This presents a problem for those who want these poems to reflect accurate autobiography.

5. chaste women: Either because Cynthia has made herself inaccessible and Propertius is seeking favors from loose women or, better, because Cynthia and her way of life has made typically moral women unattractive to the poet. It is worth noting that Propertius's final poem, elegy IV 11, will be a speech of self-justification made by Cornelia, the very example of the "chaste wife."

9. Tullus: Tullus, the nephew of L. Volcacius Tullus, cos. 33 B.C.E., is also addressed in poems I 6, 14, 22, and III 22. He represents the public world of the career politician and is appropriately addressed here in the context of Milanion's effective action. This is the world of which Tullus may have some understanding, even if he is not a lover.

9–16. Milanion, Atalanta: Milanion was the successful lover of the Arcadian huntress Atalanta. In this version, Milanion succeeds by enduring many trials, most notably by killing the centaurs Hylaeus and Rhoeteus, who tried to rape Atalanta. In the more familiar version, Milanion, like all of Atalanta's suitors, is challenged to a footrace. He wins by dropping gold apples in her path which she stops to pick up. The story of Milanion and Atalanta is a kind of mythological exemplum common among Callimachean poets; one should compare Catullus 68. 73ff, the story of Protesilaus and Laodamia. Propertius uses this tale as an illustration of what is not his condition.

18. old paths: One of the most familiar dicta for the Callimachean poet was the command not to travel the familiar path, that is, not to write in hackneyed style on familiar themes. See Appendix.

19. tempt the moon: The poet addresses an imagined company of those who have power over the moon and sacred rites. "Cynthia" is a reference to Apollo's sister, the virgin huntress goddess Diana, who as the equivalent of the Greek goddess Artemis, was also associated with the moon goddess Selene, and the witch goddess Hecate. Here the poet moves from Atalanta, a virgin huntress, to the virgin goddess by references to witches and the moon. This allows him to recall Hecate and the traditional powers of magical song. It has been argued that the programmatic allusion in these lines is to the magical power of neoteric poetry and the tradition of "scientific" Orphic song which Propertius claims is like Gallan learning in that it cannot relieve the poet's passion or bring the poet's fascination with "Cynthia" to a satisfactory conclusion.

24. Colchian song: The text is in dispute, but if this is the correct reading, then Propertius refers to the most famous of ancient sorceresses, Medea, lover of Jason, whose story was told in Apollonius's *Argonautica*.

25–30. Friends . . . .: In this new section the poet seeks aid from familiar topics in elegiac poetry: medicine and travel. For the theme of medicine, see Propertius I 1. 25–26; for the theme of travel, see Catullus 11.

28. can speak freely: Free speech was the central freedom of a citizen in the Republic. In 29 B.C.E. when the *Monobiblos* was published it was not clear, perhaps not even to Octavian, what was going to happen to the freedoms of the Republic.

29. exotic lands, over the sea: The line is a very clear echo of Catullus 101. 1.

31–36. To you the god . . . .: Propertius now addresses a new group, the world of happy lovers from which he is excluded.

33–34. our Venus. . . Love: While referring to Venus and her son *Amor*, or "Love," Propertius characteristically blurs the distinction between the woman who causes his passion, the passion itself, and the deity who presides over such passions.

I 3

Perhaps one of the best known and best liked of Propertius's poems, this combines a comic scenario with elegiac emotions and a psychological drama of passion and fear with a typically Callimachean and learned manipulation of sources. The poet has been out drinking late and Cynthia has fallen asleep when he returns. The domes- ticity of the scene and the ease of Propertius's access to Cynthia recalls a husband and wife, which is, of course, contrary to the genre.

1. Ariadne: The story of Ariadne was popular in art and had been told by Catullus in his "little epic," poem 64*. She, the daughter of King Minos of Crete, fell in love with Theseus, a young Athenian who had been sent to Crete with others as part of a yearly sacrifice to the Minotaur. The Minotaur was kept in the center of a labyrinth from which young men never returned. Ariadne helped Theseus to find his way out and sailed from Crete with him. He abandoned her on the island of Naxos when she fell asleep. She was eventually rescued by Bacchus who carried her off and married her.

3. Andromeda: Andromeda was the daughter of an Ethiopian king who was told to sacrifice her to a sea monster in order to rescue his land from flooding. She was chained to a rock on the seashore, where Perseus, after slaying the Medusa, saw her and fell in love. He won her hand in marriage by killing the monster.

5–6. Thracian women: The women of Thrace are frequently mentioned as devotees of Bacchus. After their ecstatic dancing and violent celebrations of the god, they would fall asleep. Here they are pictured sleeping on the banks of the river Apidanus which flowed into the Peneus in Thessaly, about 150 miles southwest of their home in Thrace.

9. wine-drunk feet: The situation set up here is a kind of reverse *paraclausithyron* (see Tibullus I 2): the door is open, the lover enters, the mistress speaks, and she gets the last word.

14. now Love, now Wine: The two are referred to as gods, but the second god, usually known as Bacchus, here is called by another name in the Latin, *Liber*. *Liber* means "free," and Bacchus is so named in general because the effect of wine is often to free one from normal behavioral constraints.

20. like Argos to Io's horns: Jupiter raped Io, a priestess of his wife Juno, and turned her into a heifer to hide her. Juno learned of this, asked for the heifer and ordered her guarded by Argos, a monster described as having as many as one hundred eyes. This was another story popular in murals and wall paintings.

21ff. The lover's ministrations, here including the typical lover's gift of fruit, reminds one briefly of Tibullan fantasies.

36. home to our bed: In these lines, in which Cynthia speaks for the first time in Propertius (in her final speech, IV 8, she similarly interrupts Propertius in mid-debauch), she casts their affair as an essentially domestic arrangement. She also places herself in the role traditionally

assumed by the elegiac poet: she imagines that Propertius has been unfaithful and she claims to find consolation for her unrequited love in song.

41.   by weaving with purple thread: Purple was particularly prized and was associated both with high honor and with luxury; it is the color most commonly used in Roman religion. Weaving was a domestic activity associated with chastity, faithfulness, and the devoted, hard-working wife; it was also the most common metaphor for poetic composition. Some see an allusion here to the thread by which Ariadne helped Theseus find his way out of the labyrinth of the Minotaur; see lines 1–2 above.

42.   by Orphean song: Orpheus was a Thracian (and so may recall lines 5–6 above) and the legendary master singer of the ancient world, associated with a tradition of magical and pseudo-scientific song. When he lost Eurydice, he went to the underworld to seek her. There his singing so charmed the powers below that they allowed Eurydice to return to the world above on condition that Orpheus not look back. When he did, she disappeared forever and he was left to sing of his inconsolable grief.

I 6

Tullus, the career politician addressed in I 1, has invited Propertius to follow him to foreign lands. In this poem, as Propertius refuses to join Tullus and bids him farewell, the poet can join features of the *propempticon* (or "send-off poem") with features of the *recusatio* (or "refusal poem"). Official business, often represented by travel, provided poets with an opportunity to contrast their gentle lover's life with the harsh life of the man of action; compare Tibullus I 1. 51–58. At several points, Propertius seems to have Catullus in mind: the poem in general reverses the situation of Catullus 11; lines 5–7 recall Catullus 35; and in line 27, Propertius seems to find pleasure in the dreadfully destructive feelings of Catullus 76.

1–2.   Adriatic, Aegean: The ancient Romans typically did not like sea travel because of the dangers, especially from storms. The Adriatic was notorious for its storms, especially difficult in the autumn; and the Aegean was sometimes associated with the Greek word *aigis* or "storm." Sailing and warfare are typically used as examples of the extremes to which men will go for glory or money. The ocean and the long voyage are also figures for the kind of public, bombastic, epic (military) poetry which Propertius and his generation of poets opposed.

3.   Rhipean peaks: The Rhipean mountains were a mythical range in the extreme north of Scythia and the origin of the north winds; they are associated with loneliness and extreme cold.

4.   Ethiopia: A country of Africa known for its heat; paired with the "Rhipean peaks" it makes a "universalizing doublet"—from the extreme north to the extreme south is the equivalent of "anywhere."

13.   Athens's learning: The cultural seat of the ancient world.

14.   Asia's ancient wealth: Asia was typically associated with wealth and luxury. Athens and the "fabled cities of Asia" were common places for a young man to visit in his travels about the world.

17.   adverse winds: The idea that lover's words and actions are as empty as the wind and as stable as the water was a commonplace; compare Catullus 70, 3–4.

19.   your uncle's prestige: L. Volcacius Tullus was promagistrate of Cilicia in 45 B.C.E., consul with Octavian (Augustus) in 33 B.C.E., and proconsul of Asia in 30–29 B.C.E.

20. <u>Restore forgotten allies' ancient rights</u>: This is generally taken as a reference to the degeneracy of Mark Antony's regime in Asia. Antony was defeated by Octavian at the battle of Actium in 31 B.C.E. and, presumably under Octavian's orders, the uncle Tullus has been sent to Asia to restore order and right the wrongs of Antony's rule.

22. <u>your nation's arms</u>: It is supposed that Tullus served at the battle of Actium on the basis of these lines.

23. <u>that Boy</u>: Cupid.

31. <u>gentle Ionia</u>: A country of Asia Minor on the eastern coast of the Aegean. While the geographical reference points to the range and importance of Tullus's activities, the term "gentle" is especially common in characterizing the life of the poet/lover. See also "tyrant star" below.

32. <u>Pactolus's stream</u>: The Pactolus River flowed down from Mt. Tmolus in Lydia (Asia Minor) and was fabled to be rich in gold.

34. <u>a partner in a popular rule</u>: The line may mean: "a partner in the power granted [to your uncle]," recalling a line written to Julius Caesar by the poet Gallus: "My fate, Caesar, will then be sweet to me, when you | will be a great partner in the history of Rome."

36. <u>this tyrant star</u>: Propertius caps his refusal to go with Tullus by associating Tullus's travels with terms and places that recall a luxurious and effeminate life, while returning to the language of the warrior/lover to characterize his life. While the poet says that he is not a warrior and so will not attend Tullus, his language claims both that the lover's life participates in hardships like those of which the warrior is proud and that the public man's life enjoys delicacies and ease like that which earns the lover a certain public contempt.

I 7

This poem, addressed to the epic poet Ponticus, contrasts Propertius's poems with the epic subjects and aspirations of Ponticus's poetry. Such a contrast will set the world of the poet/lover and the words associated with him (tender, soft, gentle, humble, miserable, in vain, neglect, pleasure, mistress, sorrow, complaint, loss, slavery, infamy, etc.) against the world and terms of epic (busy, hard, haughty, strong, military, accomplishment, master, threats, benefits, achievement, triumph, fame, pride, etc.). It is part of Propertius's tactic here, as it was at the end of elegy I 6, to reverse many of these associations. In doing so, he both denies to Ponticus exclusive possession of the terms associated with epic praise and reevaluates the place of pride Ponticus desires: Ponticus is a false giant. He then claims for himself true poetic priority because of the irresistible power of love and the universal success of his poems—poems which even Ponticus will admire.

1. <u>Ponticus</u>: We know little about this poet. He was a writer of epic and a friend of Ovid as well as an acquaintance of Propertius. Presumably he wrote a *Thebaid*, or a poem on Thebes. His name, which means "of or belonging to the sea," well suits the language of Callimachean polemics in which the ocean is associated with Homer and the vast and muddy scope of epic poetry.

1–2. <u>Cadmean Thebes</u>: Cadmus was the founder of Thebes, the city from which Oedipus was banished and where his sons Eteocles and Polynices fought and killed each other in competition for sole possession of the throne.

10. <u>my fame</u>: The pursuit of fame and glory, of a name and reputation, was the foundation of Roman aristocratic values.

12. <u>a learned girl</u>: The characteristic description of an elegiac lover's mistress; she best understood and was often even won over by the poet's learned artifice.

16. <u>that Boy</u>: The reference is to Cupid who typically appears with his bow and arrows; compare I 6. 23–24.

18. <u>useless the seven armies</u>: Propertius alludes to the poem on Thebes which Ponticus is writing. When Polynices attacked Thebes in order to win the throne from his brother Eteocles, he arrived with seven allies and their respective armies. In effect Cynthia will be the love poet's ally, while all the allies of Thebes will not help Ponticus.

21. <u>a late love informs no verse</u>: With this couplet Propertius looks forward to elegy I 9 and makes an extraordinary claim for the value of his poetry: not only will the young men of lines 24–25 appreciate his achievement, but the old poets who praise the traditional and martial Roman virtues will be converted and will attempt, unsuccessfully, to emulate him.

22. <u>no humble poet</u>: A proud and triumphant claim which affords a curious echo of Horace's description of Cleopatra (*Odes* I 37. 32) as she eluded Octavian's triumph, "no humble woman."

I 9

Propertius's warnings have come true: Ponticus has fallen in love. The poet takes the occasion to celebrate what amounts to his victory and the victory of love (poetry) over war (poetry). He is a prophet, his predictions were correct and now only his song can afford Ponticus any respite. Propertius begins in mocking triumph. He then adopts the tone of a *praeceptor amoris*, or "teacher of love," as he outlines the further course of Ponticus's passion. The notion of the poet/priest/prophet, or *vates*, was first introduced by Vergil in his *Eclogues*. It became, especially for Horace, an image of the poet's special abilities and responsibilities in the public realm.

1. <u>I told you</u>: A reference back to elegy I 7. 15–16.

3. <u>beggar</u>: The appropriate reversal of roles for one who celebrated victory and heroes.

4. <u>some bought girl</u>: It is doubly painful for Ponticus: not only has he fallen in love, but he has fallen for some prostitute.

5. <u>Chaonian doves</u>: Chaonia was a district of Greece opposite the heel of Italy where the famous oracle of Zeus at Dodona was located. It is disputed whether the priestesses at this oracle were called "Doves" or whether the birds were themselves the prophets. In any event, Propertius equates his words in matters of love with prophecies sent from Zeus.

8. <u>how gladly I would stammer</u>: The inherent contradiction of passion like Propertius's surfaces here: he is glad of his victory and his power as a love poet, but he would also be glad to never have fallen in love. The idea that it is love that makes the love poet eloquent is made explicit at the beginning of Book II when he says that Cynthia "alone creates my genius"; see elegy II 1. 4.

9. <u>tumid epic</u>: In the language of the Callimachean program, epic poetry was swollen with debris from everywhere, unlike the refined and slender Alexandrian verse.

10. <u>Amphion's lyre</u>: The poet Amphion, by playing on a lyre given him by Apollo, caused the stones themselves to move and arrange themselves as a wall.

11.   Mimnermus: The first great elegiac love poet, Mimnermus, wrote around 630 B.C.E.

15–16.   The meaning of this couplet is disputed. The language clearly recalls the terms of the Callimachean opposition to epic: it was muddy, like a swollen stream or like the ocean. It seems that Propertius says that Ponticus is crazy because as an epic poet he is in the midst of a flood, but he is looking for clear potable springwater as a love poet, a Callimachean poet, should. He is crazy, therefore, to think that he can drink salt or muddy water or use it to win his girl. Line 15, however, still presents difficulties. As translated, we may imagine Propertius saying that it could be worse, he might not even have success to sing of. The Latin, however, might also refer to poetry and could be translated, "what if excess (as an epic poet) was not easy?" In this case, Propertius is presumably mocking Ponticus's excess as something that comes easy but turns out to be empty. There may be an allusion here to the punishment in Tartarus of Tantalus.

19.   Armenian tigers: These tigers are proverbially savage. The willingness here to undertake all trials recalls Propertius's use of Milanion in elegy I 1.

20.   Ixion's hellish wheel: Ixion attempted to seduce Jupiter's wife Juno, and was punished in the underworld by being bound to a wheel that turned forever.

21.   Love's shaft: "Love," or "Cupid" is regularly pictured as firing an arrow into the lover's marrow when he makes one fall in love.

28.   watches kept: An allusion to the theme of the lover as a warrior: love will not allow the lover to keep a night watch for anyone but the particular beloved.

31.   Such suavity: Love's charms, their suavity, are given powers similar to those of Orpheus's lyre which, according to legend, could move trees and rocks. If we recall the allusion to magical song in the first poem, one may note that while love itself has power like Orpheus to move stone and tree, still the power of Orpheus cannot move or cure love.

I 16

This poem is one of the most unusual of Propertius's elegies. It is his example of a *paraclausithyron*, a lover's serenade late at night, usually on returning from a party, at the closed door of his girlfriend. It was a common motif in ancient comedy and a common genre in ancient poetry. Examples may be found in epigram, Theocritus's idylls, and even in the lyric fragments of Alcaeus. The typical features include a lover who has been drinking and arrives at the door of his beloved with garlands and torches where he keeps a midnight vigil, complains of the weather, alternately kisses and curses the door, and worries that his beloved is in the arms of another. The "deification" of the door and a married beloved seem to be Roman features of the genre. Catullus composed a variation on the *paraclausithyron* (poem 67*) in which a passerby greets a street door in Verona and the door recounts the scandalous adventures of its former mistress. That poem, no doubt, suggested to Propertius his similar variation. Here the door complains again of the mistress's conduct but extends its complaint to include the pathetic complaints of the lover "reciting his verse with plangent charm." This variation on the *paraclausithyron* complains about the genre at the same time that it includes an example of the lover's complaint. This is a very witty subterfuge: a conservative door, a door that used to stand for triumphs and Roman values, complains like a lover about the lovers complaining at the door. Compare Tibullus I 2; Horace *Odes* III 10, and Ovid *Amores* I 6.

1. mighty triumphs: The door immediately poses as one who values conservative Roman aspirations; one should compare Propertius's attitude to military glory elsewhere, for instance in the poems to Ponticus (I 7 and I 9) and at II 7. 13–14.

2. Tarpeia's chastity: The Tarpeian family was an old aristocratic family in Rome whose members are not heard of again after 452 B.C.E. Commentators are at a loss to discover the Tarpeia to whom this might refer, especially since the most famous Tarpeia betrayed Rome and the Capitoline to the leader of the Sabines, who she loved and who held Rome under seige during Romulus's kingship. Propertius tells his version of this legend in IV 4. Since it is impossible not to think of this faithless Tarpeia, even if there is another Tarpeia renowned for chastity of whom we know nothing, still the allusion is problematic.

3. gilded chariots: The triumphant general rode in a gilded chariot to his door.

11. reputation: A woman's most important possession, as "glory" and "fame" is a man's most important aspiration—for the typical conservative and aristocratic Roman. Compare Propertius's attitude in II 7. 19–20.

29. Sicilian rock: Either lava, of which Sicily had a great deal because of Mt. Etna, or agate, which was first discovered in Sicily.

42–44. offerings: Doorways were especially important in Roman religion and it appears to be a special feature of the Roman *paraclausithyron* to treat the door as if it were a god.

48. mourning, am famous in eternal shame: This line could stand as a summary of the elegiac poet's aspiration. Compare poem I 6. 25–26 (where "shame" = Latin, *nequitia*).

I 19

This is the last elegy on Cynthia in the *Monobiblos*. Here, as often in Propertius, death provides the occasion for measuring his passion, imagining his fears, and expressing his hopes. Compare Tibullus's handling of the same topos; for example, in elegy I 1. 59ff.

7. In that dark place, Protesilaus: The "dark place" is Hades, land of the dead; Protesilaus was a young man from Thessaly who married Laodamia but had only one day of married life with her before leaving as commander of the Greek forces from Phylace to fight at Troy for the return of Helen. He was doomed to be the first Greek killed at Troy. His ghost was then allowed to visit Laodamia for a single day, and upon his departure she killed herself.

13. the troop of beauties: On the defeat of Troy, the Greek leaders were granted by lot or choice the women of Troy as their concubines.

14. Argive men: Another name for the Greeks who fought at Troy.

I 21

Here Propertius takes a common genre of Hellenistic poetry, the literary representation of an epitaph, and adapts it to a contemporary theme: the doubtlessly common tragedy in the years of civil war of unburied and unrecovered kinsmen. The speaker is a certain Gallus; he addresses a fellow soldier, perhaps the brother of his betrothed, as that soldier flees from the seige of Perusia in 41 B.C.E. The town, which had revolted against Octavian, was surrounded with ramparts and gradually starved.

Several attempts were made to break the seige, and the Gallus of this poem apparently was killed during one of those attempts. When the town yielded, Octavian made a human sacrifice of 300 senators (according to the historian Dio) at the altar of Julius Caesar, his adoptive father. Much property was then confiscated, probably including some property that belonged to Propertius's family, which was from the neighborhood of Perusia and rich enough to attract attention.

1. You, soldier: Typically a Hellenistic epigram addresses the passerby, telling him to stop and read the sad fate of the person buried there. Propertius inverts the form: he says, in effect, "keep running and save yourself."

3. when I moan: It suddenly appears that the speaker is not dead, speaking from a tombstone, but still barely alive. In a sense, then, the generic conventions of epitaph suddenly come alive—the voice is a real voice; the fate to escape is not an abstract comment on the human condition, but a real and threatening death.

10. Etruscan hills: Perusia was located in the hills of eastern Etruria, near the plains of Umbria.

I 22

The last poem of a poetry book was often called a *sphragis*, or "seal poem," that is, a poem in which the poet identified himself by his origins and called attention to his achievements. See also Horace *Odes* III 30. This poem is addressed to the career politician Tullus, also addressed in I 1 and I 6 (see notes there), who is represented as having asked where Propertius was born. Propertius's answer is that he was born in Umbria not far from Perusia. He takes advantage of this proximity to lament again the civil war and especially the destruction of Perusia (see poem I 21, above). The *Monobiblos*, then, ends with two epigrammatic attempts by Propertius to come to terms with the brutality of the Civil War, especially as it affected him and his country's leader, the destroyer of Perusia, Octavian.

2. household gods: The Penates, a general term for all the gods worshiped in the home, were the most generally worshiped of the Roman deities. Each home held a shrine to these deities whose special province was to protect the home from harm.

4. Perusia, our country's grave: The town which was beseiged by Octavian in 41 B.C.E. See notes on I 21, above, for more details. To call Perusia "our country's grave" is a bit of an exaggeration, since it was only the aristocracy (300 senators) who were killed when the town capitulated.

7. Etruscan dust: Perusia was a town in Etruria.

9. you do not cover: And so his soul must remain on the far side of the river Styx and is not allowed to enter the land of the dead. Among other things the image is one of failed consolation, of duty still to be done.

10. Umbria: Umbria was the territory to the east of Etruria. It is likely that Asisium (a town above the Umbrian plain famous today for being the birthplace of St. Francis of Assisi) was Propertius's home.

Book II

Book II seems to have been written between 28 and 25 B.C.E. and is concerned with Propertius's developing and degenerating affair with Cynthia and with the poet's response to traditional Roman values. Readers have generally felt an increased intensity and even abandon in these poems: Cynthia is elevated to divine status by being compared with a goddess for the first time (II 2); the Trojan War plays a larger role in the poet's imagination (II 1. 13–14, II 2. 13–14, 14. 1–2); death plays a more prominent role; and examples from myth are more frequently cited, sometimes as justification for the poet's emotions. Together with this increased intensity, however, readers have also noticed a growing irony and distance, especially in the fantasies of poems 26a and 29a. Propertius continues his programmatic debate with epic, sometimes wittily expanding the figure of lovemaking-as-battle into the claim that with a naked Cynthia he will "compose long *Iliad*s" (II 1. 14), sometimes comparing his emotions with those of epic heroes (e.g., II 14. 1–10).

    The period in which Book II was written was the period in which Octavian took the name "Augustus," consolidated his power, and claimed to return the Republic to the Roman people. It was also a time when many Romans were concerned with national renewal and moral reform. Propertius's poetry, both in general and sometimes specifically (see the note on poem II 7), reflects the new pressures and realities of Augustus's regime (see elegy II 10).

    Book II is the longest book of elegies in our collection, and within it the elegies themselves get longer. Some scholars believe that the book is actually an amalgamation of two books of poetry, and the confusing state of the text may be taken to support this view. The poems are often marked by abrupt transitions. This has been variously interpreted: sometimes as a reflection of Propertius's stormy emotional life, other times as evidence that what appears as a single poem in our manuscripts is really two poems; see below on II 24 and 26. On the other hand, many poems of Book II have a demonstrably clear and mathematically regular structure.

II 1

Due to the success of the *Monobiblos*, Propertius is now a member of Maecenas's literary circle. Maecenas was a very close friend of Augustus; he was left in charge of Rome more than once during the period 36–29 B.C.E. when Octavian was absent. His literary circle included Vergil and Horace, and his name became synonymous with literary patronage. (For more on Maecenas, see Horace *Odes* I 1). Given the position of this address to Maecenas (the first poem of Propertius's new book) and its subject matter (the writing of poetry and the poet's future) one might suspect that Maecenas had become Propertius's patron. However, unlike Horace, Propertius probably did not need any financial assistance from Maecenas and there is little evidence of any intimacy between patron and poet. Maecenas is addressed only here in Book II; in Book III he loses the pride of first place and is addressed only in poem 9; in Book IV he is not addressed at all.

    Propertius begins in answer to a question from Maecenas by reflecting on the success of his first book, the *Monobiblos* (1–16); he then moves in a fairly traditional fashion to a *recusatio*, or refusal, to write epic, (17–46), followed by a description of his elegiac aspirations (47–56) and his incurable passion (57–70). He concludes with a brief address to Maecenas in which he asks Maecenas to address his tomb and so to characterize his life.

1. You: We learn in line 17 that the addressee is Maecenas.

2. my sweet book: A reference to the publication of his *Monobiblos*.

3. Not Calliope, not Apollo: Calliope is one of the nine Muses and the one particularly favored by Propertius; Apollo is the god of poetry. Roman literature in general shifted the emphasis in passages that reveal the poet's inspiration from the Muses, common in Greek literature, to the individual poetic talent; compare the beginning of Vergil's *Aeneid* ("Arms and the man I sing . . . .") with the beginning of Homer's *Iliad* ("Sing, goddess, the wrath of Achilles . . ."). Propertius makes this shift in emphasis specifically elegiac when he claims that his girlfriend creates his talent. In a sense, he says that Cynthia is his Muse, and, as noted on poem I 1, she is appropriately named for that role (Cynthia = one who belongs to or is related to Cynthus Apollo).

5. Coan silk: The finest silk came from the island of Cos where, according to Pliny, a woman named Pamphile had invented the process for unraveling cocoons and weaving the thread into material for women's dresses—"in order to make feminine clothes a form of nudity." Prostitutes in Rome were commonly dressed in sheer silk.

7. her curls: The arrangement of the hair for Roman women both took a large amount of time and served as an expression of fashion. It is frequently a subject for the moralists who disapprove of the attention given to hair and for the amoralists like the elegiac poets who can be careful observers of fashion. Ovid provides the latter perspective; Tertullian, a Christian ascetic of the late second and early third century C.E., offers an interesting version of the moralist's perspective: "Why can you not give your hair a rest? One minute you are building it up, the next you are letting it down—raising it one moment, stretching it the next. Some women devote all their energy to forcing their hair to curl, others to making it hang loose and wavy, in a style which may seem natural, but is not natural at all. You perpetrate unbelievable extravagances to make a kind of tapestry of your hair, sometimes to be a sort of sheath to your head and a lid to the top of you, like a helmet, sometimes to be an elevated platform, built up on the back of your neck." (Tertullian, *On Women's Fashion*, translated by J. P. V. D. Balsdon in *Roman Women* [London: Bodley Head, 1962] 258).

9. lyre: Playing the lyre was expected of the elegiac poet's "educated girl."

14. long *Iliad*s: The *Iliad*, being itself a long epic poem, was exactly the kind of poem a Callimachean poet should not aspire to write. Nevertheless, it was both a tale of love and battle (the battle of the Greeks against the Trojans to win back Helen).

17–78. Propertius describes his poetic choices, first in terms of what he cannot write and then in terms of his aspirations and his passion. The first part (17–46) is structured as a *recusatio*, a poetic form in which typically the poet refuses a request from his patron to write an epic in praise of either the patron's deeds or those of the leader of the state. Here Propertius preempts such a request by averring that, if he had his way, he would choose of his own to write the praise of Caesar. He illustrates this preference in twenty lines (19–38). Such illustrations could serve several purposes: they might take the place of a hymn of praise and so actually offer in smaller scope what the patron requested; they might suggest that the poet really could accomplish such a hymn if he chose and so emphasize the moral dimension of the poet's stylistic choice; and they could undermine their own content, becoming an illustration of what is undesirable in such poetic projects.

19–20. Titans: In the war which the Titans waged against the gods, and especially against the sky god, Jupiter, they piled (according to Homer) the mountain Ossa on Olympus and Pelion on Ossa in order to build a stairway to heaven.

21. Thebes: This ancient city in Greece was the home of Oedipus the king and the location of those stories about him and his family which are collectively known as the Theban cycle. This would include the war of the Seven against Thebes which was the subject of an epic reputed to be by Homer and the subject of Ponticus's epic in elegy I 7.

21. Troy: The location of the Trojan War and so of Homer's *Iliad*.

22. Xerxes: At the beginning of the fifth century, B.C.E., Xerxes, a king of Persia, dug a canal through an isthmus near Mt. Athos in order more safely to bring his fleet to Greece for an invasion.

23. Remus's first reign: Remus and his twin brother Romulus were together the joint rulers of the city that was to become Rome. In a dispute, Romulus killed Remus and so the city received Romulus's name and was called Rome. The story of the origins of Rome in a fratricide gradually became a troubling emblem of Rome's later civil wars. The story is the subject of the first books of Ennius's *Annales* (about 180 B.C.E.) and the first book of Livy's history of Rome, *From the Founding of the City*, which Livy was beginning to write at this time (28–25 B.C.E.).

23. Carthage's pride: Carthage, a city on the north coast of Africa, was a great center of Mediterranean maritime trade until it came repeatedly into conflict with the political and economic interests of a growing Rome. Its "haughty pride" is apparently a reference to the hostilities that broke out three times: after the first war (264–41 B.C.E.), Carthage was forced to evacuate its holdings in Sicily and to pay indemnities; after the second war (218–201 B.C.E), during which the Carthaginian general Hannibal made his famous march across the Alps with his elephants, it was forced to give up its navy; and after the third war (149–146 B.C.E.), it was utterly destroyed. The Roman poet Naevius wrote an epic, *The Punic War*, which treated the first war; Ennius, in his *Annales*, treated the second.

24. Cimbrian threats and the feats of Marius: The tribes of Germany, of which the Cimbri were one, troubled the Roman world toward the end of the second century B.C.E. The great Roman general Marius, credited with reconstituting and reorganizing the Roman army, finally brought the threat they represented to an end with victories over the Teutones in 102 B.C.E. and over the Cimbri in 101 B.C.E.

25. Your Caesar's: Octavian, who went by the name Julius Caesar, received the name by which we usually refer to him, Augustus, in 27 B.C.E. Assuming that introductory and programmatic poems come late in the composition of a book of poetry, one may imagine that this poem was written around 25 B.C.E. At that time, Octavian's history as a general presented some problems. His wars and victories at this time would include little more than his impressive victories over Romans in the recent civil war, a subject that entailed difficulties for any Roman. Nevertheless, he had established peace, paid his armies, and contemplated a return to normal republican government. In the lines that follow Propertius summarizes what he takes to be the most significant of Augustus's achievements.

26. my second care: At this time Maecenas was arguably the second man in Rome: during Octavian's absence he had been left in sole charge of the city from 36–33 B.C.E. and together with Agrippa from 31–29 B.C.E.

27. Mutina: In 43 B.C.E. Octavian defeated Mark Antony at Mutina and rescued Decimus Brutus (not the same man as the Brutus who assassinated Caesar) from Antony's seige. Later Antony and Octavian would be allies; still later they would fight each other for sole rule of Rome.

27–28.   Philippan civil wars: In 42 B.C.E., together Antony and Octavian defeated Brutus and Cassius, the murderers of Julius Caesar, at Philippi.

28.   Sicilian rout: Sextus Pompey, son of Pompey the Great, inherited his father's war against the followers of Julius Caesar and was defeated in Sicily in 36 B.C.E., not by Octavian, who was himself defeated, but by Octavian's older allies, Agrippa and Lepidus. After Lepidus claimed the island and dismissed Octavian, Lepidus's troops, weary of fighting, deserted to Octavian, who returned to Rome as the victor.

29.   old Etruscan race: The Etrurian town of Perusia was close to the place of Propertius's birth. During the civil wars it sided against Octavian and was beseiged and defeated in 41 B.C.E. See poem I 21 and I 22 for further details and for Propertius's feelings about the event.

30.   Ptolomaean Pharos: Pharos was an island at the entrance to the harbor of one of the great Egyptian cities, Alexandria, which had been made the seat of government by the Ptolomies. After the battle of Actium in 31 B.C.E., Octavian conquered and annexed the kingdom of Egypt.

31.   Egypt and Nile: The Nile with its seven mouths is the great river of Egypt. In triumphal processions it was usual to display effigies representing conquered countries and their cities and rivers.

33.   the necks of kings: Augustus claimed that in his triumphs he had led nine kings or children of kings. It was common to display captives in chains and to indicate royalty with gilded chains.

34.   Actium: The final sea battle against Mark Antony and Cleopatra in 31 B.C.E. brought an end to the civil wars and left Octavian in sole possession of power. The battle there became the subject of Propertius's elegy IV 6. See further the notes there.

34.   the Sacred Way: The road on which the triumphal procession passed through the forum to the capitol.

35.   warlike scenes: Maecenas did not usually accompany Octavian during the wars here cataloged; his role was to remain at Rome in charge of the city.

37–38.   Theseus, Pirithous: This is a traditional exemplum of friendship and loyalty. Theseus and Pirithous had attempted to carry off Proserpina from the underworld but were captured. Theseus was rescued by Hercules but was unable to rescue his friend. See also Horace *Odes* IV 7. 27–28.

37–38.   Achilles, Patroclus: Another traditional exemplum of friendship and love. Achilles during the Trojan War had been partially responsible for the death of his friend Patroclus. His grief and rage at this loss became the occasion for his return to the battle and his defeat of Hector, the great Trojan leader. In both of these examples the hero's attendant is killed because of the hero's activities.

39–40.   titanic tumults: An early subject for epic poetry was the battle between the Gods and the Giants, in which Jove (also called Jupiter) used his thunderbolt to blast the giant Enceladus and confine him under Mt. Etna. The battle against the Titans (the *Titanomachia*) was actually a different battle, but was often confused with the *Gigantomachia*, or battle against the Giants.

42.   Trojan source: Julius Caesar claimed descent from Iulus, son of Aeneas. Aeneas, son of Venus and Anchises, was the Trojan who escaped the destruction of Troy and came to Italy with his band of refugees where intermarriage with the native Italians formed what became the Latin race. This is the subject of Vergil's *Aeneid*, which was already underway and receiving attention and favor from important men. Propertius writes with this new literary development in mind.

43–45. The sailor . . . the farmer . . . the soldier . . . the shepherd. . . . I . . . . : The transition from *recusatio* to a description of Propertius's poetic aspirations is effected by a *priamel* (45–47), or "preamble." Here Propertius rewrites one of the most famous lyric *priamels* in Western poetry, Sappho 16: "Some say the most beautiful thing on the dark earth is an army of cavalry, others of soldiers, and others of ships; I say it is what you love."

45. narrow bed: A transference to the bedroom of the "slender muse" and the "narrow path" which Callimachean poetics valued.

46–78. The second part of Propertius's program elaborates the nature of his aspirations and his commitment to elegy. The picture he offers is one of growing morbidity; it concludes with the image of Maecenas addressing the poet's tomb. The specter of death is more frequently on the horizon of Book II than it was in the *Monobiblos*.

47. glory to die in love: This is a revision of the patriotic slogan, "it is sweet and proper to die for one's country." Here death appears (albeit unobtrusively) for the first time in this elegy.

48. my love alone: No sooner does Propertius fix his attention on the glories of his chosen way of life and profession than the sorrows of that life also appear.

50. *Iliad:* Helen was the cause of the Trojan War, after the Trojan prince Paris abducted or seduced her from her husband.

51. Phaedra's poison: Phaedra fell in love with her stepson Hippolytus and attempted to make him fall in love with her. The story of the love potion or poison is not part of the versions that have come down to us and the precise details of the allusion are obscure, although it seems that in this version Phaedra gave Hippolytus a drug which was intended to arouse his passion but instead killed him.

53. Circe's herbs: Circe, Phaedra's aunt, was a notorious witch/goddess who turned Odysseus's men into swine upon his visit to her island (as told by Homer in *Odyssey* X). Odysseus, with Hermes' help, freed his men from the spell and then lived with her for a year.

54. Medea: Another witch from mythology and again a neice of Circe. She fell in love with Jason and at his home in Iolchus rejuvenated Aeson, Jason's father, by boiling him with certain herbs. She then persuaded the daughters of Pelias, the half-brother of Aeson and guardian to Jason, to do the same to their father, but she did not give them the right herbs and he was killed by the process.

57. Medicine cures all: The topos here claims that only love cannot be healed by medicine. The exempla that follow reflect Propertius's interest in learned Callimachean poetry. They are all of the miraculous sort, meant to illustrate the extraordinary powers of medicine.

59. Machaon, Philoctetes: According to this version, Machaon, a doctor in the *Iliad*, cured Philoctetes of a festering and foul-smelling wound caused by a snakebite or by one of Hercules' poisoned arrows.

60. Philyridean Chiron, Phoenix: Chiron, a centaur and master of medicine, was the son of Zeus and the nymph Philyra. He cured Phoenix of the blindness caused by his own father when Phoenix was falsely charged with seducing his father's mistress.

61. Epidaurian god, Androgeos: The Epidaurian god was Asclepius, the god of healing, who had a sanctuary at Epidaurus. According to Propertius's version (which is unique), he was able to restore to life Androgeos, the son of King Minos of Crete.

63. Mysian youth, Achilles: The king of Mysia, Telephus, was wounded by Achilles and cured by an application of rust from the very spear that caused the wound.

65. he alone: There follows a series of allusions to incurable afflictions from mythology. As such, any reference to their cure or alleviation is the equivalent of an *adynaton*, or natural

impossibility. Taken together they suggest that Propertius's passion is forever unsatisfied, his actions are forever ineffective, and his wound is forever renewed.

66. apples to Tantalus's hand: Tantalus is reported to have committed various crimes against the gods. His punishment was to be placed in water that always receded from him when he tried to drink it and to be set underneath apples which always withdrew from his grasp.

67. the virgins' urns: The Danaids, who murdered their husbands on their wedding night, were condemned to carry water in leaky urns.

69. Prometheus: Prometheus, a Titan and trickster figure who stole fire from the gods for the benefit of men, was chained to a rock on Mt. Caucasus where a vulture continually devoured his liver which was continually restored. It may be relevant that Maecenas had written a *Prometheus*.

76. British chariot: The Celtic war chariot referred to here had been adopted by the Romans for pleasure. Maecenas's chariot is apparently embellished, an allusion to his notoriously luxurious life-style.

II 2

As a poem of praise for Cynthia's beauty this poem shares the basic impulse of Catullus 43. Catullan praise of Lesbia arises from the poet's confidence, focuses on her looks, and is joined to a background of invective; Propertian praise of Cynthia draws in from its mythological allusions a set of emotional associations entirely foreign to Catullus and is joined to a narrative of failed freedom.

2. having made peace: If love is like war and the lover like a soldier, then the end of an affair is peace and freedom.

4. Jupiter: Jupiter's amatory adventures were legendary. For the poet to forgive Jupiter is both pretentious and a momentary lapse into the attitude of the (now understanding) moralist.

6. Juno's equal: A comparison that might well describe Jupiter's view of all of his dalliances. This is the first time that Cynthia is compared to a goddess and she comes off rather well: she is likened to Juno, Athena, Brimo, and Venus.

7. Pallas: Pallas Athena, daughter of Jupiter, helped Odysseus in the *Odyssey* find his way back home to Ithaca. She wore an *aegis*, or breastplate, adorned with the head of a Gorgon.

9–10. Ischomache, Centaur: A mortal woman of whom we know little; the name occurs only here. At the marriage of Pirithous (chieftain of a Thessalian people called "Lapiths") and Hippodamia a fight broke out between the Lapiths and the centaurs resulting in the rape of several women by the centaurs. The centaurs were wild beasts, half horse and half human, noted for being lustful and fond of wine.

11–12. Brimo, Boebeis, Mercury: The text is corrupt and we do not know exactly what Propertius means here. Some editors do not accept the reference to Brimo and assume that Propertius continues to speak of Ischomache. In that case we must assume that she had an affair with Mercury. If not, then Propertius mentions a Thessalian goddess, Brimo, often associated with Hecate, Artemis, and Persephone. Mercury tried to rape her and in one version of the story failed. Lake Boebeis is on the eastern border of Thessaly.

13. goddesses whom, Paris once judged: Paris, a handsome prince of Troy, was asked to judge the beauty of the goddesses Juno, Minerva, and Venus on Mt. Ida in Phrygia near Troy.

He chose Venus because she offered him as his reward the most beautiful woman in the world, Helen, and so began the Trojan War.

16. Cumaean Sibyl: The Sibyl of Cumae was destined to live a thousand years.

II 4

The poem effects a transition to the next set of poems (5–9) which probe in more explicit detail the nature of Propertius's affair with Cynthia.

7. Here: That is, "in love." The theme that there is no cure for love is a common one in Propertius, going back to the first elegy of the *Monobiblos*.

7. Medea: The witch/sorceress who aided Jason; see above on II 1. 54.

8. Perimede's art: Another witch who is linked with Circe and Medea by the bucolic poet Theocritus.

11. This patient needs no doctors: While this may at first sound like a reprise of the major theme of II 1 and a theme common in Propertius since I 1 (namely that doctors can do the love-sick poet no good), this is actually the opposite theme: that lovers have a special blessing from the gods and need fear no harm.

13. his corpse: By a brutal twist, the divinely blessed lover who (thought he) needed no doctors turns up dead and his friends are shocked at his funeral.

14. indefensible: The Latin can mean either that love shows no caution or that no amount of caution can protect one against the devastating effects of love.

18. Delight in a boy: This is not an uncommon topic of amatory consolation.

19. In a safe boat: The imagery is familiar from programmatic passages where the small boat hugging the shore and avoiding the open sea and its large waves is an image of the Callimachean poet's opposition to the grand and bombastic.

II 5

This is the first mention by name of Cynthia in Book II and it immediately sets the stage for the new tensions and strained ambivalences to come. The poet tries and fails to get free of her. The poem is in the tradition of Catullus 8 (anger, threats, vengence), especially in its use of self-address, but it lacks that poem's comic humor.

2. your unsavory life: The Latin here for "unsavory life" (*nequitia*) is also used in I 6. 25–26 to define the poet's own aspiration (there *nequitia* = "shame").

3ff. you'll pay the price . . .: A more intense version of Catullus's threat in 8. 15ff. Propertius lays special emphasis on punishment and retribution.

7. tear you apart: Apparently Propertius imagines a new lover who, like the Cynthia of II 1. 49–50, despises faithless women.

9. Leave now: Propertius begins to speak to himself and continues through, "All pain . . . is light," line 16.

11. Carpathian: A particularly dangerous sea located between Crete and Rhodes.

17. Juno's sweet rule: Juno was the patroness of women and marital happiness. She usually appears in elegy as the deceived and vengeful wife; as the patroness of marriage, she is not commonly invoked by elegists, being found only here and in Ovid's atypical poem III 13 on the Juno-worshipers of Falerii.

18. my life: This is the Latin idiom for "love of my life."

19. not only bulls: The topos that each animal protects himself as best he can, bulls with their horns, etc., is familiar as a justification for satire and iambic, or invective, poetry.

21. I won't tear the clothes: Compare Tibullus I 10. 61–64.

23. your woven locks: On the extraordinary attention Roman women paid to their hair, see above on elegy II 1. 7.

25. Let brutes: "Brutes" is *rusticus*, which means literally "country man." This would not be an unfitting reference to Tibullus, whose interest in and love of country life was a striking characteristic. Compare the ending of Tibullus elegy I 10 with the sentiment here.

28. Cynthia . . . Cynthia . . . : Propertius rewrites some of his famous lines on Cynthia from the *Monobiblos*: I 11. 26, "Whatever I will be, I'll say, 'Cynthia was the cause.'"; I 12. 20, "Cynthia was first, Cynthia shall be last."

II 7

This poem is a good example of Propertian defiance of conventional Roman values. Until a few years ago it was generally believed that Propertius in this poem responds to the withdrawal in 28 B.C.E. of a marriage law, an early version of Augustus's later moral legislation (18 B.C.E. and C.E. 9); it now seems most likely that the law which was repealed was a tax imposed on bachelors. In either case, Propertius imagines that the consequences of the law would have been to force him to become not just a husband, a responsible Roman man, but the husband of a woman other than Cynthia. He uses the occasion to parade his life and values, his amatory glory and elegiac patrimony, in the face of sterner conservative Roman values.

3. lest it divide us: There are two possible explanations: Cynthia was already married; Propertius could not marry her because she was a courtesan.

5. "But Caesar is great": The imagined retort of Cynthia or some unnamed interlocutor. Coming immediately after the reference to Jupiter, the retort implies a comparison between Jupiter and Caesar in which Cynthia fears Caesar more than Jupiter. The implication that Caesar, at least in these matters, is both sterner and more potent than the greatest of the gods is both sacrilege and mockery.

8. waste torches at a bride's whim: The reading in the Latin and the meaning of the line is in dispute. Many prefer "waste my passion" as the figurative meaning of "waste torches"; compare the torches of the first epigram of Valerius Aedituus in the Appendix. Some prefer a different Latin text and read "in love of a wife" in place of "at a bride's whim." In any event, the poet claims that he would prefer death to the consequences of the proposed law and that the proposed law would require his marriage to another woman.

8, 9, 11. torches, parade, flute: Propertius refers to the standard features of the Roman wedding ceremony: torches were carried in the wedding procession and a double flute played at the ceremony. But there are double meanings here: torches accompanied the lover as he returned from a party to his beloved's door (see I 16) and torches are also a familiar image of passion (compare the English, "He still carries a torch for her"); the flute may also refer to the poet's pipe and so to his poetry.

9. past your closed door: By emphasizing "past" one may sense the implicit meaning that this law would have prevented Propertius from writing any more *paraclausithyra* (see I 16).

12. horn's funeral note: A special trumpet was played at funeral services; see Propertius II 13. 20.

13. sons of mine: If this poem does refer to marriage legislation, and not a bachelor tax, then this line refers to the intent of such legislation, namely to increase the birth rate among the aristocracy. If we are dealing with a bachelor tax, then Propertius takes the opportunity to offer an ethical perspective. Conservative Roman morals espoused responsible marriages by Roman citizens which would produce citizen children who would then serve and protect the country. The poet's amoral life style is here defended as a challenge to conservative values: it does not lead to marriage and so does not lead to children which would become mere "cannon fodder." This refusal prepares the way for Propertius's polemical variation on the lover as soldier topos.

16. Castor's horse: Castor and his twin, Pollux, were deities who had fought, according to legend, against the Latins in 496 B.C.E. to preserve the Republic in its early years from an attempt to reestablish the kingship. Castor's horse, Cyllarus, was a gift from Juno and considered one of the finest horses of all time.

20. more than my father's name: This is a striking assertion of the poet's willingness to renounce family, responsibility, and the social standing which some are entitled to by birth. In the Roman view of things, it is a stronger claim than it would be for us today. One's relationship to both the gods and the state were consciously modeled on the fundamental patriarchal relationship of fathers and sons.

II 10

This poem at first appears to be Propertius's first poem in support of the new Augustan dispensation, a striking contrast to the attitude adopted in II 7 above. The style is the high style of hymnic praise poetry; Augustus is now addressed as "my leader" (compare poem II 1. 25: "Your Caesar') and the poet explicitly assumes the mantle of *vates*, or poet/priest/prophet. This exuberance, however, is restrained because the avowed project is one that suits old age (line 7), it remains in the future (20) and at the poem's conclusion the poet substitutes this twenty-six-line elegy of good intentions for the promised future epic.

1. Helicon: The largest mountain in Boeotia (southern Greece) which was the site of the spring Hippocrene, inspiration of poets and home of the Muses.

2. Thessalian horse: Thessaly was noted for its war-horses. Horses were sometimes used as a metaphor for poetry.

3. troops brave in battle: Compare Propertius's attitude to military service in poem II 7, where he only wished to "serve in my love's army," line 15.

6. will suffices: Although these lines may seem to mock any poet undertaking courtly poetry on behalf of Augustus, they also lay the foundation for this poem's closure: the poem will end with the claim that the poet had the "will" to write an epic, even if Augustus must resign himself to being satisfied with the elegiac expression of desire.

7–8.   Let youth . . . maturity . . .; wars I shall sing: The form is that of a *priamel;* the content inverts the typical lyric and elegiac *priamel.* See above on II 1. 43–45.

7.   maturity: The Latin offers the incongruous claim that "old age should sing of uprisings." It is impossible that Propertius thought of himself as an old man at this time.

11.   Arise, soul, from lowliness: The Callimachean Roman celebrated the slight and insignificant in his verse and even claimed that his verse was itself nothing more than trifling; see Catullus 1. This was one way in which the poetic and stylistic program of Callimachus himself was given an explicitly political and ethical significance for the Romans.

13.   Euphrates, Parthian riders: The Parthians were a warlike people near the Euphrates River in Asia Minor. They were particularly famous for their style of fighting, one that depended solely on the cavalry. The riders, while pretending to retreat, would fire arrows backwards over their shoulders.

14.   the Crassi: Both M. Licinius Crassus, once the richest man in Rome and a member of the First Triumvirate, and his elder son were killed by the Parthians in the disaster at Carrhae in 53 B.C.E. The Parthians kept in their possession both Roman standards and Roman prisoners until they surrendered them to Augustus in 20 B.C.E.

15.   India even: India had marked the furthest eastern boundary of Alexander the Great's empire and so had come to mark the limit of Roman dreams of empire as well. We know of one embassy to Augustus from India in 26/25 B.C.E. and another in 20 B.C.E. Even if there were others at this time, the claim that India "gives her neck to your triumph" is at the very least exaggerated.

16.   Arabia's realm: In 25–24 B.C.E. Augustus ordered an expedition against Arabia. It ended in failure. If these lines were published after that failure, not only is the claim that Arabia "trembles before you" fantastic, but the description of Arabia as "untouched" becomes mockery. In any event, the praise here is exaggerated.

17.   earth's farthest borders: Most likely a reference to the western borders, that is to Britain, against which Augustus repeatedly (34, 27, and 26 B.C.E.) initiated expeditions which were never carried out.

19.   a great prophet: The Augustan poets, especially Vergil and Horace, used an old Latin religious term, *vates*, meaning something like "an oracular poet/priest" to define their serious relationship to the state, to moral reflection and political virtue. This line marks the first appearance of the term in Propertius; the next time he turns "vatic" (elegy II 17*), it is as a prophet of love.

21.   great statues: A Roman general in his triumphal procession would arrive at the statue of Jupiter Capitolinus in the temple of Jupiter on the Capitoline hill and there dedicate his golden crown of laurel leaves. Since the statue was too large to be crowned by the general himself, he would lay his crown in the statue's lap. Propertius takes this scene and pictures his own action as an even more dimunitive response: he lays garlands at the feet (not in the lap) of the statue.

23.   praise's triumph-car: The idea that a poet's praise, when just and fair, was itself a form of triumph had already been adopted by Vergil.

25–26.   Ascraean fount, Permessus's stream: Ascra was the birthplace of Hesiod, a Greek poet. In Vergil's *Eclogue* 6, a Muse initiates Gallus, whom she finds wandering by the Permessus, into poetry by leading him up Mt. Helicon above Ascra to the springs of the Permessus River: Hippocrene and Aganippe. The scene repeats the scene of initiation for Hesiod himself as Hesiod had recounted it in his *Theogony.* Here Propertius claims to remain with the lowly subjects of elegy rather than ascend, as did Gallus and Hesiod, to the lofty springs of real poetic inspiration. Compare the claim at the beginning of II 1: "Not Calliope, not Apollo . . . [Cynthia] alone creates my genius."

II 13

This remarkable elegy is sometimes treated as two elegies: 1–16, on the poet's commitment to Cynthia and to love poetry; 17–58, on the poet's pain and the vanity of life. There are, however, some good reasons to be skeptical about the division: an explicit connective ("Then"; Latin, *igitur* = therefore) joins the second part to the first; the wish that begins the second part follows easily from the wish that ends the first part; the Callimachean rejection of the "common clamor" (13) in the first part parallels the Callimachean rejection of the grandiose (19–26; see "small funeral, modest ritual," 24) in the second; and the poem's extraordinary capacity to compose the residue of emotional turmoil in coruscating images and transitions. It is this last general characteristic of the poem that convinces me to keep it as a single elegy. The first part is not so simply a celebration as some have made out. Already with "may I delight . . ." (11) pleasure and its cause are as much the purpose of prayer as they are a past reality; thereafter Cynthia appears as grieving mistress, perhaps as Polyxena, as an aged Nestor, as Venus herself, while Propertius imagines himself in the guise of the poet Linus, of Achilles, of a life-weary Nestor, of a dead Antilochus, and of Adonis. When these aspects of the poem are pulled out, it becomes clear that in addition to proclaiming a Callimachean program the poet here imagines a kind of heroic elegy; elegiac both because it values love over heroism and because in this poem the heroes are dead and all that remains is loss and grief. This is an extraordinary, if consistent, development of Propertius's initial view of elegy as primarily a form of complaint (see poem I 1).

1. Persian arrows arming Susa: Literally "Achaemenian" arrows. This is a learned Callimachean reference to Persia by means of an allusion to the founder of the clan to which the Persian kings Cyrus and Xerxes belonged. Susa was the capital of Persia. The reference is to the Parthians and their unique way of fighting by shooting back over their shoulders while pretending to flee.

3. He forbade: An allusion to the typical initiation scene in which a poet is directed to write a certain kind of poetry. For the Callimachean poet this means novel, refined, learned, polished, delicate verse. Compare Ovid *Amores* I 1.

4. Ascraea's grove: Ascra was the birthplace of Hesiod whose poetic initiation in the *Theogony* is the origin of these investiture scenes. There the Muses gave Hesiod a laurel rod and inspired him with a divine voice. The direction here to Ascraea's grove indicates that now Propertius's song will aspire to Hesiodic excellence. Compare the claim of poem II 10. 25, "My songs fall short of the Ascraean font." The following lines, however, limit this aspiration to elegiac excellence: "Not to . . . nor to . . . but to strike Cynthia dumb."

5. Pieria's oaks: Orpheus, the mythical and archetypical poet, was said to have charmed the animals with his song and to have made trees follow him. Pieria was a district of northern Thessaly associated with the Muses and where, according to some versions of the story, Orpheus was buried.

6. Ismaria's valley: Ismarus was a mountain in southern Thrace where Orpheus sang his songs and where he was, according to some versions, killed by maenads offended by his preoccupation with grief at the death of his wife, Eurydice.

8. Inachian Linus: Another allusion in the Callimachean manner. Inachus is the name of the first king and of the chief river of Argos in Greece; the adjective seems to have been used in general as a learned substitute for "Greek," just as "Achaemenian" was used for "Persian" in line 1. Linus was another mythical singer and learned poet, either the teacher or the brother of Orpheus, and a youth who met a violent death and became the subject of many dirges.

9–10: The claim that the poet's girlfriend is loved for qualities that are more than physical and that her qualities exceed what can be possessed by others goes back, in the Latin tradition, to Catullus 86; the rejection of traditional aristocratic aspirations for family fame and glory is an elegiac convention.

16. Jupiter's enmity: Compare II 7. 3.

19. family portraits: The Roman funeral procession was accompanied by the death masks of one's ancestors as an indication of the age and importance of one's family. Here Propertius reaffirms the indifference to social status he had expressed above at line 10.

20. trumpet: The special trumpet sound that indicated that the pyre was being lighted; compare II 7. 12.

21. with ivory headrest: According to archeological evidence, the corpse was often burned while lying on a couch, the headrest of which was inlaid with ivory.

23. fragrant platters: Apparently perfumes and incense were carried in on trays and cast into the fire during elaborate funeral ceremonies.

25. three books: This is the Propertian statement to which some scholars appeal as part of their arguments that what we have as Book II is really a conflation of Books II and III of Propertius's elegies.

26. Persephone: The beautiful goddess of the underworld to whom one should, according to Vergil, bring the Golden Fleece as a gift.

30. onyx jar: The corpse was annointed with perfume before being burned on the pyre; here the perfumes are referred to as "Syrian oils," a conventional epithet, because these were the most prized.

33. laurel: The tree is sacred to Apollo and to poets and its leaves were used for the triumphal crown of a victor or general.

35–36. For other instances of Propertius's fascination with his own death and with the epigrammatic view of a visitor to his tomb, see poems I 7. 25 and II 1. 78. For Propertius's pride in being faithful to one girl alone, see poem II 1. 48. The aspiration itself is a curious inversion of the conservative and outdated ideal for a Roman matron of being *univira*, that is, a woman who has had only one husband.

38. Achilles' bloody grave: Achilles, the greatest warrior and hero of Greek epic, had by his deeds and by Homer's celebration of them achieved eternal fame. His tomb was famous because Polyxena, the daughter of Priam, king of Troy, was sacrificed at it. As the elegiac competitor of epic, Propertius figures himself as Achilles; but when he does so with specific reference to Achilles' tomb, one may well wonder who is being figured as Polyxena.

43. Sister of the Three: A reference to the three sisters known as the Fates. According to ancient belief the three Fates determined the length of a person's life by spinning their life-thread, usually starting at birth, and snipping that thread at the appropriate point.

46. Nestor: Nestor, who lived three generations, saw his son Antilochus killed before his eyes while Antilochus was defending his father against Memnon. He is used here as an example of life-weariness, to localize the poet's depression. In this analogy, the external death which has made the poet cry the equivalent of "Oh Death, why come to me so late?" must be the death of

Cynthia's love for him. The passions which figure themselves in this way are in a sense murderous. But if Propertius has figured the loss of Cynthia as the death of a son, he is pursuing a Catullan tactic; see Catullus 72, 3–4 and Catullus 68, where the loss of Lesbia and the loss of a brother are paralleled with Laodamia's loss of her husband Protesilaus.

47. Ilium's ramparts: Ilium is another name for Troy.

54. snow-white Adonis: Adonis, a beautiful youth beloved by Venus, was killed by a wild boar while hunting on Mt. Idalium in Cyprus.

II 14

The textual integrity of this poem receives mixed reviews. Some, who find the last four lines so abruptly different in tone that they cannot be part of a continuous whole, print the poem as two poems; others believe the poem is neatly divided into three sections of ten lines each followed by a two-line coda. If we take the girl to be Cynthia, it seems particularly apposite that this poem celebrates a single night and not a change in the status quo (10), and the end of the poem is a return from the elegy of celebration and disdain to the elegy of complaint.

1. Not . . .: Propertius is the only one of the elegiac poets to use mythological exempla in a negative fashion as a foil to illustrate the uniqueness of his feelings; see on elegy I 1. 9–16.

1–2. Atrides, Trojan triumph, Laomedon's great labor: Laomedon was the Trojan king who built the walls of Troy; thus the city of Troy itself is referred to as his labor. Atrides is the Greek patronymic meaning, "son of Atreus," a reference to either Agamemnon, who led the Greek expedition against Troy, or to his brother Menelaus, whose wife Helen had left home with the Trojan Paris, thereby starting the Trojan War. Both allusions are apt to the Propertian analogy, since both would have rejoiced in the fall of Troy. Homer's epic, the *Iliad*, tells part of the story of this war.

3–4. Ulysses, Dulichia's shores: After the Trojan War, Ulysses, in Greek called Odysseus, wandered for ten years before returning to his faithful wife Penelope. As the first two lines referred to the *Iliad*, so these two lines refer to Homer's *Odyssey*.

5–6. Electra, Orestes, false bones: Clytemnestra had sent her son Orestes away before she killed her husband Agamemnon. Orestes returned and together with his sister Electra they killed their mother in retaliation for their father's murder. The scene alluded to here was a famous one, especially in Greek tragedy: Orestes arrives home at the very moment that Electra is grieving at Orestes' false tomb.

7–8. Minos's daughter, Theseus, Daedalian maze: The craftsman Daedalus built a labyrinth to contain the Minotaur, the bull/man monster on the island of Crete. King Minos exacted a yearly tribute consisting of youths and maidens who were sacrificed to the Minotaur. One of the youths was the Athenian prince Theseus, with whom Minos's daughter Ariadne fell in love. She helped Theseus out of the maze with a guiding thread and then sailed with him on his way back to Athens, but she was abandoned by him on the island of Naxos. There Bacchus came to her rescue. In I 3, Propertius began with a similar set of comparisons as he gazed on the sleeping Cynthia.

20. she'll come today: A reminiscence, perhaps, of Aphrodite's response to the Greek lyric poet Sappho in her "Hymn to Aphrodite": "If she flees, soon she will pursue."

23. <u>Parthia beaten</u>: A return to the militaristic concerns of the opening, but this time in terms of contemporary Roman issues. A victory over the Parthians had been desired by the Romans since Crassus lost his legions and standards there in 53 B.C.E. See further above on elegy II 13.

25. <u>Cytherea</u>: The island of Cythera in the Aegean Sea was noted and celebrated for its worship of Venus.

27. <u>THESE SPOILS</u>: Compare Horace *Odes* I 5, a poem whose ending Propertius may have in mind.

29. <u>Will my ship</u>: Venus, goddess of love, was born from the ocean; her Greek counterpart, Aphrodite, was said to have received her name from the word *aphros*, or "ocean foam." For this reason she was considered a sea goddess, and the stormy course of love was often likened to a stormy voyage at sea. See, for example, the ending of Horace *Odes* I 5. Here, however, the poet pictures himself with the harbor in sight and fearful of a last-minute disaster.

32. <u>dead before your door!</u>: The poet asks that his mistress not only lock him out, but let the poet die outside; this is an extraordinary reference to a grotesquely failed *paraclausithyron*.

II 26a

In most of our manuscripts, elegy 26 of this book is given as a fifty-eight-line poem; in some manuscripts, a new elegy is marked at line 29 of this poem. Most editors, however, divide the manuscript poem after line 20 and after line 29, giving three elegies. We have followed the consensus. Elegy 26a is a dream in which the poet recounts his thoughts on seeing his beloved drowning at sea.

1. <u>shipwrecked</u>: A shipwreck is a conventional image for a failed love affair; see above on elegy II 14, lines 29–30.

2. <u>Ionian foam</u>: The reference to the Ionian Sea is probably a verisimilar detail. If Cynthia were really sailing on the Ionian Sea, it would probably be because she was on a voyage to Greece.

5–6. <u>Helle, golden sheep</u>: Helle, the daughter of Athamas, king of Thebes, fell into the sea from a winged and golden ram on which she was riding while attempting to escape her stepmother Ino, who was jealous of her and hated her. The sea into which she fell was consequently called the Hellespont. It is the entry to the Black Sea from the Aegean and it divides Europe from Asia; Troy is on the Asiatic side.

9–10. <u>Neptune, Castor, and his brother, Leucothea</u>: All gods and goddesses to whom a sailor would pray for protection and safe passage, and to whom someone in Propertius's position would make prayers and promises. Neptune was the brother of Jupiter, whose dominion over the sea was parallel, if inferior, to Jupiter's dominion over the land and sky. Castor and his twin brother Pollux, called the Dioscuri, were patron deities of sailors. Leucothea was in her mortal life Ino, wife of Athamas, who was turned into the sea goddess while trying to escape her husband's vengeance for the pursuit of Helle described above.

13–14. <u>Glaucus, Ionian sea nymph</u>: Glaucus was a Boeotian fisherman who after eating a magic herb leaped into the sea and became a sea god. The Ionian Sea lies between Italy and Greece just below the Adriatic. The idea here seems to be that Cynthia is so beautiful that Glaucus would have offered his magic herb to her if he had caught sight of her.

15–16.   Nereids, Nesaee, Cymothoe: Nereus, the old man of the sea, was the father of the sea nymphs known as the Nereids. They were beautiful and benevolent goddesses. The names here come from Homer's *Iliad*.

17–18.   dolphin, Arion's lyre: Arion was a legendary poet from Lesbos who was robbed by pirates and cast into the sea. A dolphin, moved by his singing, rescued him and carried him to land.

II 29a

Again the manuscripts offer us a single poem while modern editors consistently divide II 29 into two poems. The first twenty-two lines, given here as II 29a, are addressed to Cynthia, "my light," and recount the poet's imagined arrest by a band of Cupids. If not strictly a dream, it is another fantasy, one which composes a desire to escape and desire to be bound in a narrative to his mistress which is simultaneously a confession of unfaithful desires and a promise to spend future nights at home.

2.   no servant: At night one would normally be attended by one's slaves, as in elegy I 3. 10.

3.   little Loves: These plural Cupids appear to have been introduced into Latin literature by Catullus; see Catullus 3. This diminutive crowd of naked boys with their dimunitive torches adds a light touch of humor which works against the claims of fear in the following line.

5–6.   torches, arrows, chains: All emblems of the lover—burning with passion, wounded deep in his bones, enslaved to the beloved.

9.   a contract: There were men employed in Rome rather like bounty hunters to retrieve runaway slaves; an allusion to such posses may be intended here.

16.   Sidonian turban: This was a nightcap with earflaps that tied under the chin.

17.   Arabian herbs: The perfumes and oils of Arabia were especially prized.

18.   those which Love made: Propertius may have in mind that other famous perfume, the one Lesbia offers in Catullus 13.

22.   nights at home: One should compare the scene and the poet's attitude in Propertius I 3, of which poem this is in some sense a rewrite. There is again a kind of domesticity in the assumptions: Cynthia is at home; Propertius is brought home.

II 29b

Continuing in the mode which we described above as a rewrite of elegy I 3, Propertius now describes how Cynthia looked in the morning, asleep, when he arrived. The poem cannot be a continuation of II 29a because the poet's motive in visiting Cynthia has changed entirely. Also, there is a time discrepancy between the poems; in 29a Cynthia is said to be waiting while in 29b she is sleeping, and in 29a Cynthia is addressed as "my light" while the narrative of 29b refers to her in the third person. This poem's narrative is similar to I 3: the poet arrives, admires the beautiful sleeping Cynthia; she awakens and berates him.

1.   alone: This marks the most significant change in the general situation from elegy I 3: Cynthia's faithfulness in I 3 is not an issue. The particulars of the scene are vague.

5. dreams: It was common practice to tell dreams to a priest or god in order to purify them of any harm they might portend to the house. The dreams are told to chaste Vesta because she was the protectress of the hearth and the home.

12. knowing one man: The outdated and conservative ideal for married women was to be *univira*, or known to one man only. Here Cynthia seems to claim such a standard for herself.

Book III

Two events, one political and one literary, help situate in its historical context the publication in about 22 B.C.E. of Propertius's third book of elegies. The first is the death of Marcellus in 23 B.C.E. He was the adopted son of Augustus, husband to Augustus's daughter Julia, and probable heir to Augustus's power and position in Rome. The importance of his death to those outside the immediate family of the emperor points unmistakably to Augustus's dynastic ambitions. The Republic and its freedoms, illusory or problematic as they may have been, were not part of the ambitions of the new monarchy. Augustus remained an ambiguous figure. He had meant peace at home, stability, attention to conservative values, and a diversion of military action away from the slaughter of civil war to the dreams of empire, the Parthians, the Indians, and the Britains at the edge of the world. He also had meant an end to the Republic, the slaughter at Perusia, the redistribution of land, a willingly deceived and obsequious Senate, and a cultural program that asked more and more insistently for the support of the poets. The second is the publication in the same year of Horace's *Odes* I–III. This extraordinary and brilliant attempt to revive something of the range and power of Greek lyric in the Latin language was a direct challenge to Propertius and his elegiac poetry. Horace's range, from intimate love lyrics to the solemn and public pronouncements of the poet/priest/prophet, the *vates*, summoned from Propertius the need to redefine and reassert the importance of his poetic task at the same time that it may have suggested to the elegist the need to explore new directions. Those new directions would finally appear in Propertius's own fourth book of elegies.

III 1

Propertius had already at elegy II 1 40 justified his refusal to write epic by explicit reference to Callimachus, and in II 34. 31–32 he had advised his friend Lynceus to imitate Philetas and Callimachus. In poem III 1 he makes his proudest and most explicit claim yet to being the Roman Callimachus and the first to write elegy in the Alexandrian manner. In doing this he echoes the language and ideals of Callimachus himself when that poet defended himself against his critics (see Appendix, "Callimachus's 'Prologue to the Aetia.'").

Critics today do not agree about the degree to which these aesthetic ideals are made part of a larger political or ethical program. While some would see Propertius's concern here as one only of style, I am convinced by arguments which find in the rejection of epic a larger ethical objection to narrow concerns with military glory, expansionist dreams of empire, and a foreign policy motivated by cries of vengence upon the Parthians. Propertius finds here in the ideals of a refined and elitist poetry an assertion of individualism which allows him to oppose the consensus of the crowd and the propaganda of the crown.

Poem III 1 is an example of Propertius's more expressly learned and Callimachean manner and the more abstract reflections on poetry that characterize book III. It is a programmatic poem addressed to the shades of Callimachus, to "him who detains Phoebus in arms," to Rome itself, and to the Muses—quite a different procedure from other programmatic poems such as I 1, I 7 or II 1. This programmatic poem, proudly justifying his chosen genre and life, makes no precise reference at all to Cynthia or his love affair.

1. Callimachus, Philitas: Callimachus of Cyrene lived and was active as a poet during the third century B.C.E. Philitas of Cos was associated both with the Callimachean ideals and with elegiac narrative and epigrams. It has been said of Philetas that no Roman poet ever read him, that he was merely a figurehead.

1. Coan mysteries: The phrase refers to the home of Philetas but does so with specific reference to religious mysteries.

3. the first priest: The claim to poetic priority was common among the Roman Alexandrian poets.

3. the pure well-spring: Pure water from a small spring symbolized for Callimachus the proper and best poetry.

4. Italian emblems: In a religious ritual the priest or worshipers would carry holy symbols and objects. Here the emblems may represent his poems' Italian content in Greek form.

5. in what cave: In Latin poetry, the cave, like the glen and the grove, was often associated with Apollo and the muses.

6. what step: A reference both to manner or tone and to the meter (the Latin term *pes*, or "foot," makes this clear).

7. him, who detains Phoebus in arms: That is, who keeps the god of poetry, Phoebus Apollo, occupied with military and epic subject matter. Since at this time Vergil had been working for at least five years on his epic, the *Aeneid*, it is thought by some that this is a polemical rejection of Vergil's new and very Augustan project.

8. by a fine pumice: An echo of the second line of Catullus's introductory and programmatic poem 1. 2: "new-slicked with assiduous pumice."

9–10. my daughter | my Muse: Literally, "Muse born of me." The standard comment is to note that here the Muse is used metonymically for the poetry. However, Propertius was never comfortable with the archaic picture of the poet inspired by the Muse: in II 1. 4, he had claimed that "[Cynthia] alone creates my genius."

10. triumphs: The second major image in this passage again recalls Vergil's *Georgics*: the poet as triumphant victor. The image, however, of "little Loves" sitting in his chariot and "a mob of writers dogging [his] wheels" provides a curious contrast with the pomp and circumstance of a real triumph. The most recent triumph in Rome at this time had been the triple triumph of Augustus in 29 B.C.E. after the defeat of Mark Antony.

13. competing, your reins let loose: Here the image of a military triumph is easily transformed into an image of an athletic victory; in so doing, Propertius recalls the Pindaric mode that Horace had on occasion adopted.

14. a wide road: The Callimachean symbol of popular, easy, unrefined, and valueless poetry.

15. annals: The early Roman epic poet Ennius had actually titled his Roman epic *The Annals*; in general, however, "annals" refer to the oldest form of Roman history, the public records of magistrates and of official events kept by the *Pontifex Maximus*, or chief priest. For Propertius's elegiac attitude toward history, see elegy II 1. 15–16.

16. Bactra: The capital of a province in Parthia, standing here for the whole of Parthia. The reference is to the fond hopes of some for a renewed war against Parthia to avenge the loss of Roman legions and standards by Crassus at the disaster of Carrhae in 53 B.C.E.

17. Muses' mountain: Hesiod was initiated as a poet by the Muses on Mt. Helicon in a scene that was frequently recalled by other poets.

19–20. soft garlands | hard crowns: A metaphoric comparison that entails the opposition of elegy and epic, of love and military, of peace and war, of banquet and arena.

25ff. who would -have known: Propertius refers in what follows to events in the Trojan War, most of which were told by Homer in his epics. The story of the Trojan horse is told in the *Odyssey*, and it was also the subject of Vergil's *Aeneid* II. Achilles' fight with the river and the dragging of Hector's body around the walls of Troy was told in the *Iliad*. The typical ancient sentiment is expressed by the Greek poet Theocritus: "Who ever would know the Lycian heroes or the long-haired sons of Priam or Kyknos, a girl, if the singers of old had not sung their battles."

25. the towers: The towers of Troy were destroyed because the Greeks were able to sneak within the city's walls by hiding some of their soldiers in a wooden horse.

27. Simois, Scamander: Two rivers of Troy. The Scamander, called the offspring of Jupiter by Homer in the *Iliad* XXI, rose out of its bank to fight with Achilles, who at that time in his rage at the death of his friend Patroclus was slaughtering Trojans in the river and blocking the river's flow with corpses (*Iliad* XXI 218–220). As the river Scamander chased Achilles across the plain, he called on his brother, the river Simois, to help him.

28. wheels befouled Hector: According to Homer, after Achilles killed Hector, the greatest of the Trojan Warriors, he would drag Hector's body around the tomb of his dead friend Patroclus three times daily. Propertius's highly allusive manner depends upon the familiarity of these stories.

29. Deiphobus, Helenus, and Polydamas: Deiphobus and Helenus were sons of Priam and minor heroes in the Trojan War; Polydamas was a counselor whose words were not heeded by Hector.

30. Paris: Paris was the youngest son of Priam whose abduction of Helen was the cause of the Trojan War. As a "lady's man" he was often portrayed as a weak warrior. The image of Paris, unequal to the weight of epic armor, might well be an image of the Propertian lover.

31, 32. Ilion, Troy: While sometimes Ilion is said to refer to the city, and Troy to the general area, the two are generally taken as equivalents.

32. twice captured by Hercules' force: Hercules first conquered Troy when King Laomedon refused the reward he had promised Hercules for ridding the country of a sea monster; the second defeat was the Trojan War familiar to us from Homer which was brought to an end when the warrior Philoctetes arrived and killed Paris with the bow of Hercules.

34. grow with prosperity: An echo of the proud ending to Horace's third book of *Odes*: III 30. 8, "I will grow green with praise."

38. <u>Apollo saw to it</u>: A return to the echoes of Callimachus with which the poem began (the Latin gives him the designation "Lycian Apollo," recalling the passage from the *Aetia*/translated in the Appendix).

III 2

Here, replete with echoes of the final poem of Horace's *Odes* (III 30), Propertius proclaims again the power of his love elegy, this time emphasizing his *ingenium*, a Latin term for "talent," "wit," or "genius." In terms of Propertius's development, earlier in poem I 7. 7–8 he had said, "I give up wit [=*ingenium*] to obey pain" and then in poem II 1. 4 he had said "[not the Muses but] my girl alone creates my genius [=*ingenium*]." The poem has three distinct movements which center around examples of poetic power (3–8), examples of luxurious living (11–14), and examples of the decay of time (19–24). Different ways of dividing the poem into eight-line sections have been suggested by critics. I offer an outline that I hope makes several other schemata accessible:

    1–2   = two lines: Introduction and transition
    3–8   = six lines: Traditional power of song
   9–10 = two lines: Success of Propertian song
 11–16 = six lines: Rejection of contemporary luxury
          11–14   = four lines: Contemporary luxury
          15–16   = two lines: Propertian values
 17–18 = two lines: Poetry's power
 19–24 = six lines: Decay of the physical world
          19–22   = four lines: Three wonders of the physical world
          23–24   = two lines: Causes of their decay
 25–26 = two lines: Immortal glory of poetry

2.   <u>girl might be glad</u>: Compare I 7. 12: "Praise me for this alone: I pleased a learned girl."

3–8.   Three mythological examples of the power of song over nature, animate and in-animate, and over the beloved.

3.   <u>Orpheus</u>: The mythological master singer of Thrace whose magical song could make the forests follow him, charm animals, and delay the rivers and winds in their swift course.

5–6.   <u>the story goes</u>: This is the story of Amphion, joint ruler with his brother of Thebes and a lyre player of such skill that he was able to charm the stones of Cithaeron, a mountain in Boeotia, to form the city walls of Thebes, the chief city in Boeotia. If Orpheus represents a kind of poetry of withdrawal, Amphion is an image of poetry put to work for the state.

7.   <u>Polyphemus</u>: Polyphemus, a cyclops with one eye in the middle of his forehead, fell in love with the sea nymph Galatea. Theocritus (who writes before Propertius) offers two versions of the story. In Idyll 11, Polyphemus attempts to woo Galatea with his song, but he fails. The story was popular in Greek comedy; two *Galateia* and one *Cyclops* are known to us. After Propertius's time, Ovid writes that the nymph hated Polyphemus as much as she loved the young man Acis. We know of no version of a successful Polyphemus, and, although such a version might have been known to Propertius, still the poet also must have known the versions of failure and complaint.

7.   <u>Etna</u>: Polyphemus's island is usually identified as Sicily, where Mt. Etna is found.

9. <u>Bacchus and Apollo</u>: Bacchus was the god of wine, often appealed to by Propertius; Phoebus Apollo was the god of poetry. See the introductory note on elegy III 1.

10. <u>a mob of girls</u>: Compare the mob of writers at elegy III 1. 12.

11–14. The poet cites three examples of luxurious living.

11. <u>Taenarian columns, ivory ceilings, gilded beams</u>: The black marble from Taenarum in Sparta was especially prized; the ivory ceilings and gilded beams point to the luxurious homes of the wealthy. Such indulgence was universally criticized by Roman moralists.

13. <u>Alcinous's groves</u>: In *Odyssey* VII, Homer tells us of Alcinous's orchard in Phaeacia. There, he says, the fruit trees never cease giving fruit and the west wind is always ripening some while it starts others into flower.

14. <u>Marcian stream, artful grot</u>: Around 140 B.C.E., Q. Marcius Rex brought water to Rome from about forty miles away by way of the great aquaduct called the *Aqua Marcia*. This water was especially prized as cool and pure. During the late Republic (as during the eighteenth century) artificial grottos became popular with fountains of piped-in water, mosaics, sculpture, and rustic decorations.

16. <u>Calliope</u>: The Muse singled out by Propertius as his special patron.

18: <u>monument</u>: The word, an allusion to Horace *Odes* III 30. 1, "Done. A monument more lasting than bronze," introduces the closing section of this elegy (19–26). This section is a *tour de force* of reference and allusion to that final poem in the just published three-book edition of Horace's *Odes*.

19–22: <u>Three of the Wonders of the Ancient World</u>: the pyramids of Egypt, the temple of Jupiter at Olympia, and the tomb of King Mausolus (from which we get the word, "mauso-leum") of Halicarnassus.

26. <u>glory by genius stands deathless</u>: The self-assurance and the emphasis on "genius" here is remarkable; it was already apparent in the secondary role given to the Muses in line 15: "The Muses are my followers."

III 4

After his vigorous opposition to poetry placed at the service of the military aspirations of Augustan Rome, the opening to this poem comes as a surprise. In the vatic tones of the poet/priest/prophet, Propertius celebrates the future success of Augustus's planned expedition against the Parthians. Throughout this pre-panegyric there are indications of irony and of a different sensibility on the part of the poet. Then, about halfway through the poem, the old Propertius comes more clearly to the fore: first, he emphasizes the futurity of that triumph over the East (a tactic he had used in elegy II 10); then, he pictures himself most indecorously lying in his girl-friend's lap, applauding as the triumphal procession goes by. The poem takes the underlying form of a programmatic *recusatio* ("I was asked to write of glorious war and Caesar, but I do not have the wit to do that") and turns it into a narrative ("Imagine the glorious war they're going off to fight; but I'm just going to wait here and watch the parade with my girl."). The next poem, III 5* begins, "Love is the god of peace and we lovers worship peace."

1. Divine Caesar: The flattery is fulsome by the standards of other poets like Vergil and Horace for whom Caesar Augustus is always the son of a god (referring to Julius Caesar, who was proclaimed divine after his death) or destined to become a god. Augustus had been careful to decline any divine honors at home in Rome.

The first line of this elegy begins just as the *Aeneid* does: War divine Caesar plots = War and the man I sing. The major difference being the second word, which in the *Aeneid* is "the man" but here is "the god." Finally, reading the first word of line 1, the second word of line 3, and the third word of line 9 we have (roughly) the opening to the *Aeneid*: Vergil wrote *arma virumque cano*; the Propertian sequence is the echo, *arma viris cano*.

2. gem-rich sea: The Indian Ocean, which was particularly noted for its pearls.

3. triumphs: Recall the Propertian triumph of elegy III 1. 11–12: "and with me in our chariot ride little Loves, I a mob of writers dogging my wheels."

4. Tigris and Euphrates: The Parthians were a warlike people near the Euphrates River in Asia Minor. Rivers frequently are taken to personify territories and the control of rivers is an image of imperialistic power. Compare, for instance, Tibullus I 7.

5. Belated: A note which may be felt to undercut the praise; the Roman standards had been in the possession of the Parthians and on display at the temple of Ahuramazda for more than thirty years.

5. Ausonian rods: Roman lictors were accompanied by the fasces, or bundle of rods surrounding an axe, the symbol of their power and authority.

6. Parthian trophies: This will refer to both the the new trophies, consisting of the arms and leaders of the Parthians, which Propertius imagines Augustus bringing home, and to the Roman standards, which by being in the possession of the Parthians for more than thirty years have become the "Parthian trophies." There may be a note of criticism or even mockery in saying that the Roman standards will come to know Latin Jove.

6. Latin Jove: Either a reference to Latin weather, since "Jove" is often used in poetry to mean "the sky god" and so "the sky and its weather," or a reference to god and country, a pair commonly called on during times of military effort.

7. war-tested prows: Tested, that is, at Actium, the final battle of the civil war, in which Augustus (then Octavian) defeated Mark Antony.

9. the Crassi: M. Licinius Crassus and his elder son were killed in the disaster at Carrhae, 53 B.C.E.

10. remember Rome's history!: Compare III 1. 15: "Many men, Rome, augment annals with your praise."

11. Father Mars: Mars, originally an agricultural god of boundaries, was both the Roman god of war and the father of Romulus and Remus, founders of the city of Rome.

11. Vesta: Goddess of the hearth and so protector of the home; the sacred fire of the state was kept burning in the temple of Vesta where it was tended by the Vestal virgins. This temple was on the Sacred Way just as it entered the Forum on the way to the Capitoline.

13. Caesar's chariot: A brief description of the typical Roman triumph appears here. The triumphant general proceeded in his gilded chariot led by four white horses, from the Field of Mars, through the Triumphal Gate, along the Sacred Way, past the temple of Vesta to the temple of Capitoline Jupiter where the spoils of the war were dedicated. The procession was accompanied by effigies and images of the conquered peoples, their rivers, cities, and gods, which would be given identifying names.

13. chariot, spoil-laden: This is a curious mistake or impropriety. The general's chariot was not filled with booty and prizes; rather, it was accompanied by barrows so filled and marked.

17. javelins, fleeing horses, bows: References to Parthians and their method of fighting, especially the notorious tactic by which they would fire arrows over their shoulders while seeming to flee.

19. your child: According to Roman legend, the goddess of love, Venus, bore to the mortal Anchises a son, Aeneas, who escaped Troy and made his way to Italy where he and his son Iulus founded what was to become the Latin people. The Julian family, to which family Augustus belonged, claimed descent from this Iulus.

21. whose labors earned them: Labor is one of the great themes of Vergil's *Aeneid*.

22. Sacred Way: The road on which a triumph proceded to the temple of Jupiter on the Capitoline hill.

III 16

In this elegy, Propertius responds to his mistress's summons at midnight. No reason is given for her demand. In the first ten lines he outlines the situation; in the next ten he toys with the topos that lovers are sacrosanct (compare Tibullus I 2. 25–32, Horace *Odes* I 22, and Ovid *Amores* I 6. 9–14); and in the final ten lines he consoles himself with the thought that his mistress (who remains unnamed throughout) will give him a proper burial. The tone is strikingly light-hearted. Compare the youths that crowd his grave at I 7. 24–25, the famous and not neglected grave of III 1. 35–38, and the humble rites and famous tomb of II 13.

2–3. Tibur, gleaming roofs, twin towers: Tibur was an old town about sixteen miles from Rome, where many of the wealthy had villas and where Horace claimed he hoped to spend his old age.

4. Anio's nymph, spreading lake: The river Anio, here personified as the river's nymph or spirit goddess, plunged down a gorge at the famous Tibur falls.

6. mauled by ruffians: For the dangers at night in Rome see elegy II 29a.

9. a whole year: This is the famous "year of separation" which has tempted many a critic to a literal interpretation and to a detailed narrative of the Cynthia affair.

11. no one who'd hurt holy lovers: Propertius begins the theme that lovers have the special protection of the gods.

12. Sciron's road: The road from Athens to Megara ran along a cliff. It was here that the legendary robber Sciron would rob travelers and push them off the cliff.

13. Scythia's shore: The shore of Scythia in what is now southern Russia was not historically a particularly dangerous place. It was far away and so potentially barbarous.

16. his lit torches: The torches of love are a familiar image, but they are not usually for the purpose of lighting one's way at night.

17. fierce mad dogs: One should compare Horace, *Odes* I 22, in which Horace claims that a wolf fled from him while he sang of his beloved Lalage.

19. scanty blood: The lover is traditionally pale and wan.

20. <u>the shut-out man</u>: Since Propertius has been summoned to his mistress, he is anything but shut out. The reference, then, is probably traditional, perhaps even to a line from a *paraclausithyron*, as well as a general reference to the poet's usual condition.

25–28. <u>common earth. . .</u>: Roadside burial was common; hence the address of many epitaphs to the passerby. The language here recalls the Callimachean aesthetic program: avoid the common and the public, find the secluded grove with the pure fountain. Elsewhere he desires a celebrated tomb: II 13. 37–38 and III 1. 35–38.

29. <u>foreign sand</u>: This is exactly the fate bemoaned in the typical Hellenistic funereal epigram.

Book IV

This is Propertius's last book of elegies and was probably written between 22 B.C.E. (the date accepted for the publication of Book III) and 16 B.C.E. (the last datable reference in Book IV). If Propertius was born in the late 50's B.C.E., he was then in his thirties when he wrote his final poems, and since Ovid refers to him in the past tense in 2 B.C.E., he will probably have died in his forties. In this book Propertius changed the direction of his poetry in several ways. He turned to Roman themes and, in imitation of Callimachus, to etiological subject matter; he worked more broadly in the Callimachean style of mixing genres by bringing mythological narrative, mime, satire, letters, and funeral speech into his elegies; he no longer wrote short, personal elegies; his two poems on Cynthia, an anecdotal narrative and a self-portrait, are no longer in the personal and subjective manner. We have chosen for our selection an etiological elegy on Tarpeia and the Tarpeian mount (IV 4); Propertius's poem on the battle of Actium (IV 6); the two elegies on Cynthia (IV 7 and 8); and the funeral apologia of Cornelia (IV 11). For some readers, Book IV is the final victory of the elegiac perspective and the final vindication of Propertius's poetry; for others, this was, if not a failure, at least an acquiescence in the demands of the Augustan regime.

IV 4

This is formally an etiological poem whose ostensible purpose is to explain the archaic name for the Capitoline hill, the Tarpeian mount. This purpose, however, only provides the occasion for telling the story of Tarpeia's love of Titus Tatius, the Sabine chief who held Rome under seige during the early years of Romulus's rule. At that time, the Romans had taken refuge on the Palatine hill with a garrison on the Capitoline hill lead by Tarpeia's father. Tarpeia, while fetching water, saw Titus Tatius and fell in love. In return for the promise that she would become his wife, she betrayed her father's garrison. Titus Tatius, however, when he had taken the Capitoline, ordered his men to crush Tarpeia with their shields.

In telling this version, Propertius chooses not to follow the more common version of the story in which Tarpeia betrays the fortress out of greed for the beautiful bracelets the Sabine warriors wore. As a result he gives voice to Tarpeia's story, a tale of uncompromising, if unrealistic and unrequited, love, a tale of passion that turns its back on patriotic and Roman virtues, and a tale of the conflict between war and love. With the major part of the poem (31–66) being Tarpeia's love soliloquy, the poem may be seen as becoming another love elegy, and Propertius may be seen as toying with a conflict between the elegiac values of the soliloquy and the more public values of the frame.

1.   grave: The grave did not exist in Propertius's day; it had been moved when Tarquin built the temple to Jupiter on the Capitoline. Propertius will explain the origin of a lost monument.

2.   Jove's ancient temple taken: Tarpeia's crime was to betray the troops on the Capitoline hill; there was at the time of Tarpeia no temple to Jove, although the hill was believed to be sacred to the god. Tarpeia betrayed a future monument.

5.   Silvanus's branching home: Silvanus was, as his name implies, a woodland spirit; he was sometimes associated with Pan. The "sweet flutes" mentioned at the end of the line confirm the sense that Propertius is constructing a pastoral setting for this vignette of love and war in early Rome.

15.   for the goddess: Tarpeia, as a Vestal virgin, would be required to fetch water for Vesta, goddess of the hearth and protector of the state.

17–18.   Would one death suffice: Many editors are unhappy with this couplet which seems to them out of place here. However, efforts to place the couplet elsewhere are not very satisfactory. Here the lines will be read as an anticipatory interjection of the poet.

19.   sandy fields: The Forum, where Tatius would have been maneuvering, was not sandy except when spread with sand for gladiatorial games. Again, a tale of the past is anachronistically set in terms only recognizable to a future perspective.

25.   to indulgent nymphs: The exact nature and purpose of these rituals is open to speculation; part of Tarpeia's purpose is, of course, to go to the spring so she may catch another glimpse of Tatius.

29.   her own Tarpeian rock: The rock was called the Tarpeian rock because Tarpeia, in punishment for her treason, was killed there. This designation is a form of pathetic anticipation.

29.   sitting: Her neglect of her work in order to sit and ponder her love places Tarpeia in the tradition of pastoral lovers.

31.   The martial fire: In her first words Tarpeia points to the antinomies she is caught up in: because of the erotic fires of her love, the martial fires of Tatius's camp have been substituted in her mind for the Vestal fires she was to protect.

33.   captive: Compare the beginning of the first poem of the *Monobiblos*: "Cynthia's eyes first captured poor me." In Tarpeia's case, a position as a captive would ease the conflict she experiences between her divided loyalties. She apparently imagines herself, anachronistically, as a captive in Tatius's triumph.

35.   Roman mountains: The seven hills of Rome.

38.   toward his right hand: The Roman agricultural writers tell us that the mane falling on the right was a sign of a spirited and desirable horse.

39.   Scylla raged: Two Scyllas are here combined. The first is Scylla, the daughter of Nisus, king of Megara. He was safe from harm as long as a purple lock of hair remained on his head. When Scylla fell in love with an enemy, Minos, king of Crete, she betrayed her father by cutting off his purple lock. The outcome, however, was no more happy for Scylla than it will be for Tarpeia: she was suspended from Minos's ship and dragged through the sea until she turned into a seabird. Her father was turned into a sea-eagle which pursued Scylla forever across the

ocean. The second Scylla was the daughter of the sea-god Phorcys, who was turned into a monster by Amphitrite, her rival in love for Poseidon. Opposite the whirlpool of Charybdis, she is represented with snarling dogs growing out of her groin. The conflation of the two stories creates an extraordinary image of sexual pathology, guilt, and desire.

41.   the brother monster's horns: Pasiphaë, the wife of Minos and the queen of Crete, fell in love with a royal bull. Aided by Daedalus, she devised a way to consummate her passion. As a result, the Minotaur, a monster which was half man and half bull, was born and kept by Minos in a labyrinth where Athenian youths were yearly sacrificed to him. Ariadne, daughter of Minos and Pasiphaë, fell in love with one of those Athenian youths, Theseus, and helped him to kill the Minotaur and escape the labyrinth by means of a thread. She, too, was subsequently betrayed by Theseus, who abandoned her on Naxos.

43.   What a warning: Tarpeia takes the point of the disastrous love affairs she recalls and expects herself to become an example of criminal behavior for the girls of Ausonia, or Italy.

45.   Pallas's flame put out: The fire of Vesta was kept in the temple of Vesta along with the Palladium, an image of Pallas Athena which was said to have come from Troy. The extinction of this fire would be a dire omen. The reference here to Pallas Athena adds to this omen a reference to the theft of the Palladium from Troy by Odysseus and Diomedes which made possible the fall of that city. Tarpeia's language foreshadows her coming betrayal of Rome and represents it as another betrayal of Troy.

47.   all Rome will be drunk: The correct reading is uncertain here. If Propertius did describe the city as drunk, he may have had in mind Vergil's similar description of the Trojans on the night that Troy was destroyed: "the city buried in sleep and wine."

48.   You: Tarpeia imagines she is addressing Tatius himself.

51.   the Magic Muse's charms: Apparently a reference to the magic of Medea, another woman who betrayed her family in order to bring aid to Jason, the man she loved. She, too, was later betrayed by Jason, who married the daughter of Creon.

53.   the purple toga: Originally the purple robe was a symbol of royalty. During the Republic, the purple toga embroidered with gold was worn by the triumphant general in his procession up the Capitoline hill. Tarpeia suggests both that Tatius should be the victor and the king of Rome.

53.   that bastard: Romulus and Remus were the twin sons of Rhea Silvia, a Vestal virgin who blamed her pregnancy on the god Mars. The Alban king, Amulius, had Rhea Silvia thrown into prison and her children thrown into the Tiber. They were washed ashore and, according to legend, suckled by a she-wolf.

55.   a foreign queen: Her fantasy has taken an extraordinary step up from her earlier imagination of merely being Tatius's captive. The language here would inevitably recall Octavian's propaganda about Cleopatra and Mark Antony, repeated in Horace *Odes* I 37.

57.   Sabine's rape: Titus Tatius, a Sabine king, was at war with the Romans because Romulus and the young men of Rome had stolen the Sabine women from their fathers and husbands during the celebration of some games which the Sabines had been invited to watch. The plan to steal the women had been conceived of by Romulus because of a shortage of women in the newly founded Rome and because the neighboring Sabines had refused to allow the Romans to intermarry. Here Tarpeia asks Titus Tatius to rape her; literally, the Latin says, "*me rape*" = "*seize me!*" Paradoxically, rape is not in ancient times defined from the point of view of the woman; it is literally a "seizure of property that belongs to the dominant male." Tarpeia's reference to the Sabine rape and her order, "seize me," are then references to the same general action—stealing women from men. In both imagined futures (as queen and as property) she attempts to find a way for her love to compete with the war that surrounds her.

59. sunder battles joined: The Sabine women did eventually sunder the battle lines drawn up by the Romans and the Sabines. They interposed themselves between their fathers and brothers on the one side and their husbands on the other and, in Livy's version, assumed responsibility for the war.

61. Hymen, start your song: The invocation of Hymen was a customary feature of the Roman wedding ceremony.

63. the fourth horn: The night watch was divided into four "watches." The fourth trumpet would announce the beginning (or perhaps the end) of the last of the night watches.

67–71. Beginning with "She spoke," Propertius uses diction and images that recall the language of epic, especially the scenes of Dido's sleepless and frenzied infatuation for Aeneas in *Aeneid* IV. That story was, at least from Dido's point of view, another tale of a betrayed lover.

69. Vesta: Given this reading, the line must mean that "the thought of Vesta nurses her sense of guilt," that is, her official responsibilities keep reminding her of what she is doing. However, many editors prefer to read "Venus" here, and with good reason. Venus had been the protector of Aeneas during his wanderings from Troy to Italy as he brought the divine fire to its new home. She was also the patron goddess of the Julian family, to which Julius Caesar and Augustus belonged. It was during his wanderings to Italy that Aeneas stayed in Carthage where Dido fell in love with him in the scene mentioned above on lines 67–71. In any event, this section of the poem ends by returning to the image of fire which had begun Tarpeia's speech.

71–72. quick Thermodon, a Thracian | Amazon: The Thermodon is a river in Cappadocia considered to be at the borders of the known world. The Amazons were associated with Cappadocia and with Thrace; however, the one was far to the east, the other just north of Greece. The reference to bare breast and torn robe as well as the destructive passion that Tarpeia feels would suggest a Bacchante, an orgiastic worshiper of the god Bacchus, rather than an Amazon, a kind of female warrior said to have removed her right breast in order to handle the bow. However, as Tarpeia plans to participate in this war by betraying Rome, she confounds the two. She is both the warrior and the bare-breasted Bacchante.

73. *Parilia*: The festival of Pales, goddess of the flocks. It was celebrated on April 21, the supposed date of Rome's foundation. The alternative spelling for the name of this festival is *Palilia*; see Tibullus I 1. 35 and the note on that line.

78. a drunken crowd leaps: Apparently the crowd of celebrants at the *Parilia*, after the feast, jumped over bonfires of straw set at intervals. It is believed that this, although it may have been treated as sport, was also part of a purification rite.

94. oh watcher: Commentators are divided as to who is meant here. There are two possibilities:

1) Jupiter, known sometimes as Tarpeian Jupiter, has just been described as keeping "vigil for his vengeance" (line 86). The Tarpeian mount is his reward for having had to endure the unjust fate of seeing his Capitoline hill taken by the Sabines.

2) Tarpeia, who could not sleep, also kept vigil, and, while her death may have been deserved, her lot in life (her fate, generally speaking) was not deserved; she was more a victim than a victor in this tawdry affair. The ambiguity of the line reflects the ambiguity of the poem whose stern and patriotic frame encloses a sympathetic tale of suffering.

IV 6

This poem is similar to poem IV 4 in two respects: both are formally etiological poems and both are structured around a central panel that accounts for the bulk of the poem. Here Propertius proposes to explain the origin of the temple of Palatine Apollo and frames his central narrative of the battle of Actium with a description of his activity as a poet and his praise for the Augustan peace, just as in IV 4 he had framed a lover's soliloquy with its Augustan judgments on Tarpeia. It is generally believed that the occasion of this poem was the celebration of the *Ludi Quinquennales*, games established by Augustus in 28 B.C.E. in honor of his victory at the battle of Actium and celebrated by Agrippa in 16 B.C.E. The temple to Apollo was dedicated on October 9, 28 B.C.E., in fulfillment of a vow which Augustus (then Octavian) had made in his campaign against the son of Pompey the Great in 36 B.C.E. The temple itself is said to have been the most splendid of Augustus's buildings, but today its site is unknown.

Interpreters of this poem are divided into two groups: the first group believes that Propertius finally yielded to political pressures and wrote a piece of hack work in praise of the Augustan settlement. These readers feel dissatisfaction with Propertius's poem because the poem makes a poor showing in comparison with the description of the same battle by Vergil in *Aeneid* VIII 675ff, or even with Horace's *Odes* I 37. The second group of readers have felt that the picture Propertius presents here is intentionally silly because Augustus is silly, his propaganda, the battle, the temple, the dreams of divinity, the whole affair was silly. In other words, the poem is ironic. For Propertius to do this in the role of Augustan vatic poet/priest, overseeing the sacrifices and rites that bring the community together in celebration of peace and victory, is so remarkable that many decline to accept this view; however, no less remarkable would be the poet's acquiescence in and obeisance to the political powers and realities that had destroyed Perusia and opposed his elegiac accomplishments. I agree with those who find the Augustus portrayed here silly and find the image Propertius offers of himself—drunk at dawn watching the morning light dance in the wine glass—far more compelling than "father Caesar," "Actian Phoebus," and Augustus, "preserver of the world."

1. The priest: Propertius begins this elegy in the high style of the Augustan poet/priest and in language that recalls Horace *Odes* III 1. With the command, "keep holy silence," the priest announces the beginning of the ceremony proper.

3. Roman garland, Philitan ivy: The Roman garland, woven of flowers, has associations with symposia and with Venus. The ivy berries were sacred to Bacchus, the god of wine and poets. Philetas of Cos was a Hellenistic poet who flourished in the third century. He was much admired by Callimachus and almost always associated with him by Propertius; see note on elegy III 1. 1.

4. Callimachus's urn: Callimachus of Cyrene was the most influential Hellenistic poet whose program of refined and learned poetry, symbolized by the water of a pure spring in his *Hymn to Apollo*, was adopted by Propertius and other Roman poets.

5. spikenard, incense: Perfume and incense were burned at the altar to attract the attention of the god and to please him.

6. woolen orb: Binding the altar with wool suggests a magic ritual, as does the number three.

7. sprinkle me: The suggestion is of a purification rite with lustral waters.

8. Mygdonian vessels: Propertius describes the music of the flute as if it, too, were part of the ritual libation; the "Mygdonian vessels" are a reference to Phrygians, a people of the east associated with the orgiastic rites of the *Magna Mater*. See Catullus 63.

10. purifying laurel: A laurel branch was used to sprinkle the lustral waters; the laurel crown was associated with the triumphant general.

10. the poet's new road: A reference both to the new direction Propertius has taken in his poetry and to the Callimachean injunction to travel the unfamiliar path.

11. I'll tell . . .: The poet here announces his etiological and his Roman theme, and so begins his poem within the poem with a traditional appeal to the Muses.

12. Calliope: Propertius's favorite Muse.

13. in Caesar's name: Both because the event which is the dedication of the temple of Apollo acrues to the glory of Caesar Augustus and because Propertius's new poetic program is aligned with the values and interests of Augustus.

15. Phoebus's harbor, Athamanian shores: Actium is located at the mouth of the Ambracian Gulf on the western coast of Greece between Acarnania to the south and Epirus to the north. The Athamanes were a people who lived to the northeast of the Ambracian Gulf. The harbor, then, extends or "flees" east and north to the Athamanian shore. At the mouth of the gulf, according to the ancient geographer Strabo, was a precinct sacred to Actian Apollo and a hill on which a temple to Apollo stood. It was here that Augustus dedicated the first fruits of his victory over Antony and Cleopatra in 31 B.C.E.

16. Ionian Sea: The Ionian Sea lies between the heel of Italy and the western coast of Greece.

18. a friendly path: On a dangerous coast the bay of Actium provided an easy entrance into a safe haven.

19. the world's navies: By September 2, 31 B.C.E., Antony and his troops at Actium were in a desperate situation. Both Antony and Octavian had about four hundred ships. Cleopatra advised a naval engagement, and on the morning of September 2, Antony and Cleopatra with seven squadrons met Octavian's fleet under the command of Agrippa. Octavian's ships were smaller and more maneuverable than the large heavy vessels of Antony's navy. By afternoon, Antony was suffering the worst of the battle: three squadrons had returned to harbor; two had surrendered. When Cleopatra with her sixty ships was seen to flee, and when Antony was not able to extricate his flagship, he followed Cleopatra to Egypt with the forty ships left in his squadron. Octavian seized and burned the five surrendered squadrons.

20. bird sign: It is said that Octavian put great store in the omens that preceeded this battle.

21. Trojan Quirinus: Romulus, founder of Rome, was deified as "Quirinus" and as a god would have been the protector of the Roman state. He is called "Trojan" because he was a descendant of Aeneas, who fled Troy with his son Iulus after the Trojan War.

22. by a woman's hand: The image of any woman, especially an eastern queen, Cleopatra, contending with Roman men was anathema, and Octavian's propaganda had made good use of the claim that Antony wished to establish a foreign queen in Rome. One should recall Tarpeia's dreams of queenship on the throne of Tatius, elegy IV 4. 55.

24. used to conquering: Octavian could claim victories at Mutina in 43, where Antony had attempted to starve out the republicans but was defeated by Octavian and others; at Philippi in 42 B.C.E., where Antony and Octavian together defeated Caesar's assassins, Brutus and Cassius; at Perusia in 41 B.C.E., where Octavian starved the Antonian forces and executed the innocent senators (see elegies I 21 and 22); and at Naulochus in 36 B.C.E., where, according to tradition,

300 ships from each side met while the troops watched from the shore and Octavian (aided by Agrippa) defeated the son of Pompey the Great.

25. Nereus double-arcs: Nereus, the sea-god, is described as the agent of the naval strategy. According to the historian Dio Cassius, Octavian advanced his fleet in a crescent-shaped formation.

27. Phoebus: Phoebus Apollo, patron deity of Augustus, was born on the island of Delos, which, according to legend, had been a floating island until it was stabilized on four pillars at the time of the labor of Leto, Apollo's mother.

29. a strange flame: Such divine fire may be taken to indicate the presence of a god. In the *Aeneid*, however, especially in Book II which tells of the fall of Troy, Vergil uses such flames ambiguously, as much to indicate the violent destruction of Troy as to suggest the glory of Rome.

31–32. hair falling, tortoise shell lyre: Apollo, as god of poets, was imagined as playing a lyre made from a tortoise shell; his long flowing hair was an image of his eternal youth.

33. Agamemnon of Pelops: At the beginning of the *Iliad*, Apollo, god of prophecy, took up the cause of Chryses, a prophet who had been condemned by Agamemnon. With his arrows he caused a plague to destroy the Greeks ("discharged the Grecian camps to greedy death pyres") and set in motion the events that led to the withdrawal of Achilles from the battle and the eventual destruction of Hector. Such a moment was as disastrous for the Greeks as for the Trojans.

35. Python: Before Apollo came to Delphi and made it the seat of his oracle, it was the shrine of Mother Earth and was guarded by a giant snake, Python. Apollo killed the snake and established his oracle there.

37. from Alba Longa: After Aeneas arrived in Italy, his son Iulus, founder of the Julian family, founded Alba Longa and became its first king. Augustus traced his lineage back to this Iulus.

38. Hector: The greatest warrior and defender of Troy, Hector was the son of the king of Troy, Priam. He was killed by Achilles at the end of the *Iliad*.

43–44. Romulus, the Palatine birds: Romulus and his twin brother Remus founded a city on the site of Rome, Romulus by building on the Palatine hill, Remus on the Aventine. When a dispute arose as to who should be the new city's ruler, both claimed that right on the basis of bird signs: Remus because he had been the first to see six vultures fly over; Romulus because he had seen twelve vultures. When Remus in contempt jumped over Romulus's walls, his brother killed him. The story became an allegory of civil war for later Romans.

46. a queen's sails: Rome was a republican aristocracy and prided itself on not being subject to royal rule. As the very term "king" was pejorative, so the idea of a "queen" was anathema.

49. Centaurs: Just as Apollo was the tutelary god adorning Octavian's ship (above, line 29), so images of Centaurs (are said to have) adorned the ships of Antony and Cleopatra. The Centaurs were a monstrous race, half man and half horse, typically noted for their drunkenness and barbarity; their traditional weapons were rocks and clubs.

54. laurel-bearing hand: See line 10 above.

56. following the bow: Some find the narrative here so abbreviated as to be silly; others find it perfunctory and inadequate.

59. father Caesar: Julius Caesar, the adoptive father of Octavian, was acknowledged to be a god after his assassination; the appearance of a comet shortly after his death was thought to be a

sign of his deified spirit ascending into heaven. Venus was the mother of Aeneas, and so of the Julian family. This deification was viewed with skepticism and amusement by many in Rome.

61. Triton: Triton, son of Poseidon, was one of the gods of the sea, usually portrayed blowing on his conch. Propertius here imagines this sea-god leading a chorus of sea-nymphs who conduct Octavian safely to shore, a kind of naval pre-triumph.

63. she seeks the Nile: The flight of Cleopatra from the battle of Actium is well attested; however, we know that she left the battle with sixty ships, a full squadron. One should compare Horace's version of the battle in *Odes* I 37.

65. what a triumph: Propertius speaks as if it would have been a disgrace for Cleopatra, a woman, to have been led in Octavian's triumph. It appears that that is exactly what Octavian wanted, and when she eluded him by committing suicide, he carried an effigy of Cleopatra with the asp which killed her in his triple triumph of 29 B.C.E.

66. Jugurtha: The African king of Numidia who, after being a protégé of Scipio (134 B.C.E.), became an enemy of Rome (111 B.C.E.) and was finally defeated by the great general Marius, brought to Rome for his triumph, and put to death in 104 B.C.E.

67. his monuments: The temple to Apollo on the Palatine and the temple to Actian Apollo on the promontory at Actium.

71. white-robed: The white toga was usual attire on feast days and white was a symbol of purity, necessary for religious propriety.

73. Falernian: A good quality Campanian wine.

74. Cilician saffron: According to Pliny, the best saffron was grown in Cilicia.

77. Sycambri: A German tribe on the lower Rhine that had recently invaded Gaul and defeated the Roman general M. Lollius in 16 B.C.E. They withdrew soon after and gave hostages to the Romans.

78. Cephean Meroe: Cepheus was the legendary king of Meroe, a town in Ethiopia, and father of Andromeda. In 22 B.C.E. the Roman prefect of Egypt, Petronius, forced the Ethiopians to sue for peace after they attempted an invasion of Roman Egypt. The Romans, however, never occupied Ethiopia or went as far as Meroe.

79. Parthia: The land where Crassus had lost the Roman standards in 53 B.C.E.

80. Remus's standards: It is generally said that "Remus" is used for metrical reasons in place of "Romulus" to stand for "Roman." However, the story of fratricide, especially as an image of the internecine strife of civil war, cannot be ignored, especially in a poem that has already made reference to Romulus and his bird signs; see above 43–44.

80–81. surrender his own, Eastern quivers: Here, as at elegy III 4. 6, Propertius refers to the dream of a conquest of Parthia which became the jingoistic locus of military aspirations in the first years of Augustus's rule.

82. future triumphs: Gaius and Lucius Caesar were the grandsons of Augustus who had been adopted by him in 17 B.C.E.

84. cross the Euphrates: The Euphrates is the longest river in western Asia. From Rome, one would travel to the eastern shore of the Mediterranean and then inland about 100 miles. Carrhae was about seventy-five miles further east across the Euphrates. We are told by Plutarch that the Parthians after the battle of Carrhae (53 B.C.E.) staged a mock triumph in which a prisoner who resembled Crassus was paraded in woman's clothing. Crassus's head and hands were cut off, sent to the Armenian capital, and used in a production of Euripides' *Bacchae*. A real tomb for Crassus's body seems unlikely.

86. the day casts its light on my wines: "He notices the gleam of sunlight in his wine glass, is faintly surprised. The light is pretty that way. Elusive, evanescent patterns; a shifting of bright images, a wavering clarity: like the poetry he loves." W. R. Johnson, *C.S.C.A.* 6 (1976) 171.

IV 7

Cynthia, shortly after her death, reappears to Propertius in a dream.

4. the roadside: Tombs were often placed by the side of the road and literary epitaphs often use this fact to address the passerby.

5: love's death rites: In the topics of consolation, sleep is taken as the first indication that the bereaved has been consoled, that he can now return to the needs of the day-to-day world. In this line Propertius indicates that he is not yet able to put aside his grief; sleep hangs over his head but will not come to him. These words seem to suggest that Propertius and Cynthia were still lovers at the time of her death; such a narrative would contradict the implications of Propertius's farewell to Cynthia in poems III 24 and III 25.

6. I complained: Complaint is the typical mode for the Propertian lover, but this line in particular recalls Cynthia's complaint at elegy I 3. 43.

8–9. Cynthia's ghost appears at first either as a kind of malignant spirit or with macabre realism as a half-burned corpse.

10. Lethe water: The dead drank from the river Lethe in the underworld, a drink that was supposed to make them forget their previous existence.

13. Traitor: One should compare Cynthia's tirade in I 3; we have here the same old Cynthia.

15–18: the watchful Subura . . .: The passage offers tempting details about their affair. Cynthia lived in the Subura, the valley northeast of the Forum between the Esquinal and the Viminal hills, a place where prostitutes could be found. Perhaps she lived in the house of a man who kept her as mistress and from whom Propertius seduced her.

23–24. no one called me back . . .: Apparently it was traditional for the survivors at a death scene to cry out loud at the moment that a dear one passed away. Here Cynthia may have in mind the story of Laodamia, whose grief at the death of her husband Protesilaus was so great that she was allowed another day with him.

25. no guard rattled: A guardian was set over a corpse with some kind of rattle to scare away either evil spirits and witches or hungry animals.

28. a black toga: Black was associated with death; we are told that a dark gray was actually the color of mourning.

29. going beyond Rome's gates: The dead could not be burned or buried within the walls of a city. It is thought that the cortege would accompany the corpse to the city gate and from there on only the family and closest friends would proceed further.

31. beg the winds: Cynthia seems to refer to Achilles' prayer to the winds that they come and fan the flames of Patroclus's pyre in the *Iliad*.

34. a broken wine jar: It was customary to break a wine jar over the ashes of the dead.

35. Lygdamus: As we know from elegy IV 8. 79–80, Lygdamus was Propertius's slave. He is to be tortured with heated metal to make him confess a plot. The torture of slaves to compel them to tell the truth was accepted practice in ancient Rome.

37. <u>Nomas</u>: She is mentioned only here and, given the context, was probably an older female slave in Propertius's household who knew about poisons and charms. She too is to be tortured.

39. <u>put herself on show</u>: Prostitutes exhibited themselves nude or in sheer clothing for the examination of their potential clients. Here Propertius's new lover, pointedly unnamed until later, is described as having exchanged the traditional dress of a prostitute for the long elaborate cloak of a well-to-do woman.

41. <u>repays with labor</u>: For the onerous task of doing the day's spinning, each slave was given daily basketfuls of wool to be returned at the end of the day as spun yarn. Here Cynthia claims that any maid who mentions her name is given unfairly large amounts of wool to spin.

43. <u>Petale</u>: Another servant mentioned only here. It is not clear whether she belongs to Propertius's household or to Cynthia's. It was customary to adorn tombs with wreaths and garlands.

44. <u>a dirty block</u>: She has a wooden block tied to her leg as punishment and perhaps so she will not be able to visit Cynthia's tomb.

45. <u>Lalage</u>: Another servant mentioned only here. The girl of whom Horace sang when he frightened off a wolf on his Sabine farm was called Lalage; see *Odes* I 22.

49. Commentators invariably note that the tone of speech changes at this point. Cynthia becomes more gentle and conciliatory. But what is really important to her and how are we to understand that importance? She claims that it is more important that she was the subject of Propertius's poetry than that she was loved by Propertius; later she asks Propertius to burn the love elegies he wrote about her.

51. <u>Fate's thread</u>: According to ancient belief the three Fates determined the length of a person's life by spinning their life-thread, usually at their birth, and snipping that thread at the appropriate point.

52. <u>Cerberus</u>: The dog who guarded the entrance to the underworld; see below on line 90.

53–54. <u>May vipers . . .</u>: It was a popular belief that the marrow in the bones of wicked people turned into snakes upon their death.

55. <u>two seats</u>: The underworld is often pictured has being divided into the places of punishment for the wicked and the field of the blessed. Cynthia claims that she is in Elysium, the part of the underworld reserved for the righteous. This claim is implicit proof that she is speaking the truth when she claims to have been faithful.

57. <u>Clytemnestra</u>: The wife of Agamemnon who was left in Mycenae while he went to lead the Greeks against Troy. However, his fleet became stuck in Aulis when the winds refused to blow and he was told to sacrifice his daughter in exchange for favorable winds. When he returned home after the war he was killed in the bathtub by his wife in return for his murder of their daughter.

57. <u>Pasiphaë</u>: The wife of Minos, king of Crete, became sexually attracted to a beautiful bull and, by being disguised in a wooden cow, was able to satisfy her lust. Her pregnancy resulted in the Minotaur.

61. <u>lutes, brass</u>: The lute and brass cymbals were associated with the orgiastic worship of the Great Mother, Cybele; see Catullus 63. They have no special connection with the underworld.

62. <u>lyre, turbaned</u>: The lyre was associated with Lydian music, and the turban, called the *mitra*, was the Lydian headband. Again, there is no special association with the underworld.

63. <u>Andromeda</u>: Andromeda's mother bragged that her daughters were more beautiful than the Nereids. As a punishment, Andromeda was chained to a rock and exposed to a sea monster. While chained, Perseus, the hero who killed the Gorgon, discovered her and turned the monster into a rock by showing it the Gorgon's head. After Perseus defeated another suitor, Phineus, Andromeda went to Argos with him.

63. <u>Hypermestra</u>: She was the only one of Danaids, the fifty daughters of Danaus, to refuse to murder her husband according to the command of her father on her marriage night. She was punished by being placed in chains from which she was finally released with the help of Venus.

72. <u>Chloris</u>: Unless Chloris is a witch used by her successor, Cynthia here finally names the woman who has taken her place. The picture of a successor, however, is difficult to reconcile with the poet's description of himself at the beginning of the poem.

73. <u>Parthenie</u>: We know nothing more of this nurse, who has never been mentioned before. There may be a covert allusion here to Parthenius, the Greek scholar and teacher who introduced Cinna and the neoterics to Callimachean aesthetics.

75. <u>Servilla</u>: Mentioned only here.

79. <u>ivy</u>: Ivy was sacred to poets and to Bacchus and is often mentioned by Propertius in association with poetic inspiration.

81. <u>fertile Anio</u>: The Anio leaves the Sabine mountais and falls down the gorge from Tibur (modern Tivoli) into the plain of the Roman *campagna*. Here it is said to fertilize the orchards of Tibur. See Horace *Odes* I 7. 12–14.

82. <u>by Hercules' power</u>: The famous temple of Hercules Victor was at Tibur, where, apparently, ivory kept its color better than at any other place.

83. <u>on a column</u>: Grave monuments were often in the shape of columns with inscriptions carved at about eye level.

87. <u>dreams that come from ivory gates</u>: The belief in two passageways for spirits to ascend from the underworld is ancient, going back to Homer's *Odyssey* and repeated in Vergil's *Aeneid*. Spirits that come through the gates of ivory are said to be true shades, while those that come through the gates of horn are said to be false. There is another and distinct notion that there are two passageways for dreams as well. Propertius has blended the two concepts, perhaps with the idea that righteous spirits are allowed to return to the world above in dreams where they tell the truth.

90. <u>Cerberus</u>: Cerberus is the monstrous dog who, chained to the inner side of the door to Hades, guarded its entrance and kept spirits from leaving. At night he was set free.

91. <u>stagnant Lethe</u>: There were five rivers in the underworld; here the Lethe seems to stand not for the waters of forgetfulness, but for the infernal waters in general.

92. <u>the boatman</u>: Charon was the ferryman who carried the souls of the dead across the river Styx in his boat.

96. <u>escaped my embrace</u>: Achilles in his attempt to embrace the shade of Patroclus (in Homer's *Iliad*), Orpheus as he attempts to embrace the receding image of Euridice (in Vergil's *Georgics*), and Aeneas as he attempts to embrace the shade of his wife Creusa in Troy and the shade of his father in the underworld (in Vergil's *Aeneid*) are all described in similar terms as vainly grasping at the air.

IV 8

For some, this poem, the last to or about Cynthia, is the culmination of Propertius's art. It is taken as evidence, together with poem IV 7, that Propertius's real strength and interest lies in his love poetry. Here Propertius returns to familiar Propertian themes: fidelity, love's battles, the powerful mistress and the enslaved lover, and Cynthia's temper, her domination, and her laws. These concerns are gathered into a narrative which begins with an account of a festival at Lanuvium and its ancient rites, and proceeds to Propertius's arrangements for a *ménage à trois* which culminates in a scene fraught with foreboding and supernatural signs; this is followed by another scene which reverses the gender roles of the typical adultery mime, and the poem ends with the final image of a triumphant Cynthia giving laws to the conquered and restoring peace to the willing and eager Propertius. Propertius closes with an ironic, elegiac version of the traditional Roman and Augustan justification of empire as the imposition of a Roman peace and laws on a willing world.

    1. the rainy Esquiline: The Esquiline, on which Propertius lived, was traversed by five aqueducts which provided Rome's water supply. The epithet "rainy" may be taken as a kind of witty mock-heroic epithet (like "Ohio, rich in Hondas") or as a reference to fountains and distribution stations where the water supply branched out to the city.

    2. New Gardens: There had been on the Esquiline a pauper's graveyard, haunted by witches and thieves until Maecenas laid out his new gardens there.

    3–4. Editors believe that these lines, which in the manuscripts follow line 20 below, are out of place and cannot be easily placed anywhere but here. The tavern is the tavern into which Cynthia will chase Propertius's lovers at the end of the poem—Propertius did not follow her and so he can say, "not with me . . . ."

    5. Lanuvium: The town of Lanuvium is southeast of Rome on the Appian Way and the site for the ritual worship of Juno the Savior. Her temple there was one of the oldest in Italy and there she was represented as a warrior goddess with goatskin helmet and a serpent at her feet. The site has been excavated and contains relics dated back to the sixth century B.C.E. Propertius here gives a basic outline of her rites: blindfolded young girls entered a cave on certain days to offer cakes to the serpent within; they proceeded to the serpent's lair by following a breeze that blew through the cave; if the cakes were accepted, the girls were proved to be virgins, and this was considered a good omen for the city. The ritual is described in detail by the third-century Greek author of *De Natura Animalium*. "Your inquisitive hour" indicates that these rites were as strange to the Romans of Propertius's day as they are to us.

    17. clipped ponies: Cynthia has decided to go to Lanuvium with another man. She rides in a carriage drawn by "clipped ponies," a sign of wealth and fashion. She is the very opposite of the girls whose virginity and offerings protect the farmers' fields.

    18. Juno, Venus: The excuse for this trip was the ritual of Juno the Savior; the real reason was erotic infidelity—Venus.

    19. what a triumph: The spectators along the Appian Way are imagined to have watched Cynthia as if she were a Roman general returned from imposing peace on a barbarian world and marching in his triumphal procession. In Cynthia's final appearance she is still the triumphant conqueror she was in her first appearance.

    20. over your stones: The Appian Way, built at the end of the fourth century B.C.E., was Rome's principle route to southern Italy. It was known to be rough and slow going.

23. <u>depilated scion's silk-hooded coach</u>: Cynthia rode in a two-wheeled vehicle covered with a silk hood that was both a pleasure vehicle and sometimes a racing carriage. Her compan-ion was a man of family, a "scion" who had a taste for the super-elegant: he had his hair plucked.

24. <u>Molossan dogs</u>: These were typically working dogs; it is another sign of the young man's luxurious ways that he pampers them and places something more than just a dog collar around their necks.

25. <u>sell his life</u>: Even people of family and position were known to become gladiators in order to save themselves from want. The idea is that the young man will soon have spent his patrimony and will sink as low as anyone can.

26. <u>when a beard</u>: Just as a smooth face was a sign of the elegant young men of Rome, so the beard was a sign, almost a badge, of the gladiator.

29. <u>Aventine Diana</u>: There was an ancient temple to Diana, the virgin goddess of the hunt, on the Aventine. She was the sister of Apollo, and so as Apollo was called "Cynthius," so Diana would have been "Cynthia."

31. <u>Teia</u>: The name is a nickname meaning one from Teos, the island from which the Greek love poet Anacreon hailed.

31. <u>Tarpeian grove</u>: A depression between the Capitoline and the Arx; the area was mostly covered with public buildings.

37. <u>Lygdamus</u>: Propertius's slave whom we met in elegy IV 7 above.

38. <u>Methymnaean wine</u>: Methymna was a town in Lesbos, an island famous for its wine and as the home of the love poet Sappho. In this *ménage à trois* there may have been some Sapphic lovemaking, alluded to by reference to this wine.

39. <u>Nile, yours was</u>: In other words, the flute player was an Egyptian; the exact text is in doubt here and Propertius may not have referred to the Nile River at all.

40. <u>artlessly elegant</u>: The phrase is a distinct reminiscence of Horace's description of Pyrrha in *Odes* I 5. 5.

41. <u>Magnus</u>: The name means, "Big Guy" or "The Great," and is here used ironically, and no doubt as a nickname, for a dwarf. Entertainment of this kind was common at dinner parties.

45–46. <u>shooting dice . . . the damn dogs</u>: It was common at dinner parties to play a game of dice. The best throw was called "the Venus"; the worst was called "the dog."

49ff. <u>the raucous doors creaked . . . .</u>: It seems that Propertius here rewrites and reverses a scene familiar to Romans from the stage. In the final scene of a typical adultery mime, the husband returns, the adulterer hides but is caught, and is finally driven off with blows, fearing for himself and for his reputation.

56. <u>taking of the city</u>: One of the most explicit and polemical characterizations of love as the equivalent of martial valor in Propertius and another reference to the imagery of triumph.

75. <u>in Pompey's shade</u>: The portico of Pompey and its gardens were popular places to meet members of the opposite sex.

76. <u>Forum's lascivious sands</u>: The Forum, which was not usually sandy (it was paved with stone), was spread with sand for gladiatorial shows and other games. These games would also provide occasions to socialize with potential mates.

77. <u>the theater's top</u>: Women sat in the upper tiers of the theater.

84. she fumigated: We return now to ritual actions of purification reminiscent of the opening scene at Lanuvium.

IV 11

This last elegy in the last book of elegies Propertius wrote was at one time held in high esteem for its noble sentiment and its high moral stance. Today, at least one critic has taken the poem as a condemnation of the life noble women were required to live. It is perhaps not out of place among the experiments of Book IV, but it is atypical of Roman elegy. It is spoken entirely by a woman and a wife and it emphasizes marital virtues. On the other hand, it deals with love, fidelity, and death—topics central to Propertian elegiac concerns and to the elegiac tradition in general. The speaker is Cornelia, daughter of a certain Cornelius Scipio and Scribonia, a woman who was later married to Octavian and was the mother of Julia. Octavian divorced Scribonia after one year of marriage because she was impossible to live with; apparently she had a temper. Cornelia's family was a prominent in politics: her father may have been the consul of 38 B.C.E.; her husband, L. Aemilius Paullus Lepidus, was *consul suffectus* in 34 B.C.E. and censor in 22 B.C.E., and her brother was consul in 16 B.C.E.

The poem is a monologue which, at least at the beginning, recalls a kind of monumental epigram in which the dead person speaks from the tomb. It also takes the form of a formal defense of Cornelia's life, complete with character witnesses. In other respects it is like a funeral *laudatio*, or praise of the dead. The poem is variously addressed to Cornelia's husband, to the judges of the dead, and finally to her family.

1. Paulus: L. Aemilius Paullus Lepidus, her husband, who is imagined as weeping at her tomb. This is the moment traditionally represented at the beginning of consolation poems.

4. inexorable adamant: It was a commonplace of consolation literature to remark on the unyielding finality of death; see Horace *Odes* I 24. "Adamant" refers to anything inflexible and unbreakable.

5. the god: Hades was the god of the underworld.

7. the ferryman: Charon ferried the dead across the river Styx into Hades for the payment of an obol, a coin of little value. For this reason, the dead were buried with a small coin in their mouths.

8. the pale door: This is not a reference to any standard portrayal of the doors to Hades; rather, it seems to be a "transferred epithet," that is, because death makes the corpse pale, the door to death is called a pale door. It is said to "shut in" the dead because they were thought to try to escape.

11. my family chariot: As a member of the family of the Cornelii, Cornelia would include among her ancestors the great Scipios of the Punic Wars and Aemilius Paullus of the Macedonian War. Here Cornelia either uses the singular to refer collectively to the triumphal chariots of her ancestors, or the Scipios may have used the same chariot in their individual triumphs. In any event, the triumphant general kept in his home the gilded chariot he rode in his triumph.

12. pledges of my fame: Usually "pledges" in these circumstances refer to the children who are both evidence and witnesses of her wifely virtues; here, however, Cornelia seems to have in mind any and all evidence of her life, including ancestors and reputation.

12. how have they helped: Another common topos of the funeral lament is the complaint that virtue did not receive its reward; again, see Horace *Odes* I 24.

17. but not guilty: Here the commonplace funeral complaint that death has taken an innocent victim allows the poem to become a defense of Cornelia's life.

18. Pluto: Another name for Hades, god of the underworld; the name means "wealth" because the earth's increase has its origin in death.

19. Aeacus: Cornelia pictures a Roman courtroom where the judge, or *quaestor*, determines the order of appearance for defendants by selecting names from an urn. See Horace *Odes* III 1. 16. Aeacus was a son of Jupiter by Aegina (less commonly said to have had Europa as his mother) and grandfather of Achilles, the great hero of the *Iliad*. Together with Minos and Rhadamanthus, he was one of the judges of the dead, so honored because of his just life on earth. See below on line 39.

21. his brothers: Minos and Rhadamanthus were sons of Jupiter by Europa; Aeacus would be their half brother. When Cornelia asks Minos and Rhadamanthus to "sit by," she refers to those colleagues and experts who sat beside the *quaestor* in an official capacity as advisors and consultants on points of law. Minos's chair is said to be beside the judge presumably because he is the older brother.

22. troop of Fates: The Eumenides, ancient gods and avenging spirits, are imagined in the role of lictors, those attendants of public officials who carried the fasces which represented their magisterial authority.

22. the listening forum: The forum is first and last a place of business. Propertius imagines that in the land of the dead all business halts and the audience sits in hushed anticipation of Cornelia's defense.

23–26. The scene here is influenced by a similar scene in Vergil's *Georgics* in which Orpheus, on the death of Eurydice, descends into Hades where his music, so beautiful and sad, stills the troubled shades and wins a temporary victory over Death: "Nay, the very halls and innermost depths of Death, the regions of Tartarus were struck dumb and the Furies with snakes woven in their hair; and Cerberus held his three mouths agape, and the turn of Ixion's wheel stopped in the wind" (*Georgics* IV 481–484).

23. Sisyphus: For a variety of trickster-like misdeeds, including the time he chained up Death itself, Sisyphus was condemned in the underworld to roll a large stone to the top of a hill, but whenever he got to the top the stone rolled back down and he had to begin again.

23. Ixion: For his attempt to seduce Juno, wife of Jupiter, Ixion was bound to a wheel which turned forever in the wind.

24. Tantalus: Either for serving the gods his own son's flesh at a banquet or for stealing the gods' nectar, Tantalus was punished in Hades by being placed in a pool of water that always receded when he tried to drink and under bunches of fruit that always rose up from his grasp when he tried to eat.

25–26. Cerberus, the silent gate: Cerberus, the dog that guards the entrance to Hades, is chained to the gate itself, so when he attacks shades trying to escape, the gate (or its lock) rattles.

27. like the sinful sisters: The daughters of Danaus who, except for Hypermnestra, all killed their husbands on their wedding night according to the order of their father. They were punished in Hades by being condemned to fetch water in urns which had holes in the bottom.

They are appropriately chosen by Cornelia since her claim is to marital fidelity. Compare Cynthia's reference to them in elegy IV 7. 63 above.

29. ancestral trophies: The appropriate place to begin a funeral speech of self-defense; wax images of one's famous ancestors were kept in the entry hall of Roman homes and worn at funerals.

30. Africa's realms, Numantine fathers: On her father's side, she was descended from the elder and the younger Scipio Africanus, both of whom received their *agnomen*, or "added name," "Africanus" for their actions against Carthage: the elder Scipio Africanus defeated Hannibal at Zama in 202 and brought the Second Punic War to an end; the younger besieged and destroyed Carthage at the end of the Third Punic War in 146 B.C.E. The younger had also earned the title "Numantinus" for forcing the surrender of Numantia in Spain in 133 B.C.E.

31. maternal Libones: On her mother's side, Cornelia was descended from the Scribonii Libones. They were not, however, a particularly distinguished family and the claim that they "set the balance" with the Scipios is highly exaggerated.

33. The *praetexta*: This robe with a purple border was worn by all freeborn children until their majority; at that time, boys put on the *toga virilis*, or "manly toga," and women at the time of marriage put on the stola.

34. a new headband: This is a reference to the coiffure of the bride; it is not certain exactly how the hair was done, but we know that the bride wore her hair parted and braided in six locks, each bound with a band.

36. Read this stone: The poet continues to recall the fiction that this speech is inscribed on a grave monument.

36. bride to one man alone: Cornelia makes reference to the Roman matron's conservative pride in being *univira*, married but once and always faithful to her husband. This ideal was honored more in the breach than in practice where dynastic marriages and remarriages were common.

37–38. Ancestral ashes . . . beneath whose legends: This appeal to her ancestors as witnesses of her virtue is more complex than it at first seems. Roman families usually burned their dead; hence ancestral ashes. However, the remains of the Scipios lie beneath monuments whose carved legends celebrate their titles and achievements. Since their achievements include the conquest of Carthage (in northern Africa), Africa itself is imagined as lying crushed beneath the grave monuments of the Scipios.

39–40. Perses, Achilles: Aemelius Paullus, father of the younger Scipio Africanus, conquered Perses, king of Macedonia, who claimed descent from Achilles. It is strange that Cornelia would call upon the defeated enemy of Rome to give witness to her character. As a result, editors frequently either move these lines or revise them.

41. the censor's law: Cornelia's husband was censor in 22 B.C.E. His censorship, according to one ancient witness, Velleius Paterculus, was notoriously weak.

49. the urn: In a Roman trial, the jurors were given three small tablets marked separately with the sign for "absolve," "convict," and "unclear." At the end of the trial, each juror placed the appropriate tablet in an urn whose contents then determined the verdict.

51–52. who towed Cybebe with a rope, Claudia: In 205 B.C.E. the black stone of the *Magna Mater*, Cybebe, was brought to Rome on a ship that went aground in the Tiber channel. Quinta Claudia, who had been accused of unchastity, prayed for a sign to prove her innocence and then single-handedly pulled the ship off of the sands with her girdle. Consequently a statue of her was placed in the temple of the *Magna Mater*.

52. <u>tower crowned goddess</u>: The *Magna Mater* is usually represented as wearing a crown with turreted walls.

53. <u>when just Vesta called</u>: A Vestal virgin entrusted with care of the eternal fire of Vesta allowed that fire to go out. Aemilia, an older Vestal virgin, assumed responsibility and, after praying to the goddess, placed her robe over the ashes. The flame reappeared.

55. <u>Scribonia</u>: Cornelia's mother, who had been married for a year to Octavian, provides the transition for a complimentary reference to the young emperor.

58–60. <u>Caesar's lament . . . tears escape the god</u>: The young Octavian (Augustus) attended the funeral. Propertius here toys with the philosophical commonplace that the gods were incapable of tears. See further on elegy III 4. 1.

59. <u>a sister worthy of his own daughter</u>: Since Cornelia's mother, Scribonia, had been married to Octavian (Augustus), her daughter by Octavian was Cornelia's half sister.

61. <u>finery's generous honors</u>: The exact meaning of this line is not clear. We know that certain privileges came to a mother who had three children. These privileges may have included the right to wear certain clothing.

63. <u>Lepidus, Paulus</u>: Cornelia's two sons, M. Aemelius Lepidus and L. Aemilius Paullus, she assumes and prays, will carry on her family line and her good name. They did, as the former was consul in 6 C.E. and the latter consul in 1 C.E.

65. <u>my brother</u>: P. Cornelius Scipio was consul in 16 B.C.E.

69. <u>the ship sets sail</u>: A reference to the boat of Charon which carries the dead across the river Styx to the underworld.

71. <u>a woman's triumph</u>: Some critics find in this expression no little irony and bitterness. To understand their perspective, one needs to recall that a man's triumph was a public event celebrated as a religious cermony in a state parade to the temple of Jupiter on the Capitoline. One should recall Propertius's imagination of Cynthia's triumph in elegy IV 8.

75. <u>do a mother's work</u>: A striking command to be given to a Roman consul and censor.

81–82. <u>let the nights suffice, and dreams . . .</u>: From here to the end of the poem there are several reminiscences of the Cynthia poems. Does married love turn out to be a sober version of elegy?

85. <u>a new bed</u>: The *lectus genialis*, a symbolic marriage bed, was placed in the atrium of a Roman home opposite the door. There the woman of the house sat to receive callers. When a widower remarried this bed was replaced with a new bed.

97. <u>I never mourned as a mother</u>: Infant mortality was, of course, very high in Rome. Cornelia takes it as a matter of pride that none of her childern died before her.

99. <u>witnesses . . . rise</u>: At the end of a speech for the defense one might ask the witnesses to rise in order to impress the court with their number.

102. <u>the honored waters</u>: Cornelia imagines that she will be conveyed across the rivers of the underworld to the land of the blessed; hence the waters that carry her are honored waters.

Sulpicia

Women always played an important role in the cultural life of Rome, whether we think of Cornelia, the mother of the Gracchi, of Lesbia and the other "learned girls" of the elegists, or of Agrippina and the powerful women of the empire. However, as at other times in Western culture and literature, the presence of women is marked primarily by their silence and their speech is usually usurped by the speech of men. An interesting and provocative reflection on this situation is offered by M. I. Finley in "The Silent Women of Rome," *Aspects of Antiquity* (New York: Viking Press, 1968) 129–142. The poet Sulpicia, however, is the exception with her forty lines of elegy. On these grounds alone Sulpicia's poetry is in a special position and should arouse no small degree of interest. Until recently, however, outside the field of classics she has been unknown; and within the field she has been treated as merely a gifted amateur.

One critic (Hinds) has astutely pointed out that the name of Sulpicia's lover, "Cerinthus," sounds like the male version of a conflation of "Corinna" (Ovid's mistress) and "Cynthia" (Propertius's mistress). From a literary point of view, two things are remarkable about her lover. First, by virtue of the pseudonym, Sulpicia's man has, in effect, no name; he is deprived of the patrilineal emblem of patriarchal order. Second, he is silent. Thus, following the norms of Latin love elegy produces here the curious situation in which the male is passive, absent, and undemonstrative, refracted in the speech of his female lover. The inevitable result of these generic norms adapted to a female speaker is a form of cross-dressing for both partners to the affair.

In some collections poems 7–20 of Book III of Tibullus are numbered as Book IV 1–14. This division is given here in brackets.

BIBLIOGRAPHY

There is no book in English on these poems, but several articles will provide useful discussion and details.

Currie, H. MacL. "The Poems of Sulpicia," *ANRW* 2. 30. 3, 1751–1764.

Fredricks, C. S. "A poetic experiment in the Garland of Sulpicia (Corpus Tibullianum 3. 10)," *Latomus* 35 (1976) 229–239.

Hinds, S. "The poetess and the reader: further steps toward Sulpicia," *Hermathena* 143 (1987) 29–46.

Santirocco, M. S. "Sulpicia reconsidered," *CJ* 74 (1979) 229–239.

III 13 [IV 7]

The collection begins here, and it is already in the middle of the story: Sulpicia, after several literary attempts to gain Cerinthus's affection, has finally succeeded. This poem appears casual in manner, and, since it has no addressee, appears to some like a diary entry. However, as Sulpicia reflects on the power of her poetry and expresses her resolve to write publicly about her love, the poem almost necessarily has a programmatic quality. Not only does she claim that her poetry has practical power in that it has had the effect of winning Cerinthus, the poem is also very consciously about publication, that is, publication by a woman. It begins explicity with the poet's concern for the speech of others, the report that will follow her desire to speak of love and the reputation she will have as a result. It is precisely in this regard that Sulpicia adopts and adapts the pose of social defiance which is typical of the elegists, but as she does, she gives it a specifically female orientation. It has been noted that references to speech ("to be said to hide," "rumors," "Let it be known") frame the poem, and much of this poem is actually in "indirect discourse." Sulpicia's concern with what is hidden and what is communicated frames the entire collection; note III 13. 1, "to be said to hide this kind of love," and III 18. 6: "desiring as I did to hide my own fire." These concerns, as expressed here, are at least in part concerns about what men will say.

1. At last: When the poet begins in *mediis rebus*, she not only suggests that there has already been a long history to this love affair, but she passes over all those poems which she says "won over [her beloved] by the pleading of my Muse." In a sense, then, she does "keep what I've written under seal."

1–2. to hide. . . , rumors that I'd laid it bare . . .: Neither of the alternatives are free from the judgment and speech of others: Sulpicia cannot simply choose silence or speech; she must simultaneously choose or negotiate the speech of others, which reveals her fear of the consequences of being found out.

3. Won over: Sulpicia apparently believes in the effectiveness of her love poetry as a practical instrument of her will. This is not uncommon, either in the genre of elegiac poetry or in the fancy of poets. To begin a collection of elegies at the point of success is unusual; elegiac expression is usually motivated by a crisis. Here the crisis may be the dangers of publication.

3. Cytherea: An allusion to Venus taken from the name of the island in the Aegean where she was said to have first landed, Cythera, and which was noted for its worship and celebration of Venus.

4. him: Who? We know from the next poem, as well as from the preceding poems in our collection, that Sulpicia's lover was Cerinthus, but it is surely an elegant piece of wit that Sulpicia here conceals the name of the very lover whose indiscreet disclosure she celebrates. One may compare Ovid's *Amores*, where the name of Corinna is postponed for five poems.

4. placed him in my arms: Elsewhere in Latin the expression Sulpicia uses here refers to bringing someone into the Senate or the assembly, that is into specifically male bodies engaged publically in specifically male activities.

5–6. Let my joys be told: An extraordinary revision of the familiar claim that the elegiac poet speaks for all lovers and so all lovers will speak his poems. See, for example, Propertius I 1. 38: [literally translated as] "Alas, with what grief he will repeat my words." In Sulpicia's reversal, her imagined speaker is not an unhappy lover but one without a beloved, and so the repetition of Sulpicia's story will not be a form of shared complaint but of displaced satisfaction. For the male elegist's view that girls will enjoy hearing his poems, see Propertius I 9. 14.

9. a little infamy: A cautious version of the elegiac poets' typical defiance and disregard of social proprieties.

10. a fitting partner: The language stresses social propriety and personal appropriateness; literally, "Let me be known to have been a proper girl with her proper boy." The language and form is that of the world of public and reciprocal (typically male) worth and worthiness. Together, they make a striking claim on the values of the very world Sulpicia seemed to defy in line 9.

III 14 [IV 8]

A poem on Sulpicia's birthday, no doubt the basis of the poem to Juno Natalis in the "Garland of Sulpicia" (III 12 [IV 6]). It is addressed to Sulpicia's uncle, Messalla, and ostentatiously reverses two typical themes of elegiac poetry: first, the birthday is unhappy; second, the town is preferred to the country. Since Sulpicia's unhappiness depends on her forced departure from Rome, one should keep in mind the social reality of Roman women: they were in general under the supervision and control of the men in their lives. For a more typical birthday poem, one may consider Tibullus I 7.

2. Cerinthus: The first mention of Sulpicia's lover.

3. What's sweeter: Although the sentiment is not typically Tibullan or Horatian, the new generation of poets certainly included men like Catullus and Ovid for whom the city's urbane life was especially prized.

4. Arretium: Messalla's country villa was in central Italy, in Etruria near the town of Arretium on the river Arno.

6. journeys: The topic has a long history in elegy from the journeys in Catullus 11 that Catullus's friends imagine, no doubt as a cure for his unrequited love, to the journeys Tibullus and Propertius do not wish to take with their adventurous patrons.

7. abducted: It is (for male readers, especially Roman males) an extraordinary conceit to figure a Roman uncle's expectation that his niece will journey with him as an abduction or rape; and in Latin, it may be argued, the implication is easily effaced or ignored due to the several meanings of the word. However, such an interpretation cannot be dismissed *tout court*, especially since the last line translates literally, "since force does not allow me to live in accordance with my own judgment."

III 15 [IV 9]

This poem is a response to the preceding birthday poem III 14. The two poems contrast in length and, pursuing this formal contrast, some critics have found the first poem coldly rhetorical and the second warmly spontaneous. I am skeptical of such judgments and suspect that the gender of the reader may have affected his reading. The poem seems to be addressed to Sulpicia's lover and friends: she will stay in Rome and celebrate her birthday there.

Latin Lyric and Elegiac Poetry: An Anthology of New Translations

4. once-skeptical: Perhaps one should hear a note of reproof. The preceding poem was, in part, an effort to persuade Mesalla, and if Cerinthus remained skeptical, he must have had some doubts about Sulpicia's powers of persuasion and poetic effectiveness. Such an implication makes an effective transition to the next poem.

III 16 [IV 10]

This poem is generally thought to be the most difficult of Sulpicia's poems and yet also the most typical. Cerinthus has been unfaithful and Sulpicia's response engages a set of shifting emotions. At first she is sarcastic; then indifferent; finally proud. The poem is often remarked for this variety and intensity of tone, which seems to dramatize both Sulpicia's divided internal responses and the external division from her lover which leave Sulpicia casting about for other personal connections in which her care is matched by the care of others.

3. the simple toga: *The toga virilis*, or "man's toga," was the unadorned dress worn by Roman males on reaching the age of majority. Curiously enough, this symbol of the dignity and privileges of the male Roman citizen was also worn by prostitutes. It was not worn by respect-able women.

3. basket-burdened: Sulpicia refers to the basket in which a spinner's daily work was contained. The wool spinning here referred to was laborious and paid poorly.

4. Sulpicia, daughter of Servius: In what is called her signature, "Sulpicia, daughter of Servius," there is both pride and bitterness. The name "Servius" recalls in Latin the designation of "slave," *servus*; "daughter of Servius" and "daughter of a slave" would be in Latin indistinguishable. Thus, at the moment Sulpicia asserts the pride of her aristocratic place, two linguistic events confound her. First, she finds herself named as if a slave or a freedwoman, the very class from which prostitutes came; second, she is named, as almost all women of Rome were named, in terms of a male domination: literally, she is "the woman of the Sulpicii who is the daughter of Servius."

5. Others: These would be the other men in her life, those who protect her and who give her status. It is worth noting that here Sulpicia asserts the same principle that concerns her in the last poem: care for others should be matched by care from others.

6. yield . . . to an inferior: Does this mean that Cerinthus was of low birth? The current consensus is that the inferior one here is the prostitute. If so, Sulpicia composes in this couplet a remarkable intersection of forces: as a lover, she imagines the posture of a combatant, fighting like a man for high place in society and refusing to yield to an inferior; however, as a woman she finds consolation in the very solicitude of men that in poem III 14 threatened her self-determination.

III 17 [IV 11]

Sulpicia is ill. As in the preceding poem, the poet adjusts herself and her emotions to a potential crisis: each couplet opposes her and Cerinthus: your devotion / my frailty; my prayer / your wish; my benefit / your indifference. The opposition remains unresolved and the poem ends awaiting the speech of Cerinthus. Illness is a typical theme of the elegists, often used to illustrate the devotion of the poet/lover; e.g., Tibullus I 5, Propertius II 28, and Ovid *Amores* II 13. Here, however, the sickbed is the scene of complaint, of absence, as if Sulpicia again intentionally reverses generic expectations. Compare the claims of Propertius II 9*.

2. vexed with fever: There is here a double reference to the fever of passion and the fever of medical illness. Compare the poem to Apollo in the "Garland of Sulpicia," elegy III 10.

3–4. I would not pray . . . : And if he does, he is presumably love-sick as well. Compare the conclusion to the Garland poem on Sulpicia's sickness: "Praises will be heaped on you I For having saved not just one life but two!" ("Garland of Sulpicia," elegy III 10. 2122).

5. What use: As in poem III 16, Sulpicia imagines here her strength in masculine terms (she can conquer disease); but then discovers her weakness in that victory (his indifference conquers her).

III 18 [IV 12]

Sulpicia's apology for not demonstrating the strength of her passion. The poem is constructed as a kind of ring (from "fervor" in line 1 to "fire" in line 6) and is unusual in that the six lines form one sentence (typically in Sulpicia, each couplet forms a sentence). As the last poem of the group, one may be tempted to find here the suggestion of a programmatic allegory: All attempts to give speech to her love have finally resulted in inadequacy; the rest is silence.

Sulpicia wishes that Cerinthus's passion be diminished if ever she did anything so foolish as what she did last night when she did not show her passion. On the surface this is an apology for what was not said and not shown, and a request that Cerinthus not take her speech and actions to heart. But the request is also an attempt to preempt Cerinthus, who must not think, "well, if that's all she cares for me, then I will care less for her." In order to do this, Sulpicia accepts an implied principle that passion should equal passion, and, consequently, if her passion was only what it seemed, then Cerinthus's passion is justifiably diminished. When put this way, we see that again Sulpicia is concerned both with the language and the thoughts of others. Her poem addresses Cerinthus both as a confession of inadequate speech and as an attempt to get the last word by preempting his thoughts. It is, then, a striking irony that even as she does this, she arrives at no positive and independent formulation of her love. Her rhetoric of challenge and confession, her language of "regret," "foolishness," and "fire" all point to what is not said.

Critics have difficulty in placing this poem within a coherent narrative of the affair. However, if this chronological uncertainty detracts from the poem's role at the end of this round of epigrams, the poem still offers a fitting closure. The collection has moved from Sulpicia's claim that silence would shame her more than indiscretion to her apology for not disclosing adequately the strength of her love. For all the generic playfulness and manipulations of speech, there remains in these poems a silence which readers may find more expressive and compelling than the posture of complete disclosure.

1. my light: While common enough as a term of affection for one's beloved in other poets, it occurs only here in Sulpicia's poems and never in Tibullus's poems.

3. if ever in my youth: The language and the careful logic recall Catullus, as does the form of the epigram in general.

"Garland of Sulpicia"
(Tibullus III 8–12 [IV 2–6])

The following comments on the "Garland of Sulpicia" are frequently indebted to the fine and suggestive study of S. Hinds, "The poetess and the reader: further steps towards Sulpicia," *Hermathena* 143 (1987) 29–46.

III 8 [IV 2]

This poem is generally thought to have been written to accompany a gift to Sulpicia on the *Matronalia*, a woman's festival celebrated on the first of March. March is named after the god of war, Mars, and so he is properly summoned to the festival. It was a day on which the slaves dined with the matron of the household, and she in fine attire received gifts from the males in her life. Sulpicia is not a matron, however, and this poem initiates an elegiac sequence which celebrates a love affair. The festival, then, may not be the *Matronalia*, or the *Matronalia* may be used as a false lead which, like the presence of Mars himself, will be changed by Sulpicia's loveliness. As a *kletic*, or invocatory, hymn to Mars turns into elegiac praise of Sulpicia, as Mars drops his weapons and Venus smiles, one may also suspect that the generic indecorum that pervades the poem adds to the prestige of Sulpicia and the erotic indecorum accrues to the praise of Venus.

1. <u>Descend from heaven</u>: A typical phrase in a *kletic*, or invocatory hymn in which a god is summoned, often to attend a festival. Here, however, the god is Mars, a divinity whose presence is at least irregular in the genre of love elegy. Compare Propertius's antithesis of love and war. Furthermore, the god is summoned to gaze upon and admire, as if to worship, his own devotee, and perhaps to consider her as an alternative to his mate, Venus.

3. <u>though Venus</u>: Venus, the goddess of love, is appropriately watching the festival in this poem: she is the true presiding deity of elegy and she is the lover of Mars, whose festival it is. Her smile is generally taken to mean that she will not be angry that Sulpicia's beauty may lead Mars to thoughts of infidelity. However, elsewhere the smile of Venus is a casual recognition of her power and ascendancy; here, too, Mars's erotic thoughts of infidelity as he gazes on Sulpicia's loveliness are reflection of Venereal power.

6. <u>his double torch</u>: The torch, together with the bow and arrow, are Cupid's typical weapons; they are often viewed as instruments of torture.

10. <u>a coiffure</u>: While the dress of Roman women remained surprisingly the same over the years, hair styles were much more variable.

11. <u>Tyrian purple</u>: The island of Tyre was noted for the quality of its purple dye.

13. <u>Vertumnus on Olympus</u>: A god of the seasons whose name is related to the Latin for "to turn, to change," and who is aptly and frequently named in this poetic situation. He is situated on Mt. Olympus where the gods were said to live.

16–20.   purple-dyed woolens, Arabian ... fragrance, gems: Traditional examples of luxury and extravagance. Since luxury is a matter of excess which depends on a standard of propriety, that Sulpicia alone ought to have these items indicates that in her case propriety is not violated, that these expenditures properly adorn her beauty.

21.   Muses: The appeal to the Muses is in the hymnic tradition and, while it literally asks for some song from the Muse, scholars have noted that it usually reflects the very song the poet is bringing to a close.

22.   Apollo: As god of poetry he presided over the Muses.

22.   tortoise shell: Lyres were made from tortoise shell.

24.   deserving of your hymn: This poem, whether intended to accompany a gift on the *Matronalia* or not, is in the end itself a gift which the poet offers. Sulpicia, who is at first the lovely worshipper at this festival of Mars, becomes, by virtue of being the object of another's gaze, first a potential replacement for Venus herself, and then the deity who supplants Mars, who owns the festival, and of whom the Muses sing.

III 10 [IV 4]

Sulpicia is sick, a common scene in elegy, and one which the male lover/poet typically uses to demonstrate the seriousness of his love. Here the poet calls upon the god Apollo to drive out the disease, calls upon Cerinthus to show his love, and promises Apollo his reward. Assuming a nonspecific speaker, we read the poem in part as an attempt to charm Apollo into coming to Sulpicia's aid, which means coming with his own charms to entice away the evil spirits which were thought to cause disease, and in part as an attempt to reassure Cerinthus that the norms of his elegiac world have not been permanently disturbed. The theme of a beloved's sickness is also taken up in Tibullus I 5. One critic has argued that Sulpicia's sickness was really her fear of unrequited love; see S. C. Fredricks, "A poetic experiment in the "Garland of Sulpicia" (Corpus Tibullianum 3. 10)" *Latomus* 35 (1976) 761–782.

1.   Apollo: Apollo was god of poetry (and so of charms), of prophecy, and of medicine. He was a young god, a representative of eternal youth, and since young men did not get their hair cut, was depicted as having long hair himself. He is summoned here as a god of healing. However, given his role in typical scenes of initiation for the Callimachean poet, his other important role as god of poetry cannot be far from the poet's mind.

2.   Come ... come!: One finds also in the Latin, twice repeated, the longer and so more noticeable formula for invoking the presence of a deity. It signals a *kletic*, or invocatory, hymn.

3–4.   you will always be | Glad: The invocatory hymn generally offers the god a deal: if you do this for me, then you will get this in return; or, since I am doing this for you, you must come and do something for me.

13.   if she should seem worse: Another reflection of the contractual nature of Roman religious practice. Cerinthus will curse if the god does not accept or live up to his end of the bargain.

15.   Fear not: Cerinthus fears both for his beloved and on account of his curses, which may earn the wrath of the gods.

15.   god's by love disarmed: The idea that gods will not harm a lover is a common topos of elegy and lyric. Typically the lover feels safe from all dangers as he walks the streets at night;

compare Propertius III 16 and Horace *Odes* I 22. Here, however, the poet reverses the topos and uses it to enjoin Cerinthus's affection.

18.   until . . . a fight: The appropriate and desirable place for tears in the elegiac world is limited to the aftermath of a lover's fight, usually portrayed as a kind of soft-core violence against women, see Tibullus I 10. 59–66.

21.   Phoebus: Another name for Apollo.

24.   to heap your altar: The poet returns to the deal or contract he offered in lines 3–4 and makes explicit Apollo's reward: he will be the envy of other gods.

III 12 [IV 6]

The poet addresses the goddess Juno Natalis on Sulpicia's birthday. Juno Natalis was the guardian spirit which followed women throughout their lives; she was the counterpart to a man's genius; see on Tibullus I 7. 49–54. The young man, Cerinthus, is present by allusion and suggestion. Consequently, the poem's putative public occasion is but an opportunity for Sulpicia to show herself off to her mystery man, and her mother's prayers are but an excuse for other silent wishes. The poem is a delicate exercise in evoking the hidden desires and pleasures of youth while invoking the god's beneficence.

1.   Birthday Juno: As a man would swear by his genius, so a woman would swear by her Juno.

2.   clever girl: The reference is to the "learned girlfriend" or *docta puella* common in elegy and lyric since Catullus's Lesbia. Sulpicia was, of course, a woman most qualified in this regard.

13.   shining purple gown: Juno is asked to come dressed in the favorite costume of Venus.

14.   thrice: The number three is often felt to have magical powers.

14.   cake and wine: Traditional offerings; see Tibullus I 10. 24.

16.   silently: We are told in the commentaries that prayers had to be made out loud for the gods to hear them; apparently this is not always the case.

17–18.   she | Burns: The description here recalls the prayer made in some love charms; for example, "As the clay hardens, as the wax melts, with one and the same fire, so may Daphnis burn with love for me," (Vergil *Eclogue* VIII 81–82).

19.   When next year rolls around: A Roman equivalent of "many happy returns."

Ovid

BIBLIOGRAPHY

We can recommend some fine general books on Ovid:

Fränkel, Herman. *Ovid, A Poet between Two Worlds* (Berkeley: University of California Press, 1945).

Mack, Sara. *Ovid* (New Haven: Yale University Press, 1988).

Rand, E. K. *Ovid and His Influence* (New York: Cooper Square Publishers, 1963).

Wilkinson, L. P. *Ovid Surveyed* (Cambridge [Eng.]: University Press, 1962).

Amores I

Ovid began writing the *Amores* at about eighteen years of age in 25 B.C.E. When he came to revise this five-book edition sometime after 10 B.C.E. into the three books we have, he apparently rearranged the order of the poems, roughly speaking, from pre-infatuation to disenchantment. In this way Ovid can construct an apparent narrative of his love affair which may also seem to parallel his attraction to the genre and his eventual abandonment of it. The first book of the *Amores* has the clearest structure as a book: it begins and ends with programmatic poems which correspond to each other and places the longest poem in the center. On either side of this poem, I 8, the other poems are arranged in pairs of success and failure: 2 with 9, 3 with 10, etc.

I 1

The first poem in an Augustan book of poetry is typically programmatic, and for Ovid's generation the poetic program harkened back to Callimachus. For these poets the choice was traditionally between epic and amatory verse. In one common Callimachean apology for not writing epic, the poet who attempts epic is reprimanded by Apollo, god of poetry, for attempting what is unsuitable to his slender talents. One may find examples of this scene in Propertius III 1 and III 3 and in Horace IV 15. Here, in Ovid's witty variation of the *recusatio*, or "refusal poem," not only does Cupid usurp the role of Apollo and the Muses, but the poet at first and uncharacteristically protests; then we discover that the poet cannot write love poetry because he is not in love. This is a playful inversion of what we take to be the normal sequence by which one first falls in love, then attempts love poetry. For the contrast between love poetry and epic, see also Propertius I 7 and I 9.

1. <u>Weapons and war</u>: A reference to the opening of Vergil's nationalistic epic, the *Aeneid*, which begins "Weapons and the hero I sing . . . ."

2. <u>in meter</u>: Epic verse was written in heroic verses, called hexameters, which maintained a continuous rhythm of six feet, while amatory verse was written in elegiac couplets, which alternated six-foot lines of hexameter with shorter, five-foot pentameter lines.

6. <u>Pierides</u>: The Pierides were associated with the Muses primarily by Vergil and Ovid (in Vergil's pastoral poems and in Ovid's exile poetry). This is the only identification of the two in the *Amores*, and they are never associated in epic poetry.

6. <u>bards</u>: The Latin term, *vates*, denoted public poetry with political and religious seriousness. See Horace *Odes* I 1. 35.

7. <u>Venus, Minerva</u>: The poet protests Cupid's meddling with his epic project by reciting a list of incongruous and humorous reversals of divine roles. In the first, the goddess of love, Venus, changes position with the virgin goddess Minerva, who is associated with war.

9–10. <u>Ceres, Diana</u>: Ceres was the goddess of agriculture and as such associated with the stability needed for civilized life; Diana was the goddess of the wild and of the hunt.

11–12. <u>Apollo, Mars</u>: This reversal is not so sharp as those above. Apollo was god of youth, of music and the lyre, but he was also the god of archery who fought with the Greeks against Troy in Homer's *Iliad*; Mars, who is not associated with music, is the Roman god of war.

12. <u>Aonian lyre</u>: The Aonian mountains in Boeotia included Mount Helicon, sacred to Apollo and the Muses.

13–16. <u>empire . . . rule the whole world</u>: With these references Ovid draws in a comparison of his poetry with the proud and public ambitions of Augustan Rome.

29. <u>myrtle from the shore</u>: Myrtle was sacred to Venus. Ovid uses the myrtle here as symbolic of love poetry, but may also have in mind Venus's role as the divine ancestor of Augustus's family.

I 4

This poem introduces a new complication in Ovid's incipient affair: his beloved has a man. Unfortunately, we cannot be certain whether this means that she was married or had an older lover and patron. Line 64 seems to refer to legal rights, but they might be the rights of a lover and patron as well as a husband's rights. However, given the conventions of the genre and the description at lines 47ff, it seems unlikely that they were married. The occasion is an invitation to a dinner party which the three will attend. This party provides Ovid with an opportunity to play the role of *praeceptor amoris*, or "love teacher," as he instructs the girl in how to act. It also provides an opportunity to explore light-heartedly the psychology of desire and rivalry.

7. <u>well-wined centaurs</u>: The centaurs were mythical four-legged beasts, human from the waist up and horses from their equine shoulders down. Pirithous, king of the Lapiths, once invited them to his wedding to Hippodamia, a princess from Atrax in Thessaly. The centaurs got drunk and attempted to abduct his bride. The story was commonly invoked as an example of reprehensible, drunken, and barbaric behavior. Ovid's assumption here of the centaurs' role is a striking use of myth; it is as if Propertius, instead of saying that Cynthia was as lovely as Ariadne, said that he felt like Theseus setting sail.

12.   Eurus: The east wind; proverbially, lover's words, which were not to be trusted, were said to be written in the wind and the water. However, the topos is usually used as a complaint ("She swears, but it means nothing," cp. Catullus 70); here it is as if the mistress is already well versed in lover's piffle.

17–20.   Watch me . . .: The signs are conventional; compare Tibullus I 2. 21–22 and I 6. 19–20.

40.   "she's mine."..: Ovid's diction here adopts the mode of technical legal language, specifically that in which a thief is caught in the act and the rightful owner takes physical possession of what is his.

53.   he'll get soused: A standard operating procedure for elegiac lovers was to get the rival drunk; compare Tibullus I 6. 27–28.

62.   to the heartless door: Ovid refers to the *paraclausithyron* or "excluded lover poem," a common scene in Roman comedy and elegy: the excluded lover, usually drunk, stands outside his beloved's door and curses, cries, wheedles, etc. See Tibullus I 2 and Propertius I 16.

I 5

There are only two poems in Augustan love elegy which describe a successful sexual encounter: this poem and Propertius II 15.

9.   Corinna: Corinna's first named entry into Ovid's love poetry is like an epiphany. Her name is taken from the name of a beautiful Greek poet whose poetry was celebrated for its complexity. The poet's method in the lines that follow and Corinna's appearance have aptly been described as a tease.

11.   Semiramis: An Assyrian queen famous for her beauty and said to be the daughter of a goddess. She was raised by doves and turned into a dove upon her death. In some versions, she was said to have been a courtesan before she became queen.

12.   Lais: She is not identified with any certainty, but is one of at least two popular Corinthian courtesans named Lais; see Propertius II 6. 1. This reference complicates our view of Ovid and Corinna: does the lover refer only to her beauty or her experience or her mercenary motives?

I 6

This poem is another *paraclausithyron,* or excluded lover poem. Compare Tibullus I 2 and Propertius I 16; the motif appears frequently in ancient poetry, as in Horace *Odes* III 26. 7. Typically the lover, on his way home from a party, stops at his mistress's door, drunk and unhappy; he entreats his beloved or the door to open to him. When his pleas are (inevitably) unsuccessful, he leaves a token of his love (verses or a wreath) and either departs or falls asleep on the steps. The genre provided endless opportunities for variation among the poets, just as the occasion provided opportunities for exploiting the numerous changes of mind that may arise under such circumstances. In Ovid's typically rhetorical version, the standard themes and figures of speech are played with; most frequently they are taken literally (see line 4), or applied inappropriately (see line 39). The lover balances between two roles: the clever manipulator of persuasion and the victim of his own tropes. In the end, he bids farewell like some actor on the stage who had completed his grand scene.

1. <u>doorman</u>: It was Ovid's innovation to have the lover address the doorman. This makes the situation immediately more rhetorical and provides the lover with opportunities to wheedle, flatter, threaten, offer deals, and so on.

4. <u>for me to squeeze through</u>: A typical source of Ovidian wit is the literalization of a metaphor or the application of a figure in an unusual context; here the typically wasted lover attempts to use his emaciation to advantage.

9. <u>fear the dark</u>: The divinely protected lover is a common figure in elegy; see Tibullus I 2. 25–28; Propertius III 16. 11–20; Horace's variation in *Odes* I 22.

11. <u>Then he laughed</u>: Cupid's interruption and the change he effects in the poet's life recalls programmatic scenes of divine investiture and Ovid's witty variation on such scene at the beginning of the *Amores*. Compare Ovid *Amores* II 18. 11.

24. <u>Night is passing</u>: Ovid introduced the refrain into the *paraclausithyron*; before, it was known in choral lyric, funeral poems, magical incantations, and so on. Since we know that young lovers actually did sing songs in the night at their beloveds' houses, one may imagine that refrains were not unknown before Ovid.

41. <u>Are you thick as wood</u>: The language is here derived from the traditional *paraclausithyron* in which the door is addressed.

47. <u>I'd gladly take your place</u>: The typical situation for the lover and the guardian is first reversed so that the lover can then offer a reversal of situation as his deal to the guardian.

53. <u>Boreas, Orithyia</u>: Boreas, the north wind, had his cult worship in Athens for having aided the Athenians against the Persians. According to the myth as recounted in Ovid's *Metamorphoses*, he first wooed Orithyia, the daughter of a king of Athens, with prayers rather than force; but when this failed he turned to violence and carried her off to be his bride.

65. <u>Lucifer</u>: The name means "bringer of light" and it refers to the morning star, Venus, which rises just before the dawn. Most of the celestial phenomena were imagined as traversing the sky behind a team of horses.

I 8

The bulk of the poem is the speech of a *lena*. This person, often called in translation a "procuress" or "madame," was any woman, from madame and brothel keeper to a nurse making introductions, who arranged meetings between men and women for her own profit. The figure is common in many literary genres from comedy and mime to elegy (see Propertius IV 5, Tibullus I 5, II 6, and Ovid *Amores* III 5), and, judging from laws relating to them, such persons apparently really existed. It is doubtful, however, that someone of Ovid's class and connections, or that any average youth at this time, would have relied on a *lena*, and the poem should probably be taken more as a literary fiction than as a reflection of Ovid's literal reality. It seems typical of these figures that they are old, alcoholic, greedy, and amoral and it is surely significant that Ovid places this poem at the center of *Amores* I. The lover overhears a *lena*'s advice to his mistress. The lover himself is only indirectly characterized, and shows a certain gullibility in his acceptance of the *lena*'s magical powers. It has been suggested that this self-delusion on the lover's part protects him from having to face the cynical and sordid motives upon which his sophisticated sexual game depends. By this interpretation, the lover himself is discredited by conveniently believing in the old woman's magic, while the old woman's advice accurately diagnoses and discredits the world of urban elegiac love. In its context in the *Amores*, this *lena*'s speech recalls Ovid's own speech of advice in *Amores* I 4 and therefore makes the *lena* a special kind of *praeceptor amoris*, an anti-professor of love (from the man's point of view), or a professor of love to women. The speech also serves the ironic function of anticipating some of the tricks Corinna will play on her lover later.

2. Dipsas: The name, which means "thirsty," was the name of a small viper whose bite caused its victims a painful thirst.

4. Memnon's mother: Memnon, king of the Ethiopians, was considered to be the son of Aurora, the dawn, who in the morning rode her chariot up the eastern sky. In a poem relatively free of mythological allusion, this establishes the lover as self-conscious and sophisticated.

5. secret spells of Circe: Ancient magic was frequently, if not predominately, used for amatory and aphrodisiac purposes. It was a fairly conventional theme in Roman poetry, and the powers here attributed to Dipsas are the standard ones.

8. poison: Traditionally, the secretions from the genitalia of a mare in heat were thought to be a love charm.

11. Believe it or not: The poet invites the reader to assess the credulity of this lover. Note below, "I believe what I hear," line 15.

20. eloquent: Dipsas is presented as a kind of immoral lawyer. The form of the speech may recall rhetorical exercises called *suasoria*, or speeches of persuasion. The speech has four parts: 23–34: take this rich lover; 35–68: take any rich lover; 69–104: how to take rich lovers; 105–108: final urgings.

29. Mars ascending: The common belief was that Mars, the red star, was malevolent, especially in regard to the plans of Venus, a planet who would be auspicious for lovers. This is no more learned or sophisticated than contemporary recourse to astrology. Other references to myth and history are standard and conventional.

39. Sabine girls: The Sabine women were often cited as examples of old-fashioned morality; Dipsas does not seem to accept the story without reservations.

41. Mars: The Roman god of boundaries became, naturally enough for a nation both expanding and protecting its boundaries, the god of war. In early Rome, the wars were against the Roman neighbors, the Sabines themselves.

42. Venus rules: Aeneas was the founder of the Latin people, who eventually established Rome. The logic seems to be that now, with Mars leading Roman youths to wage war at the ends of the earth, Venus controls Rome, and with Venus come many opportunities for promiscuity. Venus was also the founding goddess of the Julian family, of which Augustus was a member. See note on *Amores* I 1. 29.

47. Penelope: The wife of Odysseus who waited twenty years for him to return from the Trojan War; she is generally cited as the model of fidelity. In Homer's *Odyssey* she deceives the suitors who have gathered at her home by weaving and unweaving a shroud and, when the disguised Odysseus finally arrives, she tells the suitors she will marry the one who can successfully string Odysseus's bow.

64. chalk-marked heel: At a slave auction, foreign slaves were distinguished by their chalked feet.

65. family busts: Roman aristocratic families kept on display the masks and busts of their illustrious ancestors.

68. from his own lover: A handsome young man, before puberty, was expected to have a male lover. The *lena*'s suggestion is here pretty brutal: just as the young man becomes interested in girls, he must find a way to "wheedle" money from his male lover.

74. Isis: An Egyptian goddess whose worship was forbidden within the old city walls of Rome but who is mentioned often enough in love elegy because her worship entailed ritual abstinence from sexual intercourse.

86. Venus can fix it: It was a commonplace that lover's oaths meant nothing and that the gods did not punish their perjuries.

100. Via Sacra: On the *Via Sacra*, or "Sacred Way," one could find jewelry shops and prostitutes.

108. when I'm dead: Like most poets and lovers, and especially like Propertius, the *lena* closes her speech/poem and imagines her success validated at her grave.

I 9

The portrait of the lover, first as the victim of Cupid's attack, then as a soldier himself, has a long history and many variations going back at least as far as Hellenistic literature. By Ovid's time the theme was a commonplace, and in this collection one may compare Catullus 37. 13; Tibullus II 6. 6; Propertius II 7. 15; Horace *Odes* III 26. 6–8. Here and elsewhere (*Amores* I 2 and II 12) Ovid chooses to elaborate the theme at length, and, in order to do this, he chooses to vary the terms of the metaphor: at first the poet follows Cupid, then it is the girl he follows, and finally the girl is the spoils of war. While this may be a logical contradiction, it hardly seems to be experientially false and actually describes the progress of Ovid's *Amores*. Ovid's conclusion to this elaborate figure of speech is to turn it into a self-justifying argument in surprising terms. He claims that before he fell in love he was a lazy ne'er-do-well; but it was love that rescued him from this life of inactivity. This argument, of course, reverses the typical Roman objection to the amatory life. From the perspective of conservative, patriotic Roman values the amatory life had always been a life of idleness, and the poets from Catullus on had embraced the charge that they indulged themselves in idle play. Ovid's comparison here may be felt to go some way toward mocking the values of patriotic militarism.

2. Atticus: The addressee and the occasion of this poem are unknown.

13. for favoring stars: Sea travel in the Mediterranean was dangerous and unpleasant. Certain times were especially dangerous because of spring and autumn storms which could be predicted by the rising or setting of certain constellations.

19. the threshold: This siege on the threshold of a hard-hearted girl recalls one of the most common set pieces of ancient amatory verse: the scene of the *paraclausithyron*. See *Amores* I 6, Propertius I 16, and Tibullus I 2.

23. Thracian Rhesus: In a famous scene from Homer's *Iliad*, the Greek warriors Odysseus and Diomedes go out at night to gather information about the Trojan plans. Once they receive the information they need from the captured Trojan, Dolon, they kill him and then proceed to slaughter the sleeping Thracians who came to Troy with Rhesus, king of Thrace. Finally, they

kill Rhesus himself and escape with his white horses back to the Greek camp. The scene involves the flagrant deception of Dolon and particularly brutal killing. The Callimachean amatory poet was programmatically opposed to the writing of epic.

33.   Achilles: The whole of the *Iliad*'s plot is motivated by Achilles' anger at Agamemnon for Agamemnon's theft of the girl, Briseis, from Achilles.

35.   Hector: In one of the most touching scenes in the *Iliad*, Hector returns from the fighting to Troy where he meets his wife, Andromache, and his child, Astyanax. Hector takes off his helmet when it scares his child. Andromache says farewell to her husband before he returns to the battle in which he will die. Ovid alludes to a detail that he has invented, namely that Andromache places the helmet back on Hector's head.

37.   Priam's daughter: On the destruction of Troy, Agamemnon, the Greek leader, fell in love with Cassandra, the most beautiful daughter of Priam, the leader of Troy. She was a prophetess who had devoted her life to virginity but had been cursed by Apollo to never be believed. Consequently, in her prophetic rantings she was likened to a maenad, or worshipper of Dionysus.

39.   Mars: In Homer's *Odyssey* a singer tells the story of how Vulcan laid a trap for his wife, Venus, and Mars. When they were in bed together they were trapped by a net of chains. All the gods then gathered around to look and laugh.

I 10

A poor young lover, a beautiful courtesan who wants expensive gifts, a greedy *lena* or madame: the characters are right out of comedy; the theme is a common elegiac topic. Ovid begins, however, with a distinct echo of Propertius's I 3, a set of mythological references to beautiful heroines. The function of this catalog is not at first explicit, and, recalling Propertius, might seem to be praise of the poet's girlfriend. But the elaborate prelude turns out to be foil for the poet's avowed change of heart, a change occasioned because his girl has apparently been listening to the advice of the *lena* in *Amores* I 8. The poet then launches into a diatribe against the mercenary attitudes and practices of women. The romanticized world of Propertian mythology and heroines is brought into stark contrast with the world of contemporary Rome, the language of the forum, and the commercialization of love. The poet's shift from an idealized elegiac world to common Roman realities suggests the moral seriousness of satire, until his brave attack finally dwindles into the conventional claim that lovers should ask for what can be given and that the poet can offer eternal fame. Thus love even for this lover is a kind of transaction or exchange. In the end the poet yields, insisting only that his gifts not be demanded, but seem to be freely given. The view that this kind of love depends on the lover's willingness to be deceived has already appeared in the ending of *Amores* I 4.

1.   Helen, Eurotas, Phrygian sail: Helen, the wife of Menelaus, lived in Sparta near the Eurotas River and was considered the most beautiful mortal woman. She was seduced by Paris, a young Trojan from Phrygia (hence Phrygian sail), and abducted back to Troy. When the Trojans refused to return Helen to her original husband, the Greeks under Agamemnon and Menelaus embarked upon the Trojan War, which lasted ten years and ended with the destruction of Troy.

3. Leda: This wife of Tyndareus was also a paradigm of beauty. She was seduced by Jupiter disguised as a swan and became the mother of Helen and of Castor and Pollux.

5. Amymone: She was sent by her father, Danaus, to find water for the dry plain of Argos. While looking for water, an unsuccessful rape attempt was made upon her by a satyr, and a successful attempt by the god Neptune.

7. eagle and bull: Jupiter's most famous rape was in the guise of an eagle when he abducted the young Trojan boy, Ganymede. As a bull, he carried off Europa.

15. a naked little boy: For the traditional image of Cupid as a naked little boy, see also Propertius I 2. 8.

18. he hasn't even a pocket: A typical form of Ovidian wit is to develop an allusion or story in terms of literal reality.

19. not suited to . . . war: Compare the opening to *Amores* I 1.

21. at a fixed price: It seems that prostitutes worked for fixed rates and, for some philosophers, this was a point in their favor. Ovid turns the point against Corinna and all women who set arbitrary or flexible rates. The comparison here to a prostitute is generally taken as evidence that the real Corinna was not a prostitute.

25–28. Just as today one finds moral arguments, usually conservative ones, supported by appeals to nature and the world of animals (e.g., "Humans are the only species of animal that kills its own kind."), so in the philosophical traditions of Ovid's time this appeal to the behavior of irrational animals was often used to make *a fortiori* argument about appropriate behavior.

49. the Vestal virgin: According to one legend, Tarpeia, the daughter of the Roman commander defending the city against the Sabines, betrayed the capital in return for the bracelets worn by the Sabines. When the Sabines gained entry to the city, they crushed her with their shields—thereby giving her what they wore on their arms. According to another legend, recounted by Propertius in IV 4, Tarpeia fell in love with the Sabine commander.

51. one's very son: Alcmaeon, the son of Amphiarus and Eriphyle, avenged his father's death by killing his mother, Eriphyle. She had been bribed by Polynices, who offered her a necklace to persuade Amphiarus to go on the Trojan expedition even though he foresaw that his participation would mean his own death.

54. can afford: Suddenly the lover suggests the very principle of flexible pricing which he had criticized in lines 21–24.

56. Alcinous's orchard: Alcinous was king of the Phaeacians whom Odysseus visited during his wanderings. His orchards were proverbial for their fertility.

62. the fame my verses give: Compare Horace *Odes* III 30. Ovid adapts the poet's traditional claim that through his verse the poet will become immortal to the demands of the occasion.

64. you'll have what I now deny: Corinna already has, through this very poem, a fame that will last forever. The poem ends with the formula of a *stipulatio*, or formal legal promise constituting a bargain.

I 13

This kind of poem has a long history. The theme of the lover's desire for dawn to delay its light goes back to Homer's *Odyssey* and the dawn's delay at the time of Odysseus's reunion with Penelope. Typically, Ovid combines the common sentiment with an ironic perspective. Part of this irony is accomplished by Ovid's reversal of the traditional gestures of a "kletic hymn," or hymn that calls for the presence of a god. The poem may also be read as another rhetorical exercise in persuasion; compare the *suasoria*, *Amores* I 8. 20ff.

1. Gold-haired Dawn: Aurora, the goddess of the dawn, was married to Tithonus, a mortal. Ovid plays on this by suggesting that Dawn leaves Tithonus because he is too old to be a satisfactory lover.

3. Memnon's shadow: Memnon was a mythical king of Ethiopia and son of Aurora, the dawn. His name may have been connected by Ovid with the Greek command, "Halt!" [= *mimne*]. The "birds of Memnon" were said to fly from Africa to Troy each year where as an annual honor they killed each other over Memnon's grave.

11-12. Before your arrival . . .: A good example of the reversal of traditional formula in *kletic* hymns where such expressions, often marked by the repetition of the personal pronoun ("you . . . you . . . you . . .") accrue to the praise of the goddess, not to her blame.

15-16. You are the first . . .: Another formula which typically serves to amplify praise.

37. Cephalus: Ovid plays with several traditions. Aurora was said to have fallen in love with Tithonus, Orion, Cleitus, and Cephalus. Cephalus was an Athenian hero whom Aurora abducted; they had a son, Phaethon, who was Venus's attendant.

41. the moon gave her lover: Luna, the moon goddess, drove her chariot across the sky during the night. When she fell in love with Endymion, a remarkably beautiful young man, Jupiter put him to sleep eternally in a cave in Latmos where the moon visits him.

43. the sire of the gods: Jupiter extended his lovemaking with Alcmena, wife of Amphitryon, by lengthening the night. Alcmena bore Hercules as a result. The claim that Jupiter was "tired of seeing [Aurora]" is a gratuitous insult.

I 14

Corinna has botched a hair treatment and her hair has fallen out. Many critics find the tone of the poem cruel and heartless, but it is not clear that we should imagine every word spoken directly to Corinna. If *Amores* III 2 is best understood as a fantastic inner monologue, one may find a precursor of the style in this poem. In any event, the dyeing of hair and the wearing of wigs was common in Augustan Rome, and this poem may be taken as a general reflection of fashion. As an elaboration of fashion and taste, however, the poet cannot help but use language that recalls the poetic virtues of his own craft and art. After the first couplet introduces the situation, Ovid expands on the virtues of the hair that is no more: fine as silk, delicately spun, of blended color, readily managed, adaptable to a hundred styles, and best with an air of loose and wild negligence (3–21–22). The poet then imagines and laments the hair's forced and unnatural elaboration in a style that recalls the elevated diction of tragedy while describing the elevated curls of a high coiffure (23–34). The poem's last extended section turns lament for the lost hair into blame for the false artifice Corinna sought and mockery of the spectacle she will become (35–50). At this point the poet notices that Corinna is crying as she looks at the ruins of her hair, and he abruptly tries to offer consolation: time will repair the losses.

5–8. fine, delicate, spins, weaving: All these terms are used in the Callimachean program to refer to the aesthetic values of Alexandrian art.

6. fine as silk: Silk imported from China was extremely expensive in the ancient world. Because of its fineness and transparency it was often considered not befitting a proper Roman.

12. vales of Ida: A reference to the hills near Troy; it is thought that the metaphor is original and the product of personal observation.

14. a hundred styles: The arrangement of a woman's hair was extremely important and was performed by a specially trained hairdresser. See the note on Propertius II 1. 7 for further details.

16. Your hairdresser was safe: The young woman who flies into a rage at her hairdresser was a common topos in literature.

21. Thracian maenad: Women in worship of the god Bacchus indulged in orgiastic rites which alternated between peaceful scenes of oneness with nature, like that alluded to here, and wild, frenzied activities that culminated in the eating raw of a young animal. See the notes on *Amores* III 1. 23 and III 15. 17 for the poetic implications of the cult of Bacchus.

31. Apollo or Bacchus: The two gods were both young and had unshorn hair; they are generally taken as representative of youthful beauty.

33. Dione: The name for Venus's mother, Dione, was often used for Venus herself. Ovid here refers to a famous picture of Venus painted by the fourth century Greek, Apelles, and called Aphrodite Anadyomene. The picture was brought to Rome by Augustus and is mentioned elsewhere by Ovid; see *The Art of Love* III 223–224.

39–42. Ovid refers to the world of magic, popular in literary and especially elegiac contexts. The four kinds of spells he mentions are 1) poison herbs sent by a rival mistress; 2) poison water from Haemonia, the poetic name for Thessaly, a place famous for its witches; 3) illness caused by misfortune; and 4) the evil spells of an antagonist.

45. triumphant armies: Ovid again turns a mocking glance on the imperial achievements of Rome. It is not certain what German conquest he has in mind.

I 15

It was typical of Augustan poets to make their claim to an immortal reputation in the final poem of a poetry book: compare Horace *Odes* II 20 and III 30. Since Catullus it was implicit that the poet's claim to glory and fame was in some sense in competition with the traditional conservative means to the same goal, namely a career of public service in the military and in the Senate. Ovid here explicitly refutes that traditional Roman position while harkening back to many of the themes of Callimachean poetics: overcoming envy, gaining immortality, separating oneself from the common herd, etc. Unlike the typical *sphragis*, or poem setting the poet's seal on his book, Ovid undertakes a defense of poetry in general, not a defense solely of his poetry or of his chosen genre. The poem is also a kind of acknowledgment for Ovid's literary predecessors and influences.

1. biting Envy: Envy was first given poetic prominence by Callimachus. References such as this are generally taken as signaling the poet's affiliation with Callimachean poetics.

5. your father did: Ovid's father was a successful, though not exactly wealthy, member of the equestrian, or business, class. He had expected his son to follow the normal course of education, become a lawyer, and eventually win election into the Senate.

9–30. Ovid catalogs the poets who have won immortality through their verses. In each case, Ovid's description is particularly apt to the kind of poetry each wrote. The catalog of six Greek and six Roman poets is not strictly chronological. Scholars disagree about the significance of some important poets, such as Sappho and Catullus, being missing from the list.

9. Maeonides: The son of Maeon, i.e., Homer. Tenedos, Mt. Ida, and the river Simois are all at or near Troy, the site of Homer's *Iliad*.

11. The Ascraean poet: Hesiod, a poet who was particularly important for the Callimachean poets since he represented an alternative to the traditional epics of Homer, wrote a longish poem, called *The Works and Days*, about work, farming, and justice.

12. Ceres' golden hair: Ceres was the goddess of grain and agriculture; her golden hair refers to the ripe wheat in the fields.

13. the son of Battus: This is a reference to Callimachus, the great poet of the Hellenistic age, who helped revive poetry at a time when its political and public functions had gone and when it was, for the first time, primarily a written rather than a performance art.

15. the high-laced buskin: The buskin was a high-laced sandal which represented tragedy, the genre for which Sophocles was famous.

16. Aratus: A Hellenistic poet greatly admired by Callimachus and the Callimachean poets of Rome for his translation into verse of astronomical treatises.

18. Menander: An Athenian poet of the Hellenistic age who was considered the supreme writer of New Comedy, a kind of comedy of manners usually involving young lovers, stock characters, and formulaic situations.

19. Ennius and Accius: Ennius was an early Roman poet of the second century B.C.E. who wrote both tragedies and an epic, the *Annales*. He was at this time best known for his epic. Accius was a contemporary of Ennius, who wrote verse works on history, poetry, drama, and erotica. He was best known in antiquity for his tragedies. The description of him here points to tragedy.

21. Varro and his . . . Argonauts: Varro Atacinus was a poet of the first century B.C.E. Ovid refers to his translation of Apollonius's Argonautae, a Hellenistic epic in four books which told the story of Jason, "the Aesonian lord," and the Golden Fleece.

24. Lucretius: A didactic poet, contemporary with Cicero and Catullus, who wrote *De Rerum Natura*, or *On the Nature of Things*, a scientific poem promulgating Epicurean philosophy. Here Ovid echoes the Epicurean doctrine that, since all things have beginnings and ends, therefore the entire world will one day fall into utter destruction.

29. Gallus: An important poet of the generation between that of Catullus and that of Vergil. He was a political and military figure, friend of Augustus, and governor of Egypt after the civil wars, as well as the inventor (in all likelihood) of elegiac poetry as a genre. His girlfriend was Lycoris, but his work is lost to us, with the exception of a few fragments.

32. time and decay: For the general topic, see Horace *Odes* III 30.

35. herd of mankind: A reference to the Callimachean injunction to avoid the commonplace.

36. Castalian spring: Ovid refers to two symbols of poetic inspiration: Apollo's influence and drinking from a poetic spring. Both have Callimachean associations.

37. winter-shy myrtle: Ovid recalls his request for myrtle at the end of *Amores* I 1. For the convention of requesting or demanding a garland, and in general for the ending of this poem and book, compare Horace *Odes* III 30.

Amores II

In this book, the poet proceeds on his project of demystifying love, convention, and sincerity. Book II includes humorous versions of the *epicedion,* or "funeral poem" (6), the *propempticon,* or "farewell poem" (11), and (perhaps) the *paraclausithyron,* or "excluded lover poem" (19). Corinna is named nine times, more often than in any other book.

II 1

Like Books I and III, Book II begins with a programmatic poem, a humorous rewrite of the typical *recusatio,* or "refusal poem." Here again he chooses not to have Apollo, god of poetry, warn him that his meager talent is insufficient for epic; rather, his epic was going along just fine ("I had the ability, too," line 12) when he was interrupted because his girl slammed the door. In other words, epic (and the range of ideological and aesthetic associations it represents) will just make you into an "excluded lover," compel you to sing your *paraclausithyron,* and you too will come to elegy in the end. Put in this way, the poem especially recalls and seems to dramatize Propertius's addresses to Ponticus in elegies I 7 and I 9. In recalling Propertius, however, Ovid is intent on revising the traditional posture of the conventional elegist. As in *Amores* I 1, he diverts attention from the particular mistress and suggests that his interest is more general than that of other elegists. The claim, however, that the feelings of the lover are universal is directed precisely against the Propertian contradiction that his passion is both unique and representative. Similarly, Ovid finds in this poem not grounds to reject the pretentions of magical poetry and charms (compare Propertius I 1), but the reason to believe in their efficacy: elegy itself is magical. And then, with typical Ovidian wit, the origin of elegy's magic is exposed: girls are vain and want to be praised. So it is that the delicate language of the love elegist is a charm more effective than Jupiter's thunderbolts.

1. I composed this, too: The wording suggests that *Amores* I is in circulation and so suggests that this poem was written for the first publication of the *Amores* in five books, presumably published individually.

3–4. Begone I judgmental souls: The poet adopts the language and role of poet/priest (or *vates*) initiating holy rites; compare Propertius II 10 and Horace III 1.

11–12. to recount celestial battles . . .: Apparently the epic Ovid claims to be working on was a *Gigantomachy,* or Battle of the Giants; compare Horace II 12. 5–12 and Propertius II 1. 17–20. Such a poem would recount how the earthborn Giants attempted to overthrow Jupiter and how he struck them down with his thunderbolt. In Callimachus's poetic initiation, to which Ovid refers here, the poet had been told that thundering was Jove's business not the poet's.

12. Gyas: The name is actually disputed; some prefer "Gyges." In any event, he was a mythical giant with a hundred hands.

13–14.   Olympus, Pelion, Ossa: According to Homer, the giants, in attacking Jupiter, piled the mountain Ossa on Olympus and Pelion on Ossa.

17.   My woman shut me out: A reference to the typical and common scene in elegy and comedy of the *exclusus amator*, the lover outside the door of his beloved, who sings his *paraclausithyron*. With wit and psychological astuteness Ovid pictures poetic inspiration as arising not from the appearance of Apollo but from the withdrawal of the beloved.

23–28.   Songs: The Latin word, *carmina*, refers to both "songs" and "spells."

29–32.   These typical subjects for an epic poem are all taken from Homer. Achilles was the Greek warrior at Troy whose wrath became the subject of the *Iliad*; the sons of Atreus were Agamemnon and Menelaus, the leaders of the expedition to Troy; the "Man of Too Many Wrong Turns" was Odysseus, whose travels were the subject of the *Odyssey*; and Hector was the greatest of Trojan Warriors who was killed by Achilles.

II 4

The poem is not a confession at all, but a celebration of the lover's promiscuity in which women are merely extensions of male fantasies (see on lines 24 and 26). The poem's theme recalls Propertius II 22.

5–6.   The speaker's protests here recall Catullus 85. In that famous poem, however, Catullus was torn by his attraction and revulsion for Lesbia; here the Catullan ambivalence has been reflected back on the speaker himself.

10.   a hundred motives: The speaker begins a kind of catalog which in the philosophical tradition is used to represent the irrationality of the lover. Lucretius, the Roman poet of Epicurus's philosophy, says in his indictment of erotic passion, "Men, blind with desire, generally make and attribute advantages which are not really advantages to them . . . . The dark-skinned girl is like honey, the ugly and rank is unadorned, ..." (*The Nature of Things*, IV 1153ff).

15.   Sabine type: Here as in Horace's *Odes*, the conservative and austere Sabine farmer is taken as an archetype of upright moral rigidity.

17.   my lovely reader: Readers and appreciators of sophisticated verse like Ovid's were thought to enjoy his sophisticated life-style as well, but here the writer's game deserves attention, for the text leers at its imagined female reader.

19.   Callimachus sounds rustic: For an urbane Callimachean poet from Catullus on, the unlearned and unsophisticated life was epitomized by the farm.

27.   plaintive strings: Ovid refers to playing the lyre, a stringed instrument without frets. Neither playing a musical instrument nor accompanying oneself on a musical instrument was considered a respectable accomplishment for a lady in Rome.

29.   The dancer: Like musical performance, dancing, especially like this, was considered decadent and indecent.

32.   Hippolytus into Priapus: Hippolytus, son of Theseus, refused the advances of his stepmother, Phaedra, while Theseus was absent. Phaedra committed suicide, but left a note accusing Hippolytus, and when Theseus returned, he banished his son and had him killed. Hippolytus thus became a symbol of chastity. Priapus, on the other hand, was the god of fertility, traditionally represented by a figure with a large, erect phallus.

37. <u>just think</u>: This is the only example in Ovid's catalog of a flaw remedied; elsewhere Ovid portrays the particular characteristic as attractive (to him) in itself.

42. <u>Leda</u>: Leda, the wife of Tyndareus, king of Sparta, was seduced by Jupiter disguised as a swan and became the mother of Helen and of Castor and Pollux. Like Helen, she was a paradigm of beauty, but is not elsewhere attested as having black hair. See *Amores* I 10. 3.

43. <u>Aurora</u>: The goddess of dawn. Goddesses in ancient mythology are conventionally blond; however, Aurora's hair color is meant to recall the colors of the dawn sky. See also *Amores* I 13 and I 8. 4.

II 6

This poem is a parody of the standard *epicedion* or "funeral poem." According to ancient traditions, a funeral poem should contain the following:

1. Address summoning the mourners
2. Praise and lament for the dead—grief should be combined with both
    a. praise for the dead's character, accomplishments, and promise
    b. a curse upon the powers that took the beloved away (which often provides another occasion for praise)
3. Account of the deathbed scene
4. Consolation for survivors, often by turning to philosophical reflections on the nature of death and the underworld, which led to various topics such as the welcome the beloved will receive in the underworld, and
5. Description of the funeral, including the permanent memorial left in the world above.

This poem is modeled on and should be compared with Catullus 3, another funeral poem on the death of a pet. Also compare Horace's *Odes* I 24 and Ovid's poem on the death of Tibullus, *Amores* III 9. While humor is acknowledged here, readers still often feel that the poem as a whole is pathetic and touching, while the poem on the death of Tibullus is indecorous and gauche. Two recent solutions to this contrast are 1) to read the Tibullus poem as an ironic reflection on the elegiac lover and this poem as suggesting the natural love which corrects the mercenary and self-interested promiscuity of the Ovidian persona, and 2) to read this poem as a reflection on the goals and values of the Alexandrian poet.

1. <u>from orient India</u>: According to the Roman natural historian Pliny, the parrot came from India. Ovid does not choose the swan or the nightingale, both animals associated with a poet's song, but rather an unmusical bird who can only repeat what he is taught.

7. <u>Philomela, Ismarian tyrant</u>: Philomela's sister, Procne, was married to Tereus, the Thracian king, here called the Ismarian tyrant after Mt. Ismaros in Thrace. Tereus raped Philomela and cut out her tongue, but she contrived to tell her story through embroidery. When Procne found out the truth, she served Tereus his own son, Itys, for dinner. When Tereus discovered what he had eaten, he pursued the two sisters until he was turned into a bird of prey and they into swallow and nightingale. The nightingale continues, according to legend, to mourn her fate.

12. turtle dove: According to Pliny, the turtle dove was the companion of the parrot.

15. Orestes, his friend from Phocis: Orestes, when in exile after his mother murdered his father, Agamemnon, went to Phocis where he met Pylades, the son of Strophius. Their friendship became legendary.

27. quail: Known to Pliny and Aristotle as particularly quarrelsome birds.

35. raven: The raven was said to be hated by Minerva because of its enmity with the owl, Minerva's favorite bird, and was fabled for its long life. Minerva is said to be "well-armed" like her Greek counterpart, Athena. At Rome her worship expanded at the expense of Mars himself.

41. Thersites, the youth from Phylace: Thersites was the ugliest among the Greeks who went to Troy to fight; in the *Iliad* he attempts to rebuke his leader, Agamemnon, and is literally slapped down by Odysseus. The youth from Phylace is Protesilaus, the first Greek to perish at Troy. See Catullus 68.

42. Hector: The great defender of Troy who died at the hands of Achilles; his brothers included Paris himself, the abductor of Helen, and the cause of the Trojan War.

44. Notus: Specifically the south wind, but sometimes used by the poets for the wind in general.

45. the seventh day: A particularly critical day for some diseases according to ancient medical lore.

46. Parcae: Of the three sisters known as the Parcae (Fates), one, Clotho, kept the spindle whose thread measured a person's life. When the spindle was empty, or the thread cut, one's life was over.

49. dark ilex . . . in Elysium: A kind of oak tree, also known as the holm-oak or the great scarlet oak. Ovid here imagines a kind of ideal scene for a parrot in the underworld, specifically in Elysium, the land of the blessed, which was reserved for those who had lived pious lives. The scene may be derived from Tibullus, elegy I 3. 57–66.

54. long-lived phoenix: A mythological bird from Arabia said to rise again from its own ashes after dying.

55. Juno's bird: The peacock.

61–62. I pleased my mistress . . .: The language recalls the description of the typical poet/ lover of elegy.

II 7

Throughout the *Amores* Ovid has written paired poems, sometimes, as with II 7 and II 8, the poems are placed side by side in a kind of diptych, more frequently (as with II 6 and III 9) they are separated by several other elegies. In this poem, Ovid addresses Corinna and answers her charge that he has been sleeping with her maid and hairdresser, Cypassis; in the next poem, he will address Cypassis. He defends himself by citing Corinna's paranoia and suspicions and protesting his utter innocence. However, in the context of *Amores* I 4 and II 4 we see that Corinna's paranoid suspicions reflect fairly well the speaker's intentions, and elegy II 8 comes, not as a surprise, but to confirm the reader's own suspicions. Together this pair is reminiscent of scenes from comedy and mime, by which it was doubtlessly influenced. Elegy II 7 is carefully structured, and has been compared to a courtroom defense, and the speaker admits as much in the first line. The structure of this defense as follows: introduction (1–2), narration of general situation (3–10), protestation (11–16), specific charge (17–18), refutation (19–26), oath (27–28). For parallels to the charge of infidelity, see Propertius II 20 and III 15.

2. I win, of course: The attempt to discredit one's accusers by creating a tradition of their false accusations is a common rhetorical tactic.

3. back at the gallery: At the Roman theater, women sat in the upper rows, segregated from the men. Despite this arrangement, Ovid tells us elsewhere (*The Art of Love*, I 89–134) that the theater was a good place to flirt and to meet women.

6. send silent signals: Compare the elaborate plans and signals of *Amores* I 4.

15. long-eared ass: The ass may have had long ears, but he was proverbially deaf; furthermore, he was taken to be a particularly virile and promiscuous creature.

19–26. The speaker offers in his defense what ancient rhetoric identified as *eikos* arguments, or arguments from probability.

II 8

Now it's Cypassis's turn to be upset, and the speaker offers another defense. He attempts to turn his defense in II 7 into a favor he has done Cypassis, and then, with reckless abandon and bravado, the informed-upon lover attempts to get his way by threatening to inform on himself.

1. in styling hair: The speaker begins his defense before Cypassis with a reference back to his indirect compliment in II 7. 24. In *The Art of Love* Ovid spends thirty-five lines describing various hair fashions, including the complaint that he cannot cover all the different fashions since new ones appear daily.

11. Briseis . . . and the Thessalian: Achilles, "the Thessalian," held Briseis as his captive girl at the beginning of the *Iliad*. When Agamemnon, the leader of the Greek forces, insisted on taking Briseis from Achilles, he began the conflict within the Greek camp which motivates the story of the *Iliad*.

12. the lord of Mycenae: This refers to Agamemnon, and the "enslaved priestess" is Cassandra, Agamemnon's captive after the fall of Troy.

13. Tantalus's son: Agamemnon actually is Tantalus's great-grandson.

20. harmless perjury: It is a standard topos of love poetry that the gods do not take the oaths of lovers seriously. Here, as elsewhere, the speaker turns to his advantage exactly what traditionally caused lovers pain and distress; see Catullus 70 and Ovid *Amores* I 8. 85–86.

20. Carpathian ocean: So named for an island between Crete and Rhodes, the Carpathian Sea was proverbial for its storms.

II 10

Another Ovidian exploration of the poet's adversarial relationship to society and its conventional standards.

1. <u>Graecinus</u>: Probably C. Pomponius Graecinus, the *consul suffectus* of 16 C.E. and a patron of Ovid. He is addressed in three of Ovid's *Letters from the Black Sea* and may have tried in those years to ease Ovid's exile. It is unusual for Ovid to have an explicit addressee for his elegies.

9. <u>I'm at sea</u>: The lover compared to a man at sea and love compared to the ocean is another familiar metaphor; see Horace *Odes* I 5.

10. <u>I'm torn</u>: There is no verbal reference to Catullus 85 in the Latin.

11. <u>Erycina</u>: Eryx was a mountain in Sicily near a famous temple to Venus; the name, "Erycina," therefore, refers to Venus.

23. <u>I may be thin</u>: The topos remains familiar in the jug-band tune, "I may be skinny, and I may be thin, but I'm an awful good daddy for the shape I in"; and in the blues number, "cause I'm built for comfort; I ain't built for speed; but I got everything a good girl need."

31–36. <u>The soldier . . .</u>: The speaker's preference takes the form of a *priamel* (see the note on Tibullus I 1. 1–6), and uses it to oppose both conventional military virtues and conventional aspirations for wealth. See further on Horace *Odes* I 1.

37. <u>At my funeral</u>: In a poem that often glances at Propertius, especially elegy II 22, it is fitting that the speaker conclude with the familiar Propertian device of measuring his state in terms of a future epitaph.

II 11

Formally, this poem is a *propempticon*; compare Horace *Odes* I 3 and III 27 and Propertius I 17. Traditionally, the speaker of such a poem includes a curse as an expression of his anxiety and as part of his effort to dissuade the lover from leaving; when that fails, he wishes for a safe voyage (here lines 33–38). At the end of this poem Ovid adds features of another genre, the welcome home poem, the *prosphonetikon*; compare Catullus 9—plans for the return (the fantasy of lines 39–56). While both genres may be serious, this poem remains light-hearted and amusing (note the picnic on the beach). But Ovid has combined with the fairly standard set of topics a set of allusions to other poets and to the terms of Augustan poetics. Thus the girl who should remain at the shore (line 14) or only wade into the shallows (line 16) recalls Apollo's metaphorical and poetic advice to Propertius in elegy III 3. 23–24. The ocean itself is often associated with the popular, bombastic, public voice of the epic poet (see Propertius I 7 and I 9). In this context, it is striking that the alternative to a sea voyage is "to curl up in bed with a good book" (line 31). Similarly, the poet's preference for keeping the dangerous world of the high seas at bay appears in advice which itself recalls a lyric *priamel*, "Let others tell you all about such things" (line 21). This advice becomes the basis on which the poet fantasizes Corinna's return: "There, when we've poured the wine, you'll tell me story after story . . ." (line 49).

1ff. <u>the sea's evils . . .</u>: It is common in ancient curses to blame the first inventor or the first instance of a general phenomenon for present woes that may arguably result. Here Ovid's words recall epic, tragic, and Alexandrian versions of this kind of curse. In the opening lines of Euripides' *Medea* the nurse, because of Medea's present abandonment, curses the building of the ship which brought Jason. These lines were translated, with the order of incidents reversed, by the Roman epic and tragic poet Ennius. The story of Jason and Medea was told by the Alexandrian writer of epic, Apollonius of Rhodes. All of these versions were used and alluded to in Catullus's famous poem 64*, in which Ariadne, because of her abandonment, curses the first ship ever to sail. Here Ovid, in mock heroic style, recalls this tradition, as well as the elegiac tradition of the lover abandoned by his seafaring girl; see Propertius I 8.

1. <u>Pelion</u>: A high mountain in Thessaly, the country of Jason, from which the pine for the first longship, the Argo, was taken. The Argo was the ship on which Jason sailed to Colchis in order to retrieve the Golden Fleece. In Colchis he met Medea who fell in love with him, helped him at the expense of her own brother's life, returned to Corinth with him, and then was abandoned.

3. <u>Clashing Rocks</u>: Rocks which seemed to clash together and through which the Argonauts had to sail.

8. <u>dear Penates</u>: The Penates are the household gods ("dwellers of the pantry") who, with the Lares and Vesta, protect the home.

9–10. <u>Zephyrus, Eurus, Boreas, Notus</u>: The four winds from the four cardinal points of the compass: Zephyr is the west wind which blows in spring; Eurus is the east wind which blows opposite to Zephyr; Boreas is the north wind; and Notus, its opposite, the south wind.

11. <u>the sightseer</u>: This is our only clue as to why Corinna is leaving.

17–20. <u>Scylla, Charybdis, Ceraunian cliffs, greater and lesser Syrtes</u>: Proverbial dangers for sailors. Scylla, originally a sea monster with six heads and twelve feet, was rationalized as a rock in the Mediterranean between Italy and Sicily. She lived in a cave opposite Charybdis, a whirlpool which sucked in and sprayed out water three times a day. The Ceraunian cliffs were dangerous mountains on the coast of Epirus. The greater and lesser Syrtes were two large sandbanks in the Libyan gulf, dangerous for their shallows and sunken reefs.

28. <u>Triton</u>: A merman from pre-Greek mythology variously portrayed, sometimes with other Tritons in attendance on Venus.

29. <u>Leda's two fine sons</u>: Leda, mother of Helen and Clytemnestra, also had two sons, Castor and Pollux, who took part in the expedition on the Argo and upon their death became stars usually identified with the constellation Gemini. They were worshiped as the patron gods of sailors.

32. <u>Thracian lyre</u>: Thrace is the homeland of the mythological poet and singer Orpheus. He too participated in the expedition of the Argo, but is most famous for his journey to the underworld where his singing convinced Persephone to allow his wife to return to the land of the living with one stipulation: he was not to look back at her during the journey up. In Vergil's version of the story, he did look back and lost his wife a second time. Thereafter he would only grieve and sing songs of grief until he was torn to pieces by Thracian Maenads. He was taken by Vergil's generation to symbolize both the poet's power and his vulnerability.

34. <u>Galatea</u>: Galatea is a sea-nymph or Nereid. The love of the cyclops Polyphemus for her was the subject of two poems by the bucolic poet Theocritus.

36. <u>Nereus</u>: A sea-god who lives with his daughters, the Nereids, at the bottom of the sea.

44. <u>She brings my gods back to me</u>: A reversal of the common prayer, "May the gods bring my beloved back to me!" The beloved is commonly referred to as the lover's goddess.

45. <u>on my shoulders</u>: This line, together with the literal sense of the line above and the sacrifices that follow, evokes the image of Aeneas carrying his father out of Troy on his back, and later landing in Latium, with his Trojan gods.

55. <u>brilliant Lucifer</u>: Literally, "light bringer," the name here refers to the son of Aurora (the dawn) and Cephalus. In ancient mythology, all the celestial phenomena—sun, moon, dawn, night—move across the sky in chariots.

II 13

This poem and the following curse on abortion form a typical Ovidian two-scene sequence; compare poems 7 and 8 on Cypassis. In the background are the Augustan social reforms which were designed to encourage marriage and discourage childlessness. Augustus imposed penalties on those who failed to marry or who married but remained childless. From this fact and from references to abortion in the literature (usually denouncing it), the frequent occurrence of abortion in imperial Rome can be inferred. Legislative opposition to abortion (which came later) was based on the father's right to heirs and complemented by philosophical arguments based on "nature." It is this assumption of the male prerogative which motivates these poems and which characterizes their speaker. In another body of legislation, Augustus attempted to revive old Roman religious practices. These efforts entailed the suppression of eastern religions, specifically including the Egyptian worship of Isis and Sarapis. In this regard too, when the speaker prays to Isis and Ilithyia, goddess of childbirth, that Corinna survive the ordeal of her recent abortion, he appears relatively indifferent to Augustus's moral project. Formally, the body of the poem (7–26) is a prayer: invocation of Isis (7–16), worthiness as function of past services (17–18), invocation of Ilithyia (19–21), statement of worthiness (22), promise of future worship (23–26).

7–8. Isis: An Egyptian goddess whose cult spread throughout the Mediterranean during the Hellenistic period and whose importance could be felt in many, if not all, aspects of life. Her cult included mystery rites, an Egyptian professional priesthood, temples, and festival days. She was called upon especially by women in childbirth. Paraetonium was a seaport in northern Africa; Canopus was an island at the most westerly mouth of the Nile noted for its luxury; Memphis was the great center of Lower Egypt where the cult of Sarapis originated in the worship of Osiris; and Pharos was an island near Alexandria where King Ptolemy had built a famous lighthouse. Pharos was particularly associated with the ritual lament of Egyptian women for the death of Osiris, Isis's husband.

11. Anubis: A local Egyptian god of death and rebirth usually represented as a jackal.

12. Osiris: The brother and husband of Isis, a god of fertility and the ruler of the underworld; his worship was connected with that of Isis, Sarapis, and Anubis. From October 28 to November 1, the rites of Isis, the *Isia*, were celebrated at Rome. These rites reenacted Isis's search for Osiris after his murder by his brother, her discovery of his dismembered body, and her revival of his remains.

13. snake: The snake was sacred to Isis and variously used in her worship.

14. Apis: A sacred bull worshiped in Memphis. This bull, when it died, was mummified and it was believed that the bull then began a second life by the blessing of Osiris, god of the underworld. This ritual is thought to have been the origin of the cult of Sarapis.

18. Gallic laurel ritual: The poet seems to refer to the orgiastic mystery cult of the goddess Cybele. Her priests, the Galli, would wound themselves and sprinkle the laurel bushes with their blood. If this is the correct reference, then the poet has confused this ritual with the feminine rites of Isis.

22. Ilithyia: A Greek goddess of childbirth sometimes identified with Juno, sometimes with Diana.

II 14

Ovid's catalog of objections to abortion does not include moral objections. Some critics believe that the poet finally bought the official line about abortion; others that he is again mocking the serious pretensions of Augustan reforms. It has been suggested that the speaker here attempts to reassert the male superiority which he found threatened by Corinna's actions and his response in *Amores* II 13.

5. The woman who first . . .: The typical form for introducing a curse; compare the beginning to *Amores* II 11.

9. our forbears: The conservative appeal on which Augustan reforms were based.

11. to seed: According to Greek myth, after the flood, Deucalion (a kind of Greek Noah) and his wife Pyrrha repopulated the earth by throwing stones over their shoulders. The stones Deucalion threw became men; those Pyrrha threw became women.

12–13. Priam's palace . . .: Priam was the leader of Troy when it was besieged by the Greeks under Agamemnon during the Trojan War. The sea-goddess Thetis had married Peleus and given birth to Achilles, the greatest of the Greek warriors at Troy.

14–16. Ilia . . .: Ilia, or Rhea Silvia, was the mother of Romulus and Remus, the twins who founded Rome.

17–18. Venus: The Roman goddess of love who gave birth to Aeneas. Aeneas escaped from Troy at the end of the Trojan War and with a small band of followers made it to Latium where, in alliance with the aboriginal Latins, he founded the Latin race. The Caesars, who belonged to the Julian clan, traced their ancestry back to Aeneas's son Iulus, and so to Aeneas and to Venus. Augustus, who had been adopted by his great-uncle Julius Caesar, claimed and celebrated such a lineage.

27. How can you: This is now a lecture delivered to the plural, "you women."

29. the woman of Colchis: Medea, when abandoned by Jason in Corinth after having helped him gain possession of the Golden Fleece, killed her own children in revenge.

30. Procne's victim, poor Itys: Procne's husband, Tereus, raped her sister, Philomela; to avoid being caught he cut out Philomela's tongue. Philomela, however, told her story on a robe she embroidered and the two sisters sought revenge by serving Tereus his own son, Itys, for dinner. See *Amores* II 6. 7.

35. Armenia: A country in Asia Minor south of the Black Sea and west of the Caspian Sea. It was the conventional habitat for tigers.

II 17

This poem is Ovid's variation on the familiar elegiac theme of the lover as a slave. His arguments that he and Corinna, though unequals, should be joined finally uses an argument from poetry, that the lines of an elegiac couplet are unequal but harmonious, to transit into a programmatic celebration of poetry's power. The poem supplies more suggestive evidence about Corinna than any other. She is apparently Ovid's social superior (14) and (25). She is also arguably Roman: the reference to the Po, a Latin river, which would not share its banks with the Eurotas, a Greek river, some think implies this. Therefore, if Corinna was a real woman (a big supposition which this very poem makes problematic), she most probably was an Italian lady of higher social standing than Ovid.

4–5.   Paphian Aphrodite . . .: Venus, the Latin equivalent of the Greek Aphrodite, was worshiped both in Paphos on the island of Cyprus and on Cythera. Both places were said to be the place that she first came ashore after being born from the sea.

15.   Calypso: The sea-nymph in Ogygia who kept Odysseus captive for seven years, offering him immortality if he remained with her.

17.   Phthian Peleus: Peleus, who accompanied Jason on the voyage of the first ship, the Argo, saw the sea-nymph Thetis and fell in love. Jupiter, who himself loved Thetis, gave the nymph to Peleus when he learned that she would have a son greater than that son's father. Peleus and Thetis had the son—Achilles.

18.   Egeria: According to Roman tradition the second king of Rome, Numa, noted for his piety and justice, had as wife and instructor the water-nymph Egeria.

19.   Vulcan: The god of the forge was originally a god of volcanic fire. His marriage to Venus was taken as an allegory: that beauty (Venus) is joined to meticulous craftsmanship.

21.   another unequal match: Elegiac poetry was written in couplets, the first line being a six-foot hexameter, the second being a shorter pentameter. Compare Ovid's use of the same figure in *Amores* I 1.

32–33.   Po, Eurotas: The Po was a river in northern Italy and the Eurotas in the southeastern Peloponnese (southern Greece).

33–34.   Compare the Propertian version of this claim in II 1. 4 and I 12. 20.

II 18

Ovid writes to a close friend, Macer, who appears to have written an epic about the events before and after those narrated in Homer's *Iliad*. Before Ovid, Propertius (I 7 and I 9) had also written to a fellow poet, Ponticus, who was interested in epic poetry and like Ovid he exalted the importance of elegy. Ovid, picking up themes from *Amores* I 1, I 15, and II 1, tells how he has been sidetracked by Cupid and how it is not his nature to write of war. He also uses the occasion to review his poetic productions: he refers to eight of his first fifteen *Heroides*, or poetic letters in which heroines write to their heroes, and to his successful tragedy, *Medea*. Line 20 seems to refer to his later work, *The Art of Love*; if so, this will be the only poem clearly written for the second edition of the *Amores* in three books. As is usual in program poems, reference to "love" or to the girlfriend does not exclude an implied reference to the love poetry itself.

1.   magnum opus: From this, critics assume that Macer wrote of the events leading up to the opening scene of the *Iliad*. The language recalls the Callimachean poet's programmatic opposition to the large, the grandiose, the epic. The opening recalls the opening of Propertius I 7.

3.   Macer: Little is known of this close friend of Ovid, a fellow poet and tutor. He was related to Ovid's third wife and accompanied Ovid on his tour of the East between 24 and 22 B.C.E. when the poet was in his late teens and before he had given up on pursuing a public career.

5. I've tried . . .: Here begins another Ovidian variation on the *recusatio*, or "refusal poem."

12. Arms and the Man: A witty reference to the opening of Vergil's epic, the *Aeneid*: "Arms and the man I sing."

13. my tragedy: Ovid's *Medea* was generally considered by the ancient critics Tacitus and Quintilian to have been among his best works.

15. Then Cupid laughed: A recollection of Ovid's earlier *recusatio* in *Amores* I 1. 3.

19. buskins: The boots worn by tragic actors were high hunting boots laced up the front; they became symbolic of the tragic genre.

22. Penelope, Ulysses: Ulysses was gone from his home in Ithaca for twenty years: the ten years of the Trojan War and ten years of wandering. His wife Penelope faithfully awaited for his return. In a sense, this letter is the elegiac version of what Homer's *Odyssey* did not tell, and as the first letter in this context suggests that Ovid saw his *Heroides* as being in competition with the masculine heroics of epic verse.

23. Phyllis: Phyllis was engaged to be married to Demophoön who, when he left to settle his family affairs in Athens, killed herself believing that he would never return. The first two letters then form a pair from a successful and an unsuccessful lover.

24. Paris: The young Trojan Paris was married to the nymph Oenone when he abandoned her for Helen.

24. Macareus: Macareus and Canace were children of the wind god, Aeolus; they fell in love with each other and had an incestuous affair.

24. Jason: In his quest for the Golden Fleece, Jason came to Lemnos, an island ruled by women who had murdered their husbands. While he delayed there, Jason had two children by their queen, Hypsipyle, whom he then deserted. Later, after recovering the Golden Fleece with the help of Medea, the two took refuge in Corinth where Jason abandoned Medea and married Glauce, daughter of the king of Corinth.

25. Hippolytus and his father: Phaedra, Theseus's wife, fell in love with her stepson Hippolytus. When he refused her, she hung herself and left a note to Theseus incriminating Hippolytus. Theseus banished him and, using one of the three wishes granted to him by his father, wished for his son's death.

25. Dido: On his way from Troy to Latium, Aeneas was shipwrecked on the coast of Africa where he was taken in by the Carthaginian queen, Dido. After delaying in Carthage unreasonably long, he suddenly left Dido, whose suicide is told at length, including what she said with sword in hand, by Vergil in his *Aeneid*.

26. Sappho: According to legend, the Lesbian (i.e., from the island of Lesbos) poet Sappho had an unhappy love affair with Phaon which ended in his departure for Sicily and her suicidal leap from the cliffs of Leucas.

27. my friend Sabinus: A close friend and poet who wrote replies to Ovid's *Heroides*.

31. Elissa: A pet name for Dido.

33. the songstress of Lesbos: Sappho.

35. to Phoebus: Presumably, Sappho dedicated her lyre to Phoebus Apollo as a thank-offering for having won Phaon's love with her poems.

37. Paris and Helen: Paris, for judging Venus more beautiful than Juno or Minerva, was granted the most beautiful woman in the world, Helen, wife of Menelaus of Sparta. Paris visited

Menelaus's home and took Helen back with him to Troy. Such was the beginning of the Trojan War.

38. <u>Laodamia</u>: The first Greek to go ashore at Troy and the first Greek to be killed at Troy was Protesilaus, the young groom of Laodamia. Mercury brought Protesilaus up from the dead, and on his return to Hades Laodamia killed herself.

II 19

Here Ovid gives advice to a cuckolded husband in a poem cleverly dubbed by one critic, "the lament of the unexcluded lover." The poem should be compared with poem III 4. After a brief introduction, the first major section (lines 9–36) of the poem explores the oxymoron that for the lover the husband's defeat is a success that comes too easily. In the second section, the poem offers its oxymoronic advice to the husband (that he should guard his wife so that the lover can really have some fun) with the victorious implication that the advice is useless; the husband is and will be cuckolded. Here the lover's passion is not focused on Corinna or anyone else. The desire is for titillation and danger, a kind of desire that arises from boredom and the loss of eroticism. It is also possible to find in the speaker's description of the amatory life the Callimachean aesthetic program.

21. <u>shivering on your doorstep</u>: Ovid alludes to a major topos and a major sub-genre of erotic lyric: the shut-out lover who sings outside the door a *paraclausithyron*. See *Amores* I 6.

27. <u>Danae</u>: The king of Argos, Acrisius, was told that his daughter Danae's son would one day kill him. He therefore kept her shut in a bronze chamber to prevent her ever becoming pregnant. Jove turned himself into a shower of gold to enter the chamber.

29. <u>Io</u>: Jove seduced Io, the daughter of a river god Inachus, and then turned her into a heifer to hide her from Juno. When Juno learned of this, she tormented her with a gadfly and guarded her with Argus, a monster with many eyes.

32. <u>by the bucketful</u>: In programmatic poetry such an image is often used for sloppy, popular writing.

36. <u>flee when I'm pursued</u>: Sappho in her hymn to Aphrodite had been promised by the goddess that "if she [Sappho's beloved] flees, soon she will pursue." Ovid has this passage in mind.

55. <u>to wake in terror</u>: The scene alluded to here was a popular one from shows referred to today as adultery mimes. Typically, at the end, the woman's husband would return, the adulterer would try to hide, and would eventually be caught and beaten.

Amores III

Book III of the *Amores*, brings the affair with Corinna to an end. This is taken by many to allegorize the end of Ovid's interest in love elegy as a genre. While Ovid went on to write many more poems whose central themes and interest may be described as amatory, once he had completed the *Amores* he did not return to the genre. Furthermore, no other Roman poet picked up where Ovid left off. The poems of the last half of this book are frequently about failure: in III 7, the speaker is impotent; in III 8 his wit and talent no longer open doors; in III 12 his poetry is the reason that Corinna is promiscuous; and in III 14, his farewell to Corinna, the speaker asks pathetically for the last time to be allowed to enjoy his delusions. Since the collection was shortened, revised and republished after Ovid had written *The Art of Love* and his *Heroides*, or *Letters from Heroic Women*, the impression of failure and abandonment cannot be ascribed merely to biographical events.

III 1

The third book of the second edition of the *Amores* begins, as did the other two books, with a programmatic poem: the poet's encounter with the Muse of Tragedy and the Muse of Elegy in the midst of an "ancient virgin forest." The scene is a familiar and typical one for solemn initiation rites, for encounters with dangerous or benevolent gods, and for poetic empowerment, and is here modeled on Propertius III 3*. The feature of a formal debate, however, is new and it allows the poet to put in the mouth of Tragedy some apt criticisms of the poet's indulgence in elegy. Furthermore, uncharacteristic of the typical *recusatio*, or "refusal poem," here the poet accepts to some extent Tragedy's claims and seeks a compromise: "You want eternity; | All she wants is a little of my time." Ovid had already written the very successful tragedy, *Medea*.

1. ancient virgin forest: The forest was often used as a metaphor for the basic material which a poet shaped into the final product.

3. fountain: The fountain frequently figured in allegories of poetic style as the source of inspiration; the sacred, untouched, or small fountain was symbolic of Callimachean style. See Horace *Odes* I 26 and III 13.

3. a cave: The scene has pastoral and erotic associations; see Horace *Odes* I 5. The association of the Muses with a cave appears to be a Propertian innovation and here, together with the birds of line 4, helps to recall Propertius III 3, in which the poet is lectured by Apollo and Calliope to avoid epic and continue writing elegy.

8. her right foot: Apparently Elegy is thought of as being right-handed—or at least right-footed: the first line in an elegiac meter (the hexameter) is longer than the second (the pentameter).

9. translucent dress: She is dressed like a prostitute; compare Corinna in *Amores* I 5.

10. were ravishing: The poet's response to Elegy's "defects" is the typical response of the lover as portrayed in the philosophical tradition: he turns them into virtues.

14. the Lydian boot: The high-laced leather boot, or buskin, worn by tragic actors and so associated with the genre of tragedy.

15. amatory foolishness: Since at least Catullus, amatory poets reveled in the insignificance, foolishness, and immaturity of their interests.

17. The tale: Hand in hand with the poet's recognition and pride in his foolishness went the claim that it was precisely by means of broadcasting this activity that the poet would attain the eternal fame which the public man so coveted. In the mouth of Tragedy, however, such an aspiration regains the moral weight that the poets tried to deny it.

19. an onlooker marks: Another mark of status and importance for the typically ambitious Roman. The figure of the notorious elegiac poet had been adopted by Propertius; see I 7. 23.

23. thyrsus's rhythm: The thyrsus was a staff with ivy leaves, the symbol of Bacchus, and so suggestive of Bacchic rituals, including the ritual performance of tragedy in Athens. The staff was shaken by worshipers.

34. myrtle: The plant was sacred to Venus, goddess of love, and so an appropriate symbol for love elegy.

38. to speak in elegiacs: Tragic meters would include the tragic scenari and the epic hexameter; Elegy points out the irony that for Tragedy to speak to the elegiac poet in an elegy she must speak in elegiac meter.

44. confidante and procuress: For the emperor Augustus, Venus was the mother of Aeneas, his ancestor and founder of the Latin race. The implications of Venus, goddess of love, confiding in Elegy and using Elegy to procure lovers is an abstraction worth thinking through. In *Amores* I 8 the parallels between the speech of the procuress and the claims of Elegy have been noted.

45. Doors . . .: An allusion to one of the more common scenes from both comedy and elegy, the *paraclausithyron*, or "excluded lover poem," in which the lover, frequently drunk and with maudlin complaints, attempts, usually unsuccessfully, to gain entrance to his beloved's room. He may sing and recite poetry, threaten the door, the lock, the hinges, and the guardian of the door, beat the posts, attach verses or garlands to the door, but in the end he often falls asleep on the steps. For the generic type, see Propertius I 16, Ovid *Amores* I 6, and Tibullus I 2.

45. high-toned high-laced boots: An allusion to both the "high style" of tragic rhetoric and the appearance of the tragic buskin, a thick-soled leather boot.

64. I already sound like you: The compromise to be worked out is, in some sense, already achieved, and these lines may suggest the "tragic" content of this book's concern with elegiac failure.

67–68. eternity . . . : The contrast between the far and the near, the long and tedious, and the brief and engaging involves both ethical questions (about how to live one's life) and poetic questions (about the value of "apolitical" poetry).

III 2

Since an unaccompanied woman at the races would almost certainly be a prostitute, and if the woman is someone else's wife the propositions are outrageous, the scene is most likely fictional. The scene recalls for us one described in a later work, *The Art of Love*, where Ovid elaborates on the advantages of the racetrack as a "hunting ground": spectators sat close together in apparently random arrangement; contact could thus be easily made under socially acceptable circumstances. In this context, we may imagine the speaker indulging his erotic fantasies and the poet publishing those fantasies as much to reveal unacknowledged desire as to toy with a husband's erotic paranoia. The poem creates an atmosphere of erotic tension, which is not diminished even if the woman is the speaker's wife, as some have suggested. In that case, the poem's naughtiness lies in the potential impropriety of its whispered seduction in a public place.

12. grazing the turning-post: In Roman horse races, the charioteer drove his chariot from the starting blocks down the track with the center barrier on his left, counter-clockwise around a

turning-post and back; the race was usually seven laps, and twenty-four races made up the day. It was to the charioteer's advantage to make the turn with the post as close as possible to his left, or inside, wheel.

 14–15. at Pisa, once, Pelops . . .: Pisa is the district around Olympia where the Olympic games, which included chariot races, were celebrated. The myth of Pelops is a curious one to use here; it imparts an air of competition, of danger amid success, and of seduction and betrayal. Pelops wished to marry Hippodameia, but Oenomaus, king of Elis, had two reasons to thwart his daughter's suitors: he desired her himself and an oracle declared that his son-in-law would cause his death. Oenomaus's tactic was to arrange a chariot race: if the suitor could get to the Isthmus of Corinth before he caught up and speared the man, the suitor could marry Hippodameia. By the time Pelops arrived there had been twelve unsuccessful attempts to win the race to Corinth. Hippodameia, however, fell in love with Pelops and aided him by bribing her father's charioteer to loosen an axle pin on her father's chariot. Despite this aid, Pelops almost lost the race and his life when he turned to look back at Hippodameia. In the end, however, Oenomaus's chariot crashed and he was killed.

 19. the seats: Spectators sat on marble benches whose individual seats were marked only by a groove in the marble.

 20. I've brought you here: Literally, "This is the advantage to the seating arrangements in the circus."

 24. must be too long: A woman's skirt, or stola, extended to the ground and its lowest portion was a border which covered the woman's feet. For Roman women the style of their dress remained the same, except for variations of color and material, for 300 years. Prostitutes would not have worn the long stola, but rather a toga or a shorter, often transparent, stola which left their feet, adorned with anklets, exposed.

 28–29. Milanion, Atalanta: Atalanta, a huntress who wished to remain a virgin, made her suitors race her: if the suitor won, he married her, but if she caught the suitor, she killed him. Milanion tricked her by dropping golden apples in her path as he ran ahead. She stopped to pick them up, lost the race, and Milanion married her.

 30. Diana: A goddess who, like Atalanta, was a virgin huntress; she, however, unlike Atalanta, remained a virgin.

 38. racing form: A flat piece of wood on which records were kept, or a schedule of events as on a modern racing programme. Some interpret the Latin as meaning "a fan."

 43. the procession: Races were preceded by a traditional parade in which the city praetor escorted ivory images of the gods from the capitol through the forum to the *Circus Maximus* by way of the *Via Sacra*. When they arrived at the circus (literally meaning "the oval"), the parade proceeded the length of the racetrack while the spectators applauded. Here we have twelve gods, a kind of pantheon or "council of gods," for the races.

 44. time for silence: Ovid here uses the official formulaic language of a priest as he initiates a sacred ceremony.

 48. Neptune: The Italian god of water who, through his identification with the Greek god Poseidon, became the god of the sea. Poseidon is also identified as the "lord of horses."

 51. Mars: The Italian god of boundaries who became the god of war.

 53. Phoebus: The poetic name for Apollo as god of light; also the god of prophecy and of the poets.

 53. Phoebe: The female version of Phoebus, and so the poetic name for Apollo's sister Diana, goddess of the hunt.

55. Ceres and youthful Bacchus: The two major gods of agriculture. Ceres was the goddess of the grain and Bacchus the god of the vine.

56. Pollux, Castor: The brothers of Helen of Troy, who in life were famous as a boxer and horseman, respectively. They were made gods on their death and became the protectors of sailors.

57. Venus, Cupids: The goddess of love and her son, here made plural, perhaps to recall Catullus 3 where we find both plural Venuses and plural (for the first time) Cupids.

60. She nodded!: The solemn nod of a god indicates his or her inviolable promise; here one should imagine that the ivory image merely moved with the wagon's movement.

62. I will worship more: It was typical of elegy to figure the beloved as a goddess; here Ovid explores a kind of literalization of the figure. If we now add this girl to the list of twelve gods we have a phenomenon known as the "thirteenth god," or the *triskaidekatos theos*—the divinity whose power and appeal exceeds that of the pantheon. It was conventional to figure Hellenistic kings as the thirteenth god; Vergil had put Augustus in this position at the opening of his *Georgics*.

III 4

In *Amores* II 19 Ovid complains that his girl's husband does not keep a close enough eye on his girl; the man just makes it too easy. Here the topic is reversed. The underlying argument remains the same: the wise husband should grant his wife maximum freedom—in II 19 because a watchful caution stimulates the lover; in this poem, because restraint stimulates the wife.

19. Argus: When Io was turned into a cow by Jupiter after he raped her, the jealous Juno, sent Argus the all-seeing to guard her. He is variously described as having a third eye in the back of his head, four eyes, or many eyes. Mercury was sent by Jupiter to steal Io away, which he could only do by killing Argus.

21. Danae: The king of Argos, Acrisius, was told that his daughter Danae's son would one day kill him. He therefore kept her shut in a bronze chamber to prevent her ever becoming pregnant. Jupiter turned himself into a shower of gold to enter the chamber. When Acrisius learned that she had a son, he set her and her son, Perseus, adrift in a chest. The chest floated ashore and the prophecy was eventually fulfilled. See *Amores* II 19. 27.

23. Penelope: Ulysses, one of the Greek warriors of the *Iliad* and the central character of the *Odyssey*, was gone from his home in Ithaca for twenty years: the ten years of the Trojan War and ten years of wandering. His wife Penelope faithfully awaited for his return, even though her house was filled with young men all vying for her hand in marriage.

32. "what if we get caught?": The familiar Roman mime, known as the adultery mime, in which the lover is caught at the end, seems to be in the background of an allusion like this.

39. our founding fathers: The mother of the twins, Romulus and Remus, whose name was Ilia (a word which in Latin means "groin" or "private parts"), was a Vestal virgin and therefore pledged to chastity for thirty years (see note to *Amores* III 7. 21). When she became pregnant with Romulus and Remus, she claimed that the father of the children was Mars, thereby avoiding punishment for unchastity. The Roman historian Livy has the dry comment: "either she thought it was so or she said it because a god was fairly honorable as the origin of fault" (Livy I 4).

III 5

Dreams in antiquity were thought to offer access to the will and knowledge of the gods, and dream interpretation was widespread, being first attested in Homer. The symbols are normal and the interpretation offered is standard, according to what we can glean from an ancient text, *On the Interpretation of Dreams* by Artemidorus. The situation (a married man dreaming about his wife's infidelity) and its images suggest that the poem's literary origins lie in comedy. This makes the poem seem like an intruder in the *Amores*, and many believe that it is probably not by Ovid—both the manuscript tradition and stylistic features tell against Ovidian authorship despite its Ovidian manner. If the poem is not Ovid's, the Ovidian imitator was apparently one of several minor Latin poets who specialized in the imitation of particular classical poets. On the other hand, the fact that this dream seems to participate in a psychological and thematic movement wherein the dream becomes reality by poem III 8 may favor Ovidian authorship.

1. It was night: According to the ancient theory of dream interpretation, the time of night determines whether a dream is false or true. Ovid carefully avoids any precise indication of time in this poem, thereby leaving open the possibility that the dream is false.

2. terrified: The poem begins ominously but quickly transits to a picture of the *locus amoenus*, or ideal landscape, which we typically find in ancient idyllic and pastoral poetry.

15. mate: The Latin term identifies the mate explicitly as "the husband."

37. the color is right: The Latin word for a "brightly shining" girl, *candida*, would be the same word used for a "white" cow.

39. The crow: The bird is an apt symbol for an old bawd: talkative, long-lived, and a troublemaker. See *Amores* I 8.

44. adultery: This is taken together with the reference to a "husband" in line 15 to indicate that the speaker is a married man.

III 7

A poem on impotence. In antiquity as today the common response was to blame the woman; in antiquity the explanation was usually that the woman was a witch and had put a hex on the man. This poem marks the beginning of those poems in Book III which emphasize failure and a more negative attitude toward love.

8. Thracian snows: Thrace was the ancient world's equivalent of Siberia: the cold barbaric home of all the winds, especially the north wind.

21. Vestal virgin: One of six young women chosen by the chief priest, the *Pontifex Maximus*, when they were between six and ten years old to serve Vesta and to maintain their virginity for thirty years. The unchaste were punished by being buried alive.

23. Chlide: Her name is Greek and it means "luxuriant."

24. Pitho, Libas: Two more Greek names meaning "persuasive" and "dripping wet."

26. nine times: Perhaps a reference to Catullus 32.

27. Thessalian poison: Thessaly was particularly noted for its poisons and witches.

28–30. some witch: Various forms of sympathetic magic were practiced and they included piercing an image or melting a wax image.

31. Magic spells: The term in Latin for "magic spells," *carmen*, is also the term used for "poems," "charms," and "songs." It is often thought that references to *carmen* are veiled references to poetry, the power of poetry, or to stylistic debates.

39. Compare *Amores* I 5. 19–20.

41. Nestor: Nestor lived to be more than 200 years old (according to Ovid's *Metamorphoses* XII 187–188); in Homer he is garrulous, long-winded, and fond of recalling the days of his youth.

42. Tithonus: The husband of Aurora, the dawn, who was granted immortality but not youth. In *Amores* I 13 Ovid suggests that Dawn leaves Tithonus because he is too old to be a satisfactory lover.

51. Tantalus: Tantalus's "indiscretions" are variously reported, but include an attempt to deceive the gods by feeding them his own son, and an attempt to make himself immortal. He was punished by being placed in water beneath dangling fruit; the water invariably receded when he tried to drink and the fruit rose to elude his grasp.

53. What kind of man: One was supposed to be pure of body when approaching the gods, and this meant that one should abstain from sexual intercourse.

61. Phemius: The singer in Homer's *Odyssey* who was forced to sing for the suitors while Odysseus was away.

62. Thamyras: A legendary singer of Thrace who challenged the Muses to a singing contest. If he won, he was to be allowed to sleep with his choice among the Muses; if he lost, they were to take whatever they wanted. He lost and they took his sight.

79. Circe: She was the witch or enchantress who changed Odysseus's men into swine in the *Odyssey*.

III 9

Tibullus, one of the three great Roman elegiac poets, died shortly after Vergil in 19 B.C.E. and this poem is thought to have been composed shortly after his death. Structurally, it is an *epicedion*, or funeral poem (compare *Amores* II 6) in five parts: 1) address to the mourners, 2) praise and lament for the deceased—including the complaint against fate, 3) an account of Tibullus's last days, 4) the consolatory topics, and 5) a description of the funeral and memorial. Since the *epicedion* had explicit rules, the similarity between this poem and II 6 may not be important; on the other hand, since poetic effects as seemingly obvious as the parallel between these two poems are hard to overlook, one may wonder if Ovid does not intend a certain degree of criticism or parody of Tibullus. This latter view need not be utterly heartless: if the parrot is in some sense an emblem of the elegiac poet, then both Ovid and Tibullus "parrot" the genre in their literary game of *imitatio cum aemulatione*, or "imitation with competition." Here, then, the Ovidian parrot parodies for Tibullus his own parodic elegiac dirge.

1. <u>Dawn, Memnon</u>: Memnon, an Ethiopian prince, was killed at Troy by Achilles; at each sunrise Aurora, the goddess of dawn, wept tears of dew for him. See *Amores* I 13.

1. <u>Thetis, Achilles</u>: Achilles, the greatest Greek warrior at Troy, was killed there as a young man, thereby winning eternal glory but having only a short life. His mother Thetis, a sea-nymph, lamented his death.

4. <u>your sad name</u>: One of the fanciful etymologies of elegy derived it from the Greek for "He cries 'woe!'" For the Romans, as for us, the term "elegy" was associated with laments, although that does not reflect the real history or origin of the form.

6. <u>on the pyre</u>: As in the modern world, Romans were either buried or cremated. Cremation seems to have been more common.

7. <u>Venus's boy</u>: Ovid refers, of course, to Cupid.

13. <u>his brother Aeneas</u>: Both Aeneas and Cupid were sons of Venus: Aeneas's father was Anchises, a mortal; Cupid's father was one of the gods. Aeneas's son was called Iulus or Ascanius.

16. <u>Adonis</u>: There are various stories about Venus's passion for Adonis. She fell in love with him when she saw the beautiful young man hunting; one of the other gods, Mars or Vulcan, became jealous and was responsible for his death. He was killed by a wild boar and either from his blood sprang the rose and the anemone or from Venus's tears sprang the anemone.

17. <u>Poets, you see</u>: Here begins the formal praise (*laudatio*) and lament (*lamentatio*). Ovid refers to "poets" using the august term for the poet/priest/prophet, the *vates*.

21. Here begins the *sketliasmos*, or complaint against inexorable fate who took the beloved away.

21. <u>Thracian Orpheus</u>: The mythological and exemplary singer of antiquity, son of the muse Calliope. His powers of song were said to be able to move trees and tame wild beasts; he even descended to the underworld and persuaded the gods there, Persephone and Hades, to allow his wife Eurydice to return to the world above with him. He was, however, unable to refrain from looking back at her and she was compelled to return to the shadows. He is frequently used as a figure for the limits of song and the power of passion to overwhelm what song has accomplished. See also Horace *Odes* I 24.

23. <u>Linus</u>: Originally an agricultural figure who was mourned yearly at harvest time in a dirge, the "Song of Linus," whose traditional cry was *aelinon*, or "alas for Linus." There are three stories of his birth and death: son of Apollo, he was exposed by his mother at birth and devoured by dogs; son of Amphimarus, he was killed by Apollo for claiming to be as good a singer as the god; brother of Orpheus, who inherited Orpheus's abilities as a singer and teacher of Hercules, he was killed by Hercules with a blow from a cithara, a type of lyre.

27. <u>Avernus</u>: An actual lake in Campania whose fumes from volcanic remains and whose isolation led to its being associated with the black waters of Hades.

29. <u>Trojan enterprise</u>: A reference to Homer's story of the Trojan War, the *Iliad*, neatly cast as giving to the poet Homer the very thing that the warriors in his tale lived and died for: eternal fame.

30. <u>the promised shroud</u>: An oblique and appropriately elegiac reference to Penelope in Homer's *Odyssey*. She was the wife of Odysseus who had promised the suitors who came to her palace while Odysseus was away that she would choose a husband when she finished the shroud she was weaving; however, every night she unraveled what she had woven during the day.

31. <u>Nemesis, Delia</u>: Tibullus's two girlfriends, as the next line indicates, and the names by which his two books of poetry were known.

33–34. These lines refer to and imitate Tibullus I 3. 23–26. There, when Tibullus was sick, he complained to the absent Delia that her ritual abstinence in honor of the Egyptian god Isis had done him no good.

35–42. A particularly witty variation on the *sketliasmos*, or funeral curse.

45. <u>Venus of Eryx</u>: A reference to a hill in Sicily where a particularly famous temple to Venus was situated. The temple was known for its sacred prostitutes.

47. <u>Corfu</u>: In Tibullus I 3. 3–8 the poet tells of falling sick on Corfu and being left behind by his patron, the general Messalla.

47. Here the poet transits to the account of the deceased's final moments.

59. Here begins the *consolatio*.

60. <u>Elysium</u>: That place in the underworld reserved for the "blessed," heroes and poets who have earned their happiness.

62. <u>Catullus</u>: One of the forerunners of elegy, not usually thought of as an elegist proper. He was often cited for his poems, some in elegiac meter, to his beloved, Lesbia.

62. <u>Calvus</u>: Another of the early Roman elegists whose work does not survive; he was also an orator of the elegant and "dry" manner.

63. <u>Gallus</u>: Perhaps the real inventor of love elegy as we know it. He was a poet of the generation just after Catullus and just before Vergil. He wrote four books of elegies to a girl he called "Lycoris," who was Mark Antony's ex-mistress Cytheris. We have only a few lines of his verse. He committed suicide for possibly treasonous actions when he was governor of Egypt and his memory was condemned by Augustus. Ovid is, therefore, bold to mention this important poet here.

67. The poet ends with the burial and a prayer for the dead.

III 12

Here the poet complains that his poetry has done him harm as a lover. This reverses the typical elegiac claim that poetry helps the lover achieve his success, and it develops further the complaint registered in III 8 that poetry is useless. The poem depends on the ambiguous relationship between poetic fiction and reality and this has led to various interpretations of its meaning: that Corinna, like the fantastic tales of mythology, really does not exist; that the affair is all but over; that literature is harmless escapism; that the hedonistic values of elegiac poetry thwart the human desire for love. These different readings are not, of course, all mutually exclusive. His claims about Corinna depend on a metonymy of the girlfriend as the poetry (Corinna is both the girl herself and the book of poems about her), and on a metaphor (already used by Horace) that treats the book of poetry as a prostitute consorting promiscuously with whoever reads it. By this displacement from the fictive to the real, the poet claims that art does make a difference, for his promiscuous art has made a promiscuous beloved in a promiscuous world. That Ovid kept the real identity of Corinna a secret adds to the poem's ironic playfulness and makes its fundamental fiction (that Corinna now belongs to everyone) in some sense false.

1. ink-black birds: The crow or raven was a bird sacred to Apollo and associated with prophecy; black is a color of ill omen, often associated with funerals.

2. chant your curse on me: Ovid imitates a line from Propertius (II 28. 38) in which Propertius laments what he thinks is the impending death of his Cynthia.

5–6. called my own . . .: Ovid imitates other lines from Propertius (II 8. 5–6) in which Propertius complains that Cynthia belongs to another—that all his poetry was in vain.

7. my own books: Ovid again imitates a line in Propertius (II 25. 3) in which Propertius makes the elegiac poet's traditional claim that his books will make Cynthia's beauty famous beyond that of all others.

15ff. Just think . . .: A light recasting of the poetic investiture scene in which the Muse or the girlfriend in the place of a muse determines the poet's creative course; see, for instance, Ovid *Amores* I 1 and Propertius I 1.

15. Troy: Homer's great subject in the *Iliad* and the subject of Vergil's *Aeneid* II.

15. Thebes: One of the great tragic cycles from which numerous plays were produced by the Athenian tragedians; perhaps the most familiar to a modern audience are the *Oedipus Rex* and *Antigone*.

15. the glory of Caesar: One of the common topics rejected by Roman poets in their programmatic poems. Nevertheless, there seem to have been several poets willing to take up the challenge; see for instance Propertius I 7.

17, 18. Muses, Phoebus: Ovid refers to the Callimachean scene, imitated by Propertius in elegy III 3, in which Phoebus Apollo or the Muses prevent the poet from writing epic. Ovid himself always varies the characters. In *Amores* I 1, Cupid interrupts the poet's epic plans; in II 1, his girl locks him out and so forces a change in his plans; in III 1, Elegy and Tragedy stage a debate about what the poet should do.

21. Scylla: It seems that here Ovid actually is doing what he is describing; he is unleashing a new tale: Scylla, daughter of Nisus, who cut the purple lock of her father's hair, was not the same as the monster Scylla, daughter of Phorcys, from whose groin sprung forth six snarling dogs' heads.

23. wings to heels: A reference either to Mercury's winged sandals or (more likely) to the wings which Perseus obtained with the help of the three daughters of Phorcys.

23. snakes to women's hairs: A reference either to the traditional picture of the Furies (also called Erinyes or Eumenides) or (more likely) to Medusa, whose hair was a collection of hissing snakes; she was killed by Perseus.

24. Perseus on Pegasus: Pegasus was Perseus's winged horse who was born from the blood of Medusa.

25. Tityus: A giant who attempted to rape Leto, mother of Diana and Apollo. She called upon the aid of her children who killed Tityus; he was punished in the underworld by being stretched out on the ground with pegs while vultures continually devoured his liver.

26. the snaky hound of hell: Cerberus, the watchdog of Hades, had a reptilian tail and (usually) three heads.

27. Enceladus: One of the giants who attempted to dethrone Jupiter. Before Ovid he did not have a thousand arms; perhaps Ovid is again creating the fiction he alludes to. Enceladus was defeated and buried under Sicily where he still smokes and fumes.

28. treacherous maiden's voice: An allusion to the story of the sirens in Homer's *Odyssey*; their singing was said to be so beautiful that whoever heard them would never wish to go away from their voices.

29. East Wind: Another allusion to Homer's *Odyssey*. Aeolus, the god of the winds, placed the winds in a sack in order to facilitate Odysseus's journey home; Odysseus's men, however, opened the bag and their journey home was lost.

30. Tantalus: For offenses variously reported, Tantalus was punished by being made to stand in water up to his chin. Whenever he tried to drink, the water receded. Similarly, whenever he tried to eat the fruit suspended above his head, it rose up out of his grasp.

31. Niobe: The daughter of Tantalus who boasted that she had more children than Leto, mother of Apollo and Diana. Leto, therefore, told Apollo and Diana to kill all of Niobe's children. She withdrew to a mountain in Asia Minor where, as she grieved, she was turned into stone.

31. Callisto: A hunting companion of Diana who had pledged eternal virginity. She was raped by Jupiter who turned her into a bear in order to escape Juno's notice. In other versions of the story, Diana turned her into a bear as punishment. Juno was not deceived, however, and either she persuaded Diana to kill Callisto or Diana killed her by mistake. Jupiter then turned her into the constellation, Ursa Major, or "the Great Bear."

32. nightingale: An allusion to the familiar story of Philomela, Procne, and Itys; see *Amores* II 6. Philomela's sister, Procne, was married to Tereus, the Thracian king. Tereus raped Philomela and cut her tongue out, but she contrived to tell her story through embroidery. When Procne found out the truth, she served Tereus his own son, Itys, for dinner. When he discovered what he had eaten, he pursued the two sisters until he was turned into a bird of prey and they into swallow and nightingale. The nightingale continues, according to legend, to mourn her fate.

33–34. a bird . . .: Allusions to stories of Jupiter's erotic adventures: with Leda, when he turned himself into a swan (see *Amores* I 3. 22); with Ganymede, when he turned himself into an eagle; with Danae, when he became a shower of gold in order to enter her cell (see *Amores* II 19); and with Europa, when he turned into a bull (*Amores* I 3. 23–24*).

35. Proteus: Proteus, a god of the sea, who in order to escape capture would turn himself into various beings and phenomena, including flame and water.

35. dragon's teeth: Cadmus traveled to Thebes while searching for his daughter Europa. There he killed a dragon, the offspring of Ares, and was advised by Athena to sow the dragon's teeth. The men who grew from the teeth were called *Spartoi*, "the sown men," and became the ancestors of the Theban nobility.

36. fire-breathing bulls: Jason, while in Colchis in search of the Golden Fleece, was ordered by Medea's father to yoke some fire-breathing bulls, plow a field, and sow it with the teeth of a dragon. From those dragon's teeth sprang warriors whom Jason had to battle.

37. sisters who weep: When Phaethon tried to drive the chariot of the sun he lost control and Jupiter, to prevent his burning up the earth, struck him dead with a thunderbolt. He fell into the river Eridanus where his sisters grieved for him until they were turned into willows and their tears into the amber drops which are found on willow trunks.

37. ocean-going ships: An allusion to the story told by Vergil in the *Aeneid* of how Aeneas's ships were rescued from the fire of the attacking Latins by being turned into sea-nymphs.

39. the sun recoiling . . .: When Atreus and Thyestes competed for the kingship of Mycenae, Atreus served to Thyestes his own children at a banquet; the sun was so horrified that it recoiled and set in the east.

39f.   the lyre . . .: Amphion, a lyre player and son of Zeus, in an effort to fortify Thebes caused the stones to follow him by his magical music. He later married Niobe.

III 13

This poem is an anomaly in the *Amores*: it does not address any of the typical subjects or themes of elegiac poetry. It can hardly be accidental that here, at the end of the *Amores*, conservative interests in Roman religion and ritual come to the surface without amatory complications. One critic suggested almost eighty years ago that Ovid is warning his readers that he does not endorse the views of his lover. Many details of this poem contrast implicitly with the views and values of the elegist's lover. The poem immediately precedes the poet's complaint in III 14 that his mistress's infidelity has ruined the affair. Do the values of Roman society finally reassert themselves over the playful infidelities of Ovidian elegy? The possibility recalls a fundamental tension in Catullus's work.

1.   Falerii: A town in southern Etruria which stands on a narrow plateau of land surrounded by precipices about 300 feet high. The journey over mountain roads is, as Ovid says, "difficult and steep." Ovid's third wife was from Rome; therefore if this is an autobiographical reference, it must refer to one of his first two early and short marriages.

2.   Camillus: M. Furius Camillus was an early Roman general and statesman. His earliest victory was the capture of Veii, 396 B.C.E., which preceded the campaign against Falerii, a city with great strategic importance overlooking routes to Etruria. According to the historian Livy, his victory at Veii was the result of Veiian impiety and Roman piety. Just before his attack he prayed to Juno that she leave the town of Veii where she lived and follow his victorious army to Rome in return for a temple worthy of her grandeur. On his victory, Camillus allowed his troops to slaughter the townspeople all day long and on the next day sold the freeborn into slavery. Later, however, he was exiled for alleged mismanagement of the Veiian booty, an act which some believed lead to Rome's capture by the Gauls. From exile he led the army which saved Rome, and became known as the second founder of the city. He is said to have celebrated four triumphs.

3.   Juno's festival: Probably a reference to the chief festival of Juno Quiritis, the goddess of Falerii, which was held on October 7.

4.   the sacrificial cow: Cows were commonly sacrificed to Juno and the white cows of Falerii were particularly prized for this purpose.

18.   The she-goat . . . .: The etiological story Ovid tells is recounted only here. In the rite to Juno Quiritis she is apparently a bride. The festival is attested in many parts of Greece and here in western Italy it is a curious relic of Greek influence.

31.   Argive in form: An ancient writer on Roman antiquities, Dionysius of Halicarnassus (I 21. 2), describes for us the Argive origin of this ritual.

32.   Halaesus: The founder of Falerii and companion or son of Agamemnon, who led the Greek troops to Troy. On Agamemnon's return to Mycenae he was killed by his wife and Halaesus fled from Argos to Etruria. Such a tale of flight, wandering, and city walls may recall the wanderings of Aeneas from Troy to Rome. If so, one should note that Halaesus worships Juno, the goddess whose hatred pursues Aeneas in the *Aeneid*, while Aeneas is protected by his mother Venus arguably the goddess of elegy.

III 14

This poem is built on an attitude Ovid has adopted before: "Fool me! . . . Let me enjoy my gullibility." See, for example, I 4. 69–70 and II 11. 53–54. The urbane self-contradiction that he is willing to believe what he knows to be a lie as long as Corinna tries to deceive him is now the basis of an entire poem. While it is tempting to interpret this poem in its context as the penultimate poem of Ovid's elegiac career, it cannot easily be summed up simply as a symbolic rejection of love elegy—it is too much of a piece with all of Ovidian elegy from which it refuses to depart. The poem, which begins as a complaint, seems to end looking forward to the role Ovid will play as *praeceptor amoris* in *The Art of Love*, a role which is clearly an extension of the elegiac lover. Nevertheless, as Ovid comes to adopt this professorial attitude, he seems to move further from the attitude which was the original impulse of elegy, namely complaint, and which characterized especially the voice of Catullus, who is echoed here throughout.

1–4: The Latin closely echoes Catullus 76. 23–24: "No longer do I seek that, that she love me in return, or, what is not possible, that she want to be chaste."

27: Another echo of Catullus, this time of Flavius's bed rattling in the night, poem 6. 7–11.

31–34. These lines recall the advice of the *lena* Dipsas in elegy I 8.

32. my gullibility: The speaker here asks for the very same thing, "gullibility" or "credulity" (the Latin word is the same, *credulitas*), that at the end of III 12 was destroying him. There is a difference, however; he asks here to believe in Corinna's fidelity, while in III 12 others too readily believed in her accessibility. If this poem is to be read as an allegory of elegy's values and of Ovid's abandonment of elegy, its logic has yet to be fully probed.

42. Compare what is perhaps the most famous Catullan epigram, "I hate and I love," poem 85.

48–50. even if I catch you in the act . . . : Compare Tibullus I 2. 58–59: "no matter what he [the husband] sees, | He'll be unable to believe his eyes."

III 15

The final poem of the *Amores* is a kind of envoy, a farewell to love elegy. Typically, such a poem identifies the poet by reference to his origins and makes claims for the eternal fame of the poet's work. Compare Horace *Odes* III 30.

1. Mother of gentle Amores: Venus.

3. (not unsuccessful) delights: Peter Green has pointed out (Ovid, *The Erotic Poems*) that the Latin has several meanings: Nor did my delights/sensuality/verse/mistress dishonor/displease/disappoint me. The moral condemnation of elegy some would find in poems III 12, 13, and 14 should be modified by the unequivocal assertion here.

4. but hardly rustic: Ovid came from Sulmo, about eighty miles from Rome, an area known for its tough peasant stock. For the attitude of the urbane sophisticate toward the rustic boor, see *Amores* II 4. 19.

5. an ancient line: Ovid claimed descent from an old equestrian family of Sulmo.

6. <u>these troubled times</u>: During the period of the late civil wars it was especially possible for a man of humble birth to gain through military service the wealth and status necessary to be made an equestrian.

7–8. <u>Vergil . . . Catullus, and I . . . .</u>: It is curious that Ovid does not mention, especially for the second edition, either Tibullus or Propertius. Mantua was Vergil's home town, as Verona was Catullus's; Paelignian refers to the territory of central Italy which included Sulmo.

9. <u>a race who</u>: the Paeligni were leaders in the social war when Rome's Italian allies attempted to win their freedom from Rome. Such a reference to recent history recalls the ending of Propertius's *Monobiblos*.

14. <u>I call you great</u>: The contrast between a poet's humble beginnings and his grand achievement is also the cause of pride for Horace; see *Odes* III 30.

15. <u>Cyprian mother</u>: Venus, of course; here referred to in terms of one of her seats of worship, the temple at Amathus in Cyprus.

17. <u>Horned Dionysus</u>: Dionysus, the god of tragedy, wine, and ecstatic emotion, was thought to appear sometimes as a bull. His worshipers shook a thyrsus, or ritual staff with ivy leaves fastened to the tip. After publishing the first edition of the *Amores*, Ovid went on to complete his only (but very successful) tragedy, *Medea*.

Horace

BIBLIOGRAPHY

There are many fine books on Horace which introduce the reader to the major critical debates and provide further bibliography. I offer below only a representative sample of what is available. (See also the note on *Odes* IV):

Commager, Steele. *The Odes of Horace: A Critical Study* (Bloomington: Indiana University Press, 1962).

Davis, Gregson. *Polyhymnia: The Rhetoric of Horatian Lyric Discourse* (Berkeley: University of California Press, 1991).

Fraenkel, Eduard. *Horace* (Oxford: Clarendon Press, 1957, ppbk. 1966).

Perret, Jacques. *Horace*, trans. by Bertha Humez (New York University Press, 1964).

Porter, David H. *Horace's Poetic Journey: A Reading of Odes 1-3* (New Jersey: Princeton University Press, 1987).

Wilkinson, L. P. *Horace and His Lyric Poetry* (London: Cambridge University Press, 1968).

Odes I-III

Horace published his three books of *Odes* in 23 B.C.E., at a time of the greatest literary activity ancient Rome ever knew. Vergil had published his *Eclogues* (39 B.C.E.) and his *Georgics* (29 B.C.E.), and his work on the *Aeneid* was well underway. Propertius had published his *Monobiblos* (28 B.C.E.), Book II of his elegies (25 B.C.E.), and was completing Book III. Tibullus had published Book I (26 B.C.E.) of his elegies and was at work on Book II. In this context Horace had set himself the almost impossible task of reviving the spirit and importance of the essentially oral and necessarily public traditions of archaic Greek lyric. The meters were foreign to a Roman audience; the genre was considered slight; and the conditions of performance had changed. Horace faced these challenges with remarkable audacity and resources. Book I of the *Odes* begins with a metrical *tour de force*: twelve odes each in a different meter. He created varying voices or personae, including his adaptations of the voice of the *vates* or poet/priest/prophet, to imagine a full range of addressees from intimate friends and imaginary girls (always Greek) to consuls and the Roman people; and to present his voices in a range of situations from realistic conversations between friends to wholly imaginary scenes in a part Greek, part Roman world where specific human issues are generalized and reverberate with symbolism, irony, and parody. He cast his eye back upon the subjects and themes, the values and prejudices of the poetic accomplishments of others and attempted to construct a lyric world capacious enough for the individual human spirit, for the presence of friends, and for the demands of Rome, history, and the future.

Odes I

I 1

The first poem of Book I is a dedication poem for the collection of *Odes* I–III, addressed to Maecenas, who had been Horace's patron since about 38 B.C.E. Maecenas was a man of wealth, influence, and luxury whose name became synonymous with literary patronage for his support of Vergil, Horace, Propertius, and others. This poem takes the form of a long *priamel*, or list of rejected choices, in this case a list of life-styles chosen by others, which acts as a background, or foil, to the poet's own choice. The poem defends Horace's choice of lyric poetry, his third poetic genre, and predicts his immortality, but also introduces the reader to that familiar Horatian irony which makes an adequate summary of his thought so difficult.

1. Maecenas: Despite Maecenas's ancestry (which he traced to Etruscan kings) and his political prominence (as friend and aid to Octavian), he preferred to remain a member of the equestrian class and never held public office.

2. my patron: Patronage offered both material and moral support. Horace claims (*Satires* I 6) that in his case there was a special bond of friendship as well. Some scholars believe that his friendship with Maecenas cooled sometime before he published *Odes* IV.

4. Olympic dust: The Olympic games, held in honor of Olympian Zeus, were perhaps the most famous national festival in Greece. A list of winners from the origin of the games, 776 B.C.E., until C.E. 217 has been preserved for us by the historian Eusebius. They were held, like our Olympics, every four years, and the first day of competition (the second day of the festival itself) consisted of chariot races.

5. noble palm branch: The palm branch, carried by the victor as a token of his victory.

7. milling Roman crowds: Horace juxtaposes the Greek aristocratic ambition to be a winner in the Olympics with the Roman ambitions to succeed politically and/or financially. The "milling Roman crowds" were ever treated with distaste, if not contempt, by Horace.

8. the three high magistracies: Success in politics for a Roman consisted in making one's way up the *cursus honorum*, or "course of high office." The "three high magistracies" were: 1) *curule aedile*, which conferred senatorial dignity and included care of the public games, an especially good, if expensive, way to gain popularity and votes, 2) the *praetor*, who acted as the judge or presiding officer in the law courts, 3) the *consul*, or chief civil and military officer of the state.

10. Libyan threshing floors: Africa was especially important as a source of grain for the Romans; Horace imagines the trader who tries to corner the grain market and withhold or store supplies until the market price goes up.

11–12. cleave the ground with a hoe: The hard-working farmer who tilled his family plot, except when called up for military service, was a symbol of conservative values for the late Republic. The motto was, "Good farmers make good soldiers." Ironically, booty from battle became in the late Republic the way in which many "good farmers" could aspire to "Attalus's riches."

13. <u>Attalus's riches</u>: The wealth of the Attalids, kings of Pergamon in Asia Minor, was legendary. Their kingdom came to an end with the "Testament of Attalus," when Attalus III bequeathed his kingdom to Rome in 133 B.C.E.

13. <u>to cut the sea</u>: The ancients did not like sailing, which was generally characterized as a dangerous and terrifying activity. The description here is a general reference to the terrors of the sea.

14. <u>Cyprian beam</u>: Cyprus, a large island in the eastern Mediterranean near what is now Israel, was famous for shipbuilding; it was said that the island could of its own resources build an entire ship from keel to mast.

15. <u>Icarian waves</u>: The waters of the Aegean near the island of Icaros, just off the coast of Caria in Asia Minor, are sometimes churned up by "the African," a southwest wind blowing from Africa.

19. <u>Massic wine</u>: An excellent Italian wine from Mt. Massicus (now Monte Massico) in Campania.

21. <u>a wild arbute</u>: Also known as the strawberry tree for the shape of its fruit, it was valued for its shade.

22. <u>some quiet spring</u>: Some readers find here a picture of Horace himself, happily enjoying his wine in Epicurean comfort. The spring, further described by Horace as sacred and gentle, is often found in Latin poetry as a symbol for the source of divine poetic inspiration.

23–24. <u>the clarion's blast</u>: The clarion was a long trumpet, curved at the end, and used to give signals to the cavalry; the horn, or infantry trumpet, was long and straight. The contrast of lives here recalls the contrast between lyric ease and epic valor.

28. <u>Marsian boar</u>: The country of the Marsi refers to a district in central Italy, about fifty miles from Rome which was rich in game; boar was considered a special delicacy.

29. <u>The ivies</u>: The ivy was sacred to Bacchus, god of both wine and poetry. The image here simultaneously recalls the prizes of Olympia and the leisure of the gentle springs above.

30. <u>mix me with the gods</u>: In a form of "ring composition," Horace returns to the "prizes" gained through other life pursuits and co-opts them; here he achieves what the Olympic victors sought in line 6, above.

32, 33. <u>Euterpe, Polyhymnia</u>: Euterpe, here, and Polyhymnia, below, do not represent specific types of poetry; such specialization among the Muses was a later development. Their names, however, are significant: Euterpe means "sweet pleasure"; Polyhymnia means "many songs."

34. <u>her Lesboan lyre</u>: The island of Lesbos was famous as the birthplace of the Greek lyric poets Sappho and Alcaeus. They were both important models for Horace's lyric poetry. The Alcaic stanza is the most common of Horace's meters (37 *Odes*) and the Sapphic stanza the second most common (25 *Odes*). Sappho is associated with love poetry and Alcaeus with more politically engaged lyric. Lyric poetry was originally composed for sung public performance accompanied by the lyre, a stringed instrument.

I 3

This poem is a *propempticon*, or "send-off poem," on the occasion of an unknown voyage to Greece by Vergil, which becomes at line 9 a reflection on man's audacity. Horace offers three examples of the transgression of limits: Prometheus, who stole fire from the gods; Daedalus, who made wings and flew; and Hercules, who descended into the underworld.

1. goddess of Cyprus: Venus, the goddess of love and goddess of the sea, was said to have come ashore at Cyprus after her birth in the sea. She had a shrine on Cyprus at Paphus.

2. the starlit brothers of Helen: Helen of Troy had twin brothers, Castor and Pollux, who formed after their death the constellation Gemini. It was believed that they could calm the sea and so they were prayed to in time of storms.

4. the breeze from Apulia: The "Iapyx," a west-northwest wind from the heel of Italy, was especially favorable for a voyage to Greece. Apulia was Horace's native region so the reference may carry a personal note.

8. Attica's shores: Attica, the famous province of Greece where Athens, long the cultural and political center of the Hellenic world, was the capital.

14. gloomy Hyades: A constellation whose name means "rainy"; its rising and setting were associated with storms.

20. Acroceraunia's notorious crags: Acroceraunia means "Thunder Cape" (Macaulay's translation). It was notorious for the shipwrecks it caused and was often the site of lightning storms.

21. God's: For Horace and for most Romans of the time, this would be a vaguely defined, providential, and prudent deity, not necessarily any particular god.

27. Prometheus: Prometheus stole fire from heaven and brought it to earth for men in a hollow reed.

30. feverish diseases: In anger at Prometheus, the gods sent Pandora to Prometheus's brother with a jar which contained all manner of diseases and other afflictions.

33. Daedalus: A master Athenian craftsman who made wings of feather and wax in order to fly from Crete with his son Icarus. Icarus flew too close to the sun, melted his wings, and fell from the sky. See *Odes* I 1, line 15.

34. the vacant atmosphere: The second elemental violation by mankind: the air.

35. Hercules: A Greek hero, deified after his death, who was ordered to perform twelve labors (Herculean tasks). His twelfth labor was to enter the underworld or the land of the dead (man's third violation of elemental nature), and steal Hades' infernal watchdog Cerberus.

36. Acheron: One of the rivers of the underworld.

40. his wrathful thunderbolts: The Roman state had just endured more than 100 years of civil war, which had most recently taken the lives of Pompey the Great, Julius Caesar, Cicero, Brutus, Mark Anthony, and large numbers of less well-known Romans. This devastation was often ascribed to divine anger.

14

A poem on the coming of spring which is notable for its modulations and changes. The poem is in a meter which Horace used only once, a meter that contrasts long lines and epic rhythms with shorter, lighter lines. One should compare Catullus's response to spring in his poem 46 and a later darker version of spring and death in Horace's *Ode* IV 7.

1. mild west winds: Favonius, the west wind, regularly blew about the beginning of February and announced the beginning of spring. The name means "the one who brings favor."

5. Venus: As a goddess of fertility she presided over springtime, love, fertility, and gardens. She was also the patron goddess and original mother of the Julian family, of which Julius Caesar and Octavian were members.

6. Nymphs: See *Odes* I 1. 31. These woodland goddesses or demi-goddesses were often attendants of the gods.

6. Graces: Goddesses of loveliness and grace.

8. Cyclopean forge: Vulcan, the husband of Venus, and his servants, the Cyclopes, labored in their workshop below the earth to make weapons, armor, and other things for the gods. In the springtime they would be at work hammering out Jupiter's thunderbolts for the summer storms.

9. myrtle's green: The myrtle was sacred to Venus.

11. Faunus: Horace refers to the god of shepherds and farmers. His name, directly related to the name Favonius mentioned above, means "the propitious one." Sacrifices were made to him on February 13.

14. Sestius: Like Horace, Sestius served under Brutus in Macedonia during the civil war. When Brutus lost, Sestius was proscribed (condemned to death and his property confiscated), then pardoned, and finally elected *consul suffectus* (a substitute consul) for the year 23 B.C.E., the year of publication for the *Odes*. The addressees of the opening odes are significant: 1. Maecenas (Horace's patron), 2. Augustus (leader of the state and winner in the recent civil wars), 3. Vergil (poet and friend), and 4. Sestius (fellow republican who fought on the losing side in the recent civil wars and now the nominal chief of state under Augustus).

16. the storied shades: The fabled *Manes*, of whom men tell stories, were the spirits or phantoms of the dead.

17. Pluto's stifling realm: Pluto was king of the underworld and the realms of death. His name means "wealth" but his realm is meager, ghostly, insubstantial—in contrast to the blessed life of Horace's friend, the *consul suffectus*.

19. Lycidas: The name is Greek and probably stands for a type—the young and slender adolescent male particularly attractive to older men in the erotic world of Greeks and Romans.

I 5

The well-known Pyrrha ode. Horace addresses a courtesan (prostitute) whom he claims once attracted him and whom he claims he no longer desires. The scene described would recall for a Roman scenes familiar from Greek and Roman comedy: the young lover falls for a courtesan, who demands with tantrums and recriminations ever more expensive gifts, and finally finds a more solicitous and generous lover.

3. Pyrrha: Her name is related to the Greek word for fire and may have been favored as a name by Greek prostitutes.

13–14. a votive plaque: Seaside shrines contained the dedicatory offerings of those who had escaped shipwreck, usually consisting of a votive tablet picturing the scene and some inscription. Epigrams imitating such inscriptions were a common poetic genre, and this poem is designed to recall just such epigrams.

16. god of the sea: Sailors would dedicate their offerings to Neptune, the god of the sea, while lovers would dedicate their tablets to Venus, a goddess of the sea and the goddess of love. The poet may refer to either here, or to both.

I 7

Like *Odes* I 1, this poem begins with a *priamel*: other places are used as foil for the special attractions of Tibur, a suburb east of Rome where Horace had his villa and where Plancus, the addressee of the poem, was born. Like *Odes* I 4, this poem advises Plancus to enjoy the moment. The last twelve lines offer a mythological exemplum to support the poet's exhortation, but the exemplum itself suddenly contextualizes the moments we are to enjoy within the larger demands of history and politics. L. Munatius Plancus, consul in 42 B.C.E., was a prominent political figure during the final years of civil war. He was on Mark Antony's side from 41 to 32 B.C.E., when he deserted Antony for Octavian. In 27 B.C.E. he suggested that Octavian take the name Augustus, which he did. By the time Horace published his *Odes*, Plancus was probably the most important and one of the most senior ex-consuls in Rome.

1. Rhodes, Mytilene, Ephesus: These three cities are all in the eastern Mediterranean and were prominent for their cultural associations. They were all places one would visit on a tour of the East. Rhodes: An island in the Mediterranean off the southwest corner of Asia Minor. Its climate was pleasant year-round and it was a center for commerce, art, rhetoric, and philosophy. Mytilene: Capital of Lesbos, home of Sappho and Alcaeus. Ephesus: Principal city of the Roman province of Asia; its temple of Artemis was one of the seven wonders of the ancient world.

2. Corinth: Horace now moves to Greece, and his next four cities proceed north from Corinth in the south to Tempe in Thesally. Corinth is on the isthmus connecting the Peloponnese (southern Greece) with mainland Greece. It had two harbors, one on each side of the isthmus.

3. Thebes: In Attica north of Athens; it was the birthplace of Bacchus.

3. Delphi: The most famous oracle of Apollo in the ancient world; west-northwest of Thebes.

4. the Valley of Tempe: A beautiful valley formed by the Peneus River in Thesally, directly north of Delphi between Mount Olympus and Mount Ossa.

5. whole careers: His *priamel* sets up contrasts between Greece and Rome, epic and lyric, the far and the near, the grand and the humble, and so on.

5. Athens: The cultural center of the Greek world, named for Athena, the "virginal goddess." The olive, which was sacred to Athena, was given by her to Athens as a symbol of her city, and it grew well and profusely in Attica.

7. Juno's: Juno, wife and sister of the greatest Olympian god, Jupiter, claimed as her favorite cities Argos, Sparta, and Mycenae.

7. golden Mycenae: Another quasi-Homeric epithet; Homer calls Mycenae "all golden" because of its fabled wealth in the bronze age. Mycenae was the home of Agamemnon, "king of kings," and leader of the Greek expedition to Troy.

9. fertile Larissa: Larissa is a city in Thesally on the Peneus River, and so it is also a reference back to the valley of Tempe (line 4 above), but in this context, perhaps it is most

importantly associated with Achilles, the local hero of Larissa and the greatest of Greek warriors who fought at Troy and who was celebrated in Homer's epic, the *Iliad*.

10. <u>locales in the country</u>: Literally, "the echoing home of Albunea," a grotto at Tibur, sixteen miles northeast of Rome, near where Horace lived and where a fountain arose between steep rocks.

11. <u>Anio</u>: A river which goes over a series of particularly beautiful falls and rapids at Tibur.

12. <u>Tivoli</u>: The modern name for Tibur, which gets its name from Tiburnus, one of the mythical founders of the town.

18. <u>silver Eagles</u>: "Silver Eagles" are the standards carried by the first cohort of each legion (when complete, three maniples of 200 men made a cohort, and ten cohorts made a legion of 6,000). Note the contrast between the "lovely shade" and the brilliance of the army in formation.

19. <u>Teucer</u>: Teucer's father, Telamon, sent him and his brother, Ajax, to the Trojan War with the injunction that neither should come home without the other. Ajax committed suicide when he lost the armor of the dead Achilles to Odysseus. When Teucer returned home to Salamis after the war, his father cursed and banished him. He and his companions sailed to Cyprus where they founded a new city and named it Salamis after Teucer's native home. It is useful to consider how this story, as alluded to by Horace, engages themes of travel, war, oracles, passion, relaxation, and home.

23. <u>poplar leaves</u>: The poplar was sacred to Hercules, the great and famous traveler of the ancient world known for his twelve labors.

31. <u>you have suffered</u>: Aeneas in Vergil's national epic, *Aeneid*, addresses his comrades in similar words after they have been blown off course by a storm (*Aeneid* I 198–199).

I 9

This poem is commonly known as "The Soracte Ode" because of the prominence of Mt. Soracte in the poem's setting. The mountain, which rises to about 2,500 feet, can be seen from Rome about twenty-five miles north of the city on the western side of the Tiber valley. This and other details give the poem a definitely Roman color. However, the opening of the poem is modeled on a drinking poem of Alcaeus (sixth century B.C.E., Greece), with common features which include the winter, the hearth, and the wine. The friend and addressee, Thaliarchus, is no doubt a literary device (his name is Greek and means, "leader of the symposium") and he is rather unrealistically asked to do the job of a slave, namely to bring in the wood. In this unreal setting, it is not surprising to find that thematically the poem's conclusion is no longer based on Alcaeus but is Hellenistic and Epicurean (fourth century B.C.E.) and is influenced by popular genres like Middle Comedy. Critics have argued that the scene is wholly imaginary, that the unity is one of thematic alternation rather than of time and place, or that inconsistencies are a generic feature of the poem's symposiastic motifs. I find it most satisfactory to think of the poem literarily as lyric's challenge to the range of epic and personally as constitutive of the spaces in which we live, not unified by time and place, but resonating with the half-lit and symbolic presence of where we've been and where we're going. The poem has always had admirers and is generally considered one of Horace's greatest odes.

8. <u>Sabine beaujolais</u>: This mellow but plain wine from the Sabine territory is imagined as kept in a Greek amphora. Wine is often used symbolically in literary polemic.

11. <u>cypresses</u>: The cypress, sacred to Pluto, was grown in gardens and used at funerals.

12. <u>ash trees</u>: The ash grew wild in the mountains.

18. <u>parade grounds</u>: The *Campus Martius*, an open field northwest of the ancient city where the army trained and where the citizens gathered to vote. It had gradually become built up with private homes and the *Circus Flaminius*, Pompey's portico and theater, and temples to the gods; it still had open spaces between the surrounding buildings.

I 11

Here Horace combines motifs from drinking songs and Epicurean philosophy in an address to a woman or girl, Leuconoë. The girl's name is a compound of "clear, white, bright, guileless," and "mind."

1. <u>it's wrong to know</u>: The diction draws on the powerful language of religious sanction.

3. <u>Babylonian astrology</u>: Generally speaking, sophisticated ladies would consult astrologers about the future. Astrology had a mixed reception in Rome: some of the great figures in the last century B.C.E. believed or professed belief in astrology (including Sulla, Varro, Maecenas, Propertius, and Ovid), but Cicero and others were skeptical. Octavian himself expelled the astrologers from Rome in 33 B.C.E., and then had his own horoscope published.

5. <u>Tyrrhenian Sea</u>: The sea west of the Italian peninsula.

I 22

Aristius Fuscus was Horace's close personal friend, and one who enjoyed a joke. Fuscus wrote comedies, preferred the town to the country, and was a schoolmaster by profession. This poem begins with a Stoic commonplace, that the pure in heart have special protection. Horace then illustrates this cliché with a tale of how he scared off a wolf who met him while he was singing of his beloved Lalage. He concludes with the grandiloquent claim that, as a lover, he would be safe anywhere in the world. While the poem was once considered a serious expression of moral earnestness (it was even set to music and sung at funerals), its flippant anticlimax is today generally emphasized; see the comments of W. S. Anderson in the Introduction. Elsewhere Horace claims that as a poet he has the special protection and favor of the gods (*Odes* I 17*; III 4*), and other poets made similar claims about the sacred protection of lovers (for instance, Tibullus I 2 and Propertius III 16).

2. <u>Mauritanian javelins</u>: In part a vividly particular adjective (like the specification of a "Winchester rifle" in American folktales). The javelin was known as a typically Moroccan weapon.

5–6. <u>Syrtes' steaming shoals</u>: Either of two famous sea banks on the northern coast of Africa. The coast of Libya was, according to Pliny, noted for wild beasts and poisonous serpents. Cato the Younger had marched around the Great Syrtes during the civil wars in 47 B.C.E., one year before he committed suicide. Some commentators believe a reference to him must be intended.

7. Caucasus range: Another strange and exotic place; it was noted for its wild animals, particularly its tigers, and marked the far eastern edge of the Roman empire.

8. fabulous Jelum: A river of India, called "fabulous" because of the strange and marvelous tales of Indian travelers and because there, in one of his most famous battles, Alexander the Great defeated the elephants of Porus.

10. the Sabine woods: Horace had been given a villa in the Sabine woods by his patron Maecenas; here he often found retreat from the troubles and pressures of Rome. The contrast between the strange and fabulous places of lines 1–8 and the Sabine farm is typical of Horace; compare *Odes* I 7.

11. Lalage: a Greek name which means "prattle, sweet-chatter." See the last words of the poem.

14. martial Apulia: Apulia was a rugged and unhealthy region in southeastern Italy. Horace refers to Daunia, a territory in northern Apulia from which Roman legionnaries were particularly recruited and where Horace's own native Venusia was located.

15. the Land of Juba: Juba was king of Numidia in Africa; his son, Juba II, was made king of Mauretania and Gaetulia by Augustus in 25 B.C.E. Lions were conventionally Gaetulian, and Juba actually collected and wrote down tales about them.

23. sweetly smiling: Throughout the poem Horace has been recalling, exaggerating, and parodying a topos of the love poets, that lovers are sacred to the gods. Here he quotes exactly the description of Lesbia given in Catullus's poem 51, line 5.

I 24

This poem is addressed to Horace's friend and the greatest poet of Rome, Vergil, on the death of Vergil's friend Quintilius (the translation uses the older spelling Quinctilius). We do not know for certain who Quintilius was, but he is also mentioned by Horace in his *Ars Poetica* as a sensitive and candid critic of poetry. Horace's poem is considered an *epicedion*, or "funeral poem." This genre of lyric had a conventional form with certain conventional topics. These include: expressions of sympathy for those left behind, curses on the cruelty of fate, statements on the uselessness of grief, the inexorable nature of death, and the need to endure. For a fuller description, see the comments on Ovid *Amores* II 6.

2. Melpómene: Melpómene, who later became the Muse of Tragedy, was not yet so specialized; Horace probably invokes her as the Muse in general, or the Muse of "dance and lyric."

6–7. Modesty . . .: Personified virtues treated as gods. "Modesty" was personified as a god as far back as early Greek poetry (Hesiod, eighth century B.C.E.) but, as a Roman divinity, does not appear before the poets of Horace's period; "Justice" was both a Greek and a Roman divinity; "Good Faith" was a Roman deity of long standing but does not seem to be a significant Greek personification; "Honesty" was not so much a cult goddess as a divinity for poets and philosophers.

13. Orpheus: a mythological figure representative of the powers of poetry. Vergil had told his story at the end of the *Georgics*, how he descended to the underworld and by his singing had persuaded the gods there to allow his wife, Eurydice, to return on condition that he not look back until they had ascended to the upper world. Orpheus did, of course, look back and so the

"gift" was less an opportunity to revoke the laws of nature than a display of how irrevocable they are.

16.   Mercury: The messenger god, also a god of poets and of merchants; one of this god's duties was to guide the dead down to Hades. His "shuddering wand" refers to his caduceus, the herald's staff he carried as a messenger, and with which he escorted the dead to Hades.

20.   unnatural: there is no word in English that exactly captures the sense of the Latin, *nefas*: It means "impossible," "unnatural," and "impious," "contrary to divine and natural law."

I 37

This poem summons Romans to celebrate two important events in the last years of the civil war. The Roman world, which had been divided between Octavian and Antony, had been held together by an uneasy alliance from 40 until 33 B.C.E. At that time the long expected hostilities finally began. Octavian managed to portray Antony, his chief adversary, not as the leader of the opposition in a civil war, but as an adherent to the un-Roman cause of Cleopatra. Notice that Antony is not even mentioned in this poem. Their forces met off the coast of western Greece at Actium on September 2, 31 B.C.E. Hundreds of ships clashed; large armies waited on the shore. But suddenly, Cleopatra, who had followed Antony into battle, fled with sixty ships. Antony soon followed with more ships and with his war chest. His fleet took refuge in port and surrendered largely intact. Octavian's victory was celebrated by the Augustan poets as a symbol of his divine favor. He abandoned pursuit of Antony and returned to Italy to suppress uprisings there, but offered Cleopatra her kingdom if she would kill Antony. He committed suicide instead. The battle of Actium is also the subject of Propertius IV 6; see the notes there for further details.

The second event celebrated in this poem is the suicide of Cleopatra in September, 30 B.C.E. Whether Octavian really planned to parade her in his triumph is unclear. The story of the asps is suspiciously favorable for Octavian. In any event, we are told that she tried to kill herself first with a dagger, then by starvation. The asp was the easiest means to death, being quite painless.

Among the interpretations of this poem offered, one should consider the following: 1. The rhetoric acts solely to magnify the danger ("the deadly monster") and to magnify the victory ("too much a woman to allow her enemies to parade her"). 2. The Romans generally showed respect and even admiration for their enemies—after they were defeated, of course. 3. Horace composes in a single ode two propagandistic views of Cleopatra precisely because their complementary inaccuracies compel the reader to reject both extremes—the poem undermines the rhetoric of victory and allows Cleopatra herself to escape such manipulative distortions.

1.   Now . . .: Horace begins, as often, with a direct reminiscence of a Greek lyric, in this case Alcaeus's poem of celebration for the death of the Greek tyrant Myrsilos.

3.   the gods' couches: At a special feast, called a *lectisternium*, banquets were set beside couches on which images of the gods lay. The *Salii*, or dancing priests, were a college particularly noted for their feasts.

5.   Caecuban: Caecuban wine was considered by some to be the very best wine; it came from Fundi near Rome.

6. the insane queen: Cleopatra is never named in Augustan poetry. Since this was primarily a civil war, the emphasis on Cleopatra is a distortion.

7. Capitoline: The one of the seven hills of Rome where the temple of Jupiter Optimus Maximus was located. It was believed that Cleopatra had threatened to dispense justice from Jupiter's temple, not only a sacrilege to the most sacred place in Rome, but also, since she was a queen, an insult to Roman democratic institutions.

13. scarcely one ship: In fact, she left Actium with sixty ships.

14. Mareotic wine: A light wine, the most famous from Egypt, was produced in the region around Alexandria.

16. Caesar: Caesar is Octavian, the adopted son of the great Julius Caesar. In fact, Octavian returned to Rome.

20. chain: Prisoners were led in chains to the temple of Jupiter during the triumphal processions of victorious generals.

23–24. hidden shores: In fact, she did attempt to move her fleet over the Suez isthmus and into the Red Sea.

I 38

After the grand and public tone of poem I 37, Horace ends his first book of odes with this poem in praise of the umbratile life and modest aspirations. Some take the contrast between these two poems as a meaningful comment on the grand rhetoric and distortions of the former poem. Others have sought in the poem symbolic claims about love poetry in general or the plain style of composition. Still others have felt that the poem is too slight to merit much consideration.

2. wreaths: Such garlands were sacred to Venus.

4. the roses: Roses, too, were sacred to Venus.

5. myrtle: Again, this plant is sacred to Venus. The myrtle was fairly common and used at symposia to cover the odor of wine.

Odes II

II 1

This ode is addressed to C. Asinius Pollio, cos. 40 B.C.E., an active figure in politics and literature during the period of the civil wars. He was with Julius Caesar when Caesar invaded Italy in 49 B.C.E. He joined Antony after the Ides of March (the assassination of Julius Caesar) in 44 B.C.E. In 40 B.C.E. he helped to construct the treaty that reconciled, however uneasily, Octavian and Antony. By the time of the battle of Actium he was a supporter of Octavian, but in light of his earlier friendship with Antony, declined to be present at the battle itself. In the world of literature, he was a friend of Catullus (see poem 12) and his circle of young poets; he founded the first national library in Rome and was noted as a poet, a writer of tragedies, and an influential orator.

In this ode, Horace is concerned with Pollio's lost *Histories*, which traced the civil war from 60 B.C.E. down either to Philippi in 42 B.C.E. or to Actium and the defeat of Antony in 31 B.C.E. The ode as a whole, being introductory to all of Book II, suggests that its final verses were written close to the date of publication, 23 B.C.E. The attitude of the poets and even of the aristocracy toward Augustus was neither single-minded nor consistent in the years during which he twice restored the Republic (27 and 23 B.C.E.). Certainly the civil war was a disease that had affected the body politic; but the end of the civil war would for many generations appear both as a remedy and as a disease worse than war itself.

As a dedication poem, this ode praises Pollio the historian; as a programmatic poem it is a *recusatio*, or "refusal poem," that is, a poem in which a poet refuses to undertake certain topics and themes, usually serious political or epic topics.

1. Metellus's consulship: The date was 60 B.C.E. when Q. Caecilius Metellus and L. Afranius were consuls and when Pompey, Crassus, and Julius Caesar formed the First Triumverate, an illegal alliance, or "friendship," whose purpose was to govern Rome.

5. unexpiated blood: During and after the period of the civil wars, the Romans came to believe that there was in their history some crime for which Roman blood was being exacted as expiation. In one version, Romulus's murder of his brother Remus was both the unexpiated crime and the symbol of civil war.

12. Attic drama: The great tragedies of Greece were written and performed in Athens, also known as Attica.

13. premier counsel: A reference to Pollio's achievements as an orator and to the remarkable fact that, except for one prosecution of C. Cato, he was, so far as we know, always an attorney for the defense.

15. your Illyrian Triumph: In 39 B.C.E. Pollio won a triumph over the Parthini, a Dalmatian tribe. A triumph, the most illustrious achievement of a Roman general, was celebrated for victory over an important foreign enemy entailing at least 5,000 dead. It was celebrated by a parade from the *Campus Martius* to the temple of Capitoline Jupiter. After his triumph, Pollio's public activity was confined to senatorial duties and the law courts.

17. menace of horns . . .: Most scholars believe that Horace has in mind the battle of Pharsallus, where Julius Caesar defeated Pompey in 48 B.C.E. In that battle, Caesar, with 22,000 men against Pompey's 35,000 or more, halted and routed Pompey's calvary, put to flight both Pompey and his infantry, and captured 24,000 men. Pompey fled to Egypt where he was murdered.

24. Cato: This reference would seem to recall the battle of Thapsus, 46 B.C.E. There, in Africa, the remnants of the Pompeian forces joined with King Juba to create a considerable force. The rapidity of Caesar's attack not only routed the enemy, but, when Caesar's troops got carried away in pursuit, resulted in a far greater slaughter of Romans than in the battle of Pharsalus. Cato, after Caesar's victory, committed suicide. The act made him a symbol of Stoic and republican virtue, a man of principle who refused to live under Caesar, and he was so honored by Horace and by Vergil. During his lifetime, Cicero had less patience for Cato's high-handed display of inflexible intolerance: Cicero said that Cato thought he was living in Plato's republic and not in the cesspool of Rome. The battle of Thapsus became a powerful symbol for Romans of this period and later. It was in Africa where Rome accomplished some of its greatest victories: over Carthage in 146 B.C.E. and over the African king Jugurtha in 106 B.C.E. In 46 B.C.E., 100

years after the fall of Carthage, when Romans were slaughtering each other in the same place, it was easy to imagine some divine force at work. After the battle of Thapsus the Pompeian commander also committed suicide; his name was C. Metellus Scipio, grandson of Metellus Numidicus, who had helped defeat Jugurtha, and related by blood to Scipio Aemilianus, who was responsible for Rome's earlier victory over Carthage.

25–26. Juno . . . return now: It was believed that the gods of a city abandoned that city just before it was conquered. By a rite called *evocatio*, the Romans had summoned Juno, patron goddess of Carthage, out of that city during the Second Punic War.

32. Medes: A group of nomadic tribes at the eastern edge of the Roman empire; poetically they represent the Parthians, the great eastern enemies of Rome, who would feel special pleasure in Romans killing Romans.

35. Apulian blood: Apulia was the region in the southeast of Italy where Horace was born. Here it may be considered poetic and local color for Romans and Latins in general, or a special reference to Horace's countrymen, who were noted as good soldiers.

38. Simonidean dirge: Simonides of Ceos was a Greek lyric poet of the sixth century.

II 13

Sometime, probably in March, 30 B.C.E., a tree on Horace's farm fell and narrowly missed him. He wrote of that experience here and in three other poems (II 17*; III 4* and 8*). However, as is often the case in Horace, the particular mixture of irony and seriousness, here of curse, praise, and parody, is difficult to sort out discursively. This poem recalls several topics and literary traditions: the sepulchral epitaph and the epigram of escape from danger (see *Odes* I 5); the curse on the origin or inventor of evils (see *Odes* I 3. 9ff); the diatribe on the unpredictability of death; and the journey to the underworld. It is easy to feel irony in the poem's opening curse against the man who planted a tree—in Rome, as now on Arbor Day in the United States, the planting of trees was traditionally a respectably optimistic activity, something one did for future generations; see *Odes* III 22. 5*. And yet a narrow escape from death is not merely a matter for humorous exaggeration.

1. whoever planted you: The almost formulaic opening to the curse on the inventor of an evil.

1. a black day: The Latin refers to the technical term for the day on which a public magistrate could not conduct official business.

6–8. father's neck, guest's blood, Colchian poisons: Images of extreme impiety. The first involves the sacred relationship between fathers and children (the essence of what a Roman meant by piety: obligations to father, fatherland, and "God[s] the father[s]"). The second entails a violation of the sacred protection offered to guests within a house by the gods of the hearth. The third, by reference to Colchis, recalls Medea and her connections with magic, passion, and even the slaughter of her own children.

14–15. Phoenician sailor . . . at the Bosporus: The Latin text is uncertain. If this is what Horace wrote, he may have referred to the Phoenicians as typical sailors. If so, these seafarers from the eastern Mediterranean are encountering the clashing rocks at the entrance to the Bosporus.

18. Parthian: Traditional eastern enemies of the Romans, noted for their cavalry and their way of fighting by shooting over their shoulders while apparently in retreat.

22. Proserpina: Wife of Hades and queen of the underworld.

22. Aeacus: A son of Jupiter who was the grandfather of Achilles. He was so respected for his piety and justice that he was made a judge, or arbitrator among the dead, in the underworld.

25–26. Sappho, Alcaeus: The two Greek lyric poets upon whom Horace most frequently modeled his own lyrics. See *Odes* I 1. 34ff. They both wrote in the Aeolic dialect. Sappho was best known for her love poetry and marriage hymns; Alcaeus for his more political poems.

29. The shades give both the hushed, sacral wonder: Horace's friend and fellow poet Vergil had similarly pictured Orpheus's descent to the underworld at the end of his *Georgics*. Orpheus's song in lament for the death of his wife Eurydice was so moving that Proserpina agreed to let Eurydice return to the world of the living, but under conditions which Orpheus ultimately could not fulfill. See *Odes* I 24. 13.

33. the monster: Cerberus, the black dog who guarded the underworld. In art he usually has two or three heads; in Hesiod he has fifty; Horace's hundred heads is deliberately exaggerated tragic rhetoric.

36. Furies: Also known as the Eumenides, these goddesses of the underworld protected blood relationships. In Vergil's picture of the underworld, Orpheus puts the snakes to sleep.

37. Prometheus, Tantalus: Two of the famous "criminals" of the underworld, suffering eternally for their crimes. Prometheus stole fire from the gods and gave it to man. His punishment was to be chained to a rock where an eagle daily fed on his liver. Tantalus is variously accused: he tried to steal the gods' nectar, to reveal their secrets, or to feed the gods his own son at a banquet. His punishment was to be placed in water which receded from his mouth whenever he tried to drink and under fruit that moved away from his grasp whenever he tried to eat.

39. Orion: A great hunter who was killed by Diana, the goddess of hunting. According to Homer, in the land of the dead he hunts the shades of the animals he hunted while alive.

II 14

In a variation on the topics of the *protreptic* poem (see the Introduction on Horace's *protreptic* poetry in general), Horace again turns to the movement of life toward its end in death. His addressee is a certain Postumus, unknown to us but with a significant name, one that means "a child born after the death of his father." For the same general theme compare *Odes* IV 7.

5. three hundred bulls: This is a general figure of hyperbole which implies satiric criticism of Postumus's excessive and self-serving religiosity. One should compare the extravagant banquets of the priests with which the poem ends.

6. implacable Pluto: Pluto was the god of the underworld, so named because all wealth (Plutos) was felt to come from death. Any such association here will be sardonic.

7. Geryon: A three-headed monster who lived on an island in the far west with his herds of cattle. Hercules in one of his twelve labors sailed to his island, killed his dog and herdsman, killed Geryon himself, and stole his cattle. He is offered as an example of awesome strength which was nevertheless dominated by death.

8. Tityos: Like Geryon, Tityos, the son of Earth, was another being of enormous strength and size. He was killed by Apollo for attempting to rape Apollo's mother, Leto. In the underworld he was bound while vultures ate at his liver.

8–9. the gloomy water: Entrance to the land of the dead was by way of Charon's boat across the river Styx.

13–14. Mars's bloodbath, the Adriatic's roaring breakers: The two ways of life generally taken as symbols of greed and accomplishment, of wealth and glory, were the life of a soldier and that of a merchant.

16. Sirocco: Winds that blew on the Adriatic up from Africa during the autumn; see *Odes* I 3. 12.

18. Cocytos: One of the rivers of Hades; its name means "wailing."

18. Danaids: The fifty daughters of Danaus were forced to marry the sons of Aegyptus, but were ordered by their father, Danaus, to kill their new husbands on their wedding night. All except Hypermnestra did and they were condemned in Hades to carry water in jars with holes in the bottom.

19. Sisyphos: A clever trickster figure who chained up Death himself when Death came to take him. As a result no one died until the war god, Ares, freed Death. For this and other misdeeds he was condemned in the underworld to forever roll a rock uphill that always slipped from his grasp and rolled back down.

23. cypresses: Called "cursed" here because the cypress tree was sacred to Pluto and so associated with death.

25. Caecuban: A fine wine from southern Latium.

28. high priest's banquet: The college of priests at Rome had a reputation for the extravagance of their banquets. The whole poem ends with a picture that suggests that things are out of place: the wine that should have been drunk; the greedy rollicking heir; the extravagance of priestly banquets.

II 15

This poem forms an apt sequel to *Odes* II 14. Protests against luxurious living and the destruction of stern conservative values were common in Rome, especially in the last century of the Republic. Here Horace takes as his target the "real estate developers" who were destroying the Italian countryside with resorts and large building projects. He protests the palatial buildings of the rich, the proliferation of fish ponds, and the artificial gardens and parks that were destroying the vineyards and olive orchards. Finally, he turns to praise the life of his ancestors. Ideologically, this poem would seem to support the Augustan view that wealthy independence and self-indulgence are not to be preferred to the commonwealth and the general good.

4. sterile planetree: A shade tree cultivated by the rich in their parks; Horace calls it "sterile" (or "unmarried") because no vines were trained to grow on it as they were trained to grow on the elm. It might be taken as an image of the aristocracy that Augustus tried to reform with his marriage laws. There was a story that Hortensius so loved his planetrees that he watered them with wine.

6. <u>myrtle</u>: A tree used for garlands and known for its pleasant odor. See elsewhere in the *Odes*: I 4. 9, 38. 5.

10. <u>laurel</u>: Like the myrtle, another aromatic plant prized in the gardens of the wealthy. Typically, it was used for the "laurel wreath" that athletic victors received; here it only provides shade.

10. <u>Romulus</u>: The founder of Rome who is often cited as an example of agricultural simplicity.

11. <u>unshorn ancestors</u>: Horace specifically cites Cato, the great-grandfather of the Cato who committed suicide after Thapsus (see *Odes* II 1. 24). It was in following his great-grandfather's example that the younger Cato developed his reputation for Stoic severity and old Roman virtue. Both Catos denounced luxury; however, the great-grandfather wrote a book on agriculture remarkable for its emphasis on progressive and profitable farming.

14. <u>porticoes</u>: Colonnades and porticoes were traditionally limited to public buildings; the private colonnade or portico was an ostentatious symbol of wealth.

14. <u>stretch the north wind</u>: The orientation of a portico was designed to catch the cool north wind.

17. <u>Their laws</u>: In this stanza, Horace describes the proper building material for the ancient Roman: sod was used for private altars, while marble and other expensive materials were used in public buildings. Literally, "Their laws did not allow them to overlook the turf that lay ready to hand" for building altars and other structures.

II 20

According to Greek fancy, the souls of dead poets passed into swans. Horace uses this tale to imagine his own immortality in the last poem of *Odes* II Horace has joined a serious mythological representation of poetic power, swan songs, and the immortality of the soul to a Hellenistic or folktale genre of metamorphoses, here pursued in some rather grotesque and whimsical detail. As often in Horace, there are also in the background of the final verses the traditions of sepulchral epigrams in which the survivors are urged not to mourn the dead. Ennius, an early and influential writer of epic at Rome, wrote: "Let no one adorn me with tears, nor make my funeral with weeping. Why? Because alive I fly through the mouths of men." This poem seems especially present in Horace's elaboration of the topic.

2. <u>double shape</u>: He will be both bird and man, but he is also a biform poet in the way he joins Greek and Roman elements.

4. <u>transcending envy</u>: The great Hellenistic Greek poet Callimachus, who more than anyone else established the poetic agenda for Horace, Vergil, and the generation of neoteric poets who preceded them, explicitly claimed that his song transcended envy. This recollection of Callimachus's poetry is both part of Horace's credentials and a reminder that Callimachus was himself a particularly "biform poet," that is, he was especially successful at combining poetic genres which had previously been kept distinct.

5–6. <u>blood of poor parents</u>: There may be some note of humility here, especially in contrast to Maecenas, "descendant of ancestral kings, my patron and the glory of my life," as Horace put it in *Odes* I 1–2. See notes there for more on Maecenas.

6. whose name: That is, one whom Maecenas would invite or summon as a social inferior to dinner or symposia.

7. Styx: One of the dark rivers of the underworld.

13. Icarus: Daedalus, a mythical artist and inventor, fashioned wings of wax and feathers on which to fly from King Minos in Crete. During this escape his son Icarus flew too close to the sun; the wax on his wings melted and he fell to his death in the ocean.

14–16. Bosporus, Gaetulean shoals, Hyperborean shoals: The Bosporus marked the northern boundary of Mediterranean civilization; the Gaetuli, southwest of Carthage in Africa, marked its southern boundary. The Hyperboreans lived in a mythical paradise beyond the far north and beyond the cold winds of Boreas.

17–18. Colchians, Dacians, Marsian cohorts, Geloni: The Colchian river Phasis represented the eastern boundary of the known world. The Dacians were a troublesome tribe which lived north of the Danube where they came in contact with Roman cohorts, here called Marsian cohorts for the sake of verisimilar detail. The Geloni were a legendary people at the edge of the world; neither Herodotus nor Pliny knew exactly where they were.

19–20. Spaniards and Rhone-drinkers: The Spaniards and the Gauls, who would drink from the river Rhone, represented the western edge of the Roman world. Horace has now squared the compass: south (Gaetuli), north (Bosporus, Hyperboreans), east (Colchians, Dacians, Geloni), and west (Spain and Gaul).

21. empty funeral: Because the essential Horace is not dead.

Odes III

The six odes which begin Book III are known collectively as "The Roman Odes" because they all share political themes, all are written in the same meter, and none are addressed to a specific individual (as is Horace's usual practice). It is generally believed that they were written in the period after the "Augustan Settlement" (27 B.C.E.), when Octavian took the name Augustus, divested himself of the most obvious displays of his prerogatives and power, and "returned the Senate to the people." It was a period of renewal and, no doubt, hope, and Horace took upon himself the function of poetic spokesman, the role of *vates* or poet/priest/prophet, for the ideals of the new regime. As the voice of serious political poetry, these poems create a contrast with one of Horace's most popular poetic personae, the Epicurean devotee of a lascivious and wanton muse.

III 1

In *Odes* I and *Odes* II Horace used the first poem of the book to define his poetic and personal preferences in contrast to other choices. Here again he contrasts the withdrawn and restrained life he lives at the Sabine farm with the excesses and ambitions associated with Rome. This poem and its concerns look forward to the invitation to the Sabine farm that Horace sends to Maecenas in the next to last poem of this book, *Odes* III 29.

1. I spurn the masses: Horace combines Callimachean disdain for the common and popular with a religious aversion to the profane and uninitiated. Thus he constructs the voice of the *vates*.

4. virginal girls and boys: The new generation, filled with hope and promise, but in need of instruction and initiation. For a different view of the current generation, see the ending of *Odes* III 6.

5. dreaded dominion: Horace seems to have in mind the great and powerful kings of the East; this is not an apt allusion to Augustus, who still had to deal with republican longings among the aristocracy, if Horace is merely optimistic about the Augustan settlement or wholly supportive of Augustan aspirations.

6. the dominion of Jove: An allusion to a famous passage from Callimachus's *Hymn to Zeus*. This is an important reference since Callimachean artifice and playfulness had been joined by most Roman poets of the first century with an Epicurean disregard for directly political themes and subjects. It is also significant, therefore, that the poem ends by reaffirming exactly those Epicurean values of contentment and withdrawal. Thus, the poem finally composes a view of the ethical and political virtues of the life of withdrawal, that is to say, it constructs the position of the typical *recusatio* (which claims that the poet has not the talent for epic) as a position of strength.

7. Gigantic triumph: Here Horace refers to Jove's "triumph," that is, victory, early in his life over the earth-born monsters, the giants. It was an important battle in establishing his power as ruler of the gods. Augustus in 29 B.C.E. had celebrated a triple triumph for his victories: in Illyricum (33 B.C.E.) where he extended the empire to the Danube River, at Actium (31 B.C.E.) where he had defeated Antony and Cleopatra, and in Egypt (30 B.C.E.) where he had gained control of the throne and the treasury.

8. his brow: A reference to the august power of Zeus as represented by Homer in the *Iliad*.

10. the Field: The *Campus Martius* where Roman elections were held.

14. mob of clients: Important men in Rome were escorted to the forum in the morning by their clients, those whom they had protected or might protect. While the image is one of prestige and the appearance of clients at one's door implies flattery and praise, the underlying situation is one of power, potential violence, and protection.

14. impartial Necessity: Necessity, personified here as a goddess, is the inexorable force of nature and fate. See *Odes* I 4. 13ff.

16. the great urn: The *quaestor* in a Roman court determined the order of appearance for the defendants by lot. Names were written on balls which were placed in an urn; the *quaestor* drew one ball at a time from the urn. Horace uses this image here to suggest that everyone's name will eventually come up.

19. his disrespectful head: Horace alludes to the story of Damocles. He had flattered the tyrant, Dionysius of Syracuse, and so was invited to be a guest at the tyrant's banquet. In the middle of the meal, Dionysius pointed to a sword hanging by a hair over his guest's head. Such, Dionysius said, was the life that Damocles envied. The image is an interesting reprise of the poem's opening movement: while the king may suspend the sword over the heads of others, Jove suspends the sword over the king's head.

24. Tempe: A beautiful valley formed by the Peneus River in Thessaly, directly north of Delphi, between Mount Olympus and Mount Ossa. Compare *Odes* I 7. 4 where Tempe is rejected for the orchards of Anio.

27. Arcturus: A constellation whose setting in October signaled the onset of the stormy season on the Mediterranean.

28. <u>Goat Stars</u>: A constellation which rose in the middle of October.

33. <u>Fish</u>: A whimsical reference to the building projects that included villas projecting out into the sea. See *Odes* II 15 for the topic treated at length.

39. <u>bronze trireme</u>: Triremes, named for their three banks of oars, were usually war vessels; here Horace seems to have in mind a private yacht decorated with brass bindings.

42–44. <u>Phyrgian marble, Falernian wine, Achaemenian perfume</u>: All extravagant and symbolic of wealth. Phrygian marble, mottled with salmon pink, was used in some of the columns of the Pantheon. Falernian wine was a choice Campanian wine. Achaemenian perfumes were costly perfumes from Persia.

45. <u>why should I . . .</u>: After a review of the lives and conditions of life of others, Horace affirms or reaffirms his choice; thus the form of the poem recalls both a *priamel* and a *recusatio*.

47. <u>Sabine valley</u>: Where Horace had his Sabine farm, a rural retreat from the troubles of Rome.

III 3

Horace begins by praising and offering examples of men who have been "just and steadfast of purpose." The body of the poem, however, consists of Juno's great speech of reconciliation upon Romulus's entry into heaven, the reward for his steadfastness. In this speech, Juno puts aside her long-standing hatred of the Trojans, to whom the Romans traced their origins. This reconciliation, however, presents the reader with interpretive problems. First, the recent civil wars could easily be considered evidence of Juno's continuing hatred of the Romans. Second, the emphasis on human steadfastness stands in an uneasy relationship to Juno's purported change of mind. The ending of the poem is also curious: Horace claims that the subject matter belongs properly to epic and that his own rendition is a temporary form of possession by the Muse. Thus, he may seem either to disassociate himself from the very themes and purposes he has pursued steadfastly for sixty-eight lines, or to return to his own steadfastly playful lyre after this detour into epic concerns. Neither, however, explains the fact that he then continues with two more "Roman Odes."

9. <u>Pollux and wandering Hercules</u>: Mythological benefactors of mankind. Pollux and his twin, Castor, were the brothers of Helen of Troy, and were known as the Dioscuri. In their final adventure, Castor, who was mortal, was killed and Pollux, who was immortal, asked to die as well. Zeus granted that they could be alive and dead on alternate days; they are identified with the constellation Gemini. It was believed that they could calm the sea and so they were prayed to in time of storms. They had a temple in the Forum, although it was referred to as the temple of Castor. Hercules was the son of Jupiter and quintessential hero of the ancient world. He won immortality for his courage and endurance, especially in successfully accomplishing the twelve labors set upon him. Those labors are referred to here in the adjective "wandering," which may also recall the wanderings of Aeneas, hero of Vergil's *Aeneid*, another exemplar of steadfastness. Both Aeneas and Hercules were adopted as symbols of Augustus and his regime.

11. <u>Augustus</u>: Here Horace makes a rather imprecise allusion to the contemporary political world. He never actually refers to Augustus as a god, but implies as much by association, as here. Compare the attitude of Propertius; see, for example, elegy III 4. 1.

13. Bacchus: Another benefactor of mankind whose chariot drawn by tigers is taken as a symbol of his civilizing power; however, the Romans did not think that the gift of wine was simply beneficial and civilizing.

15–16. Quirinus fled Acheron: Quirinus is another name for Romulus, founder of Rome and son of Mars; on his death he was transported to heaven where he was received as a god.

17. Juno: Throughout the Trojan War the gods were divided, some favoring the Greeks, others the Trojans. Horace has Juno refer to this war as "the war prolonged by our divine intrigues" (line 29). She was the great divine enemy of Troy whose hatred went back to the "Judgment of Paris." At that time, Paris was asked to judge the beauty of Juno, Venus, and Minerva; he was bribed by Venus and received as his reward Helen, wife of the Greek warrior Menelaus and the most beautiful woman in the world. When he took Helen from her home in Sparta where he happened to visit ("the infamous guest," line 25), he caused the Trojan War. Hence the reference to him as "a doomed and adulterous judge" (line 19).

22. Laomedon cheated: Trojan impiety and unfaithfulness was traced back to the Trojan king Laomedon, who was once served by the gods Neptune and Apollo. Laomedon, however, refused to pay the gods. Troy was then attacked by a sea monster, and Laomedon was told the city could be saved if he sacrificed his daughter. Instead he asked Hercules to kill the monster in return for his famous horses. When Hercules succeeded, Laomedon again refused to pay. Hercules then destroyed the city.

26. Priam: The father of Paris and king of Troy, who refused to compel Paris to return Helen to the Greeks. Thus, what might have been settled as a private wrong became the error of both a family and a state.

28. Achaeans, Hector: "Achaean" is Homer's name for the Greeks who fought at Troy; Hector was another son of Priam and the foremost Trojan Warrior. His death at the end of the *Iliad* seals the fate of Troy.

31. my grandson: Juno refers to Romulus, also known as Quirinus. He was the son of Mars and a Trojan priestess, Ilia. Juno's hatred did not abate until after Romulus's death; the wars against Carthage in the second century B.C.E. and the civil wars of the first century were easily construed as manifestations of Juno's hatred.

36. the quiet ranks of the gods: The language recalls the Epicurean view of the gods as beings who live apart from and untroubled by human affairs.

38. the exiles: The remnants of Troy, led by Aeneas, wandered to Italy after the destruction of their city and there founded the Latin people.

42. Capitol: The temple of Jupiter on the Capitoline hill.

44. the conquered Medes: Rome's enemies in the East. See *Ode* II 1. 32.

46–48. the sea. . .: The sea refers to the Straits of Gibraltar in the west; the Nile refers to Egypt in the east and the unknown source of the Nile in the far south. Thus, Juno marks the edges of the imperialistic aspirations of Rome.

49. a nation stronger: Here Horace begins an appeal to those traditional and conservative Roman values which often concern him.

58–59. an excess of devotion: The phrase begins almost as an oxymoron, or contradiction in terms. "Devotion" (Latin, *pietas*) was the central virtue of Roman public, private, and religious life; it entailed other virtues like "justice" and "steadfastness." The notion of an excess of this virtue is a curious idea, but it is also the conceptual problem that this ode faces. Here Horace treats the rebuilding of Troy as an excess of piety toward one's ancestors. All this makes sense in its particular application, but confounds any reductive or general notion of what constitutes a "man who is just and steadfast of purpose."

60. rebuild the roofs: There were apparently rumors that Julius Caesar had contemplated moving the capital, Rome, to Alexandria or to the ancient site of Troy. Today scholars believe that these were little more than rumors and cannot find any reason for ascribing a similar purpose to Augustus.

62. evil auspices: When a city or temple was founded, the priest took the auspices, that is, he interpreted the divine will from the bird signs in the sky.

66. rises a third time: The first walls of Troy were destroyed by Apollo, Neptune, and Hercules because of Laomedon's treachery; the second walls were those destroyed by the Greeks during the Trojan War.

III 6

In some ways the last of the "Roman Odes" is the most powerful and the most pessimistic. Here Horace states with vatic clarity and emphasis the Roman belief that it was old Roman piety, represented by tough Sabine farmers and noble public temples, that created and preserved Roman military and political successes. With this he contrasts the contemporary scene, and with equal force pictures its vices, the contamination of family life, the increasing degradation of the young, and a future seemingly committed to irrevocable decline. The background to the poem seems to be the political situation of 28 B.C.E. At that time, Augustus, in his sixth consulship, began a program to rebuild the temples in Rome and may have attempted to pass his moral legislation. This legislation was intended to encourage marriage and discourage childlessness; it also made adultery a public crime.

1–2. atone . . . : For the Roman sense of ancestral guilt, see *Odes* III 3. Here that ancestral guilt takes the particular form of having allowed the temples to fall into disrepair.

3. the gods' temples: Augustus claimed at the end of his life that he had restored eighty-two temples.

9. Monaeses and Pacorus: Recent military failures at the hands of the Parthians in the East. Monaeses defeated the Roman forces of Oppius Statianus, commanded by Antony, in 36 B.C.E.; and Pacorus defeated L. Decidius Saxa in 40 B.C.E. Some believe that "Pacorus" stands in general for the Parthian leaders and that Horace must have in mind the defeat of Crassus at Carrhae in 53 B.C.E. The reason for this suggestion is that the victories of the real Pacorus were short-lived, and his defeat in 38 B.C.E. won for P. Ventidius a triumph.

12. necklaces' strings: The Persians wore necklaces as signs of bravery or distinguished service; they were, like contemporary medals, conferred by the king.

14. Dacia and Egypt: Even more recently, Octavian could claim that Rome had suffered a near defeat at Actium, which is here pictured for political reasons as a foreign war against Egypt and Cleopatra rather than as a civil war. "Dacia" may refer either to the northern tribes which followed Antony (and therefore to Actium) or to a different but related event, an incursion across the Romanian border.

21, 22. Greek dances: A reference to erotic dancing, typically by professionals at dinner parties.

23. <u>illicit affairs</u>: Horace could not have Ovid's *Amores* in mind at this time, but that is the spirit to which he refers. Compare, for instance, the young wife "seeking out young adulterers | at her husband's parties" with Ovid *Amores* I 4.

31. <u>salesman or Spanish ship captain</u>: The peddler, or door-to-door salesman, was not held in high esteem; he had ready cash and easy access to the households he visited. The sailor is another proverbially promiscuous and extravagant character.

33. <u>Punic blood</u>: Horace turns his attention to exemplars of Roman excellence from the past. Here Horace probably refers to the great naval battles of the First Punic War, 264–241 B.C.E. The destruction of Carthage, which ended the Third Punic War (146 B.C.E.) was often taken as the beginning of the Roman decline because after Carthage fell there were no more pressing foreign enemies.

35, 36. <u>Pyrrhus, Antiochus, Hannibal</u>: The great enemies and the great victories of the third and second century. Pyrrhus was defeated at Beneventum in 275 B.C.E.; Antiochus at Magnesia in 190 B.C.E.; and Hannibal, the great Punic commander who overran Italy in the Second Punic War, was defeated at Zama in 202 B.C.E.

38. <u>Sabine hoes</u>: This picture is removed both in time and place from the enticements of the contemporary city. The Sabine farmer is emblematic of conservative values and the old Roman way of life which prided itself on men who were farmers and soldiers. Cincinnatus is the great example of this ideal; he was called from his plow in 458 B.C.E. to save the Roman army, was made dictator, defeated the enemy, and returned to his farm.

III 9

This poem is a responsive lyric song in which the verses are sung alternately, here by a boy, unnamed, and a girl, Lydia. There is usually a competitive element to this kind of verse with each singer trying to top the previous singer's lines. Horace has here created a certain degree of humorous, if conventional, characterization: the boy speaks of kings, ruling, and yokes, while the girl speaks of burning, shining, starlight, and cork. For a similar poem, see Catullus 45*.

4. <u>a Persian king's</u>: Proverbial for wealth and luxury.

6. <u>Lydia, Chloë</u>: Playful names used elsewhere by Horace.

8. <u>Roman Ilia's</u>: Ilia was the mother of Romulus and Remus. Romulus was Rome's founder and first king.

10. <u>skillful lyrist</u>: This is a reference to the topos of the "learned girl," the accomplished girlfriend of the elegiac poet. By implication her performance skills may not end with the music.

13. <u>Thurian Calaïs</u>: Thurii, a city in Lucania, was known for luxury. As Ornytus's son, Calaïs is presumably a "somebody," and we see that Lydia again is interested in family standing and "fame."

23. <u>angry Adriatic</u>: The storms of the Adriatic, especially in the autumn, were proverbial; the dangers of sea travel were often used as an image for the dangers of love, since Venus was herself a goddess of the sea. See, for instance, *Odes* I 5.

III 13

"Bandusia's Spring" is a continual favorite among Horace's lyrics. It seems to gather into its sixteen celebratory lines a consideration of nature and ritual, of warm blood and cool waters, of change, death, and passion, and of Horace's appreciation for both the spring and his own poetic power. Formally, the poem recalls a hymn to a god (see especially the repetition of "You . . . . You . . . . You . . . ."); and ritually it may easily be imagined to participate in the Roman Fontinalia, an October festival at which springs were honored with garlands. Such precise religious association, however, is confounded: garlands are not blood sacrifice and the Dog Star of July (Sirius) does not suggest an October *Fontinalia*. As often in the best lyric, the poem seems to create its own occasion: as the poet celebrates the impact of this loquacious spring in the last stanza, his poetry speaks of his own power to celebrate and create fame.

9. flaming Dog Star: Sirius, the brightest star of the constellation Canis Major, "the Greater Dog," rose on July 26 and marked the beginning of the hot season, the "dog days" of summer.

III 22

This poem, reminiscent of III 13, is a dedication poem of a kind familiar from Greek sources. Usually the dedication poem maintains the fiction that it is or could be inscribed on the object dedicated; however, here the poet addresses the goddess directly and so joins typical dedicatory motifs to a kind of hymn to Diana (compare Catullus 34). The goddess herself is also a hybrid, not only as the "goddess with three shapes," but also as she combines with the proper functions of Diana (Roman goddess of the countryside) one of the functions of her Greek counterpart, Artemis, goddess of childbirth. Thus, a seemingly simple eight-line poem gathers together Greek and Italian, dedication and hymn, wild and tame, and the interpenetration of life and death, birth and sacrifice.

2. in labor: For the Italians, Juno Lucina was the goddess of childbirth, not the virgin Diana.

4. goddess with three shapes: This description summarizes the complex of Diana on earth, Luna of the sky, and Hecate of the underworld.

5. farmhouse: The farm is, of course, the Sabine farm; the dedication of a tree is a particularly Italian piety. Compare the impish impiety of *Odes* II 13.

7. a young boar: The language is meant to recall a wild animal and to that extent the promised sacrifice recalls the sacrifices of Greek hunters to Artemis. However, as commentators point out, no hunter would tempt fate by promising a particular kill on a particular day each year. Consequently, the "young boar" must be a domestic pig. The wildness imagined here is then no more real than the potential battles for which this pig is practicing. For the pathos here, one should compare the young goat of III 13.

III 26

This poem is another variation on Greek epigrams. The scene is set in a temple of Venus where the dejected lover with attendant slaves is about to dedicate the tools of his trade: songs and crowbars. By the end of the poem, however, the lover is asking for one more chance. Horace likes to capture these moments when the heart and mind change direction.

2.   soldier of Love: One of the most familiar topics of elegiac poetry. This poem is in part a response to the elegiac poet's passion.

3.   my weapons: It was customary to dedicate emblems of one's profession to the gods upon retirement. The soldier would typically dedicate his arms, the fisherman his nets.

7.   crowbars and crossbows: Crowbars are appropriate to the typical young lover of comedy who storms the barred door of his beloved's home; the crossbow would be appropriate to a soldier and recalls Cupid's weapons, but has little to do with a lover. The text is suspected by some of being corrupt, although it seems Horatian in its impishness.

10.   Cyprus: Venus's most famous home was at Paphos in Cyprus, one of two places where she was said to have first come ashore after being born from the sea.

10.   Memphis: Memphis is a surprise; although there was a temple of Venus there, it is not particularly associated with Venus. Furthermore, Memphis in the hot sands of Egypt is obviously far from the snows of Thrace in northern Greece. Perhaps there is a reference here to "Thracian Chloë" (see *Odes* III 9. 9) and to the heat of passion (see Catullus 7).

III 29

Horace opened his collection, *Odes* I–III, with a dedication to Maecenas; here at the close of his collection—in the penultimate position—he returns to his patron. In doing so he reprises themes treated and attitudes adopted throughout *Odes* I–III. Formally, the poem is an invitation poem. Maecenas is in Rome and Horace is at his Sabine farm, which was, it should be remembered, Maecenas's gift. This initial situation allows Horace to contrast the city with the country, public concerns with private symposia, the mighty and the humble, poet and politician, regret, fear and contentment, and the uncertain future with the pleasures of the present. In all of this Horace emphasizes change: its ineluctable presence in human life and its restorative function in living. He does not, however, recommend his own removal to Rome as he recommends Maecenas's removal to the countryside. Change, it seems, is a principle that must not be applied inflexibly. Throughout, Horace blends Stoic with Epicurean concerns, serious questions about how to live with humor and irony (which is itself a way to live), and praise for his patron with parody of his patron's single-minded seriousness. The final image is typically Horatian: amid the inevitable and unavoidable storms of the Aegean, Horace paddles along in his tiny skiff, protected by some divine presence and, of course, by Maecenas.

1.   Scion of Tyrrhenian kings: Compare *Odes* I 1. 1–2: "Maecenas, descendent of ancestral kings, I my patron and the glory of my life."

2.   a cask: Normally containing about five gallons!

3–4.   roses and balsam: Three requirements for a Roman banquet were wine, flowers, and oil for the hair.

6. Tibur's springs: Tibur was a suburb east of Rome where Horace had his villa; see *Odes* I 7 for an appreciation of its orchards and hills.

7. Aefula: Presumably an old Italian town between Praeneste and Tibur.

8. Telegonus the parricide's ridge: Telegonus was the son of Odysseus, who was said to have accidentally killed his father. Apparently Horace (not without irony) views the country-side through Maecenas's politicized and distanced eye.

10. a house: Maecenas had a park on the Esquiline and had built there a palace with a tower from which there was a good view of the countryside. It was from here that Nero was said to have watched Rome burn.

11–16: The invitation to the banquet is cast in Epicurean terms which reject excess and wealth in favor of simple needs and friendship.

17–19. Cepheus, Procyon, Leo: These are stars and constellations that mark the beginning of the "dog days" of summer; see *Odes* III 13. 9. Cassiopea, here represented by the star Cepheus, rose on July 9; Procyon rose on July 15; and Leo on July 30.

23. Sylvanus: The old Italian woodland deity, often conflated with the Greek god Pan.

27–28. Chinese machinations, Bactria ruled by Cyrus, and discord on the Don: These extreme and excessive concerns are ironically meant to typify the "far-fetched" worries of a public man. Bactra was a Greek kingdom that existed from about 250 to 125 B.C.E. Cyrus was a Persian king of the end of the sixth century B.C.E. The Don was a river in Scythia.

29–30. Provident . . . the Deity: This recalls Stoic ideas of divine providence and entails a belief that the world is ultimately created for the benefit of man.

34. a river: The basic image here was familiar in Callimachean programmatic poetry as an image of public epic. Here, and again at the end of the poem, the language of poetic stylistic preference is conflated with the language of ethics.

36. Etruscan sea: The Etruscan, or Tyrrhenian Sea identifies the river here as the Tiber.

43–44f. Tomorrow let the Father . . .: Compare the other versions of this topos, especially that of *Odes* I 9 and I 11.

58. African hurricane: See *Odes* I 3 for the troublesome winds from Africa.

60. my Cyprian and Tyrian wares: Particularizing epithets, like the "African hurricane" for verisimilitude which carry suggestions of Venus (Cyprus) and politics (Tyre = Carthage), the two great storms of Horace's life.

62. In the protection: The Latin word translated "protection" here, *praesidium*, is the same word used in the second line of the first poem of *Odes* I–III to describe Maecenas: "O protection and sweet ornament for my life." Thus, at the end of this poem, Horace returns to the serious political role Maecenas plays as a patron, and in doing so recalls both the opening of this poem and the opening of his book of poetry.

62. my two-oared skiff: The small boat that kept close to the shore was an image of Callimachean poetics in contrast to the open ocean of epic; again, ethics and style are brought together. It is, I think, important to note that Horace does not claim to or expect to escape the storms—that would be an unrealistic and sentimental aspiration; rather, he paddles about in his rowboat amid rising seas, secure in the protection of a god—surely, an ironic image.

63. Pollux: One of the Dioscuri, who became stars thought to protect sailors. See *Odes* III 3. 9.

64. Aegean storms: The Latin word translated "storms" is the same word that is used for political unrest and civil war, *tumultus*.

III 30

A poem such as this, coming at the end of a collection of poems and recounting the poet's origins and achievement, is called a *sphragis*, or "seal poem." Here Horace revising the language of Pindar in which the Greek poet spoke of the immortality conferred by his poetry upon others, speaks of his own immortality in comparison with the great and permanent memorials of mankind and the local religious and ritual observances of Rome. As this celebration of his own achievement expands, it returns home to his humble origins and the talk of his townspeople. The victory he predicted at the end of *Odes* I 1 is now claimed as his own.

6. <u>Libitina</u>: The Roman goddess of funerals. From the grand and impersonal immortality of bronze and pyramids, Horace moves to localize his achievement.

7–8. <u>as long as a Roman priest</u>: This is a proviso that is not often heeded by interpreters or readers: Horace sees his achievement as inextricably attached to the rituals and cultural life of Rome. This was in the poet's imagination a necessary condition for his continued growth and renewal.

8. <u>ascends the Capitoline</u>: The *Pontifex Maximus*, presumably in a national ceremony, ascended the Capitoline hill, presumably amid chants and songs, with the silent Vestal virgins, here referred to in the singular. The relationship of Horace's poetry to national events and rituals is a matter of scholarly speculation, and the fact that Horace's poetry today is no longer intimately involved in the cultural life of any "Rome" has its consequences for both understanding and relevance, and for Horace's renewal—as Horace, who must have wondered at the austere magnificence of the pyramids, knew it would.

9. <u>And this will be told</u>: Another reading of this passage would be, "And I will be spoken of where . . . ."; his townspeople in the farming country of Apulia will tell about him.

10–11. <u>Aufidus, Daunus</u>: In a manner reminiscent of the grand style, Horace identifies his home, Apulia in southern Italy, by its river, Aufidus, and its legendary founder, Daunus. Daunus, according to tradition, was an exile from Illyricum who became king of Apulia. In this way his career parallels Horace's own rise "from humble origins." See a similar reference to his humble origins in *Odes* II 20. 5–6.

13–14. <u>the first . . .</u>: The claim of primacy is the typical claim of a Callimachean poet; see *Odes* III 1. 2–4. Aeolic verse refers to the Greek lyric tradition represented by Sappho and Alcaeus; see *Odes* I 1. 34–36.

15. <u>Melpómene</u>: The particularly melifluous name of a Muse who is not thought to be particularly significant at this period.

16. <u>laurel</u>: Laurel was sacred to Apollo, god of poetry and of prophecy (especially through the oracle at Delphi), and so an appropriate patron deity for the Roman *vates*. The laurel crown in the Roman tradition would have been associated with the triumphant general rather than the triumphant poet.

Odes IV

Ten years after the publication of *Odes* I–III, Horace published *Odes* IV, his last collection of lyric poetry. In these poems he reflects much that had happened in the literary and political world of Rome since his first book. It was a period that had seen the publication of Vergil's *Aeneid*, Propertius's third and fourth book of elegies, and Tibullus's second book of elegies. It was also a period that had seen the institution of Augustus's moral and religious reforms, the return of the Roman standards taken by the Parthians from Crassus at Carrhae in 53 B.C.E., and an ongoing program of public building. In a sense, *Odes* IV is Horace's contribution to the rebuilding and renewal of Rome. Here he both reviews and rearticulates the lyric concerns of his earlier work with its emphases on private loss and private passions as well as on community and Augustus.

The poems of *Odes* IV have not generally been appreciated. Recently, however, we have had the advantage of a fine understanding of what Horace has achieved, see Michael C. J. Putnam. *Artifices of Eternity: Horace's Fourth Book of Odes* (Ithaca: Cornell University Press, 1986).

IV 1

Here Horace defines himself and his renewal of lyric interests in terms of his own past; compare *Odes* I 1, II 1, and III 1. The poem's narrative moment, then, is one that reflects on time, history, loss, and change as well as on love, lovers, and lyric poetry. The poem's form is reminiscent of a *recusatio*, but as a *recusatio* it does not reveal choice so much as necessity: "I'm too old for love." However, when Venus is not so easily sent away, the poem becomes a failed *recusatio* which makes the necessity of Venus as attractive as it is implacable. One may see in the figure of Ligurinus an image of impulses improper for a fifty-year-old man, an image of the attractions of youth, and even an image of lost youth. The poem looks to that complex moment when the poet finds himself under the sway of a Venus he thought he had escaped, feeling both the desires that shape his lyric and the lack of desire, or perhaps the desire for a lack of desire, that haunts his lyric.

1. <u>a long truce</u>: Ten years—from about 23 B.C.E. to about 13 B.C.E. A long time for a lyric poet not to write.

4. <u>Cinara</u>: Generally thought to have been a real person, a freedwoman, mentioned elsewhere by Horace with affection.

6. <u>soft to your stiff injunctions</u>: Literally, "[I who am one] now too stiff to bend to your soft commands."

7. <u>Cupidons</u>: The plural for Cupid was, as far as we know, an invention of Catullus; see Catullus 3.

9. <u>Paulus Maximus</u>: Judging by his consulship in 11 B.C.E., scholars generally agree that he would be about thirty years old at this time, that is, about twenty years younger than Horace. He was a friend of Ovid, acquaintance of Augustus, whose cousin he married, and a son of a noble family. He represents here accomplishment and propriety.

10. <u>tickle the glands</u>: Literally, "to roast the appropriate liver"; which refers to the impropriety traditionally associated with older men and women who became lovers.

18–19. <u>frame you | in marble</u>: It was traditional on a victory or success to dedicate a statue to the god or goddess who had aided you.

27. Salian priests: These were the dancing priests of Mars whose banquets were proverbial. The scenario imagined is extravagant and exotic. Compare the banquets and the dancing of *Odes* I 9. 15 and I 37.

33. Ligurinus: No doubt a fanciful name, it means "clear voiced." Compare the poet's silence in line 36.

34–36. Compare Catullus's translation of Sappho, Catullus 51.

IV 3

The poet acknowledges the gift of his peace-loving muse, Melpómene, in a poem which reviews briefly the lives and aspirations of others; compare *Odes* I 1. His fame is not that which comes from those noted forms of strife, boxing, racing, and war and triumphs, prominent in both Greece and Rome, but from song, something cherished and beyond envy, sweet and magical, as pleasant and as sustaining as breath.

1. One glance: Horace recalls a long tradition, going back to the early Greek poet Hesiod, in which men are blessed by the glance of the Muse.

1. Melpómene: This muse, addressed by Horace in his proud *Odes* III 30. 15, was later to be the Muse of Tragedy; here she stands for the Muse of Poetry in general.

3. Isthmian Games: These Panhellenic games, like the Olympic games, included competitions in boxing and horse racing. They were held at Corinth. Pindar, who is directly discussed in the preceding poem, *Odes* IV 2*, is the great epinician poet who wrote poems for victors in these games.

9. Capitoline parade: The culmination of a Roman general's triumph was the sacrifice to Jupiter Optimus Maximus at his temple on the Capitoline hill.

14–15. band of poets: Compare *Odes* I 1. 35–36. There may be here a reference to Propertius, the "Roman Callimachus."

16. envy's tooth: An allusion to the proud claim of Callimachus and of Callimachean poets to be stronger than the destructive force of envy. There may also be a more personal allusion to the fact that Horace's first three books of odes did not receive the enthusiastic attention he expected and deserved.

18. Pierian: The mythical Thracian singer Orpheus, the son of the muse Calliope, was the leader of the Thracians who were said to have established a school of song at Pieria on the slopes of Mt. Olympus. Pieria, then, became a name for the muse.

IV 7

Called the most beautiful poem in Latin by A. E. Housman, this poem on seasonal changes joins the typical concerns of a spring poem: change and momentary pleasure, with a meditation on the permanence of death. At issue is the congruity or dissonance between man and nature, the degree to which man is part of nature's cycle but not part of nature's continuity. Compare Catullus 46 and Horace *Odes* I 4.

1. have melted: Literally, "have fled."

2. leaves to the trees: The even numbered lines of this poem are, in the Latin, meterically identical to the first half of the odd numbered lines. Musically, then, the poem gives a full epic hexameter and follows it with a half hexameter. This may be felt to halt the flow of the odd lines.

5. The Grace . . .: The Graces were usually plural, and here the sisters complete the ensemble.

15. father Aeneas: Called "father Aeneas" for the piety he demonstrated as both father of Ascanius and as father of his country in founding the Latin people.

16. rich Tullus and Ancus: Tullus Hostilius was the third king of Rome and Ancus Martius was the fourth. Tullus is mentioned for his proverbial wealth. Horace is not explicit about the particular qualities that lead him to mention Ancus. It may be to the point that Ancus, as the grandson of Numa, the second king of Rome, was the first king from a royal family. As such, he may represent "family."

21. Minos: A son of Jupiter and ruler of Crete who was rewarded for his virtue and exemplary justice in this world by being made, like Aeacus (see *Odes* II 13. 22), a judge in the underworld.

23. not eloquence . . .: Torquatus, probably of the noble family of the Manlii Torquati (hence "family"), was (probably) a lawyer (hence "eloquence").

25. Diana . . .: Diana, goddess of the hunt, was also associated with the moon. She loved Hippolytus, son of Theseus, who was killed by his father after being falsely accused by his stepmother of raping her.

27–28. Theseus, Pirithous: Theseus and his companion (in some accounts his twin), Pirithous, abducted Helen, fought the Amazons, and finally attempted to carry off Proserpina, queen of the underworld, from Hades. They were held captive by Hades until Hercules freed Theseus; he could not free Pirithous.

27. the Lethaean chain: These bonds are called Lethaean for the river Lethe, or "Forgetfulness," which runs through the underworld. The waters of Lethe gave the dead freedom from the cares of their lives above; the name may also recall that the dead are usually soon forgotten above as well.

IV 10

In this lyric, the *carpe diem* theme is applied to Ligurinus, the attractive young boy of *Odes* IV 1. Compare *Odes* I 11.

3. down to your shoulders: Young men wore their hair long until they assumed the *toga virilis* on reaching maturity.

IV 15

This is the final poem of Horace's lyric career. It joins motifs and echoes from his earlier poems to poetic references to his poetic predecessors and peers in an apparent reevaluation of the public role of lyric. Michael Putnam (1986) 294, who has written feelingly and well on this remarkable poem, describes it as "an extraordinary metaphor for the Augustan Age itself, combining the traditional with the unprecedented, renewing and modifying past poetic performance just as the Augustan Age, as Horace would have us see it, re-created and re-energized the world of Rome."

1. Apollo: This scene introduces a *recusatio*. *Recusationes* can be found in Horace's *Odes* I 6* and Propertius II 1 and III 9*; Apollo is part of the narrative in Vergil's *Eclogue* VI and Propertius III 3*. Typically, as the poet is about to sing of wars, the god Apollo interrupts him to tell him that his muse is better suited to the "slender" style of lyric. The presence of Apollo gives an objective dimension grounded in the nature of the muse to the poet's refusal to write epic. It seems that for Callimachus the opposition between epic and lyric was stylistic; for Catullus the intimacy of lyric was prized in opposition to the epic disregard of intimacy; but Vergil was the first to make the Catullan opposition of epic and lyric explicitly ethical and political.

3. little sails: For the image of a tiny boat usually staying close to the shore as an emblem of the Callimachean poet, see Propertius I 11. 10* and III 9. 4*; compare also Horace's use of the image in *Odes* III 29. 62ff.

4. Tyrrhenian Sea: This may be a reference to the opening of the *Aeneid*, where Aeneas and his men are sailing Tyrrhenian waters.

4. Your epoch, Caesar: Typically, the god Apollo would here address the poet. Horace's variation may be noted as a programmatic effort to adapt lyric eulogy to the world of Augustan politics.

6–8. insignia: Crassus, in a famous and disastrous defeat at Carrhae in 53 B.C.E., lost thousands of Roman soldiers, his own life, and the legionary silver eagles to the Parthians. In 20 B.C.E. Augustus, without shedding a drop of blood, won back from the Parthians the standards they had held for thirty years. This diplomatic victory was highly regarded by Roman poets and was mentioned by Augustus himself in his *Res Gestae*. The language here recalls Vergil's *Aeneid*.

9. temple of Janus: The temple of Janus, said to have been founded by the second king of Rome, Numa, was closed when the Romans were at peace; its doors were thrown open when war was released on the world. Horace here seems to revise the traditional view by implying that peace was enclosed within a temple now empty of wars. It was closed by Augustus in 29 B.C.E. and again in 25 B.C.E., the first times in more than 200 years.

12. ancestral ways: Horace refers to Augustus's moral and religious reforms.

16. Hesperian rest: The name Hesperian, cognate with the Latin and English "vespers," refers to the land of the west, of the setting sun.

21: Danube: At this time Augustus was in the process of securing the Danube as the northern boundary of the empire running east of the Alps to the Black Sea.

22. Gaets: People who occupied the plains between the Transylvanian Alps and the Danube.

22. Silks: The Seres, whose name means "silk," were the Chinese and Tibetans who became familiar to Romans of the Augustan period for their silk.

23. Persians: Horace probably refers indifferently to various Persian people, including the Medes and the Parthians.

24. Don: The Don is a river in Scythia. One should compare the whole of this passage with Horace's invitation to Maecenas which ended Book III: *Odes* III 29. 25–32.

25. And we . . .: Horace, who began as the singular poet whom Apollo in his traditional role redirected away from epic, joins his voice with others in public celebration. The form recalls the personal "cap" of a *priamel* (which has the form, "others choose *x*, but I say *y*").

26. merry Bacchus: This god of wine was both an agricultural god celebrated for his civilizing power and a god capable of making men lose all self-restraint. Compare *Odes* III 3. 13.

27. <u>our children and wives</u>: For the importance of children as the sole representatives of future generations, see the opening of *Odes* III 1. Here the poet joins his poetic celebration to the concerns of Augustus's moral reforms and makes room for mothers as well as children.

29. <u>as our fathers did</u>: There is some dispute about the meaning of the Latin. By this interpretation, Horace claims to participate in the renewal of ancient Italian community festivals that celebrated leaders in song. We have no evidence for such festivals beyond the remarks of later Romans who believed that they had existed.

30. <u>Lydian flutes</u>: The reason for the specific reference to Lydian flutes is not clear—either for verisimilitude, or as a reference to aesthetic delight, or (as an ancient commentator suggests) because they were suited to serious themes.

31–32. <u>Troy . . .</u>: Venus was Aeneas's mother, Anchises his father. The Julian house, of which both Julius Caesar and Caesar Augustus were members, traced their lineage back to Venus. The last lines of this poem look back to Vergil's *Aeneid*, which told the story of Aeneas's wanderings from Troy to Latium in Italy, and may also recall the kind of genealogy found on ancient monuments commemorating a man's family heritage and deeds. One may also note the prominence given to both epic and symposiastic themes by the selection of details.

Appendix

Five Roman Epigrams

Before Catullus's experiments in Latin epigram and in love poetry there was a Roman tradition of epigrams written by educated public men in their spare time. "Amateur poets" they are sometimes called, and their work was often based on Greek epigrams of Greek lyric which they "imitated" but did not translate. Most of this tradition is lost to us. Fortunately, however, Aulus Gellius, a writer of the second century C.E., preserves for us four epigrams from this tradition. His *Attic Nights* deals haphazardly in twenty books with a variety of topics about which he was particularly enthusiastic: literature, philosophy, history, law, etc. In the nineteenth book he records a dinner conversation at which he was present when a well-known Spanish rhetorician, Antonius Julianus, defended early Latin epigram against a charge made by certain Greeks who were present that the Romans possessed no grace or sweetness in their verses. Julianus offered four of these epigrams to support his claim, saying "Please don't condemn us Latins of a total lack of erotic feeling as if we were some kind of wild men lacking in sexual sensations." Gellius's own evaluation of these verses recalls, perhaps polemically, the language of Catullus's circle and what we usually think of as "Callimachean" values; he said that "nothing neater, more charming, more polished or more refined can be found, in my opinion, in Greek or Latin."

The second epigram, by Lutatius Catulus ("I stopped by chance . . .") is preserved for us by Cicero in *The Nature of the Gods* I 79.

Valerius Aedituus

We know nothing of this man except for these two epigrams. In fact, given his approximate date, there is good reason to believe that his name should be "Valerius Aeditumus."

1

Attempting to tell you the love, Pamphila, in my heart,
what I ask of you, words fail my lips.
Down my roused breast runs sudden sweat:
silent, aroused, I am ashamed, I die.

2

Why hold your tiny torch, Phileros? We don't need it.
We'll go as is: from my breast shines flame enough.
Your torch the wind's savage force can extinguish
or white rain pouring from the sky;
but this fire of Venus, only Venus herself,
no other force, can quench.

Lutatius Catulus

Q. Lutatius Catulus. Born in the middle of the second century B.C.E., Catulus was a member of the Roman aristocracy. He was educated in Greek philosophy and literature and became a patron to the poet Archias. He reached the consulship in 102, but was forced to commit suicide in 87. His translations of sentimental erotic poetry are a new phenomenon among the Roman aristocracy at this time.

1

My soul's escaped. I think it's gone to Theotimus
again. Yes, there it enjoys refuge.
But I warned him not to admit
that runaway, to toss it out.
Let's go see. Yet I fear I may be caught
myself. What to do? Venus, advise me!

2

I stopped by chance to greet the rising Sun,
when suddenly on my left Roscius arose.
O Heavens, grant me pardon to say:
the man seemed more beautiful than the god.

Porcius Licinus

Although this man was a member of a fairly prominent aristocratic family, little is known about him. His other writings suggest that he opposed the senatorial class and may have supported the Gracchi.

Guardians of lambs, the sheep's tender young,
do you look for fire? Come. Why? I am fire.
All the forest bursts aflame, if my finger has touched it.
All the flock burns; all that I see.

Epigrams translated by Diane J. Rayor

Callimachus's "Prologue to the Aetia"

The malignant gnomes who write reviews in Rhodes
         are muttering about my poetry again—
tone-deaf ignoramuses out of touch with the Muse—
         because I have not consummated a continuous epic
of thousands of lines on heroes and lords
         but turn out minor texts as if I were a child
although my decades of years are substantial.
         To which brood of cirrhotic adepts
                            I, Callimachus, thus:

A few distichs in the pan outweigh *Demeter's Cornucopia*,
         and Mimnermos is sweet for a few subtle lines,
not that fat *Lady* poem. Let "cranes fly south to Egypt"
         when they lust for pygmy blood,
and "the Massagetai arch arrows long distance"
         to lodge in a Mede,
but nightingales are honey-pale
         and small poems are sweet.
So evaporate, Green-Eyed Monsters,
or learn to judge poems by the critic's art
         instead of by the parasang,
and don't snoop around here for a poem that rumbles:
         not I but Zeus owns the thunder.

When I first put a tablet on my knees, the Wolf-God
         Apollo appeared and said:
"Fatten your animal for sacrifice, poet,
         but keep your muse slender."

And
> "follow trails unrutted by wagons,
don't drive your chariot down public highways,
>> but keep to the back roads though the going is narrow.
We are the poets for those who love
>> the cricket's high chirping, not the noise of the jackass."

A long-eared bray for others, for me delicate wings,
> dewsip in old age and bright air for food,
mortality dropping from me like Sicily shifting
> its triangular mass from Enkelados's chest.
No nemesis here:
>> the Muses do not desert the gray heads
> of those on whose childhood
>>> their glance once brightened.

From *Callimachus: Hymns, Epigrams, Select Fragments,* translated by Stanley Lombardo and Diane J. Rayor (Baltimore: Johns Hopkins University Press, 1988) 65–66.

Sappho

To me it seems
that man has the fortune of gods,
whoever sits beside you, and close,
who listens to you sweetly speaking
and laughing temptingly;   5
my heart flutters in my breast,
whenever I look quickly, for a moment—
I say nothing, my tongue broken,
a delicate fire runs under my skin,
my eyes see nothing, my ears roar,   10
cold sweat rushes down me,
trembling seizes me,
I am greener than grass,
to myself I seem
needing but little to die.   15

But all must be endured, since . . .

From *Sappho's Lyre: Archaic Lyric and Women Poets of Ancient Greece,* translated by Diane J. Rayor (Berkeley: University of California Press, 1991) 57. It is Sappho #31 in Voigt, E.-M. *Sappho et Alcaeus: Fragmenta.* (Amsterdam: Athenaeum-Polak & Van Gennep, 1971).

Translators

Helen E. Deutsch is an assistant professor of eighteenth-century English literature at Northwestern University. She has previously published translations of Martial, and is the author of essays on Alexander Pope, Samuel Johnson, Horace, Propertius, and David Lynch, as well as a forthcoming book entitled *Alexander Pope and the Deformity of Authorship* (Cambridge: Harvard University Press).

Rachel Hadas is professor of English at the Newark campus of Rutgers University. Her latest book is a collection of her translations from Latin, French, and Modern Greek: *Other Worlds Than This* (New Brunswick, New Jersey: Rutgers University Press, 1994). Other recent editions of her poetry include *Mirrors of Astonishment* (New Brunswick, New Jersey: Rutgers University Press, 1992), and an enlarged edition of *Unending Dialogue: Voices from an AIDS Poetry Workshop* (Boston: Faber and Faber, 1993).

Jane Wilson Joyce was educated at Bryn Mawr College and the University of Texas at Austin. She is now associate professor of classics at Centre College. She has lectured on Lucan in many settings, and has translated his epic (Ithaca, NY: Cornell University Press, 1993). In addition, she has published two collections of poetry with Gnomon Press.

Stanley Lombardo, originally from New Orleans, is professor and chair of classics at the University of Kansas. His translations include *Callimachus* (with D. Rayor. Baltimore: Johns Hopkins University Press, 1988) and *Hesiod: Works and Days and Theogony* (Indianapolis: Hackett Publishing, 1993); he is currently translating the *Iliad*.

Mary Maxwell studied English literature at Bryn Mawr College and classics at Columbia University and the American School of Classical Studies in Athens. A winner of the 1990 "Discovery"/*The Nation* prize and the recipient of a fellowship from the Camargo Foundation in Cassis, France, her poems and translations have appeared in *The Nation, The New Republic, Pequod, Salmagundi,* and *Western Humanities Review*. She lives in New York City.

Diane Arnson Svarlien was born in New York City in 1960. She has a Ph.D. in classics from the University of Texas at Austin. She currently lives in Kentucky with her husband, John, and her son, Aaron Atticus. She has published verse translations of Propertius and Horace in *Arion, Translation, The Poetry Miscellany,* and *Exchanges*.

John Svarlien received his Ph. D. in classics from the University of Texas at Austin. He is an assistant professor at Transylvania University in Lexington, Kentucky.